IDEOLATRY

God Is *Not* Your Problem

THE CHARACTER AND NATURE OF GOD
As Revealed in His Word

by

Dr. Rich Masek

IDEOLATRY – God Is Not Your Problem
The Character And Nature Of God
As Revealed in His Word

8505 Navajo Road
San Diego, CA 92119 USA
www.DBDPublishing.com

The Words of Jesus are printed in red.

ISBN 978-0-9764062-1-1
Library of Congress Control Number: 2015920022

First Printing December 2015

Editor: Dr. Judy M. Law

DEDICATIONS

To Marilyn Benefield
For sharing her vision and reminding me of my path.

To Lisa Carol Jorden
For confirming and encouraging this work and my direction.

In Memory of Bob Grondzik
Teacher, Mentor and Friend.

In Memory of Pat Markley
For his caring guidance through some of my darkest days

To Greg Stephens
For pushing me to get the first chapter done!

To Vickie Wilsterman
For helping me create the term "Ideolatry" and being my sounding board through many years of writing.

To Geoffery Nicolaysen
For educating me in publishing and the long hours spent helping me format and lay out the manuscript.

To Dr. Judy M. Law
For her incredible patience in editing and making sure that my punctuation and grammar help me say what I really mean.

To Kenneth Copeland
For opening my eyes to Faith in the Word of God.

To My Beautiful Wife, Sheri
For her patience and support through many hours spent alone.

To My God, His Spirit and His Son, Jesus
May these words truly reflect this small part of Him, without whom I would be nothing.

CONTENTS

CONTENTS

LIST OF ILLUSTRATIONS

LIST OF ILLUSTRATIONS

LIST OF TABLES

PREFACE

This book has been a labor of love for more than a decade. I was first moved to begin this project in 1998. It was at this time that I laid out the general outline and subjects. I did some research, gathered some references and began a few lines in some of the chapters. Then the inevitable hit... LIFE! Pressures from around me presented themselves, mostly from my professional speaking and educational career and my professional work as a dentist. Needless to say, I easily succumbed to them. The manuscript, barely at its conception, lay in the heart of my hard drive as a very short series of undecipherable computer 1's and 0's and had about as much value as that code. Over the years, I looked at the files and said to myself, "I really want to write that book, but I am involved in this project and have that responsibility. Just as soon as I finish them, I will take the time to work on it." Nine years later, with nothing yet added, God was gracious to step in and get my attention.

Sheri, my wife, went to lunch with Marilyn. Marilyn had been a part of our lives off and on over the previous 15 years but knew nothing of my dream of writing a book. That day in May 2007 at lunch, she wrote out a message that she asked Sheri to give to me. That hand written note, hastily scrawled on a scrap of paper, really got my attention! It said in part:

> *"You have a gift of both artistic and creative ability. You use them in your workplace and through other venues... you have the ability to paint vivid pictures through words. Just as you have worked, researched, and compiled your book concerning dentistry, there is a spiritual book within you which will cause people to know and to grow in Christ Jesus. You have pondered the idea many times but have procrastinated - now is the time to begin arranging thoughts, scriptures, and personal revelation. It will bring glory to my Name and tremendous blessing to your life."*

I was dumbfounded to receive such an unprompted message and astonished at the completeness of her analysis of my situation. I judged the message to be one directly from the Spirit of God. I immediately opened up the "dusty" files in my computer and showed my wife the work that I had begun nine years before. She was unaware that I had already begun the project. We were both in awe. Thank you, Marilyn, for listening to the Spirit and being bold enough to act upon His direction to give me that note. Without your prompting, the seeds for this book might still be hidden deep within my hard drive and may have never seen the light of day!

That very afternoon, I became obedient to restarting the project and reorganized my files. I was so excited and motivated at a *Word from God* that I began to write that very night! Quickly, another roadblock appeared. Yes, LIFE, *again*! I succumbed, became enveloped in the demands of daily life and all too easily put the book project back into hibernation mode, but this time, I added something to my already overburdened schedule. My wife got me into a program that resulted in me pursuing a degree in Theological Studies that occupied every night with reading, writing papers and even some teaching. Again, I determined that I had no time to work on this book.

God was not to be deterred, however, and got my attention again after several more months of inactivity. One night after an evening class, another woman, Lisa Carol, approached me with a question. She was also one of my dental patients, but we had never really discussed much other than teeth. She asked, "How are you doing on your book?" I replied, "Oh, the book has been finished for a while. You have seen it in the reception room in my dental office, haven't you?" She replied, "Yes, I have seen that book, but that's not the one I am talking about! I wanted to know about the book that you are writing for God!"

Again, I was stunned. You see, Lisa Carol was also not aware of this book, nor had she had any contact with Sheri or Marilyn about the project. She said that she had been praying one day, and the Spirit impressed upon her that I was writing a book. She just wanted to know when she could get a copy!!! Needless to say, I immediately set my mind and fingers back to work on the project!

Nearly a year passed and try as I might, even with these two confirmations from different sources, I still could not get the book project to rise to the top of my priority list. Then, I inadvertently got another gentle prompting from my pastor. He asked if I would be available to teach a Wednesday night service. I emphatically said, "Yes, I would be happy to start the first of a 16-part series!" (I had outlined 16 chapters for the book at the beginning!) This supplied the needed pressure to finish the first chapter, "Acts of God," which I taught that Wednesday night.

As the book took shape, thoughts became sentences that built into paragraphs and then formed chapters. That first teaching, "Acts of God," grew into six chapters! As the work expanded, I shared my progress with Tom and his wife Vickie with whom my wife and I had many spiritual conversations. Vickie and I brainstormed to create the term "***Ideolatry***" during one of those discussions as we explored my vision and outlines for the book. Vickie became a sounding board and the first to read and critique my early drafts. She continued questioning, challenging, and encouraging me to achieve clarity and simplicity with the manuscript as we painstakingly reviewed every line of every chapter. She challenged me to refine my writing and explanations so that I wasn't the only one who could figure out what I was trying to say! Thank you for your invaluable input.

Lisa Carol and her husband Patrick constantly encouraged me to press on and helped with many chapters of proofreading, posing questions and offering commentary. Lisa never failed to remind me of the vision and ask me if I was done yet! Thank you for keeping me focused.

Thank you to my editorial team, Dave and Connie, Mitzi and Joe, David, Chris and my amazing daughters, Carolyn and Karen for struggling through my first draft and providing essential feedback.

Judy, my editor, gave me quite an education as she corrected my grammar, punctuation and continuity through the many hours of editing the final manuscript. I especially loved it when she said, "Oh, there are just a few simple changes." I then spent another 40 hours making those simple changes! Thank you for your painstaking efforts.

Finally, a huge thank you to my precious wife, Sheri, for putting up with me saying "I'll be done in 5 minutes!" while watching me peck away at my computer for 8-10 hours. Thank you for your incredible patience!

You can see that the book actually did get finished, being nine years on hold and eight more years in writing. I have been very blessed to have received the gentle reminders and encouragement to get on with one of the more important things in my life. It is much too easy to let LIFE get in the way and put God on hold. However, He is understanding and will always give you another chance, right? This appears to have been true in my case, but how much of God's blessing did I forgo as I walked outside of His desire, putting His purposes on hold while I *did my own thing*? I suppose I will have to wait a while to find out.

I am honored that you would take the time to read this book. I have been working on this for so many years and through so many seasons of life that it has been hard to maintain continuity and resolve that it would ever be finished and worthwhile. I have always had the sense that God literally told me to write it, but many times I would think as Moses did, "you want ***me*** to do ***what***?"

The intent of this book is to reinforce faith and trust in the God of the Bible. It will challenge the reader to consider what is written "between the lines" and gain a deeper understanding of God and his relationship to mankind. Tradition and "religious" views, crafted by man himself, may actually distort man's view of God's true intents toward him.

The revelation of God's character through the Bible is plainly seen in many individual passages and stories supplied by the Bible. His love, care, provision, and guidance are all supplied for the benefit of man. From Genesis to Revelation and everywhere in between, God seeks to establish an eternal relationship with man and provide for his success in every avenue of life here and in the life that is to come.

I can only hope that the message that this book brings is timely for anyone who reads it. I do not take the concepts and perspectives that I have explored here lightly. They have been well considered and life altering for me as I have searched for the deep meaning of God's Word. I present some light exploration into the Greek and Hebrew foundations of various passages and also explore some important characters and their relevance.

I have chosen the particular Biblical characters that are discussed for specific reasons. Together we will explore some of the activities of the more well-known personalities of the Bible such as Adam and Eve, Job, Abraham, King David, Daniel, and Esther. We will also look in to some of the more obscure and lesser know individuals such as Melchizedek, Gad, Nathan, Shadrach, Meshach, and Abed-nego, King Nebuchadnezzar, King

Darius, Mordecai, Haman, Korah, and Uzzah. They and their accounts convey important concepts about the protocols and procedures of the spiritual world and the way things work. We will also consider some of the teachings of Jesus, which in themselves are transformative and are the foundation upon which we build. A study of these and others Biblical characters will provide food for introspection, contemplation, and exploration.

The scope of the book expanded during the 17 years that it was being written. Much of the information was actually gathered in the living of life and study aside from actually writing. The main goal of putting all of this on paper is to bring clarity to the reader about the character and nature of God and deepen the reader's understanding of God's love for each of us.

There are many scripture references contained in the text that I placed for the convenience and clarity of the reader. Unless otherwise indicated, all scriptural quotations are from the *King James Version* of the Bible. Although it was not my goal to write a textbook on the subject, I have gone into some depth in a few chapters. Even so, I still have made every attempt to make things as easily understood as possible. Please try to persevere through my explanations as I believe that they will all make sense as you read.

Finally, I did not write this book because I am a theologian or a scholar or because I have a doctorate (which is actually in dentistry). The book did not come out of my studies for a degree in Theology. I wrote this book because I am an ordinary person that has spent a significant amount of time learning about the God that made me and what He says about Himself in the Bible. It is my hope and desire that the reader is provoked to deep consideration of the concepts presented here. The research, study, and writing I have done have brought me tremendous spiritual growth, blessing, and understanding, and I hope this book will do the same in the lives of those who read it.

Oh, by the way, I did finally get that Master's degree!

Dr. Rich Masek

IDEOLATRY

In the beginning God created
the Heaven and the earth.

And God said, Let us make man in our
image, after our likeness: and let them have
dominion over the fish of the sea, and over
the fowl of the air, and over the cattle, and
over all the earth, and over every creeping
thing that creepeth upon the earth.
So God created man in his own image,
in the image of God created he him;
male and female created he them.

Genesis 1:1, 26-27 KJV

CHAPTER 1

WHY ?

One day I had a discussion with a young man regarding faith and belief in the various philosophies and religions that exist in the world. He brought up many different ideas and concepts that had been revealed to him in a DVD he had recently acquired and was very excited to share them.

I told him I would be very interested in viewing what he had seen, but he said that one of his "Christian" family members took it from him and destroyed it because it was against the Bible. I began to discuss some of my beliefs and why I chose to follow my particular path. His response was that the things (non-Biblical) that he had been exposed to sounded very plausible and he was developing a belief in them. I asked further as to his reasoning, and he said, "I think that these teachings are more believable and more reasonable than believing in Jesus, and the God of the Bible.

As the conversation continued, I asked, "What is it about these teachings that is more reasonable than believing in God, Jesus, and the Bible?" His answer was quite revealing when he said, "Everyone that has ever talked to me about God and Christianity has been judgmental, telling me that I am a bad person for not believing. They tell me my actions and lifestyle are going to send me to Hell, and I have to be saved. These other teachings do not judge me like that. That is why they are more believable. Besides that, I have experienced a lot of bad things in life and how could a loving God let them happen to me?"

Rather than answer his question directly, I responded with these questions, "What do you actually know about God for yourself? Have you ever read or studied anything about the God revealed in the Bible?" His response was, "No, I haven't." Then I responded, "You have created your attitude toward God and what the Bible says based on what others have told you. Their views are not necessarily the truth, but they may be based on their own personal prejudices and life experience."

Then I suggested, "That is like you saying that your car is better than mine, but you don't even know if I have a car! You are rejecting God based on a lack of knowledge of who He really is." The conversation literally stopped when I asked, "How can you say that the teachings on your DVD are more believable than God, Jesus, and what the Bible says about them if you have no idea what is in the Bible? How can you make a true comparison and a value judgment when you have only experienced what someone else says about God?" He had no response.

This conversation demonstrates just one of the problems that this book intends to address. There is a great void of knowledge about the God of the Bible. Studying God's Word is essential to the knowledge of who He is. A lack of understanding of what God says about himself can lead to some very confusing thoughts about how life operates. As a result, many who believe in God also believe that He is actively working against them to force them into a change of some sort. People with this perspective or mindset may blame God for many things in their lives. Thus, the subtitle of this book, *GOD is NOT Your Problem*.

Examination of the basis of our belief system can be very revealing. Where did it originate? How did it develop? In what is it rooted? These are some of the questions for which it is essential to find answers. There are many ideas that we presume to be fact. What we don't realize is that much of that ***fact*** is actually entrenched opinion.

There is a long-standing basis for making this statement. After all, for a long time, the prevailing scientific thought was that the universe revolved around the earth! Entrenched opinion in science that is incorrect usually goes away when new theories are put forth based on newly discovered facts. However, sometimes opinions linger beyond reason and the realization of new facts. These unfounded opinions can be transformed and take on a new persona, one of *tradition*. Then, tradition can define a belief system, which we will explore in Chapter 5, *Acts of God*.

Belief is what guides your existence. You go to bed and set your alarm *believing* that it will awaken you at the right time so that you can start your day. You *believe* that when you flip the switch on the wall, light will dutifully fill the room. You *believe* that your car will start when you turn the ignition key, and you *believe* that you will have enough time to stop for coffee or a donut or bagel on the way to work. You also believe that there is enough gas to get you to the job that you *believe* you will still have once you get there.

These daily beliefs are based upon your own observations and experience of what you deem to be facts. However, some of your beliefs are based on your *perspective of these facts*. The way in which you look at something can determine what you believe about it. Your perspective is based on everything that you have learned and experienced in your life that tells you that something is true. When you accept that truth, you form a belief. A potential problem with acceptance of the truth is that you might be basing the totality of your belief on a distorted perspective of truth. In Chapter 6, *Our Universe - Relative or Absolute?,* we will explore this concept.

Another word that can be used in place of belief is trust. Still another word is faith. We all have faith and use it daily. Faith is not exclusively a *religious* concept. It is the way that things work in our universe. When you sit on a chair, you have faith that it will hold you up. Without faith, we would not get out of bed in the morning, and for that matter, we might not even go to sleep because we don't really know if we will ever wake up again! You see, faith is all around us, and we exercise it every moment of every day. Faith is a choice. The real question we all need to answer is this, "In what or in whom do I *choose* to invest my faith?"

I am sure that you have heard the phrase *preaching to the choir*. I began to write this book to some of those folks in the choir, the Christians that don't understand the what or why of their beliefs. I also wanted to do my best to bring clarity to who the God of the Bible is and what He is doing in His interactions with His creation of mankind. This is how the title, *The Character and Nature of GOD,* came about. Then, I began to realize that the scope of the book had the potential to reach those who aren't in the choir because they don't even believe in God! This is where the main title of the book, ***Ideolatry***, began to take shape. I will explain how that term came about and how I define it in Chapter 2, *Mergers and Acquisitions*.

Several times during the course of writing this book, situations from real life, like the young man that I described earlier, told me that I was on the right track. I wanted to present knowledge of God from a different perspective and explore the way in which He deals with us.

God is and always has been there for us, and exploration of what is actually written in the Bible will provide the reader with a clearer understanding of who God is and how He interacts with human kind. Goals of this work are to educate, reveal truth, promote understanding and simply provide awareness of certain aspects of God's Word while leaving the decision to the reader whether the God of the Bible is who He says He is.

CHAPTER 2

MERGERS AND ACQUISITIONS

The title of this book is ***Ideolatry***. This word has both a familiar and unfamiliar feel to it. You might ask, "Where did this word come from and what does it mean?" Etymology is the study of the derivation of the history of words and can be very complex. New words can come into a language through a variety of means including the coining of new words, borrowing from other languages, meaning changes of existing words and the blending of two words to form a new one.[1] Occasionally, a merging of ideas or philosophies can result in a new term.

The concept of merging and trying to create a harmony of philosophy, mission, and goals can be a challenge, but it is one that each individual encounters every day of their lives. We all must interact with one another, but we each see things differently. We have an idea or perception of the way things work or how the systems of our society should function. Some have a very narrow view, only concentrating their thoughts on those things that directly affect them. They greatly limit the scope of their world. Others have a broader understanding and have expanded their outlook into global events and attitudes.

Mergers in the business world are a melding of interests, ideas, events, and circumstances that presumably occur for the benefit of all parties involved. Sometimes, they come about because one individual observes a problem that needs to be corrected or finds a deficiency that needs to be augmented. Companies may even see a way to increase profits. An acquisition may occur for these same reasons, but rather than collaborating to form a new entity, one company is simply absorbed by the other.

Mergers and acquisitions might make the evening news if they are big enough. A few years ago, United Airlines merged with Continental Airlines, and it was big news. The merger of the two companies was actually through an acquisition of Continental Airlines by United Airlines. The two formed into a new combined company called United Continental Holdings. They shared a common vision and mission in that they were both air carriers, but they had different styles and methods. Merging requires a bit of give and take to accomplish a harmonious "marriage."

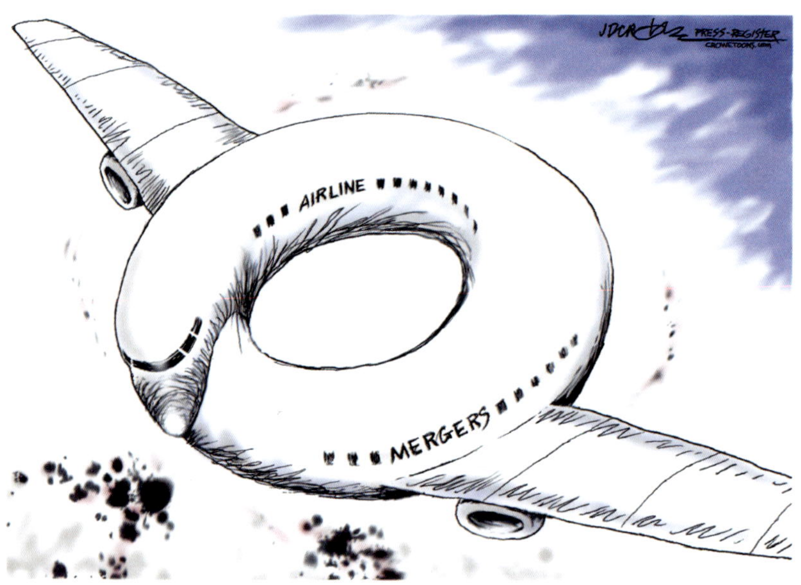

A merger is the melding together of two or more entities or ideas that blend into a new form.

Society continually evolves because of the widely varying thoughts, opinions, and understandings of individuals and groups. This evolution gives rise to new values that become belief systems. A *world view* then results from the perspective or lens through which life is then observed and experienced. Through human reasoning, society adjusts to accommodate the merger of these world views.

This merging is reflected in the word used in the title of this book, ***Ideolatry***. The concept encompassed within the term is important because it identifies an extremely pervasive attitude and prevalent world view. This world view is the reason that this book exists. Often, the coining of a term comes from the need for a unique descriptor. *Ideolatry* addresses this as it merges two notions that share a common heritage, which is the human mental process. The mind, will, and emotions of man unite through thought to form *ideas.* Thoughts *merge* in the mind to stimulate an emotional attachment or *acquisition* of the idea.

Let's consider the word *idea*. One definition from *Random House's Dictionary.com* indicates that ideas stem from the mind of man through contemplation, meditation, and observation of his surroundings.

idea *(noun)*

> *Any conception existing in the mind as a result of mental understanding, awareness, or activity.*[2]

Another word that can describe the acquired emotional attachment to an idea is the word, *idolatry*, as defined by the *Merriam-Webster Online Dictionary*.

idolatry *(noun)*

> *1) the worship of a physical object as a god.*
> *2) immoderate attachment or devotion to something.*[3]

The combination of these two concepts and a subsequent merger of the two descriptive words leads to idea + idolatry = *ideolatry* that is defined by the author as follows:

ideolatry (ī dē äl' ətrē) *(noun)*

> *1) the worship, attachment, or devotion to a concept originating and existing in the mind as a result of mental understanding, awareness, or activity.*
> *2) the worship or devotion to the thoughts and intents derived from the human mind.*
> *3) the worship of the human intellect.*[4]

The merger of these two terms helps identify a pervasive attitude of our society today which promotes the worship of the human intellect. The intent of this book is to reveal the effects of *ideolatry.* Man has an insatiable thirst for knowledge and understanding of his surroundings and his existence. His ability to invent, adapt, persevere, and prosper within his environment has been remarkable. Most, if not all advancement of the human condition, comes from thoughts and ideas that emanate from the deep recesses of the mind of man. However, there is truly something much higher than the thoughts of the human mind.

People either buy or rent a home or other lodging. In fact, some even build apartment buildings or high rises. We have learned all the science and technology, created all the necessary tools, gathered all the required parts, pieces, and elements to accomplish amazing feats of engineering. However, we don't seem to give much thought to the architect who designed it all and made it work. We don't care! We have created durable nests that protect us and have made ourselves comfortable. Blueprints and regulations are just hoops that we must jump through to get what we think we want, and the architect isn't really very important to us.

Many live their lives as if all that they have done or achieved will last forever. Well, if forever ends with the loss of our lives, then they are right! They will have taken care of all of their needs during those years. However, by any definition, *forever* exceeds the length of their lives and their family generations, both past, and future.

Science tells us that our world has been around for billions of years, not just from our first birthday to our last. Some of us accept that our last breath is just that - the last - and that's it! Some don't want to accept that kind of finality and figure if they explore and try different stuff, like creating an elixir, mummifying their bodies or deep-freezing their heads until some amazing scientific discovery brings them back to life so that their last breath won't actually be the end.

Scientific man's quest is to understand the universe, where it came from and where it leads. However, he is a bit on the stubborn side, refusing to acknowledge what he cannot see, touch, feel, explain, or prove. The discipline of modern science has portrayed an air of arrogance and demonstrated conceit that steadfastly refuses to acknowledge even the possibility that God, as the architect or the higher power, provided intelligent design. Instead, science prefers to assume happenstance, evolution, or even alien research (SETI).[5] The path of science and technology might lead people to believe that while seeking immortality they will eventually discover the answers to all questions and act as creators rather than acknowledge a higher power.

However, Man did not create himself, nor did his science or technology! His thoughts and ideas are in constant flux as his understanding and experience grows. Many times over the centuries, his *ideolatry* has insisted that the world lines up with his intellectual view of the universe. Many times, he has been wrong, absolutely wrong. After all, we have since discovered that the earth is not the center of the universe, and the world is actually not flat!

Intellectual people invest faith in something, and that is the science of the human mind engaging their *ideolatry*. Meaning and the reason for their existence is the thing they seek, but they have a terrible time trying figure out how to find it. This is frustrating because they refuse to consult the architect. The God of the Bible is in reality the Architect, the Higher Power. The discovery that the human mind is not the supreme entity comes from submitting to and understanding this Higher Power.

Being written in the seventh Biblical millennium (about 7000 years since the Biblical timeline of creation), this book does not pretend to create or establish any absolutes that have not already been revealed throughout the ages. What it does offer is an attempt to be nonreligious and non-traditional in its perspective, breaking away from the thoughts of man and seeking an understanding of a "Higher" or "Absolute Truth." This perspective is based on texts of the Bible, giving consideration to the scope of scripture and the manner and intent in which the God of the Bible deals with Man, His ultimate creation.

These perspectives are not taken from traditions, religions, religious thought or preconceived ideology or theology. They are derived from careful consideration of the motivations, thoughts, and intents that are revealed when the biblical account is taken as a whole. There will be some detailed word-by-word scrutiny of Biblical accounts to understand better God's intent that is the expression of His *character and nature*. However, the goal in this writing is to examine the primary thread that is presented in the Biblical text. It runs from Genesis Chapter 1:1 where we see the beginning of the Biblical creation account to the end of the book of Revelation where we see a new earth and a completion of this small slice of eternity.

I invite you to temporarily suspend your "traditional" belief system, your personal prejudices and your religious or non-religious upbringing and be open to understanding who the God of the Bible actually says He is, rather than what and who men say that He is. It is a journey of enlightenment, revelation, excitement, understanding, joy, faith, and change. Revelation will be gained from enlightenment, understanding will lead to excitement and faith and joy will increase from a change in the way you know ***The One*** who made you and ***His*** design for your life.

Mankind has a problem and you just might be part of it! Placing the human intellect on a pedestal and worshipping its potential is the core of "Ideolatry" and can severely diminish man's ability to be completely fulfilled. This is not to say that the accomplishments of man have not been remarkable, but there is more to this universe than man alone.

The human mind cannot and will not determine the answers to all of the questions it poses, nor can it determine its own eternal existence. These are in the realm of God. Everything in existence now, in the past and the future is found in Architect's hand, God's hand. Take some time to get to know the Architect because He drew up the plans, and He can show you how everything is supposed to work!

Let's take the next steps together and explore God and His Word without our filters of prejudice, bias, and presumption. Do your best to arm yourself with an open mind and relinquish your preconceptions. As you read, you have everything to gain if you agree and nothing to lose if you don't. Base your examination, not on traditions or opinions or you own ***"Ideolatry,"*** but on what God's Word reveals about Him even if you don't think that He exists!

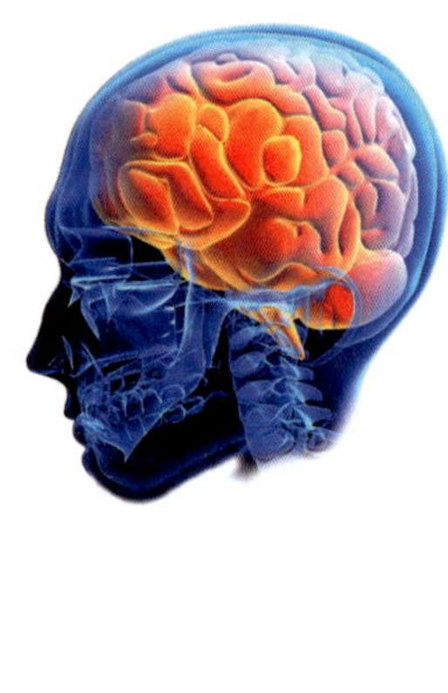

Man has a tendency to elevate his thoughts and ideas above everything else. This can result in the worship of the human intellect or ***"Ideolatry."***

CHAPTER 3

HOW IS YOUR RECEIVER?

Life is changing at an astounding pace. Technology is one of the prime factors in the increased speed of life. There are so many varieties of technology with one of the most common and pervasive among them being the ubiquitous cell phone. These amazing devices come in almost innumerable varieties, from a simple telephone to an amazing computer device that allows texting, video, and voice communications and serves as an entertainment center and a general hub of life.

These are truly amazing times that we live in. The technologies of the future will become even more amazing, but the ability for all of the technology to function rests on the concepts of transmission and reception. Reception can be achieved in two major ways. The first is a ***wired*** connection which is a physical connection between devices. It can be most easily understood by considering a light switch which connects the electricity from the transmission wires that enter your home to your lights, appliances, and other electrical devices. Another wired connection is the standard telephone which connects to a wall jack or a TV cable.

Another type of connection is the ***wireless*** connection. This is like the remote control for your TV, garage door opener, computer, or cell phone. Without this wireless technology, much of the world that we now know and take for granted would not exist. However, even before this current age of wireless everything, wireless communication existed and flourished. The telegraph and then the common radio were the first uses of this amazing technology. For the sake of simplicity, we will skip a few inventions and discussions of electronics and electrical theory and move on to the familiar radio.

In very basic terms, the radio signal begins by sending an electric signal from a microphone. The microphone element vibrates at varied frequencies and generates electric energy that is fed into an amplifier and then to a transmitting antenna that emits an invisible *signal* of a specific frequency into the air. Another antenna attached to a radio picks up the signal when tuned to the same frequency. The radio is then able to detect and decode the signal and reproduce the original sound vibrations from the microphone through the radio's speaker. This is a wireless transmission of what we now know as *data*. The data in this case is a simple voice message, simple only by comparison to the massive amounts of data from computers and videos and other sources that we deal with today.

A "wireless connection" is a signal that travels through the air, but it cannot be detected or put to use without the correct equipment that is "tuned in" to receive it.

It's Out There

We now have a little perspective on receiving, but what is being ***sent***? The sending device is called a transmitter and the radio is called a receiver. The signal that is sent is not visible to the human eye or perceptible to other senses, but it is there, nonetheless. There are two essential factors that are required to send (transmit) information and then to receive (decode and reproduce) the information. In the case of a radio transmission, input from a microphone or other source is fed into an amplifier that is connected to an antenna. The signal from the antenna is picked up by the coils in the radio that is tuned a specific station. The signal is then amplified and connected to a speaker so it can be heard. Discoveries over the last 100 years have revealed the presence of *signals* in the air all around us that come to us from space. However, the discovery of these space signals is predicated on one thing, the ability to detect them with a receiver.

You can probably locate 40 or 50 radio stations on your car radio dial if you are anywhere near a large city. There are several television stations that are transmitting their signals as well. Most areas of the country have technology with the ability to connect to your cell phone and provide service to send voice and pictures and data to your device. Large amounts of information are needed to send voice into the air and even more is needed to send video. Wireless internet connections can send truly enormous amounts of data through the air. Do you feel it? Do you see it? Do you smell it? No, you don't. But does your lack of ability to personally sense its presence negate its existence? No, again!

The concept of *reception* is extremely important to our discussion as the wireless technology requires the ability not only to send but to receive. Wireless devices do not function unless they can receive. Evidence of this is most plain when your cell phone call drops and disconnects your connection and conversation. Needless to say, reception is critical if you are to use the information that is being transmitted. However, what do you know about the information that is being transmitted. Where is it? What does it look like? You might even say, "I can't see it, so is it really there?"

Tuning In

Certainly you ***know*** that it is there, but how do you know? Did someone tell you it is there? Did you believe what they told you? Or is your belief based on evidence? And from where does that evidence come?

You have to be able to receive the signals.

Truly, there is a point to all of these questions, and it is that there are massive amounts of data swirling in the air all around us. The data is invisible, but not undetectable.

The reason that you can detect the existence of all of this information is that you have a receiving device that is tuned to the same frequency as the sending device and you can selectively *receive* want you want. You can watch a television program. You can listen to the radio. You can talk on your cell phone. You can send and receive text messages. You can connect to the internet and then view, download, upload, and send information at will.

Why? Because you have the proper receiver!

You can acknowledge that all of this invisible information is in the air around you. However, you must accept it by faith. You have to use faith because without a receiver (which you purchase on faith) there is no tangible evidence! You know that it is there. However, to verify it you have to be able to detect it and that takes a functional receiver.

The spiritual realm operates in part in the same way as radio waves and wireless technologies. The Spirit of God is everywhere, and He is constantly sending signals. However, traditional understanding, prejudice, or bias can interfere with your spiritual receiver and lead to spiritual blindness. The spiritual world is all around you, but without the right receiver or detector, you will never know that it exists. People may talk about spiritual things. They might even share stories with you about their interactions (or shall we say in technological terms, "downloading of experiences"). They might even tell you that you should experience these things, too. It would be like recommending that you watch a particular DVD movie or television program. However, if you don't have a TV or a DVD player with a monitor or computer, you can't receive it, play it or experience it.

Avoiding Interference

Interference is the term that is used in the electronics realm to describe the interruption of signals that are sent but not completely received. The receiver may not be tuned in correctly, but there may also be some physical impediment that blocks the signal such as a building. We still know that the signal is "out there," but we are just in a technological "dead zone" and can't receive it.

An emotional or mental fog or "cloud of interference" can act like a dead zone and block a person from physically seeing what is plainly around them. However, there is life, experience, and freedom outside the cloud. The cloud is frequently thrust upon us by our environment, peers, and caregivers, but it can also be self-imposed for a variety of reasons. Breaking free from the cloud of interference and an obscured view of reality can sometimes be difficult to accomplish. This is not so challenging when it comes to things that are easily observed in the physical realm, but the presence of this cloud of interference is a particular problem in the unseen spiritual realm.

Turning On And Tuning In

Transmissions are going on all of the time from virtually everywhere around you, but you must activate the detector or the receiver. Your receiver must also be able to differentiate between the massive amounts of signals that surround you. There is no way to pull in the signal and enjoy the content unless the receiver is tuned in to the correct signal. It must also be properly equipped with a functional speaker or display.

Getting into alignment to receive signals in the spiritual realm is more difficult and requires more effort. However, the same principles hold true. You must have a receiver, a "spiritual detector," which is not obscured by clouds of interference that prevent the transmissions from getting through. Some of these clouds can have devastating effects upon a person's life and "God Concept."

The receiver must also be prepared and tuned in to the right source. Radio waves are generated by man-made devices that man can understand and are routinely taken for granted in the world today. The simple fact is that radio waves are no more physical than the spiritual signals "sent" from God. Both types of transmission require a receiver to detect and decode the invisible signal. Fortunately, God created us as spiritual beings and provided us with a way to receive and experience His signals. If we choose, we can see with a *spiritual mind's eye* display and hear with *spiritual ears.*

The biggest problem man has is whether or not he chooses to turn on his receiver and tune it in to the right "channel" to receive from God. There are many factors that can block reception even though we have the right detector and the ability to receive. Many clouds cause interference and prevent reception. Some clouds are based on relationships, some on upbringing, and some on environment. These clouds get in the way and create a lot of static even for those who do acknowledge His presence. It can cause us to lose our spiritual connection and lose out on the Truth and Counsel of God's Word, which is the best information there is to provide fulfillment in our lives.

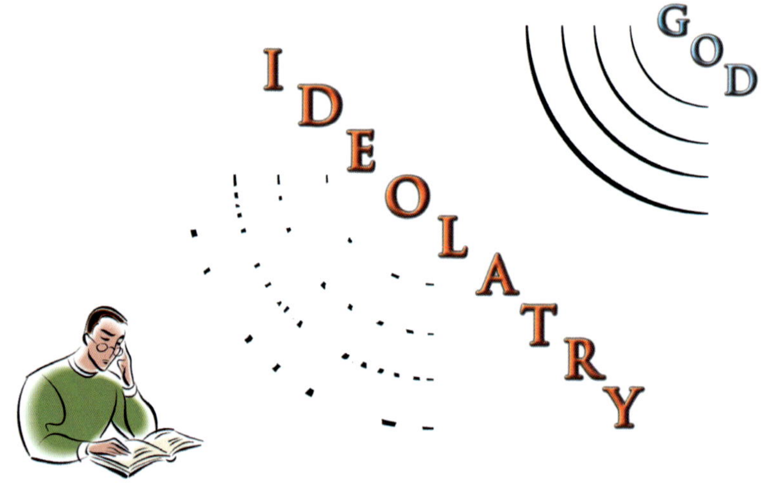

*Personal **"Ideolatry"** blocks our reception of God's Word.*

Are you ready to tune in to God's *signal* and to exercise faith in something that you can't see, feel, taste, smell, or hear? You place your faith in your technology every day. Today, consider investing your faith in something that has eternal consequence. It will take effort on your part, a desire to meet your spiritual needs and a decision to be open to study and hear what God is saying to you. God is always trying to get our attention especially through the distractions of life. Try setting aside your clouds of interference and turning your receiver on. Embrace your faith and dive in to explore how you actually see God in your life. Dare to discover whether or not your view of God agrees with who God says He is.

CHAPTER 4

HOW DO YOU SEE GOD ?

There are so many factors that influence how we see God. Influences from every aspect of our environment shape our senses and the way we see everything around us. Family life from birth is arguably the most powerful, having tremendous influence on our perceptions, world view and understanding of God, His character and nature. Daily interactions, with or without a family unit, shape our world. Some enjoy a nurturing and supportive family while others have endured ranges of abuse. Some grow up abandoned and lost in *the system*. Still others are raised in families where crime and/or drugs are the normal way to survive, and they are subjected to enormous peer pressure.

Everyone has a story full of disappointments, challenges, high points, low points and reasons why they are the way they are. We must all play the game of life with the circumstances we are given as no one chooses where they are born and raised. However, at some point in time regardless of circumstance, we are all faced with decisions, personal life decisions, which shape our futures. There can be a great temptation to compare our own circumstances with those of others and feel cheated. Most of us can probably look at some person or circumstance and cast blame on them for who we are. It can be difficult or seem impossible to overcome our personal circumstances. We can accept or reject them, but at some point, we are faced with the reality that we are personally responsible for what we think and do.

The majority of people probably do not find themselves in the extremes of life. Certainly, everyone experiences something within their pre-adult lives that they did not like or wished had been different. Yet, most would likely consider their family lives to be "normal."

The Influence of Family

Consider the following family dynamics involving a "*normal*" family of four with two boys. Minimal demonstration of caring and nurturing was given to either son during their early formative years. They were both well taken care of with all of their physical needs met, but communication, encouragement, involvement, and emotional support were largely absent. Neither parent was raised with any of these non-physical support systems, so they were inexperienced, unknowledgeable, and unequipped to know how to provide them.

The older brother had the high expectations of a first child placed upon him. He endured high demands and critical disapproval from his father and he was constantly in trouble for the mistakes that he made. He was coddled, excused, and rescued by his mother, who tried to overcome the harsh interactions of the father. The younger brother was largely left on his own with little positive or negative interaction. He felt ignored and emotionally abandoned because all attention (albeit negative) was focused on his brother.

The older brother grew to shirk responsibility and personal accountability as a result being constantly rescued. He had a guarded relationship with his father although he enjoyed a significant camaraderie with him as the first son. His view of God developed into one of disapproval in that he was conditioned to believe that nothing that he ever did was right. Therefore, because of his mother's rescuing he expected that someone would always take care of him and his problems no matter what he did.

The younger brother was not emotionally nurtured and was largely ignored. He still had the same stern relationship with his father, but without the privileged interaction that the older brother enjoyed. After observing the trouble that befell his brother, he just tried to stay out of the way and not be noticed. He was unaware of his mother's continual rescuing of his brother and never seemed to receive the same attention. His view of God was that He was stern and lacked tenderness and nurturing. He always felt insignificant and unloved. He believed that he had the responsibility to perform, but there wasn't going to be any help from anyone. God was, therefore, cold, demanding, and unloving.

The family had a spiritual life that did not include the father. Weekly duties of observance were enforced by the mother in a cold, authoritarian, mainstream religion. Their environment created a view of authority that directly translated to their differing individual views of God.

Both boys saw completely different aspects of the same two people (their parents). Each had different experiences with authority and responsibility. Each formed impressions that became their world view as a result of their experiences. They naturally acquired different views of God and His character as a result of the modeling of their human interactions. Their acquired views of the world around them influenced their understanding of God created their own reality.

The "Life Filter"

What you live with is your reality. However, is your reality a reflection of truth, or is it founded in misunderstanding or outright deception? Personal reality can become the *Life Filter* through which everything is seen and understood. One of our greatest challenges in the journey of life is to discover real truth and reshape our experiential reality to conform to the truth. Today, *absolute truth* can be a very difficult concept since there is a growing tendency toward relativism and the absence of absolutes.

Sadly, many are deceived and never take the time to explore and discover truth. Instead they merely live within the confines of the cloud of their own *Life Filters*. Consider a woman sitting in a park with trees, flowers, and the beauty of nature around her. However, there is a fog or cloud that completely engulfs her. It restricts her *world view* and limits her comprehension of her surroundings. She is unable to see the beauty that exists outside of her cloud.

The cloud represents the obscured view of reality that can occur because of our *Life Filters*. A clouded perception of truth can be created from the *Life Filters* of tradition, religion, culture, or even the general distractions of life in the same manner. A spiritual world view of *relative truth* that is based on experience rather than on a foundation of *real truth* can follow. It then becomes very easy to be deceived into living a misdirected life with flawed understanding based on the biased perceptions and inaccurate observations that come from that relative truth. This powerful, deceptive influence can prevent us from being able to see and experience the freedom that is given to the believer by God through Jesus Christ.

A cloud of "Life Filters" that may include tradition, religion or culture can limit our world view. They can prevent us from seeing and experiencing what surrounds us and understanding the real truth of God.

2 Corinthians 5:17 explains what God's gift of a relationship with Jesus Christ provides to us.

2 Corinthians 5:17

Therefore if any man be in Christ, he is a new creature: old things are passed away; behold, all things are become new.

We get outside of the cloud when we leave our "Life Filters" and "renew our minds" to really understand the promises that God provides to us in His Word. Knowledge of the Bible can completely transform our world view and anchor it in God's truth. The King James Bible explains this in Romans 12:1-2.

Romans 12:1-2

1 I beseech you therefore, brethren, by the mercies of God, that ye present your bodies a living sacrifice, holy, acceptable unto God, which is your reasonable service.
2 And be not conformed to this world: but be ye transformed by the renewing of your mind, that ye may prove what is that good, and acceptable, and perfect, will of God.

The Message Bible explains it with more detail:

Romans 12:1-2 *(MSG)*

[1] So here's what I want you to do, God helping you: Take your everyday, ordinary life — your sleeping, eating, going-to-work, and walking-around life — and place it before God as an offering. Embracing what God does for you is the best thing you can do for him. [2] Don't become so well-adjusted to your culture that you fit into it without even thinking. Instead, fix your attention on God. You'll be changed from the inside out. Readily recognize what he wants from you, and quickly respond to it. Unlike the culture around you, always dragging you down to its level of immaturity, God brings the best out of you, develops well-formed maturity in you.

There is much that competes for our time and attention that obstructs our "reception" and deters our focus from things that are more important. Removing hindrances to our reception is a key issue to "renewing our minds" and understanding truth. Peeling away our Life Filters by clearing the cloud or fog allows us to appreciate what surrounds us. The result is a completely new experience giving way to a new reality that is not based upon experience and perception but is based in Truth.

There are aspects of God's character and nature that cannot be seen because of the filter of our life experiences. The Life Filter does not necessarily create a true representation of who God is, but nonetheless, for the individual, it is their perception of God. It has been said that "your perception is your reality." The fact is that God will meet us wherever we are. However, it is up to us to change and be open to receive aspects of His character that we may be emotionally, intellectually, or spiritually unable to accept because of our life experiences. Therefore, to understand the truth about God, it is essential that we study His Word.

The images on the previous pages show that even though we might be looking, we may miss something that is hidden. Our Life Filter may cause us to miss out on important aspects of the totality of God in much the same way. We must overcome the filters that alter our perceptions and create a skewed perception of God.

It may be easy to identify with the Biblical stories and characters that give God the appearance of being cold, indifferent, and punishing. It would then be more likely for us to assume the same from God when considering our personal circumstances. However, God will meet us where we are even if we continue to see Him through our Life Filter. However, there are broad areas of God's character and nature that cannot be experienced without releasing or resetting those filters.

God – The "Higher Power"

Everyone that has the mental capacity must deal with the concept of a supernatural *Higher Power*. Acceptance of whether or not God exists is a matter of faith regardless of the decision. God may be acknowledged as a *Higher Power* or a Deity that must be obeyed, placated, and worshiped. The choices and conclusions develop fairly early in life based on family structure, values, "religious" upbringing, peer influence, cultural influences, and the like.

Some people rebel against their early exposure to the concept of God. Others embrace these experiences throughout their lives. They may maintain a belief in what they were originally taught without challenge or exploration. Some only begin to understand the concept of God as they mature because there was a God void or *Godlessness* early in their lives. Still others simply deny the existence of the God of the Bible altogether. Acknowledged or not, God created man to have fellowship and a relationship with Him, and there is a place in man that only God can fill.

Man is driven to fill the God created hole or void that is inside him. He will find a substitute and fill that hole with some other type of "god" if the true God is not allowed to fill it. Instead of worshipping God as the higher power, the man that rejects God may adopt a substitute, a distorted concept of who God is. He or she might adopt a *god concept* which might involve a thing, an activity, a single being or variety of beings. Other god concepts might include nature, the inherent goodness of man, humanism, everything is "god," a "universal" truth or possibly even a specific human that has risen to "godlike" status such as in ancient mythology. Still other concepts might include a variety of activities or pursuits that attain a "god" status in an individual's life such as sports or even one's career.

One's view of the existence of God, the meaning of scripture and how God deals with man is developed based on many factors. As a higher power, God is frequently seen as a fatherly or motherly being or a combination of the two. The "Parent God" image that is subsequently created might be largely based on the father, mother, or other authority figure relationships of the individual. Those that were raised in a close, traditional, nurturing family environment with a strong, affirmative male influence might develop a positive concept of a "Father God" as referenced in Isaiah 9:6 and Ephesians 4:6.

Isaiah 9:6

For unto us a child is born, unto us a son is given: and the government shall be upon his shoulder: and his name shall be called Wonderful, Counselor, The mighty God, ***The everlasting Father,*** *The Prince of Peace.*

Ephesians 4:6

One ***God and Father of all,*** *who is above all, and through all, and in you all.*

Family, peer, work or a host of other relationships in the life of an individual might influence the "Father God" concept in other ways. This realization is quite important, especially from a Judeo-Christian perspective which is based upon the Old Testament of the Bible. An individual's view of God as a Father will directly affect his or her interpretation of Biblical writings. It may also influence his or her beliefs regarding God's interaction with mankind in general and His interaction with individuals in particular. An individual's view and interactions with persons of authority or concepts of authority are directly influenced by his or her family unit or lack thereof.

Shaping Our "Life Filters"

The following tables list some common human attributes and attitudes. These are characteristics that might be found in a father, mother, authority figure or even a peer. The expression of these traits will have an effect upon the development of a person that creates his or her unique set of Life Filters. Different attitudes and feelings will manifest depending upon the way in which a person responds to the influence of a particular characteristic or combination of characteristics.

Common emotions, reactions, and traits shape many things about who we are, how we think, what we feel, how we cope and what we believe.[6] As a result, there is a strong correlation between the relationship or the lack thereof that we have with our parents, authority figures, and peers and the way in which we understand and view the spiritual world and God himself.

Table 1 lists some positive Life Filter influences and their effects. Table 2 illustrates the possible effects of negative Life Filter influences and attributes on an individual's view of God. These influences may come from any of a number of sources and can have detrimental effects on a person's general world view and create a significant distortion of the scriptural depiction of God.

Table 1
Positive Influences

Positive Influence or Attribute	*Therefore Your View of God Might Be*
Affectionate	*Tender*
Caring	*Nurturing*
Compassionate	*Empathetic*
Encouraging	*Supportive*
Fair	*Just*
Faithful	*Trustworthy*
Forgiving	*Forebearing*
Giving	*Generous*
Gracious	*Merciful*
Grateful	*Rewarding*
Honest	*Truthful*
Loving	*Loving*
Patient	*Tolerant*
Stable	*Unwavering*
Tender	*Gentle*
Tolerant	*Accepting*

Table 2
Negative Influences

Negative Influence or Attribute	*Therefore, Your View of God Might Be*
Abusive	*Punishing*
Angry	*Disapproving*
Frustrating	*Provoking*
Gloomy	*Woeful*
Hostile	*Angry*
Indifferent	*Disinterested*
Judgmental	*Condemning*
Overwhelming	*Menacing*
Rebellious	*Antagonistic*
Rejecting	*Dismissive*
Selfish	*Demanding*
Stingy	*Withholding*
Troubled	*Oppressive*
Untrusting	*Unreliable*
Unworthy	*Unaccepting*
Victimized	*Unjust*

It is a very difficult, if not an impossible task to interact with God and scripture without the influences of this life filter "baggage" that we all carry. A cloud of personal ***Ideolatry*** emanates from the sum total of all of these and other factors. One might imagine that the lack of positive influences might distort our view. However, how much more distorted might our view become if we are confronted with a barrage of negative attributes throughout our lives?

Table 3 illustrates how the absence of some of the positive traits might further influence and even promote a negative Life Filter view of God.

Table 3
Influences That are Absent

Positive Attribute	*A Lack of May Cause or Result In*	*Attitudes That May Develop*	*Therefore, Your View of God Might Be*
Acceptance	*Despair*	*Rejection*	*Oppressive*
Affection	*Rejection*	*Unloved / Cold Hearted*	*Not Loving*
Caring	*Neglect*	*Apprehensive*	*Indifferent*
Compassion	*Coldness*	*Victimized*	*Uncaring*
Discipline	*Chaos*	*Carelessness*	*Demanding*
Encouragement	*Discouragement*	*Hopelessness*	*Disapproving*
Fairness	*Bias*	*Prejudice*	*Unjust*
Faithfulness	*Doubt*	*Untrusting*	*Unreliable*
Generosity	*Selfishness*	*Miserly*	*Stingy*
Good	*Evil*	*Rebellious*	*Destructive*
Graciousness	*Inconsiderateness*	*Selfish*	*Harsh*
Kindness	*Cruelty*	*Aloofness*	*Vengeful*
Inviting	*Guarded*	*Anxious*	*Fault Finding*
Mercy	*Brutality*	*Hostility*	*Enraged*
Patient	*Intolerance*	*Impatience*	*Overbearing*
Sincere	*Deceptiveness*	*Unreliable*	*Distrustful*
Sympathy	*Apathy*	*Unconcerned*	*Hardhearted*
Tenderness	*Harshness*	*Hurt*	*Severe*
Tolerance	*Resistance*	*Defiance*	*Punishing*
Trust	*Distrust*	*Suspicious*	*Judging*

The results of positively modeled influences can reinforce a positive attitude toward God assuming the individual acknowledges that God exists. The presence or absence of these and other attributes and influences shape an individual's opinions of God. These factors create perceptions that influence a person's view of both the existence and character of God. They will also profoundly affect a person's understanding of scripture and the perception of how God deals with man. A truly successful understanding of God, His purpose for and relationship with the individual human spirit requires a separation from these influences.

This is not easy, but God does provide us with the tools we need to accomplish this "humanly" daunting task. They are found in His Word, the Bible. However, the totality of our *Life Filter*, our cloud of ***Ideolatry,*** prevents us from even acknowledging Him and keeps us from seeing the bigger picture of God's true character. We must be careful and not allow our *Life Filter* to reflect the adage, "You can't see the forest for the trees."

Try a different approach instead and consider God as nurturing and tender-hearted, providing emotional and spiritual support in Biblical accounts. Try hard to recognize the completeness of His nature rather than only the fragment that you may currently comprehend. As you move through the rest of this book, be open-minded to view God in ways that your emotions and life filters may not understand. If you are someone that does not acknowledge God, this will block your discovery. Please try to be open and let the Truth of God's Word explain itself.

The interpretation of God that an individual adopts emanates from the perspective gained through family, peers, education, and their environment. It has been said that "Perception is Reality."The fact is that there is a supreme and all-encompassing "Reality" or "Absolute Truth," which is God. However, man's concept of truth tends to change based on his perceptions and perspective.

Life Filters are a big part of the formation of the "reality" of the individual. Overcoming the burdens of these *Life Filters* can go a long way toward reshaping reality into alignment with actual truth. It is a challenge that is worth the effort. You can certainly learn from your past experiences, but you should not let them completely define you and your life. Search out the things that have negative influences on your reality and see them for what they are, not the persecution or punishment of God but the failings of imperfect men and women like yourself. Turn the page on your life filters and let your "Reality" be shaped by "Real" truth *(see p. 76)*.

Future chapters will explore the concept of "truth" that is created based upon individual or collective perspectives and will begin with an exploration into the truth about the *"Acts of God."*

CHAPTER 5

ACTS OF GOD

I lived in the Los Angeles area in the 1970's while attending the University of Southern California Dental School. My first career choice while in high school and the first year of college was electronic engineering. I had a deep fascination with the field of electronics and computers and had worked part-time as a technician. Computer electronics was just in the birth canal relative to where it is now, and I really wanted to be a part of the coming computer revolution. However, calculus and I did not get along well and neither did engineering physics. Fortunately for me, God had other plans. I soon found myself adrift and disconnected from my previous five years of dedication to that singular goal. Although I was not listening to Him particularly well (if at all), I was at least malleable enough to stumble along the path that He laid out for me.

I was raised in a mainstream, denominational religion and always thought I had a pretty good handle on understanding what God was all about, and I thought I knew where I fit into the scheme of things. After all, the traditions of the church were absolute and the doctrines unwavering. I was under the impression that I needed to be controlled and spoon fed by those in spiritual authority over me, and I was convinced that I didn't have much value as an individual.

Although I was instructed through three years in a religious school and ten years of weekly classes, the one thing that was missing was an encounter with the Alive and Risen Jesus. I only knew the one who was still hanging on the cross. I was carrying a load of guilt that I could only unload on Saturday afternoon to some soft, yet stern voice in a dark closet. Needless to say, I did not enjoy a personal relationship with God or Jesus. It was always filtered through the relationship, expectations, and demands of another person or organization. I thought I was a Christian because I was a member of a church!

My path took me in a direction that I was not expecting as I left the plan for engineering and stepped out into the unknown. My first semester toward my new career path in dentistry at USC began in January 1971 with undergraduate studies. I had not yet been accepted into dental school, but I was taking the necessary steps. I did get accepted and graduated from USC Dental School in 1976 and have enjoyed 39 years of practicing dentistry as I write this. However, my dental career is not the focus of this writing.

"Natural" Disasters

Something quite tragic occurred during my first semester at USC. I was getting ready for the drive to school on the morning of February 9, 1971, when the 6.6 magnitude earthquake hit Sylmar in the San Fernando Valley area of Los Angeles. The destruction was on a massive scale by recent California standards with the destruction of large freeway overpasses, streets, and buildings. Sixty-five people lost their lives.[7]

A few years later on October 17, 1989, California experienced another massive earthquake measuring 6.9. It occurred during the warm-up of the 1989 World Series between the Oakland Athletics and the San Francisco Giants. Sixty-three people were killed and 3757 injured.[8, 9] The Northridge Earthquake occurred in 1994 causing more than $20 billion in damages, 57 deaths, and 9000 injuries.[10] The Gulf States were devastated with Hurricane Katrina in 2005, leaving at least 1883 people dead and a staggering $81 billion in property damage and losses.

The world experienced the massive destruction of the Tsunami in Sumatra, Indonesia, on December 26, 2004, killing an estimated 225,000 people in 11 countries.[11] More recently, Japan was devastated with a 9.0 earthquake on March 11, 2011, with more than 18,000 deaths and 12,000 missing and presumed dead.[12] Just a few months later, the US was hit with the largest number of highly destructive tornadoes in a season, a phenomenon that also manifested worldwide.[13]

What do these and other such disasters have in common? They are all referred to as "Acts of God" by the world legal system and insurance companies. These days, with the major effort on the part of the world to eliminate the existence of God from the planet, many of the definitions are being attributed to "natural forces" and leaving God's name out of it, but there is still a sense and belief that God, however an individual may define him, is responsible for the destruction. Let's look at what are actually considered *Acts of God* and how they are defined by the *American Heritage Dictionary*, the *'Lectric Law Library,* and the *Columbia Encyclopedia*.

Act of God *(noun)*

A natural event, not preventable by any human agency, such as flood, storms, or lightning. Forces of nature that no one has control over, and therefore cannot be held accountable. This phrase denotes those accidents which arise from physical causes, and which cannot be prevented.

Where the law casts a duty on a party, the performance shall be excused, if it be rendered impossible by the act of God, but where the party by his own contract engages to do an act, it is deemed to be his own fault and folly that he did not thereby provide against contingencies, and exempt himself from responsibilities in certain events and in such case, that is, in the instance of an absolute general contract the performance is not excused by an inevitable accident or other contingency, although not foreseen by, nor within the control of, the party.

A manifestation especially of a violent or destructive natural force, such as a lightning strike or earthquake that is beyond human power to cause, prevent, or control.[14, 15]

Act of God *(noun)*

In law, an accident caused by the operation of extraordinary natural force. The effect of ordinary natural causes (e.g., that rain will leak through a defective roof) may be foreseen and avoided by the exercise of human care; failure to take the necessary precautions constitutes negligence, and the party injured in the accident may be entitled to damages. An act of God, however, is so extraordinary and devoid of human agency that reasonable care would not avoid the consequences; hence, the injured party has no right to damages. Accidents caused by tornadoes, perils of the sea, extraordinary floods, and severe ice storms are usually considered acts of God, but fires are not so considered unless they are caused by lightning.[16]

This language represents a pervasive attitude that has been instrumental in turning multitudes of people away from a relationship with the true God because of a lack of understanding. They have been conditioned through religious tradition, popular science or just plain ignorance that when a disaster occurs, it must be an "act of the gods" as seen in the lore of primitive populations. This prejudice and lack of understanding has given rise to many practices of superstitious cultures that offer sacrifices to appease the gods, stave off destruction and win favor. Assuming no personal responsibilities for their own actions and assuming that occurrences were at the whim of a god, those in power would sacrifice other people's possessions and even other people in their unending quest for appeasement of those gods. These sacrifices were intended to atone for some wrong doing or to appease a god that just felt like being angry.

Does this mean that God uses "natural" disasters to "punish" mankind for wrong doing? Are earthquakes, lightning strikes, extraordinary floods, tornados, severe ice storms, hurricanes, tsunamis, or volcanic eruptions evidence of the anger of God? In our wisdom and understanding of the forces of the natural world around us, we would mostly answer, "No." However, some religious people might still claim them to be God's judgment. How about financial calamity, abuse, sickness, disease, accidents, premature death, or starvation? Are these payments handed out as God's justice? How does God operate relative to the human race within this world that we live? According to traditional religious wisdom, these events are simply acts of retribution or punishment by the God of the Bible. However, the true God states very plainly something that is quite different in the Bible.

Hosea 4:6a

> *My people are destroyed for lack of knowledge: because thou hast rejected knowledge, I will also reject thee…*

This verse just might put a different spin on our understanding. These questions of God's complicit behavior are at the heart of this discourse. However, just whose "god" is getting the blame for these "acts of God"? The prevailing scapegoat is the God of the Bible, but there are many systems that have a "god" at the center of them. These systems are generally known as religions. There have been untold attempts to both qualify and quantify the term *religion*. However, what is religion?

Religion

For centuries, perhaps from the beginning of time as we know it, mankind has understood that there is something bigger than himself at work in the universe. There have been many approaches that he has employed to seek and understand that "higher power." Virtually all of these methods fall under the description of religion. Let's examine some definitions that include some historical etymology or origins of the word *religion* from the *Merriam-Webster Online Dictionary* and *Dictionary.com*.

religion *(noun)*

> *The origin of the word religion is from the Middle English* ***religioun****, from Anglo-French* ***religiun****, Latin* ***religion-****,* ***religio*** *is supernatural constraint, sanction, religious practice, perhaps from* ***religare*** *to restrain, tie back.*[17]
>
> *A set of beliefs concerning the cause, nature, and purpose of the universe, esp. when considered as the creation of a superhuman agency or agencies, usually involving devotional and ritual observances, and often containing a moral code governing the conduct of human affairs.*
>
> *The body of persons adhering to a particular set of beliefs and practices, something one believes in and follows devotedly.*[18]

Perhaps then, considering these definitions, *religion* will help us find the answers to some of the perplexing questions of God's complicity in the events and circumstances that we observe. However, it is interesting to note that one of the roots of the word religion is from the Latin *religare*, meaning to *tie back or restrain.* One connotation of this might actually be to tie or bind the individual to the tenants or the specific doctrines of that religion which could be a favorable or unfavorable concept. This binding might help an individual overcome unhealthy desires or actions on a positive note. Another more literal and negative inference might speak to a disturbing motive of religions in general. Religions are created by man and actively work to control their members.

Each religion has its own definition and description of its related deity. However, the world in which we live has many gods. A religion that serves a single god is called ***mono***-theistic. Religions that have many gods are called ***poly***-theistic. Some religions deny the existence of any god and are, therefore, called ***a***-theistic. Definitions of religion that many consider too broad, too narrow, too tolerant, too intolerant, too inclusive, or not inclusive enough abound. Some wish to include studies of science, such as cosmology or ecology as religions. Suffice it to say, there is absolutely no universal agreement as to what the term *religion* actually refers to, much less to the deity that may be associated with it.

Regardless of these side issues, religion is at the core of many people's values and belief system, and further exploration is necessary for a more complete understanding of the influence of religion. Each individual religion has a common theme and a shared system of beliefs to which the followers subscribe. This means that they employ a set of codes or doctrines or standards with rules of conduct and regulations of various sorts. Original core beliefs may be supplemented by traditions that are created by the leaders of the religion or possibly groups of men or women who are in leadership or positions of influence. A religion may be based solely on the teachings or philosophies of an individual. Other religions may develop from traditions that have been handed down through generations. Sometimes, they are simply born out of philosophy or a school of human thought or simply personal prejudice or preferences. The traditions that are handed down to subsequent generations may become additional doctrines within the established religion. Jesus spoke about this in Mark 7:13.

Mark 7:13 *(NIV)*

Thus you nullify the word of God by your tradition that you have handed down. And you do many things like that.

The primary focus of a religion is its deity or god. This god is the central figure of the religion that the followers serve. The doctrines are generally based on the teachings or the personality of that individual or figure. Service and worship of that central figure are generally required in ***mono***-theistic religions whereas ***poly***-theistic religions worship multiple gods.

Based on the definitions above, other activities might be considered religions of sorts. A job, career, philosophy, sports activity (can be players or spectators, as the word *fan* is short for fanatic), or any obsessive activities such as video games, hobbies, or even sex can actually become an individual's religion. One of the definitions of religion suggests that it is, "Something one believes in and follows devotedly." This indicates that anything that dominates an individual's time, energy, attention, and money has the potential to become his or her religion or even a god in his or her life. Religion could be considered the pursuit of meaning or the focus of purpose and devotion of an individual's life. It is a system of beliefs that has been created by man or mankind to pursue those things which he does not understand and define his purpose and relationship to the world and existence that surrounds him. By default, these thoughts and ideas, personalities, and leaders act as the deity of the religion. Whether a personality, an idea, or system of thought, worship is required, and for our purposes, the thing or being that is served will be referred to as the god of the religion.

God and Religion

Everyone serves a god directly or indirectly. However, there is no absolute consensus among religions about what the definition of *god* is. The definition varies for each religion. For example, there was once a television commercial in which games and players for the latest football weekend were being advertised. The main figure was a player who described the upcoming games and the excitement that fans would experience as they watched. He then described his own experience while watching the games as his *religion*. He was actively promoting the *religion* of football!

However, does the true God occupy these religions or agree with these human activities? Does God adapt Himself to all of man's different subjective views? Does God conform to various human views of established religions? Here is what the Bible says about God and man in Romans 1:20-22 through the apostle Paul.

Romans 1:20 - 22 *(NIV)*

> 20 *For since the creation of the world God's invisible qualities-- his eternal power and divine nature-- have been clearly seen, being understood from what has been made, so that men are without excuse.* 21 *For although they knew God, they neither glorified him as God nor gave thanks to him, but their thinking became futile and their foolish hearts were darkened.*
> 22 *Although they claimed to be wise, they became fools.*

God is quoted in the Old Testament book of Isaiah 55:8-9 as saying that his thoughts and ways are very different than ours. The thoughts and concepts that we as humans consider so significant, important, and valid are carnal or worldly and not necessarily accurate when considered in light of the view and perspective of God.

Isaiah 55:8-9

8 For my thoughts are not your thoughts, neither are your ways my ways, saith the LORD. 9 For as the heavens are higher than the earth, so are my ways higher than your ways, and my thoughts than your thoughts.

The human mind can be easily deceived and convinced of its superiority and self-sufficiency, which is the core of ***Ideolatry***. The human mind is an awesome thing indeed and capable of great feats of understanding and wisdom, but it is no match for the One that made it. Let's revisit the *Dictionary.com* definition of *religion* and explore it in a little more detail.

religion *(noun)*

A set of beliefs concerning the cause, nature, and purpose of the universe, esp. when considered as the creation of a superhuman agency or agencies, usually involving devotional and ritual observances, and often containing a moral code governing the conduct of human affairs.

This definition of religion acknowledges a god. However, it is neither established nor directed by a supernatural God. It is all *man* centered. Even though humans think that they possess all wisdom and understanding, they still come face to face with the Old Testament revelation of Proverbs 21:2.

Proverbs 21:2 *(NIV)*

All a man's ways seem right to him, but the LORD weighs the heart.

Suffice it to say that the definitions of religion that do exist provide no indication that religion is an institution that has been established by the true God. So then, if man wants religion, how should it be described?

A proper definition should focus on the institution of religion as it is established by man. Man creates the doctrines, sets up the rules, propagates the traditions and enforces the observance of those rules and doctrines. There are many religions and many different perspectives that they portray. Consider the author's definition of *religion*:

religion *(noun)*

Religion is man's organized set of rules and doctrines designed to direct or control its adherents. It is attempt to look outside of himself to discover a

> *meaning for his existence that transcends his own physical nature. It is man seeking God and doing so through carnal, human thought and mindfully inspired means. Religion is man's interpretation of his deity and the intents of that deity, however that deity is defined. (The Author)*

Christianity is considered by many to be a religion. However, it is not a religion. It is much different. It is not founded upon man's desire to find God. It is not based on rules and doctrines. Christianity is a personal relationship with Jesus, the Christ, based on His teachings as they are revealed in the Bible. It is God reaching out to man to establish a relationship with His Son, Jesus Christ. It is not a man-made organization.

Truth

If we will accept the possibility that religions are man made and that the counsel of God is correct, we will find great insight that goes beyond our capabilities of human reasoning. We can press through the confusion of man's perspective and actually learn what may be the truth. However, we must first deal with the concept of "*Truth*." The definition of the word truth may vary to fit a specific argument such as *relative truth*, but the *Merriam-Webster Online Dictionary* defines *truth* this way:

truth *(noun)*

> *Fidelity, constancy; sincerity in action, character, and utterance; the state of being the case - fact; a transcendent fundamental or spiritual reality.*[19]

The counsel of the Bible tells us that God cannot lie in Numbers 23:19, or in other words, He is incapable of anything but the ***truth***. According to the Bible, everything emanates from God; therefore, there is possibly a more accurate way of expressing this thought. Whatever God says becomes absolute ***Truth*** by default.

Numbers 23:19

> *God is not a man, that he should lie; neither the son of man, that he should repent: hath he said, and shall he not do it? or hath he spoken, and shall he not make it good?*

There are a multitude of biblical references that support and point to the word, works, law, commandments, and Spirit of God as being true or truth *(see Appendix Chapter 5)*. Here are just a few:

Psalms 119:142

Thy righteousness is an everlasting righteousness, and thy law is the truth.

Psalms 119:151

Thou art near, O LORD; and all thy commandments are truth.

Psalms 119:160

Thy word is true from the beginning: and every one of thy righteous judgments endureth for ever.

Deuteronomy 32:4

He is the Rock, his work is perfect: for all his ways are judgment: a God of truth and without iniquity, just and right is he.

John 8:32

And ye shall know the truth, and the truth shall make you free.

John 14:6

Jesus saith unto him, I am the way, the truth, and the life: no man cometh unto the Father, but by me.

John 17:17

Sanctify them through thy truth: thy word is truth

Romans 1:22-28 gives a very detailed view of the relationship of man to the Truth of God. It describes in great detail the path that mankind takes when it rejects the notion that God's Truth is absolute.

Romans 1:22-28 *(NIV)*

22 Although they claimed to be wise, they became fools 23 and exchanged the glory of the immortal God for images made to look like mortal man and birds and animals and reptiles. 24 Therefore God gave them over in the sinful desires of their hearts to sexual impurity for the degrading of their bodies with one another. 25 They exchanged the truth of God for a lie, and worshiped and served created things rather than the Creator — who is forever praised. Amen.

26 Because of this, God gave them over to shameful lusts. Even their women exchanged natural relations for unnatural ones. 27 In the same way the men also abandoned natural relations with women and were inflamed with lust for one another. Men committed indecent acts with other men, and received in themselves the due penalty for their perversion. 28 Furthermore, since they did not think it worthwhile to retain the knowledge of God, he gave them over to a depraved mind, to do what ought not to be done.

The Word of God, the Bible, provides some excellent instruction and insight about life to enhance our human understanding. However, the tendency that we all have is to trust more in what we can see than the instruction that we receive through the spiritual understanding that the Bible provides. This is virtually programmed in us from a very early age. In childhood, the "terrible twos" are a manifestation of a connection to only what is observed and an expression of personal will. The adolescent years frequently bring a rejection of authority and wisdom gained from those who have already had experience in living life. Proverbs 3:5-7 tells us to listen to wisdom and good counsel and rely on God's direction.

Proverbs 3:5-7

[5] Trust in the LORD with all thine heart; and lean not unto thine own understanding. [6] In all thy ways acknowledge him, and he shall direct thy paths. [7] Be not wise in thine own eyes: fear the LORD, and depart from evil.

As a result, we can have a renewing of our human minds and an opening up of our thoughts to embrace the spiritual truths in 1 Corinthians 2:12-16 that God desires to reveal to us.

1 Corinthians 2:12-16

[12] Now we have received, not the spirit of the world, but the spirit which is of God; that we might know the things that are freely given to us of God.

[13] Which things also we speak, not in the words which man's wisdom teacheth, but which the Holy Ghost teacheth; comparing spiritual things with spiritual. [14] But the natural man receiveth not the things of the Spirit of God: for they are foolishness unto him: neither can he know them, because they are spiritually discerned. [15] But he that is spiritual judgeth all things, yet he himself is judged of no man. [16] For who hath known the mind of the Lord, that he may instruct him? But we have the mind of Christ.

The Concept of Absolutes

When the Truth of God is rejected, the *wisdom* of man is exalted. It can be found in the philosophies and thought revealed in humanism, evolution, situational ethics, situational truth, relativism, scientific thought, scientific theories or postulates to name a few. These may become secular religions of sort. All of them share a common thread, one that propagates the notion that nothing is absolute. *Relativism* is a core tenant giving rise to *situational* truth. It suggests that truth actually changes depending upon the participants, observers, and the circumstances in the following *Merriam-Webster Online Dictionary* definition.

relativism *(noun)*

A theory that knowledge is relative to the limited nature of the mind and the conditions of knowing; a view that ethical truths depend on the individuals and groups holding them. [20]

Situational Truth

Scientific thought is in constant flux with new discoveries that lead to new understanding and theories based on acquired knowledge. Knowledge itself is the subject of scientific study through a branch of philosophy known as epistemology here defined in the *Merriam-Webster Online Dictionary*.

+ *(noun)* (epis·te·mol·o·gy, i-ˌpis-tə-ˈmä-lə-jē)

The study or a theory of the nature and grounds of knowledge especially with reference to its limits and validity.

Scientific thought and knowledge are somewhat rhetorical in nature in that its language intends to influence people toward its assumptions, understanding, and theories. Rhetoric sometimes can infer deception, but not always so as seen in this *Merriam-Webster Online Dictionary,* definition.

rhetoric *(noun)* (rhet·o·ric, ˈre-tə-rik)

Language that is intended to influence people and that may not be honest or reasonable.

The art or skill of speaking or writing formally and effectively especially as a way to persuade or influence people.

This philosophical view of knowledge was discussed in an essay by Robert L. Scott, Director of Graduate Studies, Department of Speech-Communication, University of Minnesota in 1967. In his work, he discussed the concepts of truth and knowledge as they relate to rhetoric. In it, he discusses ethical dilemmas that might lead a person to alter truth or even lie outright to achieve the greater good. This kind of discussion leads to the concept of situational truth which defines that which is right as a function of the circumstances. The following statement articulates his definition of situational truth.

> *Man must consider truth not as something fixed and final but as something to be created moment by moment in the circumstances in which he finds himself and with which he must cope. Man may plot his course by fixed stars, but he does not possess those stars; he only proceeds, more or less effectively, on his course. Furthermore, man has learned that his stars are fixed only in a relative sense.*[21]
>
> *Robert L. Scott*

From the standpoint of this philosophical argument, we can see that there are no absolutes in the eyes of man. This is one reason why ***Ideolatry***, which is embodied in the above quote, is such a problem. There is no standard by which to compare and evaluate. Man's truth tends to be based in his experience, and the variable nature of experience leads away from absolutes. To no surprise, this attitude is in direct contradiction to the declarations of the Bible, the Word of God. Everything is subject to change, and rules are only valid "in the moment" in this manner of human thought and life. They are subject to change at any given time without any prior notice! It would seem that this kind of thinking could lead to a great deal of chaos or confusion as to whose view, understanding, and decision processes would be the most valid in any given situation. What a challenge this is to any sense of order. However, is order required or is order simply a desire of man?

Situational Truth rests on Relative Truth or Relativism.

The order provided by religion is focused on man's wisdom and provides differing spiritual and moral codes, themes, and focuses of worship, whether deity-centered or not. There is still a collective *god* or focal point, and we can see that the characteristics of the religion's *god* vary according to the doctrines of that particular philosophy. All of this leaves us with a challenge to determine whose philosophy, system of thought, religion, belief system or *god* is the right God and where the message of truth really exists.

In its quest to become the center of man's worship, can religion provide specific answers to the questions that plague us regarding God's responsibility for the disasters, the "Acts of God," which opened this chapter? Religions do provide answers and define who God is. However, traditional beliefs frequently hold God responsible for pain and suffering that can't be easily explained. Religions are not instituted by God, however. They are man-made entities or organizations that man uses to address the problem of understanding God and also to control his surroundings. As a result, since God does not actively defend Himself, He gets blamed for the bad things. However, in the mind of mankind, the human intellect and science get the credit for the good things. This is the ultimate expression of "***Ideolatry***."

Science does not acknowledge or accept the premise of God since it explains everything relative to the physical, not the spiritual. However, if a source cannot be found in a situation such as an *accidental* death or other inexplicable catastrophe, God still tends to get the blame because it is convenient. Can science explain "Acts of God" or shed light on who God is or if He exists at all? How could it draw any absolute conclusions with the shifting definition of truth that science provides. According to science, there are ***no*** absolutes as we will see in the next chapter.

Regardless, let's give science a chance, and we may get some further insight. Perhaps the objective perspectives of scientific observation and theories will lead us to the truth. Science should be able to rationally explain who or what is actually responsible for the calamities referred to as "Acts of God" rather than the subjective claims of religion. Someone or something must be responsible. The answers to our questions about "Acts of God" will surely be answered in science.

Chapter 6

OUR UNIVERSE RELATIVE OR ABSOLUTE ?

The non-science minded reader might be inclined to "glaze over" and check out when there is a scientific discussion of this sort. Try to allow this chapter to speak to you as you read it. Every effort has been made to keep the discussion simple and easy to understand. The goal is to help the reader understand the basics of ways in which the world operates. And besides, there are pictures!

Much of what we *know* about our surroundings and our universe has been derived from man's experience through centuries of observation, exploration, thought, and philosophizing. Collectively, this is what has *evolved* into what we know today as modern science. It fills a void that is present within us, one that our intellect demands to be filled. This emptiness drives an insatiable thirst for comprehension of the nature of the universe in which we live. Vast amounts of time, energy, thought, and resources, both natural and financial, have been spent in attempts to fill the void. Logically then, we should find some answers in science.

When approaching the problems presented by the natural world and the universe, science always seems to start with the presupposition that the God of the Bible does not exist. Scientific theory is actually careful to ignore *even the possibility* that God is actually the creator. Science has even created its own starting point for the universe. It is defined as the ***Big Bang***. Stephen Hawking, the famed physicist, says the following in his book, *A Briefer History of Time*.

> *The eventual goal of science is to provide a single theory that describes the whole universe. However, the approach most scientists actually follow is to separate the problem into two parts. First, there are laws that tell*

us how the universe changes with time. (If we know what the universe is like at any one time, these physical laws tell us how it will look at any later time.) Second, there is the question of the initial state of the universe. Some people feel that science should be concerned with only the first part; they regard the question of the initial situation as a matter for metaphysics or religion. They would say that God, being omnipotent, could have started the universe off any way He wanted. That may be so, but, in that case, God also could have made it develop in a completely arbitrary way. Yet it appears that God chose to make it evolve in a very regular way, according to certain laws. It, therefore, seems equally reasonable to suppose that there are also laws governing the initial state.[22]

The Universe of Science

Hawking speaks here about the development of the universe and states that science addresses how it changes over time. He also seems to acknowledge the omnipotence of God and that God set things up in the universe to work according to certain *regular* or consistent laws. (Perhaps this a leaning toward acknowledgment of absolutes?) In the following passage, Hawking further identifies the quest of mankind for knowledge about the universe in which we live.

But ever since the dawn of civilization, people have not been content to see events as unconnected and inexplicable. We have craved an understanding of the underlying order in the world. Today we still yearn to know why we are here and where we came from. Humanity's deepest desire for knowledge is justification enough for our continuing quest. And our goal is nothing less than a complete description of the universe we live in.[23]

Man's desire for knowledge and his desire to define his own existence do not lead him to discover truth about the true God, however. Man seeks a *god* to serve, frequently one of his own making. The void that science keeps trying to fill exists within each one of us. It is a God-shaped hole. However, the void will certainly not be filled through science as evidenced by Hawking's further commentary when describing the origin of the universe.

Correspondingly, if, as is the case, we know only what has happened since the big bang we cannot determine what happened beforehand.

> *As far as we are concerned, events before the big bang can have no consequences and so should not form part of a scientific model of the universe. We should, therefore, cut them out of the model and say that big bang was the beginning of time. This means that questions such as who set up the conditions for the big bang are not questions that science addresses.*[24]

The assumption stated here is that science *knows* what has happened since the Big Bang, which supposedly occurred millions of years ago. At one time, science also claimed to *know* that there were only four elements in the universe, *fire, earth, water,* and *ether* or air. At that time, everything revolved around these four elements. It might also be prudent to add that scientists believed that the world was flat, the earth was the center of the universe and the sun revolved around the earth!

During those periods of history, there were certainly many observational factors that supported these theories and solidified them into ***fact***. Not the least of the influences was the dominance of religion and the imposition of a dominating and sequestering concept of God upon science. During those times, one of the goals of religion was to control thought and dominate the people. Centralizing science under the umbrella of religion was an effective way to both control and stifle serious investigations.

Obviously, these were ill-formed sets of suppositions and theories that are clearly erroneous based on our current understanding and perspective. Fortunately, we have learned a bit more about the universe than man knew at that time due to the noble efforts of the scientific process and thought. However, from past events, it would seem evident that in a few hundred years or less, scientists will say the same about the understandings of our time. If science is right about there being no absolutes, then even history teaches us that current conclusions and theories should not be taught as absolutes.

It seems that science declares absolutes when it suits its purpose, but still does not want to deal with the question of God. Man or science cannot explain God because God defies explanation in human terms. Science defers the problem of God to others (philosophers and religious folk) whom it actually seems to disdain and mock. It is also quite arbitrary about its parameters of exploration. It wants to start only where it thinks it knows something and ignores anything that occurs prior.

The relationship of religion to science seems to have reached the far opposite apogee relative to the extreme of religious dominance over science in previous ages. The pendulum swing has now sought to eliminate religion not only from science but from the very fabric of society in general. The *evolved thinkers* of science exclude God's manual, the Bible, as counterproductive because it has been distorted by religious thought. However, its truth still provides valuable insight regarding creation.

It's A Matter of Faith

Let's get back to the *Big Bang*. How can we actually know what happened with certainty? Is this claimed knowledge absolute? How can science truly be that arrogant in its assertion, especially as we look at the flawed thinking of past generations of scientists? Was a reporter from the National Geographic magazine there to actually witness this occurrence? Of course not! This theory is based on conclusions made solely from man's observations.

According to Cosmology, the study of the universe in its totality, the *Big Bang* theory states that all of the matter of the universe was condensed into an object the size of the nucleus of an atom (some say the size of a golf ball or so). This condensed matter is referred to as a ***singularity***, and is at the center of a *Black Hole*. This *infinitely dense and infinitely hot singularity* simply sprang into existence when there was no time or space as we observe today. Shortly after appearing out of nowhere, it began to expand rapidly, much like inflating a balloon, until it exploded. This rapid expansion propelled matter outward from the epicenter has ever since, slowly cooling as it travels through space.

Science maintains that there are no absolutes, however, the *Big Bang*, which many in science claim to be the beginning of the universe, seems to have been established as fact and taught in our schools as an *absolute truth*. Can we really say that today's perspective is the truth and that we with certainty *know* these things about our origins and our universe? No! Science accepts it based on educated guesses or theories derived from what can actually be observed. There just may have been a *Big Bang,* and this may actually be an accurate representation of what occurred *after* the beginning of creation. However, the argument that the *Big Bang* is the *beginning* is not valid because the singularity existed *before* the *Big Bang*. Look at the Biblical account of creation that is described in Genesis 1:1-2.

Genesis 1:1-2

> [1] *In the beginning God created the Heaven and the earth.*
> [2] *And the earth was without form, and void; and darkness was upon the face of the deep. And the Spirit of God moved upon the face of the waters.*

The *Big Bang* does not actually contradict the creation account in the Bible. It is feasible that a vast amount of time transpired between the verses of creation in Genesis 1:1 and 1:2 *(see p. 80)*. God is the only one that was actually there and He had a complete view of the activities. The problem is that science has completely excluded God from the discussion. The concept of God creating everything as it now stands seems repulsive to science. If science were to start with the assumption that God actually did create everything and then proceed to try to understand His creation, things would be quite different! However, for science, God is certainly an *inconvenient truth*. After all, no one in science even attempts to answer the question as to where that infinitely hot and infinitely dense ***singularity*** that initiated the *Big Bang* came from in the first place. If this theory is correct, then this is when creation actually began!

However, solely from the perspective of mankind, it really does require quite a lot of faith to claim to know what happened millions of years ago and to maintain such certainty about it. Perspective is the key issue here, perspective *relative* to man's observations. To a great extent, our perspective defines our reality or at least our understanding of that reality. However, if God and His perspective are denied, a complete lack of any absolutes ensues, and the door is left wide open for anyone's opinion to be claimed as truth. Anyone with enough charisma, persuasion, plausibility, or rhetoric can attempt to take God's place and fill the void in man. History is replete with such examples. All it takes is a convincing argument, and those arguments are based completely on the observations or perspectives of man.

The creation of theories based on observation is the foundation of science. Once a theory is accepted, it nearly becomes a doctrine and almost absolute. This is how evolution and the Big Bang have come to be taught as givens. It is interesting that those who would stress the lack of absolutes and that relativity is the law of the land would then subscribe to a philosophy of evolution that requires as much *faith* as any religion does to believe!

It's All Relative – Observational Truth

Albert Einstein, the noted thinker, physicist, mathematician, and acknowledged genius, proposed the Special Theory of Relativity. His famous formula, $E=mc^2$, changed much of what science had previously considered absolute truth. "Special Relativity" in this sense does not mean moral relativism such as is found in some philosophies that espouse situational ethics where truth is relative to a situation or where there are no moral absolutes. Einstein's theories actually deal with matter and observations. So then, why are Albert Einstein and the theory at relativity pertinent to a discussion of the character and nature of God?

Albert Einstein's Special Theory of Relativity, which was put forward in 1905, and his General Theory of Relativity from 1916 are the most demonstrative examples of the concept of relativism. These most famous of all scientific theories of the 20th century are used to explain the origin of the universe as we observe or understand it. These theories are preached as a *gospel* of sorts in circles of scientists and evolutionists. These are quite involved theories, and any serious discussion of them is well beyond the scope of this book, but an essential component of these theories is the relative nature of truth in observations and a total lack absolutes. Let's just scratch the surface of the concept of relativity and get a better understanding.

We will get a good idea of what relativity is all about if we examine this example involving a moving object and a stationary observer. This scenario is modified from Steven Hawking's example in his book, *A Briefer History Of Time.*[25] Let's consider a train station at which a woman is sitting in a chair on the platform overlooking the tracks. A train is coming toward the station on the tracks but is not going to stop at the station. The train will be going right on through at a speed of about 30 miles per hour (the actual speed is not important. It is just for reference and visualization). The train has a club car, and there is a man in it who can be seen through the window bouncing a ping pong ball with a paddle on a table. We will analyze the perspectives of each of the people involved in this scenario. From the perspective of the ping pong player, the ball is simply bouncing up and down. The woman in the chair observes the train as it moves past her, and through the windows, she observes the man bouncing the ball with the paddle.

The woman sees the ball moving up and down, just like the player. However, from her perspective the ball is not only moving up and down, but it is also moving at 30 mph down the track with the train. She observes both the vertical and horizontal motion of the ball while the player only notices the vertical movement. The exact same activity is taking place, but the interpretation by each of the observers is completely different!

A train is moving on the tracks toward the train station and a woman is observing the train going by while she is seated on the train platform.

A man bounces a ping pong ball up and down and only sees vertical movement. However, as the train goes by, she sees both the vertical and horizontal movements of the ball.

Another possibly simpler analogy might be of cars driving on a freeway passing a stranded motorist. Driver 1 is cruising along at the legal speed limit of 65 miles per hour. He sees in the rearview mirror that there is a car approaching from behind on the left. The car passes him at 70 miles an hour. Does he perceive Driver 2 to be traveling at 70 mph? No, he sees Driver 2 slowly pass him, traveling only five mph faster than him which is the difference between their speeds. However, Driver 3, sitting in a stalled car on the side of the road, feels them speed by at their full speed that seems really fast! So, who is right and what is the truth?

The Right Perspective

The position of the observer is critical in describing the action that is taking place. Which observations are correct? Whose observation is true? There are many perspectives to any situation, and *truth can be stated relative to the observer and the observer's experience*. However, does this mean that actual truth is relative to a situation? Do the rules change because of our experience? Absolutely ***NOT !*** The ***experience*** of the observer does not define truth. The man who is bouncing the ball with his paddle on the train actually observes the least detail and, therefore, the lowest level of the *truth* of the activity. The woman at the train station sees a little bit more detail of the actual activity from her wider frame of reference. The real truth is actually ***least seen*** by those who are ***closest*** to the situation or problem. When we are close to the situation, we are blinded by our own observation, perspective, bias, and personal challenges.

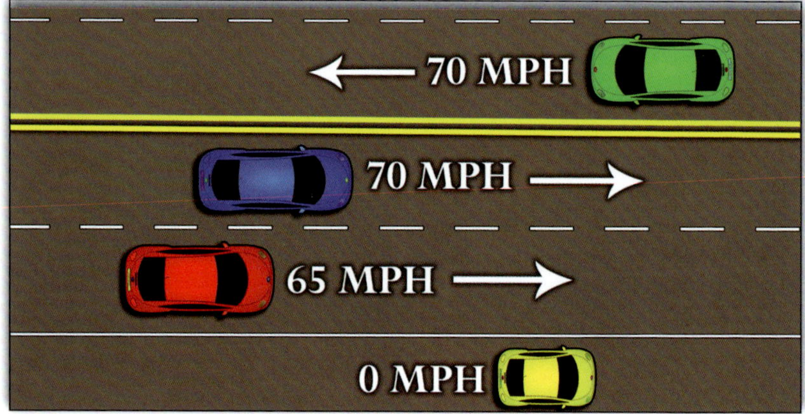

The cars on the opposite sides of the road pass each other at 135 - 140 mph. The cars on the same side only pass each other at a relative speed of 5 mph. Each driver has a different perspective of motion, but only the stalled driver sees the actual speed of each car!

The same holds true for the drivers in the second example. The two drivers in motion only perceive that they are traveling at a five mph difference in speed relative to one another. The stationary driver, however, has a completely different perspective on the activity. He observes them traveling at 65 mph and 70 mph relative to his stationary position. Now, think about someone driving at 70 mph on the opposite side of the freeway. The moving cars pass each other relatively at 135 - 140 mph!

Think about it. God observes these scenarios from an entirely different perspective. He actually sees both the perspective of the drivers, the man on the train and the woman on the platform, but He also sees outside their individual perspectives. He sees them moving on a rotating earth and the rotating earth moving around the sun in the solar system and the solar system moving through the universe. There may very well be even more to His perspective than we are aware. He has a perspective that gives him a higher view of the truth, the real and complete ***truth***! God's perspective is truth regardless of our observation, and God's truth is absolute!

God's Word reveals higher levels of truth to us than we can observe. The truth of His word *rightly* defines His character *separate* from our experience! This is where we see the conflict between the world's definition of "Acts of God" with the reality of what is actually happening and the origins and causes of those events. All of the religions that exist have doctrines and traditions that are formed and shaped from a particular perspective. Science also comes at the various issues of our surroundings from its own perspective. As we see from the train example, perspective really does matter as it has a great deal of influence upon the understanding of a particular situation. However, it does not necessarily reveal the total and complete truth. Armed with this knowledge, it becomes increasingly difficult to simply accept a claim of truth in a situation. This is certainly the case when the claim has been derived from perspectives that are not privy to all of the facts, but that are actually derived from limited observations and limited understanding.

Actually, God has the complete perspective, the absolute perspective. In reality, God is *the definition* of absolute as described in the Bible. James 1:17 states that with God there is no variation.

James 1:17 *(ASV)*

> *Every good gift and every perfect gift is from above, coming down from the Father of lights, with whom can be no variation, neither shadow that is cast by turning.*

God is not *relative.* He is absolute and without variation. He has a complete view of everything, but we do not. Our view is hindered by many factors that include our environment, education, observations, and preconceptions. All of these define our perspective and create our personal ***Ideolatry***. We are fundamentally incapable of seeing real truth in the world and the universe that we live in without God's help. As hard as we may try, on our own we can only understand God framed within our own experience and personal perspectives. In other words, on our own, everything *we think* is relative to our experience. This is why God has given us the Bible, His Word. He wants us to see and truly understand from His point of view and from His absolutely true perspective.

If we dare to consider that what God says in the Bible is true, we just might find that our observations and perspectives are not the truth! The God of the Bible actually has a very different perspective than we do. He desires that we enjoy completeness through a relationship with Him. However, Man seeks to explain his existence relative to his own observations and from his own perspective. The pride of man leads him to ignore the void that is within him, the *God-shaped hole* that yearns to be filled for man to be made complete. He wants to make himself the center of his own universe and elevate his ***Ideolatry.*** Instead, he simply reveals his self-centered, stubborn, and rebellious nature.

As we have seen, science has shown that there are actually differing levels of *knowledge* or *relative truth* based on the perspective of the observer. According to the science of relativity, each observer has his or her own unique version of the truth based on observational perspective. It would seem quite reasonable then that the perspective and observations of the individual in the previous chapter, *Acts of God*, helps to define who gets the blame for catastrophes, calamities, and disasters.

Regardless of whether or not an individual accepts God to be real, somehow the inexplicable is more easily tolerated if He is said to be in control. However, the God of the Bible transcends human understanding, and His Word can lead us to a realization of *real* truth rather than *relative* truth and a deeper understanding of life. When we discover and understand the Bible, the operator's manual provided by God, we can discover the truth and perhaps get a bit closer to understanding the real *Acts of God*.

Considerations

- There are many perspectives to any situation.
- Truth can be stated relative to the observer and his experience.
- Truth is least seen by the observer closest to the situation.
- The experience of the observer does not define the truth.
- God's perspective is truth regardless of our observation.
- God's character and nature are separate from our experience.
- God's Word is *Truth*.

So, where did the stuff come from that allowed the Big Bang to happen? We don't have that answer, but it would seem obvious that there must be another force at work that science does not understand or want to acknowledge. Observations and conclusions that are based on science are not absolute. They are subject to the interpretation of the observer. If the "singularity" at the origin of the Big Bang that science claims did exist, it is not unreasonable to believe that it came from God. Regardless of the conclusions drawn about God versus the Big Bang, a commitment of faith is required to accept either one.

Multiple versions of Truth can cause confusion.

Certainly, there is much speculation about the origins of the universe, but any deeper discussion of this is not within the scope of this work. However, there is another aspect of creation that we definitely need to deal with. It has to do with a much more personal aspect of our existence. It is a trait of human nature which relates to accountability and personal responsibility. Each of us must deal with it as this trait is built into the core of our being and to a great extent governs our activities and relationships. The early history of man from the Biblical account will shed a great deal of light on this universal trait of *free will* that all of us share. As we explore this uniquely human trait we will get closer to the understanding we need to overcome our ***Ideolatry***.

Wisdom is the principal thing;
therefore get wisdom:
and with all thy getting
get understanding.

Prov 4:7 KJV

...That the God of our Lord Jesus Christ, the Father of glory, may give to you the spirit of wisdom and revelation in the knowledge of Him, the eyes of your understanding being enlightened. . . .

Ephesians 1:17-18 NKJV

CHAPTER 7

IT'S NOTHING PERSONAL

Scientific ***observations*** create ***perspectives*** that are combined with existing understanding through ***relativity,*** and the result is scientific ***truth***. Therefore, scientific "truth" is not absolute but is always subject to change. Science seems to use rational explanations of the physical universe to avoid having to deal with the problem of God. We have touched on science and the physical universe, planets, stars, and the Big Bang, but these things do not directly influence us too much in our day-to-day lives.

Observation ⇨ Perspectives ⇨ Relativity ⇨ Truth

Relationships, activities, health, finances, work environments and life circumstances hold increasingly more sway over our lives and affect the state of our spiritual being. Observations, perspectives, relativity, and truth definitely do play important roles in our beliefs and actions, but there is an element that more profoundly influences the status of the events that surround our lives. It is an element that may actually have more importance than the rest. It is the matter of accountability or *personal responsibility,* and it may be heavily involved in what we observe occurring around us and happening to us. Although many times it is uncomfortable for us to accept personal responsibility, this discomfort does not make it any less true. Deflection of personal responsibility and the consequences of denying that responsibility have been pervasive in society from the beginning of time. It is a key element of our common human nature.

Relativity or relativism would imply that the rules change for each situation, so how can personal responsibility be an issue? When there is a continually evolving concept of truth, how can someone be held accountable? Taken to the extreme, when individual perspectives are all defined as truth because each observer has his own version of truth, there is no standard by which to compare and evaluate. If there is no standard, there can be neither personal responsibility nor accountability!

Relativism and its ensuing ambiguity are not characteristic of the God of the Bible. He actually holds us accountable, and mankind does not like that. This accountability is found in God's initial dealings with man in the Old Testament. It is then reinforced in the Law provided to Moses (Exodus 19-23), partially described in the Ten Commandments. It is also present in the New Testament teachings of Jesus. However, God's requirement for accountability began long before the Law and the Ten Commandments. Biblical history reveals to us the first two acts of disobedience which carried accountability at the beginning of the book of Genesis.

The Ultimate Con

The objects of deception and choice are first described in the narrative beginning in Genesis 2:8. God makes it a point to draw attention to two particular trees. One may argue what kind of trees these were, however, this is irrelevant to the situation.

Genesis 2:8-9

> [8] *And the LORD God planted a garden eastward in Eden; and there he put the man whom he had formed.* [9] *And out of the ground made the LORD God to grow every tree that is pleasant to the sight, and good for food; the tree of life also in the midst of the garden, and the tree of knowledge of good and evil.*

The first declaration that God made requiring personal responsibility or accountability is found in Genesis 2:16-17 as He continues in the narrative about the conditions and directions that involve one of the trees.

Genesis 2:16-17

> [16] *And the LORD God commanded the man, saying, Of every tree of the garden thou mayest freely eat:* [17] *But of the tree of the knowledge of good and evil, thou shalt not eat of it: for in the day that thou eatest thereof thou shalt surely die.*

Take note here regarding God's instructions as to the handling of the tree. He specifically stated that all of the rest of the garden was available to Adam and Eve, but this tree was not. He carefully stated that if they ***ate*** of the tree, they would die. Adam and Eve could choose to be obedient or disobedient. This is where personal responsibility was first established.

Man made an excuse, which was truly a self-deception, to justify his own actions of disobedience. This deception is revealed in the remainder of the narrative. It gives us a great deal of insight into this area of personal responsibility. It is also our first example of deflection of personal responsibility or accountability onto another. However, in Genesis 3:1-3 note also that both observation and perspective play a great role in this situation.

Genesis 3:1-3

1 Now the serpent was more subtil than any beast of the field which the LORD God had made. And he said unto the woman, Yea, hath God said, Ye shall not eat of every tree of the garden? 2 And the woman said unto the serpent, We may eat of the fruit of the trees of the garden: 3 But of the fruit of the tree which is in the midst of the garden, God hath said, Ye shall not eat of it, neither shall ye touch it, lest ye die.

What is the woman's response relative to the challenging question posed to her? She accurately stated that they were allowed to eat of all of the trees of the garden except one. However, her understanding or perspective of what she heard (or was taught) was not accurate. She added to the original instruction given to the man and stated that she was not even able to touch it without the penalty of death. Her understanding of the instructions given to Adam in Genesis 2:16-17 was faulty. It is also interesting to note that she was not surprised by the fact that the serpent spoke to her. She succumbed to the deception in Genesis 3:4-6.

Genesis 3:4-6

4 And the serpent said unto the woman, Ye shall not surely die: 5 For God doth know that in the day ye eat thereof, then your eyes shall be opened, and ye shall be as gods, knowing good and evil. 6 And when the woman saw that the tree was good for food, and that it was pleasant to the eyes, and a tree to be desired to make one wise, she took of the fruit thereof, and did eat, and gave also unto her husband with her; and he did eat.

Observe that the woman, who apparently was not given all of the information needed to make the correct, obedient choice, was deceived into taking her action. It is important to note that when God gave the instruction not to eat of the fruit of this tree, He stated that if they did they would surely die using a single instance of the word ***die***. However, when the serpent was in the process of deceiving Eve, he said that they would not *die, die*. The Hebrew word for *die* written once intimates the beginning of the process of death which could carry on for a while. However the use of the double *die, die* carries a different connotation. It implies that physical death will occur immediately.

This was actually true. God did not say that they would die immediately (*die, die*) if they ate of the fruit of the tree, but that the process of death would begin. Satan told Eve the truth, in that she would not die an immediate death (*die, die*). It is likely that neither Adam nor Eve had actually witnessed any physical death up to this point so they may not have even known what *die* or *die, die* really meant. The deception was complete when the serpent capitalized on Eve's lack of understanding of God's meaning, and she ate of the fruit.

She was lured and manipulated by the conversation of the serpent that was filled with just enough truth to sound accurate but with just enough twisting of God's meaning to make a bad decision. Up until this time, the man and woman had only ever known and experienced the goodness of God. They were unaware that evil existed. Later in God's Word, in Hosea 4:6, we see an explanation of the perils of this situation.

Hosea 4:6

> *My people are destroyed for lack of knowledge: because thou hast rejected knowledge, I will also reject thee, that thou shalt be no priest to me: seeing thou hast forgotten the law of thy God, I will also forget thy children.*

Although this passage speaks in a different time and has other connotations and implications, the principle of the words spoken here is unmistakable. This verse tells us that giving in to some other thought or desire reflects a lack of accurate knowledge and rejection of God's counsel. The lack of knowledge of the woman allowed her to be deceived by the serpent. In part, she understood that the serpent promised they would be like gods knowing good from evil. However, she probably also came to realize the difference between the progressing physical and spiritual death

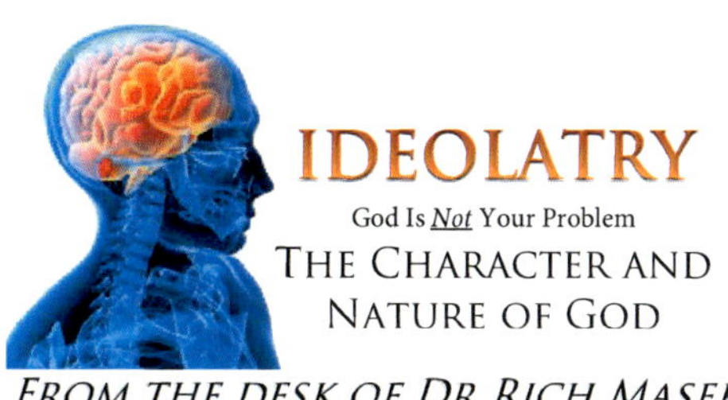

FROM THE DESK OF DR RICH MASEK

RE: ADDENDUM

Dear Reader;

I would like to thank you for purchasing and reading Ideolatry.

It is extremely important to me that Ideolatry is accurate in its discussion of God's Word. Shortly after printing, an error was noted on pages 58-59 that led to some confusion. I am sorry that this was not caught in the editing process, but I have made the appropriate corrections on this addendum. Please forgive me for any confusion that this may create in your study.

This corrected spread can be attached to the affected pages with double stick tape or a glue stick if desired. Just be sure to push the crease fully into the binding before attaching.

Please feel free to contact me anytime through my e-mail address, DrRich@ideolatry.com.

Thank you for your understanding.

Sincerely,

Dr. Rich Masek

DBD
PUBLISHING
Division of Dentistry By Design, Inc.
8505 Navajo Rd San Diego, CA 92119
619-797-1771 info@DBDPublishing.com 888-237-3228

The woman was apparently not given all of the information needed to make the correct, obedient choice. God stated that if they ate, they would *surely die*, using a double instance of the word *die*, meaning, *dying you will die*. The Hebrew word for die, written twice, *die, die*, meant that spiritual death would be immediate and that the *process* of physical death would begin. When the serpent questioned Eve about God's instruction, *she replied with a singular die*, meaning that physical death would be immediate. It is unlikely that Adam or Eve had witnessed any physical death up to this point, so Eve may not have even known the difference between *die* and *die, die*. Then the serpent told Eve that she would not *die, die*, directly contradicting God's words and further confusing her perception.

When he denied God's words, the serpent lied to Eve, knowing that God *did not say* that they would die an immediate physical death. Then the serpent added the enticement of something true and supposedly desirable, *the knowledge of good and evil*. The deception was complete as the serpent preyed upon Eve's lack of comprehension. She ate of the fruit and did not immediately die. The serpent had gained Eve's trust because nothing physically changed, even though the process of physical death had begun. He deceived Eve by taking advantage of her lack of understanding.

Up until this time, the man and woman had only ever known and experienced the goodness of God. They were unaware that evil existed. Eve was lured and manipulated by the conversation of the serpent that was a lie combined with just enough truth to sound correct. Later in God's Word, in Hosea 4:6, we see an explanation of the perils of this situation.

Hosea 4:6

My people are destroyed for lack of knowledge: because thou hast rejected knowledge, I will also reject thee, that thou shalt be no priest to me: seeing thou hast forgotten the law of thy God, I will also forget thy children.

Although this passage speaks in a different time and has other connotations and implications, the principle of the words spoken here is unmistakable. This verse tells us that giving in to some other thought or desire reflects a lack of accurate knowledge and rejection of God's counsel. The lack of knowledge of the woman allowed her to be deceived by the serpent. In part, she understood that the serpent promised they would be like gods, knowing good from evil. However, she probably also came to realize the difference between the immediate spiritual and progressing physical death that God warned of when He said, ***die, die,*** and the lie that Satan, through the serpent, mixed with truth to distort, to confuse and deceive. God set in motion the order of the universe in which we also live. Lack of knowledge of those boundaries will lead to our destruction.

It Was Their Choice

Turning back our attention to the Genesis account, we find that the man had the knowledge of God's will as indicated in his words. However, he chose to invoke his own will, in opposition to the will of God. He was fully aware of the instructions of God regarding this tree and freely made the choice to disobey the commands of God and chose to follow along with his partner's deception. How much different the world would be if the man had properly communicated the instruction to his mate, followed the will of God and withstood the temptation to follow in his own human will and wisdom! You might want to second guess their actions and think that you would have acted differently. Don't be deceived and fool yourself. It is quite certain that the free will choice of any of the rest of us would have been the same or worse. Just look at your own life and see the results of some of your own *free will* choices!

Nonetheless, to whom was the direction about the tree and the garden given? Was it not the man? The man was created first, and the woman was created out of him to become an equal partner. God gave the instruction to the man. In light of this, it would seem clear that the man had the responsibility to clearly communicate God's instruction to his new partner. Therefore, it is evident that he did not seem to understand or want to accept that the responsibility was his.

The next few verses in Genesis 3:7-12 reveal a time of reckoning, and we can see how one mistake can lead to another in an attempt to cover-up disobedience, better known as sin.

Genesis 3:7-12

[7] And the eyes of them both were opened, and they knew that they were naked; and they sewed fig leaves together, and made themselves aprons. [8] And they heard the voice of the LORD God walking in the garden in the cool of the day: and Adam and his wife hid themselves from the presence of the LORD God amongst the trees of the garden. [9] And the LORD God called unto Adam, and said unto him, Where art thou? [10] And he said, I heard thy voice in the garden, and I was afraid, because I was naked; and I hid myself.

that God warned of *(die)* and the immediate physical death (***die, di***e) that Satan used to distort and confuse. Very simply stated, a lack of knowledge of the order and boundaries that God set in motion at the beginning of the creation in which we also live will lead to our destruction.

It Was Their Choice

Turning back our attention to the Genesis account, we find that the man had the knowledge of God's will as indicated in his words. However, he chose to invoke his own will, in opposition to the will of God. He was fully aware of the instructions of God regarding this tree and freely made the choice to disobey the commands of God and chose to follow along with his partner's deception. How much different the world would be if the man had properly communicated the instruction to his mate, followed the will of God and withstood the temptation to follow in his own human will and wisdom! You might want to second guess their actions and think that you would have acted differently. Don't be deceived and fool yourself. It is quite certain that the free will choice of any of the rest of us would have been the same or worse. Just look at your own life and see the results of some of your own *free will* choices!

Nonetheless, to whom was the direction about the tree and the garden given? Was it not the man? The man was created first, and the woman was created out of him to become an equal partner. God gave the instruction to the man. In light of this, it would seem clear that the man had the responsibility to clearly communicate God's instruction to his new partner. Therefore, it is evident that he did not seem to understand or want to accept that the responsibility was his.

The next few verses in Genesis 3:7-12 reveal a time of reckoning, and we can see how one mistake can lead to another in an attempt to cover-up disobedience, better known as sin.

Genesis 3:7-12

7 And the eyes of them both were opened, and they knew that they were na
ked; and they sewed fig leaves together, and made themselves aprons. 8 And
they heard the voice of the LORD God walking in the garden in the cool
of the day: and Adam and his wife hid themselves from the presence of the
LORD God amongst the trees of the garden. 9 And the LORD God called
unto Adam, and said unto him, Where art thou? 10 And he said, I heard thy
voice in the garden, and I was afraid, because I was naked; and I hid myself.

> *[11] And he said, Who told thee that thou wast naked? Hast thou eaten of the tree, whereof I commanded thee that thou shouldest not eat? [12] And the man said, The woman whom thou gavest to be with me, she gave me of the tree, and I did eat.*

The man and woman made their choices, and they were ***their choices!*** It cannot be said, "The devil made me do it!" This was a freewill choice made under the influence of deception emanating from a lack of clear understanding of the instructions of the Words of God. They received exactly what the deception of the serpent had promised, but as with all deception, they did not receive what they thought they would!

Innocence Lost

Be careful about what you wish for because you just might get more than you bargained for! The choice Adam and Eve made led them down a path that destroyed everything that they had. The promise of the serpent came true. However, they really did not understand what the enticing promise of the knowledge of good and evil really meant. They were never intended to understand. Had they been obedient and trusted in God's counsel, they would never have been faced with the ugly truth.

A painful choice of disobedient rebellion let them immediately understand that they had done evil, and their innocence was lost forever. Their first reaction was to hide from God as they covered themselves. They knew fear for the first time in their lives. This is the natural order of things. Evil flees and hides itself from good, waiting for an opportunity to deceive and destroy when good is not looking. Evil cannot stand in God's presence and actually runs away from God. This is where justification and deflection of responsibility originate. They are tools used to try to avoid having evil or sin exposed.

Self-deception is the next step in trying to avoid facing the consequences of disobedience. The man knew that he was responsible for his actions, but his first reaction when confronted, was to deflect that responsibility to God Himself as he blamed the woman for his error. He basically said, "Hey God, you gave her to me. She told me to eat it, and I simply followed her instructions, so it's your fault!" To get to the bottom of the issue, God continued the conversation with the woman in Genesis 3:13 and asked her what happened.

Genesis 3:13

And the LORD God said unto the woman, What is this that thou hast done? And the woman said, The serpent beguiled me, and I did eat.

The woman was quite truthful and accurate in her reply to God. She did not cast blame on the man as the man had done to her. She did blame the serpent for beguiling her, but that was actually correct. She seemed to be a bit more forthright in her response. God begins to deal with each of the participants in the situation in Genesis 3:14-20. The man, the woman, and the serpent all suffered the consequences of their actions.

Genesis 3:14-20

*14 And the LORD God said unto the serpent, Because thou hast done this,
thou art cursed above all cattle, and above every beast of the field; upon thy
belly shalt thou go, and dust shalt thou eat all the days of thy life: 15 And I
will put enmity between thee and the woman, and between thy seed and her
seed; it shall bruise thy head, and thou shalt bruise his heel.*

*16 Unto the woman he said, I will greatly multiply thy sorrow and thy
conception; in sorrow thou shalt bring forth children; and thy desire shall
be to thy husband, and he shall rule over thee.*

*17 And unto Adam he said, Because thou hast hearkened unto the voice of
thy wife, and hast eaten of the tree, of which I commanded thee, saying,
Thou shalt not eat of it: cursed is the ground for thy sake; in sorrow shalt
thou eat of it all the days of thy life; 18 Thorns also and thistles shall it
bring forth to thee; and thou shalt eat the herb of the field; 19 In the sweat
of thy face shalt thou eat bread, till thou return unto the ground; for out
of it wast thou taken: for dust thou art, and unto dust shalt thou return.
20 And Adam called his wife's name Eve; because she was the mother of all
living.*

Even though Adam and Eve found themselves in dire straits as a result of their disobedience in Genesis 3:21-24, God was still determined to help them. He plainly told them that the penalty for their disobedience would be death, but God still found a way to keep them alive for as long as possible. He was legally obligated to allow their deaths to occur. Otherwise, He would contradict His own Word. The curses that Adam and Eve would endure were a direct, legal result of their sin, not God's action.

Genesis 3:21-24

[21] Unto Adam also and to his wife did the LORD God make coats of skins, and clothed them. [22] And the LORD God said, Behold, the man is become as one of us, to know good and evil: and now, lest he put forth his hand, and take also of the tree of life, and eat, and live for ever: [23] Therefore the LORD God sent him forth from the garden of Eden, to till the ground from whence he was taken. [24] So he drove out the man; and he placed at the east of the garden of Eden Cherubims, and a flaming sword which turned every way, to keep the way of the tree of life.

Adam and Eve were now changed. They stepped into a different level, possibly even a different class. God clothed them and acknowledged that their state had been altered. God said that the man had become as "one of us." We will find later that the "Us" God is speaking of is His three-person nature, God the Father, God the Son and God the Holy Spirit. Do you remember the first time you realized that you did something wrong or saw something that you wish you never had? Once it is done, it can't be undone. For Adam and Eve, there was no going back on their sin. Their sin separated them from God, and their innocence was forever lost.

There was another tree that was in the garden, the *Tree of Life*. Eating of this tree would have given Adam and Eve eternal, physical life. However, their life would have been in a fallen state, separated from God's fellowship. This would have cursed their offspring with the same fate. God did not want to let the man and woman eat of the *Tree of Life* and live forever in their sinful state, so they were expelled from the garden.

It is important to note that previously in Genesis 1:26-27, God stated that man and woman were created in His image and likeness, but they were not endowed with the knowledge of good and evil.

Genesis 1:26-27

[26] And God said, Let us make man in our image, after our likeness: and let them have dominion over the fish of the sea, and over the fowl of the air, and over the cattle, and over all the earth, and over every creeping thing that creepeth upon the earth. [27] So God created man in his own image, in the image of God created he him; male and female created he them.

The knowledge of good and evil came as a result of their disobedience. Man and woman and all of their descendants had now become completely responsible for their own actions relative to good and evil. We all now have that knowledge and are personally responsible for making the right decisions when faced with the temptation to do evil or we will suffer the consequences.

Adam and Eve were in a beautiful state of ignorant bliss or innocence when they had no knowledge of the difference between good and evil. They could not do evil in any area except that of disobedience of God's direction about eating the fruit of the tree because God made a specific decree or directive about that act. The personal responsibility of man then became a central thread running parallel to God's central thread throughout the Bible. God is setting the stage to restore man back to his original condition of innocence, and more importantly, to fellowship with God Himself. He never wanted man and woman to hide from Him in shame. Man's disobedience to God, his Creator, would forever be known as sin.

Things were inevitably going to get worse for man, however, as sin took hold through the generations. Adam's sin carried a higher weight and penalty than did Eve's deception. Adam's sin would be passed down through the ages because his blood line became tainted and his offspring were born outside the beauty and safety of the garden. They were born into the curse that Adam brought upon them.

The First Murder

Next we see Adam's son involved in the second recorded transgression in the Bible in Genesis 4:9-13.

> **Genesis 4:9-13** *(NIV)*
> *9 Then the LORD said to Cain, "Where is your brother Abel?" "I don't know," he replied. "Am I my brother's keeper?" 10 The LORD said, "What have you done? Listen! Your brother's blood cries out to me from the ground.*
> *11 Now you are under a curse and driven from the ground, which opened its mouth to receive your brother's blood from your hand. 12 When you work the ground, it will no longer yield its crops for you. You will be a restless wanderer on the earth." 13 Cain said to the LORD, "My punishment is more than I can bear."*

God proclaimed that Cain was now under a curse as a result of his action. However, it may be just as important to see what the text does ***not*** say rather than what it does say. The text does not say that God cursed him! It records a simple observation on the part of God. He was simply informing Cain of what he had brought upon himself and how his actions affected and impacted his life. God did not demand his life in exchange. In fact, He stated that if anyone else were to kill him, they would call upon themselves the even more dire consequences of sevenfold vengeance (Genesis 4:15). What we are left to wonder is what might have been if Cain had immediately accepted the responsibility for his action.

What if Cain were to have responded differently to God when asked about the whereabouts of Abel? God obviously already knew what Cain had done, just as he already knows what you and I have done. He was offering Cain an opportunity to accept the responsibility of his action by admitting to it. Perhaps that admission of guilt and a corresponding regret or ***repentance*** may have led to a different outcome.

Cain instead deflected the responsibility and denied his action with a flippant response in, "I don't know; am I my brother's keeper?" (Genesis 4:9). Where do you suppose that Cain learned to deflect his responsibility? Perhaps he learned from his father, Adam. Caught in his lie, Cain sealed his fate and put himself onto the path of destruction. In essence, he created his own fate. In later chapters, we will see more of this pattern of human deflection or defensiveness as we examine other examples of destruction or cursing attributed to the hand of God.

What was the Act of God in Cain's situation? Was it a direct action that God took against him for his sin, or was it an act that preserved Cain's life in spite of the sin? According to the text, God did not directly punish Cain. He merely informed him that he crossed a boundary that carried with it automatic consequences.

Cause and Effect

Our legal system puts laws in place to rule the conduct of people in our communities and country. Each law carries with it a consequence or penalty for the transgression of that law if it is broken. Who is responsible, and whose *action* is it when a penalty is prescribed for breaking a law? Is it the Legislature for making laws? Is it the president or governor in office at the time? Perhaps the judge that pronounced the sentence is responsible. Or could the responsibility be that of the person who broke the law? It is not the responsibility or fault of the car company if you drive into a wall because you were distracted while driving! Proverbs 26:2 describes a direct cause and effect relationship that is at work in our world.

Proverbs 26:2b *(BBE)*

. . . .so the curse does not come without a cause.

This verse points to a cause and effect relationship. A curse will not come unless there is a cause. The cause comes from the actions of the individual and not some outside agency, influence, or force. While we all value the protections that our legal system provides when we see a perpetrator go free, it may seem that the legal system is built around relieving a person of his or her personal responsibility or lessening the consequences of his or her actions. These protections safeguard us from convicting an innocent person. However, God does not have this problem as we see in Hebrews 4:12.

Hebrews 4:12

For the word of God is quick, and powerful, and sharper than any twoedged sword, piercing even to the dividing asunder of soul and spirit, and of the joints and marrow, and is a discerner of the thoughts and intents of the heart.

God is able to know beyond doubt the innocence or guilt of a person to the point of intent, not just actions. However, He deals with us in an entirely different way than the legal system of the world does. Even when we are guilty, God does everything in His power to make it right for us, not by using technicalities of the law, but by paying the penalties for us and suffering the consequences Himself as we see in John 3:16-17.

John 3:16-17

16 *For God so loved the world, that he gave his only begotten Son, that whosoever believeth in him should not perish, but have everlasting life.*
17 *For God sent not his Son into the world to condemn the world; but that the world through him might be saved.*

God posted bail for us and then let Jesus stand trial for our sins. Jesus bore the punishment, and through God's grace, we go free. This is the *Mystery of Jesus* and the power of the love of the real God of the Bible. God puts His love into action and is willing to accept the blame (because of man's limited perspective) for events that are not His doing. We discover the heart of God through this thread of truth in which He lays out His plan to restore His eternal relationship with man.

Getting a true perspective of God's character requires that we examine our own understanding. These two stories represent the first expressions of the concept of ***Ideolatry***. Adam and Eve put their own intellectual understanding above the explicit direction of God. They chose to give more weight to their minds and to worship those thoughts above God. Cain did the same when he reacted out of jealousy and killed his brother. All three of them had their own perspectives and versions of truth which they chose to obey. Unfortunately, they were all wrong.

We develop our own book of personal Ideolatry using our own version of truth. We tend to base that truth on relativity influenced by our various situations, observations, perspectives and experience. Our Ideolatry affects our views of both God and His character.

We all have our own notions of truth as we have seen from our discussion of relativity and perspective. The impersonal notions of relativity may make us think there is nothing personal going on. In reality, our existence, life, and spiritual disposition are actually very personal. Our biases or preconceptions affect our views of both God and His character. God truly is many things to many people, but at the same time, He does not change the rules for any of us. He reaches out to us in His compassion. However, if we don't really know Him, we do not know what to expect or how to recognize Him when He does.

So let's take a deeper look into how you personally experience God.

CHAPTER 8

WHAT GOD DO YOU KNOW ?

Have you had problems in your life and gone down a path that you know is not right, or you think that God does not approve of? You may have observed that things have not gone so well for you. You may have followed that path, and maybe to you, He is the ***God of Wrath*** or the ***God of Punishment*** as you meet one bad circumstance after another. Perhaps someone has wronged you. You may have suffered at the hand of another through lying, cheating, or frank abuse. You might want God to avenge your suffering. For you, He is the ***God of Vengeance*** or the ***God of Retribution,*** and you keep looking for God to penalize those people. Perhaps you have realized that many of your own failings and shortcomings have actually been forgiven, and you experience Him as ***God the Forgiver***. However, you still go through a lot of trials, and you also see Him as the ***God of Testing.*** Maybe nothing seems to go right for very long, if at all, and you blame God, seeing Him as ***God the Enemy.***

There are many more ways in which we can perceive God and draw conclusions about His character. Each of these situations can give rise to a different view or understanding of who God is in our own life. Perhaps you lost someone in your life that was very important or close to you, and you may not have understood why. You may consider that God is responsible for this loss and hold Him accountable, seeing ***God as the Life Taker***. You may have brought children into the world, or you have been rescued from dire circumstance or disease and you see Him as ***God the Life Giver***. Maybe you know someone, a good person, who always seem to get a raw deal, and you see ***God as Uncaring***. These examples might lead us to the conclusion that most of our attitudes and understanding about who God is actually emanates from our personal experiences or the experiences of those who we observe or know. Right or wrong, your perception can be your reality and shape your understanding and attitudes.

So, what is your perception of the character of God? How do you see Him? Are you willing to consider the possibility that your view of Him is based on your life experience and may not be accurate? Surely, you can see it is almost natural to have a very subjective way of assessing and understanding God. How are we to tell if these assessments are correct or not? Where is our authority or instruction on the subject? Does our authority come from individuals, tradition, religious thought/doctrine or the Bible? It would seem that the most accurate source would be the Bible, God's word and the words of Jesus.

Table 1 **Which God Do You Know?**	
The God of Wrath?	God, My Enemy?
The God of Testing?	God, The Punisher?
The Uncaring God?	God, The Life Taker?
The God of Retribution?	God, The Life Giver?
The God of Vengeance?	God, The Forgiver?

Table 1 lists some of the attributes of God discussed above. Most of these are negative attributes that might be derived from personal experience. The Bible also presents a variety of situations that might lead the reader to see God in many of these same ways. We see terrible things attributed to God in which He either causes, or at very least allows, all of the bad stuff to happen. Therefore, bad things must be part of His character, right?

Wrong!

Many of these are *situational* descriptions that are frequently attributed to God's *character*. However, the situations that might lead one to these conclusions do not actually describe His character. You may have observed other circumstances or situations in the text of the Bible that lead you to question God's character. How then do we reconcile the apparent conflicts in the activities described in the Bible and His actual character? That is what this book is intended to explore. Let's start with some fundamentals and see what God is all about. Well, maybe not, all about, because we do have a diminished capacity relative to God. We will never fully understand Him until we meet Him face to face, and maybe not even then!

Names Tell It All

What do we actually know about God? He has many descriptive names that are found in the Bible. They are shown here in Table 2.

Table 2
The Biblical Names of God

Jehovah-Elohim	Creator – Mighty and Strong
Jehovah-Hoseenu	The Lord – Our Maker
Jehovah-Eloheenu	The Lord – Our God
Jehovah-Adonai	The Lord – Our Sovereign
Jehovah-Tsidkenu	The God of Righteousness
Jehovah-M'kaddish	The Lord Who Sanctifies, Makes Holy
Jehovah-Rapha	The God of Healing (The Lord that Heals)
Jehovah-Jireh	The God of Provision
Jehovah-Shalom	The Lord – Our Peace
Jehovah-Sabaoth	The God of Hosts (Angels and Men)
Jehovah-Nissi	The Lord – My Banner
Jehovah-Shammah	The Lord is Present
Jehovah-Rohi	The Lord – Our Shepherd

We see the first description of God's character in the first verse of the Bible, Genesis 1:1, where He is God the Creator, *Jehovah-Elohim* in the Hebrew. We also see another very important, key characteristic of God in Genesis 1:3. God employs a particular method that would seem foreign to our intellect in the process of creating all that we see and know as our reality. Our understanding is that things are created by the manipulation of other things that are already in existence, an assembly or re-assembly of existing stuff. However, God created out of nothingness. There were no building blocks, so to speak, for Him to work with. No concrete, hammers, nails, wood, or steel. No dirt, rocks, water, or even air to breathe!

How did this occur? Science would have us believe that creation was a result of the *Big Bang*. This appears reasonable enough since this theory seems to describe that which we can readily observe. Some building blocks or raw materials were present in order to create something else. The *Big Bang* requires a starting point and comprehensive rules of order to explain and satisfy the need for our intellectual understanding. So how does science determine what the building blocks are, and where they came from? Stephen Hawking has told us that it is not the business of science to deal with the actual origin of the universe or to attempt to explain the sudden appearance of the material needed for the big bang, no matter how infinitesimally small it may have been. Hawking said that science feels that this concept is better left to the metaphysical or religious folk *(see p. 41)*.

Origins

God is the one who created whatever it was that began things, but science is unwilling to acknowledge this as fact. Science strives for explanations based on *human* understanding that is evidenced by its reluctance to deal with the material necessary to actually have a big bang. Through the Planck Collaboration of the European Space Agency, science declares the age of the universe to be 13.82 billion years old.[26] In the fervor of science to rationalize, describe, and understand the universe, it has developed theories over the last few hundred years to explain what it has observed in the universe. This is truly astounding!

However, the process does not verify the conclusions that are drawn. An amazingly short span of a few hundred years is extrapolated back to the beginning of time (13.82 billion years) and called ***fact***! Admirably, science endeavors to do what science does best and explain what it observes and postulate what "may have been" and "what might be." Certainly, a great number of benefits to mankind have come from this quest. Our current world of technology and convenience, industrialization, and health would not exist without science (although some may argue that we are no better off, just living under different threats, challenges, and rules).

Science proclaims, "This is ground zero and everything started here with the *Big Bang.*" The consequence is denial of God's existence and total disregard for His involvement with creation. So what do the conclusions of science and the *ideolatry* of man and have to do with the character of God? Actually, nothing!

Free Will

While the ideolatry of man does not influence the character of God, there is an aspect of His character that doesn't get much coverage. It is His willingness to let us exercise our free will to think, speak, go, do, believe, deny, agree, or disagree with the true realities of His universe. This expression of our God given-free will can bring us delight or cause us immeasurable pain, and the choice is ours. The manifestation of this free will is first noted in Genesis when God *allowed* Adam and Eve to disobey His Word. (It was not a suggestion that they disobeyed. It was a direct command, and we will explore this concept of God *allowing* things to take place in the next chapter). Even before this situation with Adam and Eve, there must have been this same willingness on God's part to permit free-will behavior. We witnessed it in the fall of Lucifer when he exerted his own free will against God as described in Isaiah 14:12-14.

Isaiah 14:12-14

12 How art thou fallen from heaven, O Lucifer, son of the morning! how art thou cut down to the ground, which didst weaken the nations! 13 For thou hast said in thine heart, I will ascend into heaven, I will exalt my throne above the stars of God: I will sit also upon the mount of the congregation, in the sides of the north: 14 I will ascend above the heights of the clouds; I will be like the most High.

Understanding Your View

There were consequences in both examples, but the behavior was permitted. Free will dictates that we are permitted to pursue our own course. It also demands that we assume responsibility for those choices. You cannot have it both ways. You cannot expect to exercise free-will and blame God for the consequences. If your view of God is that He is in absolute control of everything, then He is responsible for ***your*** choices, and you would not actually have a free will. Every move that you made and the totality of the outcome of your activities would be dictated by God. In that case, you would have no personal responsibility for your actions. You are simply a puppet in His hands, and He doles out punishment or blessing simply on a whim.

On the other hand, if your view of God is that He is loving, merciful, offering forgiveness and guidance to you to improve your life, then God is your helper, not your punisher. ***Your view of God determines whether or not you will receive from Him or run from Him.*** God makes some specific recommendations about this subject. He is prompting you to educate yourself. The benefit of giving heed to this counsel is to gain a right and correct understanding that will keep you from embarrassing yourself with costly mistakes simply coming from ignorance. The suggestion can be found in 2 Timothy 2:15.

2 Timothy 2:15 *(NIV)*

> *Do your best to present yourself to God as one approved, a workman who does not need to be ashamed and who correctly handles the word of truth.*

Other aspects of God's character are also found in the names by which He is identified in Table 2 *(see p. 69)*. He is not only the *Creator* of the universe. He is our *God* and *Maker*. He is *Present* in our lives (not removed or hidden). He is the epitome of *Righteousness* because whatever He declares is right. He is the *Healer* to our spirits and our bodies and makes *Provision* for our physical needs. He is the *Lord of our Peace,* and He is the *God of Hosts* (all of the inhabitants of heaven and earth). God is our *Banner* (like a place to gather in victory), and He is our *Shepherd* (one who cares for us like a flock and will reach out to find any who are lost). Through His Spirit, He actively works to influence our decisions, sanctify us and make us Holy. To sanctify us means to set us apart, as if in a special place. He is *Sovereign*, meaning He is supreme, absolute, unlimited, unrestricted, and boundless. However, although God is unrestricted in what He *can* do, He has made it clear that He has chosen to limit Himself by His spoken and written Word that He will not go against. We will go in to much more detail on this aspect of God's character later.

A Jealous God?

None of these Biblical names that describe God's attributes have any negative connotations. However, there are some instances not listed above that seem to. God is a jealous God *(Exodus 20:5),* and He is vengeful *(Deuteronomy 32:35; Romans 12:19; Hebrews 10:30)*. It is important to note the differences in our understanding of these words in our conversation today versus the meanings in the Bible. Portraying God as jealous or taking vengeance is not what we might think. The jealousy of God described in Exodus 20:4-6 is far from what we experience.

Exodus 20:4-6 *(NKJV)*

> *4 You shall not make for yourself a carved image – any likeness of anything that is in heaven above, or that is in the earth beneath, or that is in the water under the earth; 5 you shall not bow down to them nor serve them. For I, the Lord your God, am a jealous God, visiting the iniquity of the fathers upon the children to the third and fourth generations of those who hate Me, 6 but showing mercy to thousands, to those who love Me and keep My commandments.*

Our jealousy is demonstrated when we desire to have something that does not belong to us. We experience it when someone else has a better car, job, house, better-looking spouse, more fame or more money than we possess. We are jealous or covet those things that we don't have. God does not get jealous over what He does not have. He is protective over those whom He created and is faithful to them. God jealously guards over us against the deception of the devil who tries to direct our attention away from Him. His jealousy is to our benefit. It is actually a positive attribute.

A God of Vengeance?

The vengeance of God in action is much the same as His jealousy. His vengeance is not directed at man but at sin. The recompense associated with vengeance that is described in Deuteronomy 32:35 is a result of the transgressions of the people.

Deuteronomy 32:35 *(NKJV)*

> *Vengeance is Mine, and recompense; Their foot shall slip in due time; For the day of their calamity is at hand, And the things to come hasten upon them.*

God is revealing the effects of sin upon them. Calamity will come upon them. They will fall, and payment for their actions is rapidly coming due for them. The references in Hebrews 10:30 and Romans 12:19 both refer to this passage in Deuteronomy and warn that we should not seek vengeance upon those who act against us. The wise counsel of Romans 12:19 and Hebrews 10:30-31 tell us that vengeance should be left to God.

Romans 12:19 *(NKJV)*

> *Beloved, do not avenge yourselves, but rather give place to wrath; for it is written, "Vengeance is Mine, I will repay," says the Lord.*

Hebrews 10:30-31 *(NKJV)*

[30] For we know Him who said, "Vengeance is Mine, I will repay," says the Lord. And again, "The Lord will judge His people." [31] It is a fearful thing to fall into the hands of the living God.

We are told not to avenge ourselves but to leave the business of judgment and payment for transgression to God, who knows all of the details and can rightly assess or judge the situation and the sin. He is the only one that is in the position to rightly make a determination in an objective manner. Our determinations are based on bias and incomplete information. We are prone to react from hurt or offense that is an emotional point of view and not necessarily based in truth.

The Angry God of Wrath

The word *wrath* is mentioned many times in the Bible and in various contexts. The common theme throughout these examples is God's wrath. Wrath is always set against sin, not people as we see in Romans 1:18-19.

Romans 1:18-19 *(NKJV)*

[18] For the wrath of God is revealed from heaven against all ungodliness and unrighteousness of men, who suppress the truth in unrighteousness,
[19] because what may be known of God is manifest in them, for God has shown it to them.

People that regularly and actively engage in sinful activities will come up against the wrath of God which is directed at their sin as described in Ephesians 5:3-7. It may sometimes look as if "God is out to get us," but He is not.

Ephesians 5:3-7 *(NKJV)*

[3] But fornication and all uncleanness or covetousness, let it not even be named among you, as is fitting for saints; [4] neither filthiness, nor foolish talking, nor coarse jesting, which are not fitting, but rather giving of thanks. [5] For this you know, that no fornicator, unclean person, nor covetous man, who is an idolater, has any inheritance in the kingdom of Christ and God. [6] Let no one deceive you with empty words, for because of these things the wrath of God comes upon the sons of disobedience. [7] Therefore do not be partakers with them.

God shows that He is not being wrathful toward Believers, but actually supplies a way for them to avoid the consequence of His true wrath against sin. Romans 5:8-9 and 1 Thessalonians 5:9-10 clearly state that through the substitution of Jesus' blood for our own, God pours out His love and saves us as believers from the wrath that will come upon sin.

Romans 5:8-9 *(NKJV)*

[8] But God demonstrates His own love toward us, in that while we were still sinners, Christ died for us. [9] Much more then, having now been justified by His blood, we shall be saved from wrath through Him.

1 Thessalonians 5:9-10 *(NKJV)*

[9] For God did not appoint us to wrath, but to obtain salvation through our Lord Jesus Christ, [10] who died for us, that whether we wake or sleep, we should live together with Him.

Who Is God To You?

God is known by the names that exemplify His character. They are descriptions of a caring, loving, nurturing, protective, and ever present Supreme Being that holds your best interests in the highest regard. A foundational issue for each of us is to understand our view of God and how that view continues to be defined in our lives.

If your view is governed by your denomination and the traditions of religion, the view of a family member or your own personal experience, you may get confused and may even be very angry with God. However, if your view is established by your own personal knowledge of God based upon the Bible, the book that He provided for you as a user's manual, you can develop confidence and faith. Do not trust your eternal relationship to someone else's perspectives, including those presented in this book. Instead, find out for yourself and endeavor to ***know*** how God really acts in this realm and to understand the God that you choose to either serve or reject.

Later chapters will discuss the effects of sin and its results upon mankind more. God's nature is to guide you and prevent these effects by giving you all that is necessary for you to avoid the repercussions. You cannot enjoy the benefits if you do not accept Him and receive them. Your view of God is what helps to determine what you can receive of the things that He has provided for your benefit. Many people assume that God allows or disallows things to occur in their lives. Some believe that He does nothing in their lives and that we are just left on our own. Some have a hard time making a distinction between God's wrath, His jealousy, His vengeance and His love.

If God allows bad stuff to happen, are you experiencing His wrath? If so, how does it relate to His love for you? These wide and varied viewpoints and questions need clarification, validation, and answers. An examination of what is really happening in your life is necessary. Discovery of what God actually does or does not do will help you to further understand His character, the events that you observe and the decisions that you make. An essential factor in this discovery process is letting go of the baggage that holds you back.

Your *Life Filters (observations, perspectives, and experiences)* can become your *Ideolatry* and control your life and your very existence if you let them. *Life Filters* can redefine your perception of truth and block your way or you can choose the *Absolute Truth* of God's word. Which will it be?

Upon which version of truth will you base your life?

Change can allow you to see more clearly. The red filter page to the right represents your *Life Filters.* As you peel it away, on the page below you will reveal what your *Life Filters* might be hiding from you.

Change
Perspectives

and

Remove
"Life Filters"
To See

REAL
TRUTH

Clearly

... They received the word with all readiness of mind, and searched the scriptures daily, whether those things were so.

Acts 17:11 KJV

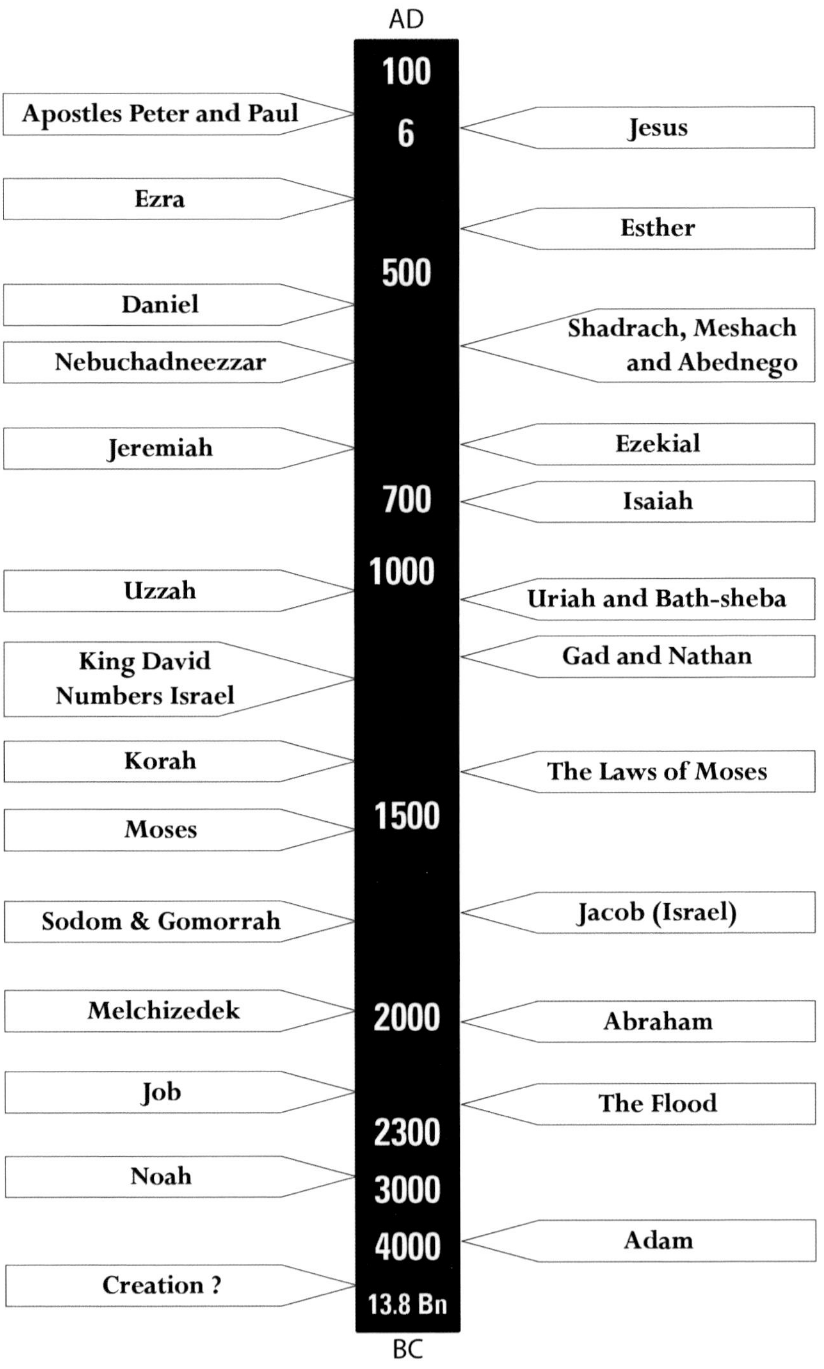

A relative timeline of approximate dates for the people and events discussed in this book.

CHAPTER 9

GOD – THE ACCOMPLICE ?

Why did God let this happen? God didn't stop it, or him, or her, or them! God allowed me to get sick with cancer, heart disease or some other malady! Why did God allow the destruction? God let them hurt me! God let him or her die! How could a good and loving God allow such terrible things to happen to us?

The concept associated with the word *allow* can give the impression that someone or something else is in control, and the one who has something happen to them had no personal responsibility in the situation. Nothing could be further from the truth. Personal responsibility is actually a major part of the concept of *allowing*. Furthermore, the action of allowing requires that a person or entity actually has the legal right or ability to allow or not allow something to be done. The action of allowing something to take place is not passive. It requires making a conscious choice to permit, alter, or tolerate an action or the enforcement of authority regarding a particular situation.

Let's look at an example of the application and potential misapplication of the word *allow* with which we can easily identify. Let's say that we are dealing with your teenaged boy who wants to use the family car. The car belongs to you, and you have the authority to grant or deny its use. You can make the choice to allow the use of the car, but you might make stipulations as to its use such as obeying the law and driving defensively. You may even impose a time limit or curfew. Let's also assume that you gave good instructions, explained the rules and were sure to make clear your terms and conditions.

It could be safely said that in this situation you did not ***allow*** him to drive drunk or drive too fast and get a speeding ticket, to come home two hours late or even carelessly cause an accident. Legally, however, you may be liable for the accident because he is under age and your responsibility. However, you did not ***allow*** the actions that he may have chosen to engage in or fallen prey to. He has ***free-will*** to choose and may abuse the freedom that came from your decision to ***allow*** him the use of the car. You began with a position of confidence and trust because of the education and wisdom you had instilled into your teen. You empowered his ***free-will*** in this situation because it was within your power to do so. You provided instruction and education as to the expectations that came with the privilege of driving the car. In this respect, you ***allowed*** the activity, but did you become an ***accomplice*** to the ensuing situation?

The teen driver will suffer the direct consequences of a drunken driving charge, a speeding ticket or an accident. Those will go on his driving record and affect the insurance (that you are probably paying for!). Surely it could be said that you, as the car owner, are responsible for anything having to do with the car because you had the choice to lend it or not. However, if we go down that path, we are shifting the personal responsibility away from the teen driver.

Are you really to blame for the actions of the driver because you ***allowed*** the use of the car? Are you an accomplice to the actions? Absolutely not! You may feel responsible because he is your child, but you gave instruction and guidance that he refused, ignored, or disobeyed. You enabled the use of his ***free-will*** based on your instruction, guidance, and trust that he ultimately betrayed. In God's terms, this would be called sin because your teenager fell short of the expectations and commands that were given along with the privilege.

We will discuss the implications of this example a bit more, but first let's examine the definitions of the terms we are using. This is critical for our understanding as we read or communicate these concepts of allowing and being an accomplice.

It's Just Semantics

Some believe that the use of a particular word is not all that important or that it is "just semantics." However, semantics is a fundamental problem that we humans have when we communicate with one another. The intellectual concepts, emotional context and the resultant meaning of words that we use are crucial to any level of accurate understanding when we attempt to write, learn, teach, or just converse with one another. Consider this definition of *semantics* from the *Collins English Dictionary*.

semantics *(noun)*

> *The branch of linguistics that deals with the study of meaning, changes in meaning, and the principles that govern the relationship between sentences or words and their meanings.*[27]

Semantics is important but some are not careful or are even quite thoughtless about their choices of words. They simply assume that everyone who hears them understands the meaning and intent of what they say.

Someone might think, "After all, I know what I mean by the word that I used. You should understand that same meaning as well." However, this kind of an attitude brings about an abundance of problems. The incorrect choice of a word in a particular situation could lead to quite different or unexpected results as we have probably all experienced. Misunderstandings, hurt feelings, misdirection, or general confusion can result from the incorrect application of a single word. The entire point of using words is the accurate transference of thoughts, ideas, and emotions from one individual to another. *(Care has been taken to be clear and understandable as to intent and meaning in the writing of this book, but some things will still be misread or miscommunicated because of our individual frames of reference, understandings, or differing viewpoints.)*

The following saying illustrates a problem of perception and understanding in communicating that can lead to confusion and misinterpretation.[28]

"I know that you believe you understand
what you think I said,
but I'm not sure you realize
that what think you heard
is not what I thought I meant."

Likewise, it is important for us to understand the meaning of the word, *allow,* since many times, God is said to *allow* something, implying that God is an *accomplice* to the action. The verb, *to allow,* carries with it a number of nuances as evidenced in this dictionary definition.

allow *(verb)*

To give permission to or for; permit; to let have; give as one's share; grant as one's right; to permit by neglect, oversight, or the like; to admit; acknowledge; concede: to allow a claim; to take into consideration, as by adding or subtracting; set apart; Older Use. to say; think; Archaic. to approve; sanction; to permit something to happen or to exist.[29, 30]

- *To let do or happen; permit*
- *To permit the presence of*
- *To permit to have*

Other sources, such as the *Collins Thesaurus of the English Language* and *WordNet* offer another definition. This definition is the one that is generally applied to God in the sense of "Why did God *allow* this happen?"

allow *(verb)*

Make it possible for something to happen through a specific action or lack of action.[31, 32]

This definition of *allow* gives the connotation of being in agreement with or an accomplice to a specific action. Let's look at what it means to be an accomplice from the *Webster's New College Dictionary* and *Wikipedia*.

accomplice *(noun)*

A person who knowingly participates with another in an unlawful act; partner in crime. At law, an accomplice is a person who actively participates in the commission of a crime, even though they may actually take no part in the actual criminal offense. At law, an accomplice has the same degree of guilt as the person he or she is assisting, is subject to prosecution for the same crime and faces the same criminal penalties.[33, 34]

So the important question is this, "Does God allow things to happen in the sense that He is an active *accomplice* or is God passively involved in *allowing* something to happen? Let's go back to the story of the teen driver and see how it relates.

Action or Consequence?

The driver scenario provides a good analogy as to God's interaction with man. God is in the position of the parent, and we are the teen driver. God enables our free will to act as we see fit but also provides instruction and guidance to help us make the right decisions. As we will see later, He has voluntarily relinquished His Will to us and purposely limited His legal authority to allow us free will. God has empowered us to exercise our ***free will*** in this world to rebel against Him and disobey His direction or even deny Him altogether. He has set up conditions under which we can function and some boundaries within which we operate.

In His wisdom and understanding of how things are set up, God did make quite a few "suggestions" to us to make our lives fulfilling and rewarding. It is up to us to heed the warnings, suggestions, or commandments and make the right choices. There are many things that occur in our lives that are the results of our choices. He does not ***allow*** bad things to happen. We do as we make choices that either enhance our lives or destroy them. This is a free-will, cause and effect relationship that connects consequence with choice. Very important suggestions or recommendations made by God are tied directly to free will *choice sets* of cause and effect. This means, if you choose an action, you reap the consequence of it. One example is found in the book of Deuteronomy 30:15-20.

Deuteronomy 30:15-20 *(NIV)*

15 *See, I set before you today life and prosperity, death and destruction.*
16 *For I command you today to love the LORD your God, to* ***walk in his***
ways, and to keep his commands, decrees and laws*; then you will*
live and increase, and the LORD your God will bless you in the land you
are entering to possess.
17 *But* ***if your heart turns away and you are not obedient****, and*
if you are drawn away to bow down to other gods and worship them, 18 *I*
declare to you this day that ***you will certainly be destroyed****. You will*
not live long in the land you are crossing the Jordan to enter and possess.
19 *This day I call heaven and earth as witnesses against you that* ***I have***
set before you life and death, blessings and curses. Now choose
life, *so that you and your children may live* 20 *and that you may love the*
LORD your God, listen to his voice, and hold fast to him. For the LORD is
your life, and he will give you many years in the land he swore to give to
your fathers, Abraham, Isaac and Jacob.

God emphatically states that you should "Now choose life, so that you and your children may live."These verses also appear to contain threats of punishment. However, we have a choice in the matter, and we are responsible for the outcome based on the choice we make. Therefore, at least for the moment, we should try to consider what might be read as a threat in a different light and instead consider it a warning of what will happen as a result of a free will choice. It is prudent, therefore, to start with an assumption as to the *rightness* of God, otherwise known as *righteousness,* and then frame our questions and discoveries within the context of this verse in Proverbs 26:2.

Proverbs 26:2b *(BBE)*

. . . .so the curse does not come without a cause.

Tuned In Discernment

We have all heard the expression, "stuff happens" in one form or another. This expression tends to imply that everything is random and that there is no way to know what causes something. Therefore, there is no personal responsibility. This leads to a conclusion contrary to the verse in Proverbs which states that things happen for a reason. Observing only from our limited perspective and understanding may lead us to wrongly blame God or attribute to bad luck those things that are actually within the Human Realm of responsibility and influence. If we alter our point of view, we may more easily comprehend the true reality of a situation and discover that ***things don't just happen without a cause***. Our lifelong challenge is to *stay in tune* with truth and reality and thus avoid self-deception. The best way to accomplish this is to turn our attention to the understanding of God and His Word.

Where do we go with this, and what is our next step in discernment?

God has been gracious to give us everything that we need to operate here on earth. Next to salvation through Jesus, one of the next most important gifts is truth from the Holy Spirit. The Gospel of John deals with this aspect of the Holy Spirit and provides us with a deeper understanding of God's plan. Let's look at John 16:13.

John 16:13

Howbeit when he, the Spirit of truth, is come, he will guide you into all truth: for he shall not speak of himself; but whatsoever he shall hear, that shall he speak: and he will shew you things to come.

Let us then search the Truth, the Word of God, as stated in John 17:17, to determine the reality of His nature, the truth of His purpose and dealings with us and our responsibilities.

John 17:17

Sanctify them through thy truth: thy word is truth.

Do you remember our discussion of science and the Big Bang? Science was not going to grapple with that difficult human question, "Where did the universe actually begin?" Instead, science has chosen to select a point at which they can state "this is ground zero" and endeavor to explain what happened from there. Albert Einstein, in all of his brilliance, found that his original Special Theory of Relativity did not fully explain some aspects, primarily the behavior of light and gravitation. Consequently, he had to modify it to the General Theory of Relativity. The dogmas of science have continually evolved, trying to understand the world around us. Although preached as absolute truth, they have been in constant flux, merely representing the current *best guess* to explain what is seen.

We must be careful to avoid a starting point of understanding God based on our best guess about Him that might be based on personal experience, prejudice, tradition, or religion. Because of a lack of knowledge of who God is and how He works, there have been many, many approaches that man has explored to understand and engage with God. Our quest is to discover explanations for what we observe around us. However, our starting point must be defined by the Bible, the Word of God, and we must use it as our final authority on these and all matters to which it applies. The Word is God's user or *life manual* for our existence, and it will do us well to heed its instruction. We may indeed have a problem with the concept presented in Proverbs 26:2 which states that "*the curse does not come without a cause.*" Does this verse really mean that every curse (negative circumstance) that comes into our lives must be internalized and be blamed on us individually? Are we required to always be that introspective and self-incriminating?

The simple, confusing answer is yes and no! So let's get some understanding and look at what the curse is in Deuteronomy 11:26-28.

Deuteronomy 11:26-28

26 Behold, I set before you this day a blessing and a curse;
27 A blessing, if ye obey the commandments of the LORD your God, which I command you this day:
28 And a curse, if ye will not obey the commandments of the LORD your God, but turn aside out of the way which I command you this day, to go after other gods, which ye have not known.

Later on, in Deuteronomy 28:1-66, God outlines the benefits (blessings) and problems (curses) that are associated with obedience and disobedience. We will discuss these in detail in a later chapter, but for now, let's understand that God is making it very plain that disobedience carries with it effects that are not desirable and have potentially grave consequences. Furthermore, He explains in Deuteronomy 30:19 that the choice is in our hands.

Deuteronomy 30:19

I call heaven and earth to record this day against you, that I have set before you life and death, blessing and cursing: therefore choose life, that both thou and thy seed may live.

Everything that happens in this world has a cause and an effect. Landing on the street is an effect that jumping off of the curb will cause. Many times the cause may not be clear and obvious. Ignorance or negligence (which are actually choices) are other reasons why undesirable things may occur. Look at this scenario as an example:

A severe accident occurs as a car driven by a young female driver runs into a group of cyclists after she turns the wrong way on to a one-way street. Her car strikes and kills the lead cyclist and injures several more.

Was there a cause associated with this curse? Most definitely! Why did God take the life of the cyclist? Here is the backstory that none of the cyclists knew.

The young woman was very upset at the surprise breakup with her fiancé that had happened 15 minutes earlier. Her focus was on the radical change in her life. She wanted to communicate with her girlfriend who was at work and could not talk on the phone. Instead of calling, she chose to text her friend a message while driving. She failed to notice the ONE WAY - DO NOT ENTER sign while she was texting and the next thing she knew, she had collided with the cyslists.

Did God allow this accident to happen? Did God take the life of the cyclist? "No" is the answer to both questions. The driver exercised her free will to make a careless and distracted choice which ended with destruction and death (a curse). The only part that God had in this scenario was His gift of *free-will* to her at birth. He was not responsible for her actions or choices. She was!

Were any of the cyclists at fault for the driver's actions? No, they were not. Could they have taken action to avoid the curse coming upon them? Maybe yes or maybe no.

The lead cyclist, who was also the organizer of the ride, considered several routes that included riding on two-way streets which he felt would be better to view traffic. At the last minute, the route was changed by group persuasion to the ONE WAY street because they assumed it to be safer. This choice ended with the collision.

God had foreknowledge of the development of this situation. One could infer that the lead cyclist was *directed* or *warned* to take the two-way street route. In this situation, the Grace of God that might have saved lives and injuries was overlooked.

This scenario is fictitious although based on an actual incident. Most of us can remember a time when we allowed our attention to be diverted and something happened that we did not intend. Most will also acknowledge that at some time they felt a prodding to change a plan, alter a routine and go another way or do just do something different, only to find out later that they avoided something unpleasant. That prodding is the Grace of God leading us to avoid a problem if we will just listen and act.

Every situation that we face may not be as obvious and direct in its cause and effect relationship. Other problems might involve sickness or other health challenges or diseases. The cause for these curses may be more obscure or it may be very obvious that the individual is responsible. There is little argument that someone who spends his or her life smoking or abusing alcohol would likely suffer the self-inflicted curse of liver disease or lung cancer.

However, having a child born with a developmental defect is another, more obscure matter. Are the parents at fault in some way? Did they do something wrong during the pregnancy? Was it nutritional? Was it genetic? Are the grandparents or the great grandparents responsible? Was it environmental through radiation or pollution in origin?

There are so many issues (curses) in a deteriorating and decaying world for which we cannot readily assign responsibility. However, one thing is certain. There is a cause for each and every one of them, and God is never one of the causes. We may not always able to find the answers to our questions. However, this is where God's character and love really shine through to help us overcome those curses.

So let's look to the Bible to find some instruction on His true character and nature. We will find that we should not use Him as a scapegoat, making Him an accomplice to our problems, pointing a finger and saying, "Why did God ***allow*** that?" On the contrary, God presents Himself to us as a solution to those problems. We can gain much more insight into the reality of the things that are working behind the scenes as we study some of the challenges that characters in the Bible have encountered.

Chapter 10

REASON, REMEMBRANCE AND RESTORATION

The God of the Bible has a ***Reason*** for what He does. He ***Remembers*** what He said, and His goal is the ***Restoration*** of Man. In other words, He has a purpose and a plan for everything. Nothing that God does is done by accident. God acts with forethought and makes His purposes known to man through His Word, the Bible. His purpose for us is first revealed through His design in the Bible which begins with general creation in Genesis 1:1, and culminates in the creation of man and woman in Genesis 2:22. Adam and Eve were amazing but imperfect beings, complete with free will. Although created in the image of God, they fell into sin because they refused to heed God's direction. God's purpose is evident as He outlines His plan of restoration throughout the rest of the Bible text. It culminates through those who desire the "water of life," the free gift spoken of in Revelation 22:17. It would be unreasonable to have created man and simply dumped him on the planet, letting him flounder and fail in sin. However, some people may feel that this is exactly what happened, but the God of the Bible is a reasonable God who provides direction, guidance, and restoration.

How is God reasonable? What does God provide for us regarding direction or instruction? The Ten Commandments are rules of conduct or laws, but are they absolute or is there some *wiggle room*? What is God's way of providing restoration? Will He negotiate with us about the specific circumstances of our lives? After all, there are reasons that things happen that are out of our control, and they are no one's fault, right?

These are very legitimate questions, but the answers do not always seem so simple. We will start our exploration and search for the answers with the definition of the word *reasonable*.

First, let's examine the uses of the word *reason,* which occurs as both a noun and a verb. As a noun, it refers to the ***why*** of something. It describes knowing the purpose, goal, or motivation for why something happens, occurs, or exists. This is the most common usage of the word and the most readily understood. As a verb, reason means to discuss, influence, or persuade. It is not commonly used in conversation. The *Merriam-Webster Online Dictionary* gives the following uses for the word, *reason*.

reason *(noun)*

> *A statement or fact that explains why something is the way it is, why someone does, thinks, or says something, or why someone behaves a certain way.*

reason *(verb)*

> *1a) to take part in conversation, discussion, or argument 1b) to talk with another so as to influence actions or opinions.*
> *2) the power of comprehending, inferring, or thinking especially in orderly rational ways.*[35]

Reasonable is an adjective and is used to describe one who uses reason. The *Merriam-Webster Online Dictionary* gives the following definitions for the adjective *reasonable*.

reasonable *(adjective)*

> *1a) being in accordance with reason , 1b) not extreme or excessive*
> *2a) having the faculty of reason 2b) possessing sound judgment.*[36]

Based on these definitions, it is safe to conclude that a reasonable person is able to take part in a conversation, influence actions, comprehend, think orderly and rationally, and possesses sound judgment. That seems to fit God, doesn't it?

The God of Reason

It is easy to accept that God has a reason (the noun form) for what He does even though we might not understand it. However, *reason* as a verb is more difficult to understand relative to God. We first see its appearance with man's desire to engage God in discussion. During a conversation with his friends, Job replies that he understands a lot of things, but he wants to plead his case and ***reason*** directly with God in Job 13:1-3.

Job 13:1-3 *(NKJV)*

[1] Behold, my eye has seen all this, My ear has heard and understood it. [2] What you know, I also know; I am not inferior to you. [3] But I would speak to the Almighty, And I desire to reason with God.

God encourages us to talk with Him and seek His wisdom and guidance.

No specific conclusion is drawn from this verse in Job, but later God enters into the narrative in Isaiah 1:16-20. God gives direction and encourages man to reason with Him. His purpose is to convince man, through persuasion based on His own promises, to adopt a particular viewpoint.

Isaiah 1:16-20 *(NKJV)*

[16] "Wash yourselves, make yourselves clean; Put away the evil of your doings from before My eyes. Cease to do evil, [17] Learn to do good; Seek justice, Rebuke the oppressor; Defend the fatherless, Plead for the widow.

[18] "Come now, and let us reason together," Says the Lord, "Though your sins are like scarlet, They shall be as white as snow; Though they are red like crimson, They shall be as wool. [19] If you are willing and obedient, You shall eat the good of the land; [20] But if you refuse and rebel, You shall be devoured by the sword"; For the mouth of the Lord has spoken.

God is neither making a demand in these verses nor is He making a threat. Rather, He is simply stating that the behavior of man determines his outcome, and He is making recommendations that will yield the most desirable results. God wants to interact with man, establish a dialogue, and *reason* with him to help with his understanding of the situation.

God says, "Let us approach this situation together, and let Me guide you through it." To paraphrase, God is basically saying:

> *Come on, Man, let's talk about this. Put away your sin and evil, do things right like I told you and you will be free of the penalties of sin. But if you don't listen to Me and believe Me when I say that I know what I am talking about, you will be destroyed. Let's talk and have a conversation about this so you will understand.*

The reasonable God desires a relationship as a loving mentor, guiding man to success. Today, God establishes a dialogue with us through the reading and study of His Word. In the beginning, God talked directly with Man in the Garden. He verbally reasoned with him through direction and advice that was for his benefit. He gave instruction, and the consequences for ignoring that instruction in Genesis 2 regarding one very specific item in the Garden, the Tree of the Knowledge of Good and Evil.

The Tree in the Garden

Genesis 2:8-9

> [8] *And the* LORD *God planted a garden eastward in Eden; and there he put the man whom he had formed.*
> [9] *And out of the ground made the* LORD *God to grow every tree that is pleasant to the sight, and good for food; the tree of life also in the midst of the garden, and the tree of knowledge of good and evil.*

There was an epic struggle regarding this particular tree. It bore fruit that God had forbidden Adam and Eve to consume. The significance of the tree, and the circumstances that surrounded it, set the course of human kind and its interaction with God. There was a choice given to Man, one that allowed him to exercise his free will and his personal responsibility. That choice was whether or not to obey the directive of God not to consume the fruit of the tree as recorded in Genesis 2:16-17.

Genesis 2:16-17

> [16] *And the* LORD *God commanded the man, saying, Of every tree of the garden thou mayest freely eat:*
> [17] *But of the tree of the knowledge of good and evil, thou shalt not eat of it: for in the day that thou eatest thereof thou shalt surely die.*

God provided a rather compelling reason for avoiding the eating of the fruit of that tree as the narrative continues in Genesis 3:1-13. He was very careful to let Adam know that an effect would come (the curse of death) if they acted and ate the fruit. However, God knew that the problem was not the fruit of the tree itself. Rather, it was what the ingestion of its fruit would yield.

Genesis 3:1-13

1 Now the serpent was more subtil than any beast of the field which the LORD God had made. And he said unto the woman, Yea, hath God said, Ye shall not eat of every tree of the garden?
2 And the woman said unto the serpent, We may eat of the fruit of the trees of the garden:
3 But of the fruit of the tree which is in the midst of the garden, God hath said, Ye shall not eat of it, neither shall ye touch it, lest ye die.
4 And the serpent said unto the woman, Ye shall not surely die:
5 For God doth know that in the day ye eat thereof, then your eyes shall be opened, and ye shall be as gods, knowing good and evil.
6 And when the woman saw that the tree was good for food, and that it was pleasant to the eyes, and a tree to be desired to make one wise, she took of the fruit thereof, and did eat, and gave also unto her husband with her; and he did eat.
7 And the eyes of them both were opened, and they knew that they were naked; and they sewed fig leaves together, and made themselves aprons.
8 And they heard the voice of the LORD God walking in the garden in the cool of the day: and Adam and his wife hid themselves from the presence of the LORD God amongst the trees of the garden.
9 And the LORD God called unto Adam, and said unto him, Where art thou?
10 And he said, I heard thy voice in the garden, and I was afraid, because I was naked; and I hid myself.
11 And he said, Who told thee that thou wast naked? Hast thou eaten of the tree, whereof I commanded thee that thou shouldest not eat?
12 And the man said, The woman whom thou gavest to be with me, she gave me of the tree, and I did eat.
13 And the LORD God said unto the woman, What is this that thou hast done? And the woman said, The serpent beguiled me, and I did eat.

Whether the passage is taken literally or metaphorically, the result is the same. Eating the fruit of the Tree of the Knowledge of Good and Evil destroyed mankind's innocence. The fruit was unlike any other food.

It was like a spoiled piece of meat that when eaten, festered, and caused sickness and disease. However, the sickness was not physical, but spiritual. It was like a *virus* that was incorporated into their very beings and into their souls. They became carriers, spreading it to all of their descendants. The serpent was so persuasive because of the nature of this insidious *disease*. He wanted to cause this disobedient action on the part of the Woman and the Man so that they would seal their own destruction.

Who was the serpent that wreaked havoc upon mankind and why would he want to do this? The serpent is not identified here, but he is made known in Revelations 12:7-9. However, his identity was not fully appreciated by those in the Old Testament because they were without any revelation of his existence. We will explore this idea in more detail later.

Revelation 12:7-9

> [7] *And there was war in heaven: Michael and his angels fought against the dragon; and the dragon fought and his angels,* [8] *And prevailed not; neither was their place found any more in heaven.* [9] *And the great dragon was cast out, that old serpent, called the Devil, and Satan, which deceiveth the whole world: he was cast out into the earth, and his angels were cast out with him.*

We now know who the serpent was but why did he set out to deceive Eve? The Devil or Satan, also known as Lucifer, knew the difference between good and evil himself before this encounter with Eve. Satan in the form of the serpent *chose* to engage in the sin of deception or lying. Man and Woman had not yet sinned when the Woman was deceived by the serpent. The deception was effective. It led to sin that made the Man and the Woman aware of the concept of Good and Evil. With their innocence now removed, they now became responsible for their actions, and subject to the penalties of disobedience. This realization begs another question, "Why did God put that specific tree in the Garden?"

The Tree might have been placed there as a test of the commitment and obedience of Man. However, the Tree of Life was also there in the midst of the Garden. If the man and woman had eaten the fruit of that tree first and then the fruit of the Tree of the Knowledge of Good and Evil, they would have had eternal life in a corrupted state, which is the condition of Satan. Considering the gravity of the choice of Man, there must have been a more compelling reason than just a *test*.

God tells us in the Bible that other beings were present in the universe before the creation of Man and Woman. These were heavenly beings, such as angels and a variety of other spiritual beings. One of the most precious and exalted of those was Lucifer (the Devil or Satan). He lost his status when he fell to his own conceit and self-importance as he exalted himself above God. A description of his fall is found in Isaiah 14:12-14 *(see p. 71).* Additional descriptors are found in Ezekiel 28:12-19. There is some disagreement among scholars as whether or not this passage refers solely to Satan, or the results of Satan's influence on an earthly king. However, for the purpose of our discussion, since the description of the spiritual condition and end state of the fallen being is basically the same as that of Satan, we will assume it to be referring to Satan.

Ezekiel 28:12-19

12 Son of man, take up a lamentation upon the king of Tyrus, and say unto him, Thus saith the Lord GOD ; Thou sealest up the sum, full of wisdom, and perfect in beauty. 13 Thou hast been in Eden the garden of God; every precious stone was thy covering, the sardius, topaz, and the diamond, the beryl, the onyx, and the jasper, the sapphire, the emerald, and the carbuncle, and gold: the workmanship of thy tabrets and of thy pipes was prepared in thee in the day that thou wast created.

14 Thou art the anointed cherub that covereth; and I have set thee so: thou wast upon the holy mountain of God; thou hast walked up and down in the midst of the stones of fire. 15 Thou wast perfect in thy ways from the day that thou wast created, till iniquity was found in thee.

16 By the multitude of thy merchandise they have filled the midst of thee with violence, and thou hast sinned: therefore I will cast thee as profane out of the mountain of God: and I will destroy thee, O covering cherub, from the midst of the stones of fire. 17 Thine heart was lifted up because of thy beauty, thou hast corrupted thy wisdom by reason of thy brightness: I will cast thee to the ground, I will lay thee before kings, that they may behold thee.

18 Thou hast defiled thy sanctuaries by the multitude of thine iniquities, by the iniquity of thy traffick; therefore will I bring forth a fire from the midst of thee, it shall devour thee, and I will bring thee to ashes upon the earth in the sight of all them that behold thee. 19 All they that know thee among the people shall be astonished at thee: thou shalt be a terror, and never shalt thou be any more.

We still have to address the question of why God put that tree in the Garden. This is especially puzzling since God undoubtedly knew that Man was going to be disobedient and sin. Sin had entered God's creation before the introduction of human kind, but the sin of Lucifer (Satan) did not automatically corrupt the human world in which we live. The corruption of God's new creation, Man, was the goal of Satan after his fall. He had previously sinned, and he was not going to tolerate a sinless creation of God. He saw that ***dominion*** had been given to Man and Woman over the realm of the Earth to which he had been cast (Genesis 1:26).

Satan was jealous of the power that God had invested in these new creatures and immediately set out to steal God's gifts to them as well as their very lives. His goal was to destroy God's creation and steal back the authority in the earth realm that God had given to Man, His new creation, but this is where God's justice came into play. Both of the Trees were present in the Garden because God is a ***just*** God. He follows the rule of law, which emanates from His mouth. If He did not follow His Words, He would be a liar and ***unjust***. Sin was already an influence within the universe due to Lucifer's rebellion. The new creation of the Earth and Man had not yet been corrupted by sin. God legally permitted the possibility of rebellion (read this as free will) within this new realm. He had to be just and fair to the rest of the beings that were already in existence. They had been aware of the sin of Lucifer and been subjected to his deception and rebellion. God could not create a separate world that would interact with the existing spiritual world without allowing the same possibilities of deception and sin. Thus, the *opportunity* to know Good and Evil was necessary.

Satan put all of his cunning to work as he influenced Man and Woman to choose disobedience and fall as they did. He did it by dangling the "carrot of knowledge" in front of Eve and Adam, enticing them through their intellect, to the detriment of their spirit. The method has changed little over the centuries, except for the type of carrot that is dangled. The lust of knowledge is still paramount in the minds of men. The world as we know it would be far different if the Man and Woman made a different choice, but they did not. Don't think you would have been any different if it were you. You would have made the same choice!

It is interesting that Adam and Eve chose Knowledge over Life when they disobeyed God. It still happens today as science is driven to seek knowledge, but you can still choose Life!

Opportunities to fail and fall are presented to us every day of our lives. We are constantly faced with decisions and choices. However, the presence of the opportunity to sin does not guarantee that you will. You can still choose what is right. Adam and Eve did not choose rightly, but chose instead to know Good and Evil. Because they ate the fruit of the Knowledge of Good and Evil, God was forced to expel them from the Garden for their own protection. God wanted to prevent them from ending up in a state of perpetual and eternal sin, as is the state of Satan. Satan was successful in the short term. He did regain the authority of the Earth Realm from Man and accomplished his physical death.

God immediately set His plan of Salvation in motion, furthered by Noah, Abraham, Moses and the Law, and ultimately Jesus. It was designed to save Man and restore him to his originally created state. However, God does not force *His Salvation* upon any man, it only comes through the conscious, deception influenced, free-will choice to follow Him.

Remembrance Encouraged

God said He would eliminate transgressions of Israel and forget their sins in Isaiah 43:25-26. He challenged them to prove themselves worthy and justified in light of their sins. Then, He says something very curious, "Put Me in remembrance...." Does God have a bad memory? Why does He need to be reminded if He made this plan in the first place?

Isaiah 43:25-26

> [25] *I, even I, am he that blotteth out thy transgressions for mine own sake, and will not remember thy sins.*
> [26] *Put me in remembrance: let us plead together: declare thou, that thou mayest be justified.*

God begins His challenge by talking about remembrance. God says in this passage that man is to remind Him of His promises, discuss the situation as in a court of law, and speak out in either agreement or disagreement with His word. This statement can be seen two ways. One inference is that God is almost sarcastically saying that if they were to argue their case for self-justification they would fail as they remember and examine His word. The other inference is that if man agrees with God, he will be cleansed and made right or righteous, and he will be ***justified***.

To better understand what God is trying to say to us in the Bible, information about the translation of specific words can be gathered from a *Strong's Exhaustive Concordance of the Bible.*[37] It lists the specific words used in the original text and definitions of those words. The Hebrew word translated *justified* in verse 26 is the Strong's word designated OT:6663, defined here:

"justified" - *Strong's* OT:6663 צָדַק, *tsadaq* (tsaw-dak')

> *a primitive root; to be (causatively, make) right (in a moral or forensic sense): KJV - cleanse, clearself, (be, do) just (-ice, -ify, -ifyself), (be turn to) righteous (-ness).*

The passage in Isaiah was specifically written to Jacob and the people of Israel about being right or cleansed, but the principle holds true throughout the Bible. The central theme is the same that God revealed and established with Adam in the beginning. God basically says, "Do what I recommend to you and you will be in good shape. Ignore Me at your own peril." God took His recommendations to a higher level when He formally established a Covenant agreement with man through Abraham in which God guaranteed that He would fulfill His promises. In order to receive God's forgiveness as described in Isaiah 43:25-26, we must remember His word and discuss it with Him.

God gave an extensive list of laws (613 in total) that included the better known Ten Commandments. He gave them to man because man was very legalistic, actively looking for ways to get around His decrees.

Man constantly seeks loopholes to excuse his disobedience relative to the intents of God and His covenant. To dissuade this rebellion, God created the laws in great detail to address virtually every conceivable situation. These laws effectively closed the *loopholes* and made man completely responsible for himself. The Law made man liable for the penalty for his own sin, which is death.

This resulted in a seemingly hopeless situation for man. He could not possibly observe the entire Law without error. Man still found himself in the same situation that he was in since the fall of Adam. However, now there was an added pressure. God made His requirements abundantly clear through the Law. Sin would not be tolerated by God. Man now had accountability or personal responsibility for his actions. Later, God declared that He had a way to fix Man's situation, even in the midst of these staggering requirements. Ezekiel 16:59-60 tells us that even though man breaks the covenant by disobeying the laws, God will continue to keep up His part to save and restore Man.

Ezekiel 16:59-60

> 59 *For thus saith the Lord God; I will even deal with thee as thou hast done, which hast despised the oath in breaking the covenant.*
> 60 *Nevertheless I will remember my covenant with thee in the days of thy youth, and I will establish unto thee an everlasting covenant.*

Think about how unfair this is to God as a party to the covenant. A covenant or agreement in our world is breached if one party does not hold up his or her end of it. Failure to perform carries a variety of legal remedies that are laid out in detail when the agreement is signed. They have negative repercussions upon the one that breached the agreement. Failing to make your payments is an example of a breach of covenant, and you may lose your car or house as a result because the stronger of the covenant partners imposes the penalties for non performance.

This is not how God chose to work with His covenant, however, and that is certainly of great benefit to man. He did something that is completely contrary to the way that man thinks and acts. He set a plan in motion to fix man's errors of non-performance through sin even though man regularly messes it all up. He outlined the details in His Word though His promises, and He tells man to put Him in remembrance of them. However, when He says to put in Him in remembrance, He is ***not*** saying that He is the one that needs the reminding. God is letting man know that ***he*** (man) needs reminding of God's goodness and provision. Man needs to make himself aware of God's word which clearly states that in spite of the sins of man, He will honor His part of the bargain. God established the covenant as *everlasting* because He is in the business of *restoration*.

God can remember His words and His promises to you, but you can't remember something you never learned. You will need to learn them first!

But, It's Not My Fault!

There may be things that have happened to you in your life that are completely out your control and that you can't fix. These may be very bad or painful things over which you had no control. You may blame God for allowing these things to happen to you and even think that He is not paying attention to your situation. However, God is aware of these circumstances, and He wants you to be restored and made whole again.

He was and is powerless to intervene in these situations because He granted ***free will*** to both you and those who brought bad things upon you. If He were to have intervened on your behalf, He would have overridden the free will of those other people. He will not do that to them or to you. We are not responsible for the actions of others, but God has put all of us into a position of responsibility for our own actions.

We can certainly point to others and say, "It is their fault. They did this to me." However, it is ultimately up to us to choose how to deal with the circumstance. This may not seem fair or even right, yet we have all heard of people that have overcome seemingly insurmountable odds to achieve success and fulfillment. You can be that person when you accept the grace that God has provided to you through Jesus and follow the leading of the Spirit of God. Regardless of your situation, God will show you a path, and if you are willing, you can receive it.

God is not the source of problems even though sometimes in the Bible it appears that way. The real causes of your problems are rebellion, selfishness, hatred, arrogance, disobedience, and every other self-centered sin committed by you or others that have harmed you. People will sin against you, abuse, hurt, and betray you, but God never changes and will never let you down. God is the constant in this universe, and He reaches out to you in the midst of your circumstances. He said to reason with Him and put Him in remembrance of His promises. Reasoning with God regarding your circumstance is to remember His provision for you.

In reality, God wants to restore you. He provides you with the tools to overcome your circumstance and be successful in every way. He wants you to be the person He created you to be, not a person that is an angry, hopeless creature that has become the product of his or her own circumstances. God offers you restoration, the choice to believe and accept is yours alone. However, based on some situations described in the Bible, it is sometimes difficult to believe that God is not against you.

To illustrate this, we will explore two examples from the Old Testament. Before examining these examples and going into further discussion of restoration, it will be helpful to gain a little understanding of basic Hebrew grammar.

It's All In The Words

The study in the next section considers the attributes of *voice* and *mood* of Hebrew verbs and inferences that are made at the discretion of the translators. An in-depth discussion of Hebrew is not within the scope of this book but can be pursued by the reader if desired. This will be an important but very superficial treatment of Hebrew grammar.

The characteristic or attribute of a verb's voice is described as *active, passive, or reflexive.* The attribute of mood is described as *simple, causative,* or *intensive*. Stems indicate these attributes of the verb. One such stem is the "Qal" stem. A verb in the Qal stem is in the *active voice*, meaning that it is associated with an action, but not a *causative* action.

This means that the one described as speaking is not causing the activity, or in grammatical terms, the subject of the verb is not causing the action to take place. The discussion that follows relates to verbs that have the Qal stem and are, therefore, not causative in Voice.

Restoration Provided

Restoration frequently follows on the heels of repentance and turning back to God. We will examine two examples that promise complete restoration and success over oppressors and natural adversities. The first example is in Jeremiah 30 and the second is in Isaiah 43.

The tables in the following discussion are derived from the *Hebrew Interlinear Bible.*[38] This Bible version shows the actual Greek and Hebrew words as they are translated in the *King James Version*. Also, in conjunction with the English translation, it provides the reference number from the *Strong's Exhaustive Concordance* and the pronunciation. It is then possible to compare the original Greek or Hebrew to the English words used in the translation.

Jeremiah 30:1-3

> [1] *The word that came to Jeremiah from the LORD, saying,* [2] *Thus speaketh the LORD God of Israel, saying, Write thee all the words that I have spoken unto thee in a book.*
> [3] *For, lo, the days come, saith the LORD, that I will bring again the captivity of my people Israel and Judah, saith the LORD: and I will cause them to return to the land that I gave to their fathers, and they shall possess it.*

This prophetic word sets the tone of the rest of this prophecy, offering both a warning and a promise from God. These verses warn of a "captivity" of Israel and Judah. They attribute both the cause of the captivity and the subsequent release to God. The same Hebrew word, *Strong's* OT:7725 שׁוּב, *shuwb* (shoob), is first translated, "that I will bring again" and then rendered again as "and I will cause them to return." It is translated many ways in other scriptures, and the rendering is dependent upon context. Therefore, it is subject to the understanding or bias of the translator.

"that I will bring again" - *Strong's* OT:7725 שׁוּב, *shuwb* (shoob)

a primitive root; to turn back (hence, away) transitively or intransitively, literally or figuratively (not necessarily with the idea of return to the starting point); generally to retreat; often adverbial, again.

Jeremiah 30:3 - Hebrew Interlinear Bible

English	*For,*	*lo,*	*the days*	*come,*	*saith*	*the Lord,*
Hebrew	כִּי	הִ®נֵּה	יָמִים	בָּאִים	נְאֻם	יְהוָה
Strong's	3588	2009	3117	935	5002	3068
Pronounced	Kiy	hineeh	yaamiym	baa'iym	n'um	Yahweh

English	*that I will bring again*		*the captivity of*	*my people*	*Israel*
Hebrew	וְשַׁבְתִּי	אֶת	שְׁ®בוּת	עַמִּי	יִשְׂרָאֵל
Strong's	7725	853	7622	5971	3478
Pronounced	wshabtiy	'et-	shbuwt	'amiy	Yisraa'eel

English	*and Judah*	*saith*	*the Lord:*	*and I will cause them to return*	*to*
Hebrew	וִיהוּדָה	אָמַר	יְהוָה	וַהֲשִׁבֹתִים	אֶל
Strong's	3063	559	3068	7725	413
Pronounced	wi-Yhuwdaah	'aamar	Yahweh	Wahshibotiym	'el-

English	*the land*	*that*	*I gave*	*to their fathers,*	*and they shall possess it.*
Hebrew	הָאָרֶץ	אֲשֶׁר־	נָתַתִּי	לַאֲבוֹתָם	וִירֵשׁוּהָ
Strong's	776	834	5414	1	3423
Pronounced	haa'aarets	'sher-	naatatiy	la'bowtaam	wiyreeshuwhaa

The word OT:7725 is translated as many, sometimes very different English words in the *King James Version* of the Bible. The following is a list of those words. Note the wide variation of interpretation of this word.

KJV - ([break, build, circumcise, dig, do anything, do evil, feed, lay down, lie down, lodge, make, rejoice, send, take, weep]) again, (cause to) answer (+again), in any case (wise), at all, averse, bring (again, back, home again), call [to mind], carry again (back), cease, certainly, come again (back), consider, continually, convert, deliver (again), deny, draw back, fetch home again, fro, get [oneself] (back) again, give (again), go again (back, home), [go] out, hinder, let, [see] more, needs, be past, pay, pervert, pull in again, put (again, up again), recall, recompense, recover, refresh, relieve, render (again), requite, rescue, restore, retrieve, (cause to, make to) return, reverse, reward, + say nay, send back, set again, slide back, still, surely, take back (off), (cause to, make to) turn (again, self again, away, back, back again, backward, from, off), withdraw.

This Hebrew word has the Qal stem, which indicates that the verb is not causative. Since the English personal pronoun, " I," is not written as a separate and distinct Hebrew word in Jeremiah 30:3, it is inferred with this translation.

This verse presents contradictory actions if God is personally causing the "captivity" in the beginning of the verse and then personally breaking the "captivity" at the end. Since the Hebrew word, OT:7725 וְשַׁבְתִּי, *shuwb* (shoob), has the Qal stem, it is not causative in mood and does not support the notion of causation by God in either situation. Therefore, reading Jeremiah 30:3 without the use of " I," the inferred personal pronoun, in the sections, "that I will bring again" as well as "and I will cause them to return," is not unreasonable and completely changes the understanding. It shifts from God personally causing the return after invoking a punishment to God simply making a statement that the events will occur.

Next, observe the usage of the word captivity. There are two ways to look at the concept of captivity. First, it can refer to exile or a state of imprisonment by an enemy. Second, it can refer to God *taking captive*; that is, God taking Israel or the dead for His own possession, to protect them and provide for their prosperity as in Ephesians 4:8 which speaks of the resurrection of Jesus.

Ephesians 4:8

Wherefore he saith, When he ascended up on high, he led captivity captive, and gave gifts unto men.

The first of these interpretations of the word captivity is a negative punishment while the second is a positive blessing. In this case, the verses in Jeremiah refer to the negative meaning of captivity.

The attribution of the cause of the captivity to God, as a negative event, can be explained through the perspective of the writer/translator. Do you remember the discussion of relativity and perspective? (*see p. 46*). Modification of the verse as follows, produces a different meaning that puts God in the position of informing about an event rather than claiming responsibility for it.

Jeremiah 30:3 *(modified without the inference of the pronoun, " I ")*

For, lo, the days come, saith the Lord, that will bring again the captivity of my people Israel and Judah, saith the Lord, and will cause them to return to the land that I gave to their fathers, and they shall possess it.

The *days,* not God, will bring their captivity. God, in this sense, is informing of a coming event, not saying that He has caused that event. With the removal of the " I " after the first "saith the Lord," the verse could read, *"For, lo, the days come, saith the Lord, that will bring again the captivity of my people....".* This is reasonable because then the verse does not make a contradiction in action. God identified their sins as the problem in Jeremiah 30:15. Therefore, after they overcame their sins, it is consistent that the God of blessings would declare their return to their land and prosperity in Jeremiah 30:3-4.

Jeremiah 30:3-4

3 For, lo, the days come, saith the Lord, that I will bring again the captivity of my people Israel and Judah, saith the Lord, and I will cause them to return to the land that I gave to their fathers, and they shall possess it.
4 And these are the words that the Lord spake concerning Israel and concerning Judah.

The warning of Jeremiah 30:3 refers to the extended captivity that Judah and Israel are about to realize fully. The promise is that their captivity will be reversed, and they will overcome and continue to exist as a distinct people. Let's closely examine Jeremiah 30:15-18, in which the reason for the captivity is given, and God describes His restoration.

The Real Cause

Jeremiah 30:15-18

15 Why criest thou for thine affliction? thy sorrow is incurable for the multitude of thine iniquity: because thy sins were increased, I have done these things unto thee.

16 Therefore all they that devour thee shall be devoured; and all thine adversaries, every one of them, shall go into captivity; and they that spoil thee shall be a spoil, and all that prey upon thee will I give for a prey.
17 For I will restore health unto thee, and I will heal thee of thy wounds, saith the Lord; because they called thee an Outcast, saying, This is Zion, whom no man seeketh after.

> [18] *Thus saith the Lord; Behold, I will bring again the captivity of Jacob's tents, and have mercy on his dwellingplaces; and the city shall be builded upon her own heap, and the palace shall remain after the manner thereof.*

The restoration described in these verses from the *King James Version* is something to rejoice over. Everything that was lost due to sin and iniquity is reinstated, and those who have come against Israel and Judah are themselves overcome. However, Jeremiah 30:15 clearly states that God did all of the afflictions that He also claimed to take away, just like the translation of Jeremiah 30:3. This is another of many situations where God gets the reputation as the one who causes destruction through cursing while also being identified as the one who does restoration through blessing. It is generally accepted as truth that God does both cursing and blessing, although this may seem contradictory, like a confusing double standard. Let us examine Jeremiah 30:15 in this passage in a little more depth for some deeper understanding.

Jeremiah 30:15

> *Why criest thou for thine affliction? thy sorrow is incurable for the multitude of thine iniquity: because thy sins were increased, I have done these things unto thee.*

Jeremiah 30:15 - Hebrew Interlinear Bible

English	***Why***	***criest thou***	***for***	***thine affliction?***	***is***	***incurable***
Hebrew	מה־	תִזְעַק	עַל־	בְשִׁךְר		אָנוּשׁ
Strong's	4100	2199	5921	7667	9999	605
Pronounced	Mah	tiz'aq	'al-	shibreek		'aanuwsh

English	***thy sorrow***	***For***	***the multitude of***	***thine iniquity:***	***were increased,***
Hebrew	בךְמַכְא	עַל	רב	נךְעֲו	עצְמø
Strong's	4341	5921	7230	5771	6105
Pronounced	mak'obeek	'Al	rob	'woneek	'aatsmuw

English	***because***	***Thy sins***	***I have done***	***these***	***things***	***unto thee.***
Hebrew		יךְחַטֹאתַ	עָשִׂיתִי	אֵלֶה		:ךְלָ
Strong's	9999	2403	6213	428	9999	3807a
Pronounced		chaTo'tayik	'aasiytiy	'eeleh		laak

Look specifically at the structure of the verse and note the words, "***I have done*** these things unto thee." This is speaking of the afflictions and disaffections described in Jeremiah 30:1-14. On the surface, it appears that God is saying to the people, "Why are you complaining? You should know that your sorrow is inconsolable because of your iniquity. And because you sinned, I did all of this to you."

The words *is*, *because* and *things* were added for clarity by the translators. This is indicated by the OT:9999 designation shown in the *Hebrew Interlinear Bible* chart for Jeremiah 30:15. Colons and commas were also added for clarity. The word that is translated, *I have done* is *Strong's* OT:6213 עָשָׂה, `*asah* (aw-saw'). It is a word with very broad applications. It can have a great variety of meanings as noted below.

> ***"I have done"*** - *Strong's* OT:6213 עָשָׂה, `*asah* (aw-saw');
>
> *a primitive root; to do or make, in the broadest sense and widest application (as follows):*
>
> **KJV** - *accomplish, advance, appoint, apt, be at, become, bear, bestow, bring forth, bruise, be busy, certainly, have the charge of, commit, deal (with), deck, displease, do, (ready) dress (-ed), (put in) execute (-ion), exercise, fashion, feast, [fighting-] man, finish, fit, fly, follow, fulfill, furnish, gather, get, go about, govern, grant, great, hinder, hold ([a feast]), indeed, be industrious, journey, keep, labour, maintain, make, be meet, observe, be occupied, offer, officer, pare, bring (come) to pass, perform, pracise, prepare, procure, provide, put, requite, sacrifice, serve, set, shew, sin, spend, surely, take, thoroughly, trim, very, vex, be [warr-] ior, work (-man), yield, use.*

None of the definitions or meanings of OT:6213 עָשָׂה, `*asah* specifically attaches the personal pronoun " I " to its meaning. These applications are wide-ranging and might reference an individual person, or just as easily, might reference a group of people, an inanimate object, event, or action. Such examples are seen in many scriptures *(see Appendix Chapter 10)*.

It is reasonable to assume that the action described in Jeremiah 30:15 was done by God. It is written, "***I have done*** these things unto thee." The perspective of the translator and the prevailing understanding during the time that this was translated was that God was both the blessing agent and the cursing agent. However, it is not unreasonable to look at the verse in a slightly different context. Simply removing the implied personal pronoun " I " from the Hebrew word, OT:6213 עָשָׂה, `*asah*, which assigns the action to God causes this verse to take on a completely new meaning.

Jeremiah 30:15 *(Original KJV Translation)*

> *Why criest thou for thine affliction? thy sorrow is incurable for the multitude of thine iniquity: because thy sins were increased, I have done these things unto thee.*

Modified without the " I " but a little awkward in reading.

> *Why criest thou for thine affliction? thy sorrow is incurable for the multitude of thine iniquity: because thy sins were increased, have been done these things unto thee.*

A slight rearrangement of the words can clarify the meaning and make the verse less awkward to read. This is frequently done by the translators and was actually done with this verse as well. The literal KJV translation of the Hebrew words in their written order is as follows:

> *Why criest thou for thine affliction? is incurable thy sorrow for the multitude of thine iniquity were increased: because thy sins, I have done these things unto thee.*

If this word order is maintained, the attribution to God is even less apparent if the " I " is removed. Also, remember that there is no punctuation such as commas in Hebrew.

(Modified and more readable)

> *Why criest thou for thine affliction? thy sorrow is incurable for the multitude of thine iniquity were increased: because thy sins have done these things unto thee.*

The word that is translated *I have done* (Strong's OT:6213) also has the Qal stem and is, therefore, not causative in its mood. Even if the " I " is retained within the passage, the subject pronoun " I " is not the cause of the "things done unto thee," which is the object of the sentence. The actual cause was the sins of the people. God was not responsible for the afflictions of the people.

They were certainly punished for their sins against God, but He did not actively (not causatively) bring the afflictions against them. The law of cause and effect is at work here. Acts of disobedience and rebellion (sin) had already been assigned a penalty. The afflictions came as a result of the people's actions. These actions opened the gates for their affliction and destruction to enter without the intervention of God.

Jeremiah 30:16

Therefore all they that devour thee shall be devoured; and all thine adversaries, every one of them, shall go into captivity; and they that spoil thee shall be a spoil, and all that prey upon thee will I give for a prey.

Clearly, this verse states that those who "devoured" Judah and Israel would themselves be devoured and that all of their adversaries would be captive, spoiled, and made into a prey. In other words, the ones that came against them and created the afflictions would be destroyed. If God is the one that actually brought all of the destructive afflictions upon them as stated in Jeremiah 30:15, He is indeed an adversary, a spoiler, and a devourer. If God was the one that brought about the destruction and devouring in the first place, the retribution against Israel and Judah's adversaries that is declared in verse 16 would actually be God devouring and destroying Himself. This is neither logical nor possible. God would be warring against Himself if that were the case.

God is portrayed by the translation in these passages as the one that brings both blessing and cursing. As a result of this and other similar portrayals, Man continues to view God as both an ally and an adversary at the same time. However, Jesus offers a clue to the truth of the situation through His words in Mark 3:23-26.

Mark 3:23-26

23 And he called them unto him, and said unto them in parables, "How can Satan cast out Satan? 24 And if a kingdom be divided against itself, that kingdom cannot stand. 25 And if a house be divided against itself, that house cannot stand. 26 And if Satan rise up against himself, and be divided, he cannot stand, but hath an end."

God is no more divided against Himself than is our true adversary, Satan. The concept of God providing blessings to man, after pronouncing a curse upon him, is double-minded, contradictory, and divided. God truly does offer blessings to man, but there are conditions. Those conditions are obedience to the Law in the Old Testament and faith in Jesus in the New Testament. God is not the one who brings blessings, just to take them away with curses or vice-versa. God offers blessings and warns of the consequences of the rejection of those blessings through disobedience and rebellion. Disobedience and rebellion, otherwise known as sin, are the work of the corrupted soul of man, assisted by deception from our adversary, Satan.

Disobedience can be a result of the work of the adversary Satan against us, but it can also be attributed to the corrupted nature of man as a result of the fall of Adam. Man has the capacity to be self-centered and self-willed, leading himself into disobedience and rebellion against God. However, we should be aware that the influences of Satan are also there to help man fall into sin. God, on the other hand, has provided His direction to keep man out of trouble in 1 Corinthians 10:13. He has provided a way for us to resist the temptation to sin and has given us a means of escape.

1 Corinthians 10:13

There hath no temptation taken you but such as is common to man: but God is faithful, who will not suffer you to be tempted above that ye are able; but will with the temptation also make a way to escape, that ye may be able to bear it.

The essence of this narrative in Jeremiah is that the sins of the people brought about their captivity and that the captivity itself would cause them to reflect upon their sins. This reflection would in turn cause their hearts to repent and turn back to God and then be restored back to their rightful possessions and position with Him. It becomes quite clear that the passage of Jeremiah 30:15 which states, "*. . . because thy sins were increased, I have done these things unto thee*" can also be read "*because the increase of thy sins has done these things unto thee.*" Sin is the true culprit that produced the curses, not God.

God is not the enemy. He does not bring about curses and destruction as tradition might suggest. If God had been doing what appears to be written, He would be "a house divided against itself," working against Himself. (More will be discussed on this subject in Chapter 23, "It's Just Not Fair!") When the totality of God's plan is taken into account, it can be seen that He is warning of impending danger, calling to repentance, and giving direction toward freedom and success.

Jacob Cursed

Our second example of restoration is found in Isaiah 43:22-28. It not only tells us to plead together with God to be justified, but also identifies God as the source of the reproaches, defilement, and curse of Israel.

Isaiah 43:22-28

> 22 *But thou hast not called upon me, O Jacob; but thou hast been weary*
> *of me, O Israel.* 23 *Thou hast not brought me the small cattle of thy burnt*
> *offerings; neither hast thou honoured me with thy sacrifices. I have not*
> *caused thee to serve with an offering, nor wearied thee with incense.* 24
> *Thou hast bought me no sweet cane with money, neither hast thou filled me*
> *with the fat of thy sacrifices: but thou hast made me to serve with thy sins,*
> *thou hast wearied me with thine iniquities.*
> 25 *I, even I, am he that blotteth out thy transgressions for mine own sake,*
> *and will not remember thy sins.* 26 *Put me in remembrance: let us plead*
> *together: declare thou, that thou mayest be justified.*
> 27 *Thy first father hath sinned, and thy teachers have transgressed against*
> *me.* 28 *Therefore I have profaned the princes of the sanctuary, and have*
> *given Jacob to the curse, and Israel to reproaches.*

Verses 27 and 28 state that the problem began with the sin of the "first father" (probably referring to Adam) and was propagated by the teachers. The curse, reproaches, and defilement came about as a result of this sin. Verse 28 refers to being "profane," or "breaking one's word" (Strong's OT:2490 חָלַל, *chalal* [khaw-lal']). This word has the Piel stem, which is in the intensive active in mood. This indicates a deliberate, rather than passive, action. The question is, who is doing the deliberate activity of profaning or breaking of his or her word? Is it God breaking His word with intent, or is it the "princes of the sanctuary" that profaned and broke their word through sin?

Isaiah 43:28 - Hebrew Interlinear Bible

English	*Therefore I have profaned*	*the princes of*	*the sanctuary*
Hebrew	וַאֲחַלֵּל	שָׂרֵי	קֹדֶשׁ
Strong's	2490	8269	6944
Pronounced	Wa'chaleel	saareey	qodesh

English	*and have given*	*to the curse*	*Jacob*	*and Israel*	*to reproaches*
Hebrew	וְאֶתְּנָה	לַחֵרֶם	יַעֲקֹב	וְיִשְׂרָאֵל	לְגִדּוּפִים׃ ס
Strong's	5414	2764	3290	3478	1421
Pronounced	W'etnaah	lacheerem	Ya'qob	w-Yisraa'eel	lgiduwpiym

The definition of Strong's OT:2490 does not specify the personal pronoun " I " be attached. In the vast majority of the 143 instances in which this Hebrew word appears in the *King James Version*, it is not associated with the word, " I ."

"Therefore I have profaned" - *Strong's* OT:2490 חָלַל, *chalal* (khaw-lal')

a primitive root [compare OT:2470*]; properly, to bore, i.e. (by implication) to wound, to dissolve; figuratively, to profane (a person, place or thing), to break (one's word), to begin (as if by an "opening wedge"); denom. (from* OT:2485*) to play (the flute):*
KJV *- begin (men began), defile, break, defile, eat (as common things), first, gather the grape thereof, take inheritance, pipe, player on instruments, pollute, (cast as) profane (self), prostitute, slay (slain), sorrow, stain, wound.*

Isaiah 43:27-28 might be read as follows if the reference to " I " is removed, not attributing to God the blame for the afflictions. Compare the King James rendering to one in which the implied " I " is removed.

Isaiah 43:27-28
27 Thy first father hath sinned, and thy teachers have transgressed against
me. 28 Therefore I have profaned the princes of the sanctuary, and have
given Jacob to the curse, and Israel to reproaches.

Isaiah 43:27-28 *(Implied " I " Removed and arranged for easier reading)*
27 Thy first father hath sinned, and thy teachers have transgressed against
me. 28 Therefore have the princes of the sanctuary profaned, and have given
Jacob to the curse, and Israel to reproaches.

The choice to attach the personal pronoun " I " to the word is again subject to the perspective of the translator. If the assumption is made from the outset that God both blesses and curses, God will be found guilty of pronouncing curses and destruction. On the other hand, if the assumption is made that God is offering blessings to man and that there is an adversary seeking to destroy man, the inferred " I " would not be written, and God would not receive the blame for these actions.

Punished Into Worship?

The perspective of the original writer or conveyor of the events is a key factor in understanding the truth of God's written Word, the Bible. We also must reconcile the perspective and the understanding of the translator. The following passage in Joel 2:21-32 is a great message of hope and restoration. These are wonderful verses of hope, deliverance, provision, abundant prosperity and spiritual insight. However, in the midst of these very positive and uplifting encouragements, God is once again given the attribution of creating the problem in the first place as written in verse 25. God is given the blame for sending "his great army," the locusts, cankerworms, caterpillars, and palmerworms, to wreak havoc on the people and their food supply.

Joel 2:21-32

21 Fear not, O land; be glad and rejoice: for the Lord will do great things.
22 Be not afraid, ye beasts of the field: for the pastures of the wilderness do
spring, for the tree beareth her fruit, the fig tree and the vine do yield their
strength.
23 Be glad then, ye children of Zion, and rejoice in the Lord your God: for
he hath given you the former rain moderately, and he will cause to come
down for you the rain, the former rain, and the latter rain in the first
month. 24 And the floors shall be full of wheat, and the fats shall overflow
with wine and oil.
25 And I will restore to you the years that the locust hath eaten, the canker-
worm, and the caterpiller, and the palmerworm, my great army which I sent
among you.
26 And ye shall eat in plenty, and be satisfied, and praise the name of the
Lord your God, that hath dealt wondrously with you: and my people shall
never be ashamed. 27 And ye shall know that I am in the midst of Israel,
and that I am the Lord your God, and none else: and my people shall never
be ashamed. 28 And it shall come to pass afterward, that I will pour out my
spirit upon all flesh; and your sons and your daughters shall prophesy, your
old men shall dream dreams, your young men shall see visions: 29 And also
upon the servants and upon the handmaids in those days will I pour out my
spirit. 30 And I will shew wonders in the heavens and in the earth, blood,
and fire, and pillars of smoke.
31 The sun shall be turned into darkness, and the moon into blood, before
the great and the terrible day of the Lord come. 32 And it shall come to
pass, that whosoever shall call on the name of the Lord shall be delivered:
for in mount Zion and in Jerusalem shall be deliverance, as the Lord hath
said, and in the remnant whom the Lord shall call.

The clear implication in verse 25 in the middle of this passage is that God is saying, "I am glad that you finally got your act together. I spent years destroying your crops and stores of food so that I could punish you, break you down, beat you into submission and even kill many of you. Yes,

I sent all of that destruction upon all of you, but don't worry about the fact that I have beaten you up and killed some of your family and friends, just call on my name, worship Me and I will fix it!"

The word, Strong's OT:7971 שָׁלַח, *shalach* (shaw-lakh') is used in the latter half of verse 25 and is translated ***"I sent."*** Once again the definition shows that the use of the personal pronoun " I " is not specified in the Hebrew word, but is again implied by the writer/translator. The construction of the verse from the *Hebrew Interlinear Bible* helps to better understand the meaning of the verse.

Joel 2:25 b - Hebrew Interlinear Bible					
English	*my army*	*great*	*which*	*I sent*	*among you*
Hebrew	חֵילִי	הַגָּדוֹל	אֲשֶׁר	שִׁלַּחְתִּי	בָּכֶם:
Strong's	2426	1419	834	7971	871a
Pronounced	cheeyliy	hagaadowl	'sher	shilachtiy	baakem

"my army" - *Strong's* OT:2426 חֵיל, *cheyl* (khale)*; or (shortened)* ***chel*** (khale) *a collateral form of* OT:2428*;*

> *an army; also (by analogy,) an intrenchment:* ***KJV*** *- army, bulwark, host, + poor, rampart, trench, wall.*

"I sent" - *Strong's* OT:7971 שָׁלַח, *shalach* (shaw-lakh')

> *a primitive root; to send away, for, or out (in a great variety of applications):* ***KJV*** *- any wise, appoint, bring (on the way), cast (away, out), conduct, earnestly, forsake, give (up), grow long, lay, leave, let depart (down, go, loose), push away, put (away, forth, in, out), reach forth, send (away, forth, out), set, shoot (forth, out), sow, spread, stretch forth (out).*

Both of the words translated as *my army* and *I sent* are personally attributed to God. This makes it look like He is the one that sent the curse. The restoration does come later in the following verses, but God is being accused of causing the destruction in the first place. This is like beating and starving your sons or daughters and maybe even killing one of their sisters or brothers because they have been disobedient. Then, after the ones that are still alive are sufficiently terrorized, you promise to feed them and maybe even give them a new car!

What an absurd thought! Unfortunately, this is the prism of religion and tradition through which many people view God. It's no wonder that many people turn away from the God of the religious! In reality, the sins of the people brought the destructive penalty upon themselves. The sins opened up the avenues for the curses to come.

It is clear from the entire passage that God is in the business of restoring and delivering people from the error of their ways and bestowing great blessings upon them. Mankind faces problems that are self-inflicted due to rebelliousness, selfishness, greed, and all forms of sin. The results of man's actions are already programmed like a cause and effect relationship. This is expertly facilitated by the true enemy of man, Satan. The great army spoken of in Joel 2:25 is not an Army of the Lord, and He did not send the destruction. It was the army of destruction that was activated by the sins of the people.

God will restore the holes and broken places of your life if you will let Him.

The 3 R's

Is God the one that brought your problems and circumstances upon you? Is He an accomplice to them? If He did do all of that to you or *allowed* it to happen, how can you really be held accountable for your decisions and reactions? The things that have happened to you are out of your control, and they are not your fault, so God should cut you some slack, right? However, God's Word says something different.

Reason with God, He wants you to talk to Him about the specific circumstances of your life, but not with the rebellious intent of blaming

Him or trying to change His mind. He loves you, and He wants to reveal His solutions to your problems.

You start with a textbook and become familiar with its contents when you are learning a subject in school. If you do not do your part and read the book or listen to its words, you will not learn the subject. When you ask questions of your teacher, you are not trying to change the teacher's mind on something, you are reasoning with that teacher, seeking understanding to increase your knowledge and wisdom. You listen to the teacher's instruction and study.

In the same manner, the purpose of reasoning with God is to allow His wisdom to reshape your understanding. However, you must actively seek God for Him to reveal Himself to you. This is done the same way that you learned in school, through God's textbook, the Bible. It provides the foundation through which you can reason with Him. As you ingest His Word through the gates of your eyes and ears, you will realize that His way is the only way that you will find true peace and happiness in your life.

Remembrance is only possible if you had knowledge to begin with. Reasoning with God through studying His Word, teaches you what His promises are, allowing you to receive them as your own by faith. It helps you to keep the promises that God makes to you fresh in your mind and spirit.

It is through ***Reasoning*** with God and ***Remembering*** the promises that He has for you that you can experience true ***Restoration*** in your life. An opportunity for God to praise and affirm you comes in the wake of your reasoning with Him and bringing His promises into your remembrance. God uses this method to *test* you - not to find evidence for punishment, but to find evidence for praise, affirmation, and grace. This will become apparent as we explore Job's trials and testing in the next chapter.

Chapter 11

TRIALS AND TESTING
WHAT'S UP WITH JOB ?

So who is Job and how does Job fit in with this discussion? As we will see, he lived around the time of Abraham and was considered a righteous man. At first read, the beginning of the book of Job appears to be some "cosmic game" between Satan and God. Here we see Job, a man minding his own business, enjoying life, serving God one day, and the next day his world explodes. Is this some chess match with Job being the pawn for the entertainment of the universe? No, this book is a vital part of our understanding of the activities that take place in the heavenly realm and the importance of our attitude in the way we conduct our lives. We will also discover more about the notion that God is an accomplice to the evil that takes place in the world and look into whether or not God *allows* bad things to happen. Job 1:21 is often quoted when things go awry.

Job 1:21

> *. . . . Naked came I out of my mother's womb, and naked shall I return thither:* ***the LORD gave, and the LORD hath taken away****; blessed be the name of the LORD.*

Declarations of Job

Job stated that "the Lord gave, and the Lord hath taken away." This statement is used when people become frustrated, confused, or simply don't understand what just happened to them. It is considered a very spiritual comment, and at face value, it gives that appearance. It also would appear to be a very humble statement as well, acknowledging God's *sovereignty* and His complete control over everything. This statement attributes the problems that we face as originating with God, implicating Him not only as the accomplice, allowing the action, but actually the one who does the action. However, is this statement correct?

What is Truth?

Everything in the Bible is inspired by the Holy Spirit of God Himself, and every word in the Bible is *truly stated*. However, every word spoken is *not actual truth*. This might not sit too well with some, but it is accurate nonetheless. Let's take a look at a couple of examples of this concept before we discuss more about Job.

The first example is one that we have already covered in a previous chapter. It is of Eve's conversation with the serpent in Genesis 3:3. Eve said, "But of the fruit of the tree which is in the midst of the garden, God hath said, Ye shall not eat of it, neither shall ye touch it, lest ye die." This is truly stated. Eve did say this, however, what she said was not entirely true. God said that He forbid them to eat of the fruit of the tree. He did not say anything about not touching it. Eve spoke out of a lack of understanding or a lack of knowledge of the truth of God's instruction to Adam. Therefore, Eve's statement was in error, and that part of her statement is false based on what is written.

Another example, found in Genesis 27:19, involves an encounter Isaac had with his son Jacob when he was old and failing in sight. The recording of a particular statement that Jacob made was true in that he *did* say it, but *what* he said was *not true*. It was a deception. It is truly *stated,* but it is *not a true statement*.

Genesis 27:19

> *And Jacob said unto his father, I am Esau thy firstborn; I have done according as thou badest me: arise, I pray thee, sit and eat of my venison, that thy soul may bless me.*

Jacob pretended to be his brother Esau with the purpose of deceiving his father, Isaac. He created a ruse with his mother to steal his father's blessing and the birthright of his brother Esau. The name Jacob means heelcatcher, supplanter, or *deceiver*. This passage provides clear evidence of why this description fit him. This characteristic ascribed to him through his name, is probably why God changed it to Israel when he became faithful and obedient to Him. However, this also shows us an example of a statement in the Bible that is not true. Jacob's statement is a total lie. It is true that he said it, but what he said was *not the truth*.

Neither the validity of the Bible nor truth of the Bible narrative is diminished in any way because of this narrative of a lie. This distinction is important because some doctrines, attitudes, and beliefs are actually based on passages of the Bible that are not statements of truth. Sometimes it is hard for us to conduct our lives, follow the correct path and find success. It is impossible when basing some of our belief system on a falsehood. This concept is especially important in the book of Job. As we will see, there are several statements that have spawned incorrect teachings, and if not properly understood, these can prevent people from receiving what God has provided for them. A kind of false humility can result by following an errant idea and can prevent a person from engaging his or her faith to receive God's promises.

Observations vs. Truth

The Biblical account points out that Job was a righteous man, perfect and upright, fearing God and rejecting evil. The first few verses of the book (Job 1:1-4) describe the greatness of his wealth and prosperity that he had undoubtedly obtained by being faithful to worship and serve God.

Job 1:1-4 *(CEV)*

> *[1] Many years ago, a man named Job lived in the land of Uz. He was a truly good person, who respected God and refused to do evil. [2] Job had seven sons and three daughters. [3] He owned seven thousand sheep, three thousand camels, five hundred pair of oxen, five hundred donkeys, and a large number of servants. He was the richest person in the East. [4] Job's sons took turns having feasts in their homes, and they always invited their three sisters to join in the eating and drinking.*

As the narrative continues, we begin to understand the dedication and faithfulness that Job demonstrated toward God. He was continuous in his care over his family and prayed for them before the Lord. This concern was based on fear and doubt for them potentially sinning and cursing God. Job 1:5 describes Job's continual custom of care over his family.

Job 1:5 *(NIV)*

> *When a period of feasting had run its course, Job would send and have them purified. Early in the morning he would sacrifice a burnt offering for*

each of them, thinking, "Perhaps my children have sinned and cursed God in their hearts." This was Job's regular custom.

Later, Job reacts to great devastation that comes upon his possessions, his family and himself in Job 1:19-22.

Job 1:19-22 *(ERV)*

[19] A strong wind suddenly came in from across the desert and blew the
house down. It fell on your sons and daughters, and they are all dead. I
am the only one who escaped to come and tell you the news!" [20] When Job
heard this, he got up, tore his clothes, and shaved his head to show his sad-
ness. Then he fell to the ground to bow down before God [21] and said, "When
I was born into this world, I was naked and had nothing. When I die and
leave this world, I will be naked and have nothing. ***The Lord gives, and***
the Lord takes away*. Praise the name of the Lord!" [22] Even after all*
this, Job did not sin. He did not accuse God of doing anything wrong.

Job made the statement, "the Lord gives, and the Lord takes away." Job was revealing his version of the truth of the situation based on his own limited perspective while he was in great distress. The narrative explains that Job did not sin and did not accuse God of doing anything wrong. However, this is a critical statement by Job that reveals his level of understanding. Let's explore the actual events that occurred to generate this disaster and that subsequently led Job to make this statement.

So, What's the Problem?

Without divine revelation, Job could not possibly have been aware of the activities in the heavenlies that are revealed as the narrative develops. It is important to note that Satan enjoyed direct access to God during a time which predated Abraham, Moses, the Law, and the Ten Commandments. According to Job 1:6-11, Satan presented himself along with a troupe of angels, and God addressed him directly, inquiring of his activities.

Job 1:6-11 *(ERV)*

[6] Then the day came for the angels to meet with the Lord. Even Satan was
there with them. [7] The Lord said to Satan, "Where have you been?"
Satan answered the Lord, "I have been roaming around the earth, going
from place to place." [8] Then the Lord said to Satan, "Have you noticed my
servant Job? There is no one on earth like him. He is a good, faithful man.
He respects God and refuses to do evil."

[9] Satan answered, "But Job has a good reason to respect you. [10] You always protect him, his family, and everything he has. You have blessed him and made him successful in everything he does. He is so wealthy that his herds and flocks are all over the country. [11] But if you were to destroy everything he has, I promise you that he would curse you to your face."

This part of the account provides us with a great deal of spiritual insight. There is no indication that Job had any revelation of the struggle that was occurring as Satan sought to create mischief. Just think about this for a moment, based on the narrative Job did not even know that Satan existed, much less that he had access to God to level accusations against the human population of the earth! Job lived at a time when, in general, there was very little known about spiritual things. By contrast, we now have a great deal of knowledge about spiritual activities because we see these things more clearly through revelation and the lens of time.

Job knew and believed that God existed because Adam would have certainly passed down stories of his experiences with God when he was in the Garden of Eden. Knowledge of Satan and his activities with God appear to have been absent, however. There probably would have been an account of a talking snake, but the activities going on in the throne room of God where not known.

Job was operating in faith in that he both acknowledged and worshiped God. The ignorance of the interchange between God and Satan was not Job's fault because he had no revelation of it. His ignorance is actually part of the reason that Job was described as good and faithful. However, another spiritual principle is at work here as well, one from which Eve also suffered. Ignorance is not an excuse that can buy a pass to avoid the consequences of that ignorance. A lack of revelation or understanding may relieve an act of sin, but not the consequences of acting contrary to spiritual law. In the same manner, a lack of understanding of the destructive potential of radiation does not prevent injury or death if a person is overexposed to a radiation source. Ignorance does not mitigate the consequences. The prophet Hosea reinforces this concept.

Hosea 4:6a

My people are destroyed for lack of knowledge.

This verse in Hosea clearly explains that destruction results from our ignorance of spiritual things. There is nothing that actually states or implies that ***God*** would destroy anyone for that lack of knowledge, just a warning that destruction will occur. The verses in Job that occurred long before the word from Hosea came give us the insight that we need to understand the origin of the destruction. God told Adam and Eve that the penalty for disobedience (sin) to His command is death, immediate spiritual death, and in the earth realm, eventual physical death. The verse in Hosea clearly explains why destruction came upon Adam and Eve. Death resulted because Eve was deceived through a lack of knowledge, and Adam freely sinned by disobeying God's instruction. Let's look in Romans 5:13 and 6:23 for more revelation of this concept.

Romans 5:13 *(CEV)*

> *Sin was in the world before the Law came. But no record of sin was kept, because there was no Law.*

Romans 6:23 *(GWT)*

> *The payment for sin is death, but the gift that God freely gives is everlasting life found in Christ Jesus our Lord.*

These verses in Romans give us a perspective that applies to Job. There is a difference between the actions and challenges that Job faced and those of Adam and Eve. Eve was deceived, but both she and Adam were disobedient to God and sinned. On the other hand, Job is described as being a righteous man who had not sinned. Romans 5:13 describes the relationship between the Law and sin and the consequences of sin. If there is a law in existence and that law is disobeyed, then sin results, and the penalties for that sin apply. By contrast, if there is no law, then no sin can result, and there is no penalty.

However, there must be more to it than that. There was no sin because there was no law that he disobeyed. In short, Job did not sin. Therefore, these problems were not the result of the penalty of sin. Then why did Job encounter all of the problems he had when he was without sin? The destruction must have come as a result of something else.

Invaluable insight into what is actually occurring and where responsibility lies is provided in Job 1:6-11. The conversation between God and Satan is very telling. Satan was possibly quite agitated as he is brought face to face with the activities and lifestyle of Job and the success of his life to this point. He seems to have occupied his time by wandering "from place to place" in the earth, possibly looking for ways to cause trouble and catch someone in his or her words or deeds (Job 1:7). Additional insight regarding the activities of Satan and his intents is revealed in the New Testament. The activity described in 1 Peter 5:8 sounds very similar to what is seen in Job.

1 Peter 5:8 *(ERV)*
Control yourselves and be careful! The devil is your enemy, and he goes around like a roaring lion looking for someone to attack and eat.

Is It Jealousy?

God used Job as an example of a good and faithful man when Satan came before Him. Satan then used this information to taunt God as Job's protector. Even deeper behind the scenes, there may have been a backstory that involved Satan's past. Hypothetically, God might have been saying to Satan, "Look at the situation we are in. I created you in all your splendor with great advantages, abilities, and beauty. You had everything from the beginning, including great favor with Me. Then, you turned on me. You really messed things up. Look at Job, this descendant of my Man-type creation. He has it together, in spite of not having the position and knowledge that you have."

Whether or not this hypothetical backstory is true, Satan, in essence, replied to God, "Maybe he is good and faithful, but Job serves you because you are protecting him. If he has problems in his life that are severe enough, he will curse You!" Satan then complained in Job 1:10 that God was unduly protecting Job with a hedge of protection and blessing. He revealed one of his strongest characteristics, jealousy. Satan is accusing God of giving Job an unfair advantage. Then, he pushes further and accuses Job of being fickle. He tells God that Job will turn on Him if He will simply take away Job's possessions. The next interchange between God and Satan in Job 1:12 gives us even more insight into the struggle that is occurring in the spiritual realm.

Job 1:12 *(NKJV)*
And the Lord said to Satan, "Behold, all that he has is in your power; only do not lay a hand on his person."

What is Legal?

God told Satan that Job's possessions were in his power and that he had power over them. God specifically stated that Satan did not have authority over Job's own person, however. God restricted Satan's activity from touching Job, himself. How is it that his possessions, his family and their possessions were in Satan's power but his person was not? This verse clearly gives the impression that Satan had the capability of bringing evil against Job's person, but in this situation, he lacked the authority to use it. His tail was tied so to speak.

God is very precise about words. To God, semantics is a very serious issue. He says what He means and means what He says. He does not speak idle words and only honors words that are accurate or legal. Legally, we will see that Job's words and actions opened the door for Satan to exercise authority over him, and in essence, he gave his permission. God heard the complaint of Satan in Job 1:10-11.

Job 1:10-11 *(ERV)*

> [10]*You always protect him, his family, and everything he has. You have blessed him and made him successful in everything he does. He is so wealthy that his herds and flocks are all over the country.* [11] *But if you were to destroy everything he has, I promise you that he would curse you to your face.*

Satan only brought up issues surrounding the work of Job's hands, his house, and his substance. Satan did not bring up anything about Job's person. God already knew that Job had unknowingly allowed Satan to have authority over him in both his possessions and his person. However, God protected Job by not revealing any more about the situation to Satan than what he had already discovered. The principal that can be applied to this situation of protection is actually articulated in Proverbs 29:11.

Proverbs 29:11

> *A fool uttereth all his mind: but a wise man keepeth it in till afterwards.*

God was looking out for Job by not revealing any more than was legally required. Job was under the power of Satan as a result of his own words and actions. It was not sin that made him vulnerable. Rather, it was fear and doubt. God never *allowed* Satan to have access to Job. God chose to limit Himself, to make Himself powerless to prevent it because He made man with *free will* and because of His commitment to His own spiritual law. (This concept will be discussed in greater detail in chapters 18 and 19.) God also could not prevent Adam and Eve from committing their sin due to their free will. However, He could protect Job from things of which he was not yet accused.

Nonetheless, there are consequences for being contrary to spiritual law, and a lack of knowledge on the part of Job could not prevent those consequences. We are all responsible for our actions and our words, whether they be words of faith or words of fear and doubt. These concepts have far reaching implications that bear further exploration, but first let's see what happens to Job at the hand of Satan in Job 1:13-19.

Job 1:13-19 *(NIV)*

13 One day when Job's sons and daughters were feasting and drinking wine
at the oldest brother's house, 14 a messenger came to Job and said, "The oxen
were plowing and the donkeys were grazing nearby, 15 and the Sabeans
attacked and carried them off. They put the servants to the sword, and I am
the only one who has escaped to tell you!"
16 While he was still speaking, another messenger came and said, "The fire of
God fell from the sky and burned up the sheep and the servants, and I am
the only one who has escaped to tell you!"
17 While he was still speaking, another messenger came and said, "The
Chaldeans formed three raiding parties and swept down on your camels
and carried them off. They put the servants to the sword, and I am the only
one who has escaped to tell you!"
18 While he was still speaking, yet another messenger came and said, "Your
sons and daughters were feasting and drinking wine at the oldest brother's
house, 19 when suddenly a mighty wind swept in from the desert and struck
the four corners of the house. It collapsed on them and they are dead, and I
am the only one who has escaped to tell you!"

The first calamity was the loss of livestock and servants that came at the hand of the Sabeans, with whom there is no indication that Job had any previous hostilities. Neither Satan nor God had a physical hand in this destruction. Satan's authority does not extend to actual physical activity, but as with Eve, he had the ability to influence humans to enact his destructive will. The second calamity is described by the servant as the "fire of God." However, nothing else states that God sent the fire. This was the perspective or observational reality of the servant and not certain truth.

It could have been a meteor strike or a bolt of lightning. However, he probably attributed anything that he did not understand to God.

The perspectives of these servants and other characters throughout the Bible are important to understand. Beliefs and doctrines can be formed from their observations and perspectives that are recorded in the Bible. However, these impressions of God may not actually be true.

The god of This World

Job, his family or their servants have had no revelation regarding the conversation that God had with Satan. Consequently, there was no understanding that this destruction did not come at the hand of God. In this situation, Satan likely had the ability to influence natural forces. Throughout the ages, casual, non-critical reading of this passage has built the case that God is responsible for the destruction. God receives the blame for it even though the narrative clearly states that Satan was responsible.

Adam and Eve gave up the authority of the earthly realm to Satan when they fell to his deception in the garden of Eden. From that point on and until the death and resurrection of Jesus, Satan had control of the earth, except when men by faith in God would exercise their God-given, Holy Spirit endowed authority. Evidence of that authority is provided during the temptation of Jesus in the wilderness in Matthew 4:8-10.

Matthew 4:8-10 *(NIV)*

> *8 Again, the devil took him to a very high mountain and showed him all the kingdoms of the world and their splendor. 9 "All this I will give you," he said, "if you will bow down and worship me."*
> *10 Jesus said to him, "Away from me, Satan! For it is written: 'Worship the Lord your God, and serve him only.'"*

Jesus identified his tempter as Satan, who could not have offered the kingdoms of the world to Jesus in exchange for His worship if he did not have that authority. Otherwise, Jesus would not have been tempted. In 2 Corinthians 4:4, Satan is described as the "god of this world" which also implies the same authority.

2 Corinthians 4:4 *(TLB)*

> *Satan, who is the god of this evil world, has made him blind, unable to see the glorious light of the Gospel that is shining upon him or to understand the amazing message we preach about the glory of Christ, who is God.*

More Calamity

The third calamity in Job 1:17 came at the hands of another warring faction, the Chaldeans. Similarly, the servants were killed, and the livestock and camels were taken. Finally, Job 1:19 describes another "natural" disaster, a great wind. It toppled the house in which Job's sons and daughters were feasting. The narrative states that the young men were killed, but the servant claims to be the only one to have escaped alive. Therefore, it is reasonable to assume that the daughters were also killed in the tragedy. The interchange between God and Satan did not include any specific discussion of authority over Job's children. However, Job continually interceded for his seven sons and three daughters. Logically speaking, he must have felt that there was cause for his concern. It would, therefore, seem rational to assume that his ten children had also opened the door to Satan's direct authority over their persons. Otherwise, God would have informed Satan that he had no power over their lives. Job was understandably quite distressed about this devastating and unimaginable turn of events as we see in the continuation of the account in Job 1:20-22.

> **Job 1:20-22** *(ERV)*
> *[20]When Job heard this, he got up, tore his clothes, and shaved his head to show his sadness. Then he fell to the ground to bow down before God [21] and said, "When I was born into this world, I was naked and had nothing. When I die and leave this world, I will be naked and have nothing. The Lord gives, and the Lord takes away. Praise the name of the Lord!"*
> *[22] Even after all this, Job did not sin. He did not accuse God of doing anything wrong.*

It is hard to even comprehend that all of this devastation could occur so rapidly in the life of a person. However, in spite of it all, Job actually proved Satan wrong by his reaction. Rather than curse God to His face as Satan had predicted, Job actually humbled himself and worshiped God. Although we do not have any indication of Satan's reaction from the narrative, this certainly must have really annoyed him.

Understanding Perspective

We now have a little more perspective on the circumstances and activities presented up to this point. Let's turn our attention back to the statement by Job that started this chapter, "The Lord gives, and the Lord takes away."This statement, as we have seen, is *truly stated*, but it is not entirely a statement of *truth*. The Lord did give to Job. He was the source of the blessings that Job enjoyed as a result of his obedience to the principles of God. There was no written law to observe at this point in time, so we cannot say that Job observed and performed it. However, what we can say is that Job displayed a reverential fear and gave wholehearted worship to God. Job's faith in God is what brought His blessings and wealth to him.

It is equally obvious that the Lord did not "take away" as Job declared. Satan did. Job knew only of God. He did not know of any other spiritual entity besides God, in this case, Satan. Therefore, Job assumed that God was both the *giver* and the *taker*, and he made his decree to that effect. However, Job did not sin because he was not falsely accusing God. He was only acting on the assumptions that he made from his limited perspective based on his understanding. This was Job's point of reference or his *experiential truth*.

Job's perspective might be comparable to that of the ping pong player or the stationary motorist in the examples of relativity *(see p. 47)*. Remember both the player and the train station observer were witnessing the same activity; however, both were aware of different levels of truth. The train station observer had a more complete view of the activity, and the player who was closer to the situation actually had less information. In this way, a more complete picture of the actual truth of the interchange between God and Satan, and Satan as the causative agent was not within Job's perspective or understanding. Job's conclusions are, therefore, understandable, based on his limited information and his observational perspective.

This perspective is part of the reason that Job was described as good and faithful. So what gave Satan the right to cause all of this destruction? Was God *testing* Job just to see how he would react as many have claimed about this narrative? Was God playing a sick cosmic game with Job, his family, and his possessions? Certainly not! The narrative clearly states that God was not inflicting the destruction. Satan had authority over these aspects of Job's life and was pouring out this devastation upon him. However, why would all that Job had possessed be in Satan's power? Perhaps Job's own actions and words will give us some clues.

The Power of Words

As we have seen, Job was not privy to the conversation between God and Satan. There was no rule of law that was established since God's Law was provided centuries after Job lived. Because there was no law that Job disobeyed and his attribution of the destruction to God was only based on his perspective and limited understanding, Job did not sin. However, there were still consequences as a result of his *misalignment with spiritual principles*. This misalignment was what gave Satan the authority to act on Job's possessions, servants, and family. Job was actually operating in *fear and doubt*.

Fear and doubt are the *spiritual forces* that allow Satan to operate in our lives because doubt is the complete opposite or a counterfeit of God's *spiritual force*, the force of *faith*. While humble and worshipful toward God, Job was actually acting in fear and doubt. He *"rose up early in the morning, and offered burnt offerings according to the number of them all: for Job said, It may be that my sons have sinned, and cursed God in their hearts. Thus did Job continually"* (Job 1:5). Job's actions were noble as he interceded for his children, but it would seem reasonable to assume that his children gave him some cause to think that they were in need of such intercession. However, even though there is no description of such actions, his activities were still motivated by the *fear* that his children may have cursed God. Let's continue with the narrative and see what occurs as Satan "turns up the fire," so to speak in Job 2:1-3.

Job 2:1-3

> [1] *Again there was a day when the sons of God came to present themselves before the LORD, and Satan came also among them to present himself before the LORD.* [2] *And the LORD said unto Satan, From whence comest thou? And Satan answered the LORD, and said, From going to and fro in the earth, and from walking up and down in it.* [3] *And the LORD said unto Satan, Hast thou considered my servant Job, that there is none like him in the earth, a perfect and an upright man, one that feareth God, and escheweth evil? and still he holdeth fast his integrity, although thou movedst me against him, to destroy him without cause.*

One can only imagine the tension that must have been present at this interchange. Satan had just been before God, challenging Him, making accusations against Job, even though Job's character and integrity are described here as "perfect and upright" in the *King James Version*. The words *good and faithful* in Job 1:8 *(ERV)* and *perfect and upright* in Job 2:3 *(KJV)* come from the Hebrew word, OT:8535.

> ***"perfect"*** - *Strong's* OT:8535 תָּם, *tam* (tawm);
> *complete; usually (morally) pious; specifically, gentle, dear:*

This word does not mean *sinless* or without error as might be understood from the *King James Version*. If Job was *perfect,* as we might understand the word, he would also have been without any error, making no mistakes. This was not the case because Job operated in some level of fear and doubt, just as we do. The account of Job never claims him to be a totally sinless man, only that he did not sin by accusing God of wrongdoing (Job 1:22). Jesus was the only sinless man to walk this earth. Misunderstanding seemingly minor details can lead to errant doctrines and beliefs.

It would appear that Satan was still looking for mischief as he wandered "to and fro in the earth, and from walking up and down in it" (Job 2:2). Clearly, Satan had unlimited access to the earth realm and its inhabitants. As he observed the results of his handiwork in Job's life, Satan had the full expectation of seeing Job fall into a state of rejection of God, just as he had done himself with no provocation. Satan did not expect to see Job reacting to this devastation with humility and worship, a clear indication of the quality of Job's character.

God once again pointed to the character and integrity of Job, reminding Satan of his unfair accusations and attempts to get Him to destroy Job without cause. The word translated, "although thou movedst me," at the end of Job 2:3 is the Hebrew word סוּת, *(cuwth)* (sooth), Strong's OT:5496.

> ***"movedst"*** - *Strong's* OT:5496 סוּת, *cuwth* **(sooth)**
> *perhaps denominative from* OT:7898*; properly, to prick, i.e. (figuratively) stimulate; by implication, to seduce: (Translated in the KJV as - entice, move, persuade, provoke, remove, set on, stir up, take away).*

None of these instances of the word imply that God actually "did" the action. Satan was trying to get God to do it. He was trying to invoke some legal argument that would force God into taking action against Job. God pointed out that Satan was accusing Job and trying to get God to act *without cause.* Do you remember the verse in Proverbs 26 that told us that a curse does not come without cause? God prevented Satan from acting in any way toward Job where there was no cause. It was a legal decree, based upon God's own words.

Satan was convinced that Job would ultimately fall and curse God and demanded that sickness and disease come upon him in Job 2:4-8.

Job 2:4-8

[4] And Satan answered the LORD, and said, Skin for skin, yea, all that a man hath will he give for his life. [5] But put forth thine hand now, and touch his bone and his flesh, and he will curse thee to thy face. [6] And the LORD said unto Satan, Behold, he is in thine hand; but save his life
[7] So went Satan forth from the presence of the LORD, and smote Job with sore boils from the sole of his foot unto his crown. [8] And he took him a potsherd to scrape himself withal; and he sat down among the ashes.

God then told Satan that everything but Job's life was *in his hand* using the Hebrew word OT:3027 יָד,(*yad*) (yawd). This word implied that Satan had a degree of "power" over him, but it was not absolute.

"in thine hand" - *Strong's* OT:3027 יָד,(*yad*) (yawd);

a primitive word; a hand (the open one [indicating power, means, direction, etc.], in distinction from OT:3709, the closed one); used (as noun, adverb, etc.) in a great variety of applications, both literally and figuratively, both proximate and remote.

It would appear that Satan's goal was to separate Job from God. Notice the specific wording in Job 2:7 in which we see that Satan left the presence of God, and Satan *smote* or hit Job with a disease. Satan was the "doer" of the action, not God. He used every tool and every bit of authority available to him to construct circumstances that he was certain would cause Job to turn and curse God. He was not alone in this assumption. Job's wife was of the same mind in Job 2:9-10.

Job 2:9-10 *(ERV)*

[9] His wife said to him, "Are you still holding on to your faith? Why don't you just curse God and die!" [10] Job answered, "You sound like one of those fools on the street corner! How can we accept all the good things that God gives us and not accept the problems?" So even after all that happened to Job, he did not sin. He did not accuse God of doing anything wrong.

Sometimes, the ones that are the closest to us are so moved with the apparent hopelessness of a situation that they inadvertently help to do

Satan's work for him! Job had enough problems already without his wife berating his integrity, telling him to curse God and die. She was in total agreement with Satan!

Job responded in the same worshipful humility as before, but he still answered with an error in his words. Again, he did not sin, but he incorrectly attributed the evil that had befallen him to the "hand of God," rather than the true source, Satan. Once again, from Job's point of view, we see something that is *truly stated*, but it is not *true.*

Job's friends arrived to comfort him and witness the depth of his grief. They did not even recognize him and remained with him speechless for seven days! Job finally broke the silence and proceeded to lament the day he was born, even his very existence. He then revealed something that pervades our conversation even today. It is a statement that seems innocuous on the surface. It was just an observation or a declaration of the facts. However, there are far-reaching implications of his words, as well as emotions, beliefs, and motivations behind the statement. Job gives us *the clue* that tells us why Satan has power over him in Job 3:25.

Job 3:25

For the thing which I greatly ***feared*** *is come upon me, and that which I was* ***afraid*** *of is* ***come unto me****.*

Job 3:25 *(GNT)*

Everything I fear and dread comes true.

Fear and doubt are the spiritual elements that open the door to attacks from Satan. Evil in the world feeds on fear, just like blood to the mythical vampire, sucking the life out of everything in its path. We only have to look through history to discover that fear is the basis of control that evil and oppressive men have used over the centuries. Every person who rises to power through aggression and conquering does so through fearful intimidation and force.

These evil men have their power through the systematic and planned exploitation of fear. Fear inspires hate, distrust, suspicion, doubt, insecurity, and every evil thing that occurs. Fear opens the door for the manifestation of all sorts of problems in our own lives. Fear is in direct conflict with love and the opposite of faith. Fear and doubt are what Satan and every evil work thrives upon. Faith is the force that God responds to and that brings blessings, life, and prosperity.

The next several chapters of the Book of Job consist of a variety of discussions between Job and his friends. They offer a multitude of counsel and advice for Job to follow, intending to help relieve him of the burden of his suffering. Eliphaz reminded Job of the encouragement and support that he himself had provided to others. He also pointed out that mortal man is not more *just* than God, nor is he more pure than God, Who is supreme. However, within his encouragement he also made a statement that is *contrary to the truth*. He correctly attributed redemption and deliverance to God. However, he also attributed the evil that he observed to God which is clearly contradictory to the narrative that we have already discussed. Eliphaz made the following statement in Job 5:17-18.

Job 5:17-18 *(CEV)*

> [17] *Consider yourself fortunate if God All-Powerful chooses to correct you.*
>
> [18] *He may cause injury and pain, but he will bandage and heal your cuts and bruises.* [19] *God will protect you from harm, no matter how often trouble may strike.*

God does correct, but not in the way Eliphaz describes. He thinks that God beat Job up and then healed him. However, God did not cause Job the injury and pain. It came from Satan! Job's friend, Bildad, then followed with his own observations about Job's situation. In essence, he pointed out that Job brought all of this upon himself because he must have sinned. After all, he said in Job 8:6 and 20 that if Job was pure, God would help him and that He would not cast away an innocent man.

Job 8:6, 20 *(ERV) (Bildad speaking)*

> [6] *If you are pure and good, he will quickly come to help you.*
> *He will give your family back to you.*
>
> [20] *God does not support evil people, and he does not abandon the innocent.*

Bildad's observations about God in these two verses are correct. However, his assessment of Job was not. This is another situation where something is truly stated but not true. However, Job replied that he did believe that Bildad's advice was correct as he struggled with making himself just before God in Job 9:12.

Job 9:12 *(GNT) (Job speaking)*

He takes what he wants, and no one can stop him; no one dares ask him, "What are you doing?"

Job said that God takes away and asks who can challenge him. However, it is clear that Satan is the one that did the taking away. Job made a statement that was based on his observation and understanding, but he was not correct in his statement because his perspective was incomplete. Job spent the next few verses in a quandary. He struggled with his perception that God is both the giver and the taker. He believed within himself that he had lived an upright life and worshiped God, but he just doesn't seem to be able to figure this out.

Here is the problem. Job was continually *looking to himself for justification*. He was trying to figure out through his own actions how to *make himself acceptable* to God. Zophar, another of Job's friends, also continued to reinforce the idea of Job's self-justification in Job 11:14-15. He said that God cannot be figured out and that if Job would simply get himself free of iniquity (sin), he would be accepted and restored. He was still saying that Job could somehow make himself acceptable.

Job 11:14-15 *(ERV) (Zophar speaking)*

[14] Put away the sin that you still hold on to. Don't keep evil in your tent.
[15] If you will do that, you could look to God without shame.You can stand strong and not be afraid.

Job replied with an extensive analysis of how history has shown that God raises up kings, princes, judges, counselors, and even nations, just to take them down again as if it were by the whim of God. He saw the righteous laughed at, robbers prospering, and those that provoked God living in prosperity and security. Then, he went on to rebuke his friends in Job 13:4-5, 15 and reinforce his own trust (faith) in God.

Job 13:4-5, 15 *(ERV) (Job speaking)*

[4] But you men try to cover up your ignorance with lies.You are like worthless doctors who cannot heal anyone.

[15] I will continue to trust God even if he kills me. But I will defend myself to his face.

Job still believed God was both the blesser and the curser. However, when he heard the accusations of his friends, he seemed to get even more convicted about his life and the way that he had lived it. Some of his conviction was in defense of what he saw as his own righteousness, his self-justification. However, as the conversations continued, it appears that faith is growing in him as well. He trusts God and displays the faith that he does have even though he still does not understand. What an amazing testimony in light of his perspective that God has both blessed him and cursed him. He still maintained his integrity toward God, even to his death. No wonder God was proud to display him as an example of an upright and perfect man in the face of Satan!

Job's perspective and understanding was revealed through his words. He was expecting to be justified by his actions or his *works*. To be made acceptable by works is to be motivated by fear and doubt and to deny *faith*. As we have seen, fear and doubt are the opposite of faith, and that is what empowers Satan.

Job was still conflicted between self-justification and faith. He was trying to do both, not really understanding the principles of faith. However, he went so far as to declare in faith that he knew that he would ultimately be found right in Job 13:18. However, he still thought that this justification would be due to his own actions.

Job 13:18 *(GNT)*
I am ready to state my case, because I know I am in the right.

Job seems to be going through a transition in his speech. He has endured an onslaught of criticism and reproach from his friends. They repeatedly told him that he was at fault and must be in sin. Otherwise, God would not have been chastising him in such a manner and would free him from his terrible circumstances. Still, Job was sure of his deliverance from the problems that he faced, stating by faith, "I know that I am in the right" or justified (Job 13:8).

The Redeemer

Job sensed that awareness of his trials and tribulations (at the hand of Satan) would be of benefit to future generations. He wanted his struggles to be written in a book. He spoke creative seeds of faith in Job 19:23 and 25 that gave birth to the Bible, the book in which his account is contained. Not only that, he had an awareness that went beyond his self-justification, and he spoke of a redeemer. Just what is a redeemer?

The word, *redeem*, has a number of extended meanings. A person might redeem a coupon at the grocery store or redeem a winning lottery ticket. These uses of the word are included in the first meaning. However, Job spoke of the redeemer in light of the second application.

redeem *(verb)*

1a) to buy back, repurchase; 1b) to get or win back.
2a) to free from what distresses or harms: as 2b) to free from captivity by payment of ransom, 2c) to extricate from or help to overcome something detrimental, 2d) to release from blame or debt: clear, 2e) to free from the consequences of sin.

Job knew that there was a redeemer for him, one who would ultimately make him acceptable to God by paying the price of his sins for him (Job 19:23, 25). This is the true sense of the word *redeemer* in the Bible. If each of us had to stand responsible for our own sins, then we would all be doomed to an eternal death. The fact that we have a redeemer, one who will pay the debt of sin on our behalf, offers us hope.

Job 19:23, 25 *(NKJV)*

23 *Oh, that my words were written! Oh, that they were inscribed in a book!*

25 *For I know that my Redeemer lives, And He shall stand at last on the earth.*

Wow! What a revelation Job declared in these verses. This is a clear reference to our redemption from sins through faith in Jesus, who would soon walk the earth! He still had limited understanding of the spiritual world, but God gave him the revelation of his Redeemer! He saw through time and knew that Jesus, his Redeemer, would walk upon the earth. That should make some tingles go up and down your body! This revelation could only come about through Job's faith and his dedication to God.

Job continued to rebut accusations as Eliphaz berated him and attempted to indict him of his iniquity. Together, they bemoaned the apparent prosperity of the wicked and compared it to the sufferings of Job, yet Job maintained that the wicked would eventually get their just rewards. Eliphaz made observations about the blessings of God coming upon the righteous. However, Job maintained that he still needed to get his act together and then made one very interesting observation about the power of spoken words in Job 22:28.

Job 22:28

Thou shalt also decree a thing, and it shall be established unto thee: and the light shall shine upon thy ways.

Job brought life to this principle in at least two instances. The first was destructive when he said, "For the thing which I greatly feared is come upon me" (Job 3:25). His words were a manifestation of his heart posture when he continually entertained fear for his children (Job 1:5). This fear is what opened the door for the attacks of Satan. The second declaration was creative and life giving when he spoke of the book and his Redeemer. The creative force of the spoken word was first revealed to us when God spoke the world into existence (Genesis 1:1). Job's final declarations came to pass because he operated according to the pattern that God established in creation. Job actually was righteous before God, and his words were spoken in faith!

Job proclaimed his righteousness, faithfulness, and integrity and finally his three older friends, Eliphaz, Bildad, and Zophar, relented. Elihu, the younger of the group, had kept quiet out of respect for his elders. However, he eventually became angered and could no longer hold his tongue because Job still justified himself. Elihu continued to cite God's glory, righteousness, and all-powerful nature in Job:32:1-3.

Job 32:1-3 *(CEV)*

1 Finally, these three men stopped arguing with Job, because he refused to admit that he was guilty. 2 Elihu from Buz was there, and he had become upset with Job for blaming God instead of himself. 3 He was also angry with Job's three friends for not being able to prove that Job was wrong.

Then, God took over, and He pointed out how much He does, oversees, creates, and is responsible for. He also pointed out that Job's own right hand could not save him. God chastised Job for contending with Him. Job finally realized that his own mouth had been the source of the problem all along in Job 30:4.

Job 40:4 *(ERV)*

I am not worthy to speak! What can I say to you? I cannot answer you! I will put my hand over my mouth.

God went on to point out Job's inabilities and shortcomings and challenge Job's attitude of self-justification in Job 40:9-14.

Job 40:9-14 *(God speaking)*

9 Hast thou an arm like God? or canst thou thunder with a voice like him?
10 Deck thyself now with majesty and excellency; and array thyself with
glory and beauty. 11 Cast abroad the rage of thy wrath: and behold every
one that is proud, and abase him. 12 Look on every one that is proud, and
bring him low; and tread down the wicked in their place. 13 Hide them in
the dust together; and bind their faces in secret. 14 Then will I also confess
unto thee that thine own right hand can save thee.

God presented a challenge to Job to prove that he was as mighty and powerful as Him. He provided several examples of global activities over which Job had no power. He then told Job that if he was not able to do these things, then he was also incapable of saving (redeeming) himself. Job ultimately acknowledged the fact that he had a Redeemer and that his Redeemer (Jesus, as we will come to know) would walk the earth.

Why Me?

Job's certainly lived his life in a respectful fear and worship of God, but we have no knowledge of him before the attacks on him. It is also reasonable to expect that he did operate in faith toward God, albeit mixed with a significant amount of self-justification. His self-justification may have been the fundamental reason that Job was under the power and authority of Satan. He may never have come to realize that he had this attitude had he not been met with the challenges posed by Satan.

Job's inclination was to bemoan his situation by saying, "Why Me?" His lack of understanding was revealed when the pressure was applied. He was conflicted by what he believed to be true about God and what he saw in the circumstances. Coupled with Job's belief that God is both the *blesser* and the *curser*, this confusion left Job at a loss.

A person might say, "God *allowed* the tribulations of Job to reveal what was in Job's heart."This might lead to the conclusion that God also caused it all from the beginning and that He set up Satan to do his work on Job so that Job could get things right. This is traditional, religious thinking and is not consistent with the delivering, restoring, and loving heart of God.

God did know what was going to occur with Job. He probably did make a plan. However, just because He saw that it was going to happen and made a plan to fix it does not mean He caused it! He couldn't interfere because of free will. God could only show more of Himself to Job until he got enough comprehension (Job 42:1-6). He left the conclusions and the heart changes to Job.

Job 42:1-6 *(ERV)*

[1] Then Job answered the Lord: [2] "I know you can do everything. You make plans, and nothing can change or stop them. [3] You asked, 'Who is this ignorant person saying these foolish things?' I talked about things I did not understand. I talked about things too amazing for me to know.
[4] You said to me, 'Listen, and I will speak. I will ask you questions, and you will answer me.' [5] In the past I heard about you, but now I have seen you with my own eyes.
[6] And I am ashamed of myself. I am so sorry. As I sit in the dust and ashes, I promise to change my heart and my life."

Job never cursed God through all of his trials. He only attributed to God things for which He was not responsible. He repented of his claim of self-justification when he realized that it was due to his error and lack of understanding. Within his limited view or perspective, he had tried to explain things about God which he could in no way understand. Many people do the same thing today. However, he finally relinquished to God that which belonged to Him alone and began to realize his own place in the scheme of things. He gave up the notion that he had the capability of making himself acceptable to God and prayed for his friends (Job 42:7-10, 12). As a result, God was able to restore him double what he lost.

Job 42:7-10, 12a *(ERV)*

[7] After the Lord finished talking to Job, he spoke to Eliphaz from Teman. He said, "I am angry with you and your two friends, because you did not tell the truth about me, as my servant Job did. [8] So now, Eliphaz, get seven bulls and seven rams. Take them to my servant Job. Kill them and offer them as a burnt offering for yourselves. My servant Job will pray for you, and I will answer his prayer. Then I will not give you the punishment you deserve. You should be punished, because you were very foolish. You did not say what is right about me, as my servant Job did." [9] So Eliphaz from Teman, Bildad from Shuah, and Zophar from Naamah obeyed the Lord. Then the Lord answered Job's prayer. [10] Job prayed for his friends, and the Lord made Job successful again. God gave him twice as much as he had before.

[12] The Lord blessed Job with even more than he had in the beginning.

This humility, faith, and trust in God's redemptive power is what God accepts from Job. God rebuked Eliphaz, Bildad, and Zophar because they foolishly spoke wrongly about Him. Even so, God provided them with a means of escape through sacrifice and Job's prayer for them. God accepted Job when he repented of his self-justification, and He turned (reversed) his *captivity* or overwhelming attacks when he prayed for his friends. Because of Job's trust and faithfulness, God restored him double what he had before the attacks of Satan.

Downloading Apps From Job

App #1 ***Trust in God. He is not the source of the evil that befalls us. Don't live in fear. God is interested in your faith and faithfulness.***

Job was initially motivated by fear, likely due to observations he made regarding his family. His approach to God was more one of appeasing an angry or hostile deity as he gave *preventive offerings* on behalf of his children. Later, he realized that his perception of God was not accurate. His friends offered a confusing variety of both errant and accurate advice. He refused to agree with the mistaken observations and was finally able to discern the truth, accepting that God was not the source of his problems. His restoration was quite miraculous once he really got it right!

Job's continual intercession for his family was him being fearfully full of care for them. However, the New Testament gives us clear instructions regarding this very situation. We are told to "be careful for nothing" in Philippians 4:6-7 and to be humble and cast our care upon God in 1 Peter 5:5-7. This means to pray, relinquish your concerns and anxieties, and trust in Him for wisdom and peace to get you through your situation.

Philippians 4:6-7 *(GNT)*

6 Don't worry about anything, but in all your prayers ask God for what you need, always asking him with a thankful heart. 7 And God's peace, which is far beyond human understanding, will keep your hearts and minds safe in union with Christ Jesus.

1 Peter 5:5-7 *(GWT)*

5 Young people, in a similar way, place yourselves under the authority of spiritual leaders. Furthermore, all of you must serve each other with humil-

ity, because God opposes the arrogant but favors the humble. [6] Be humbled by God's power so that when the right time comes he will honor you. [7] Turn all your anxiety over to God because he cares for you.

App#2	***Become spiritually aware of your life and the influences upon it. Satan hates Godly traits and actively works to destroy those who trust in God.***
App #3	***Speak and act according to faith in God and His word. Fear and doubt are the opposite of faith and empower Satan.***

Something even more powerful was revealed in 1 Peter 5:8. We need to be aware, sober, and vigilant, knowing that the devil is always on the lookout for someone that he might devour. However, he cannot devour you unless you give him permission.

1 Peter 5:8

[8] Be sober, be vigilant; because your adversary the devil, as a roaring lion, walketh about, seeking whom he may devour. . . .

App #4	***Be humble before God. A person cannot make himself or herself acceptable to God through works. You cannot save yourself by your own power or actions (your "right hand"). You cannot make yourself acceptable no matter how good you are or how hard you try.***
App #5	***Walk in faith. Faith sustains in the midst of tribulation.***

None of us are spared from circumstances that cause suffering. We live in a fallen world, spiritually speaking. Bad things will happen no matter how diligent we are because we are not perfect, and we make mistakes. God provided Job's Redeemer and our Redeemer, Jesus, to restore us and empower us. He gave us tools (weapons) with which to overcome our circumstances as we see in 2 Corinthians 10:3-5.

2 Corinthians 10:3-5 *(NIV)*

[3] For though we live in the world, we do not wage war as the world does.
[4] The weapons we fight with are not the weapons of the world. On the

contrary, they have divine power to demolish strongholds. [5]*We demolish arguments and every pretension that sets itself up against the knowledge of God, and we take captive every thought to make it obedient to Christ.*

App #6 Repent and proclaim your faith in God. God is able to restore those who acknowledge him because this is the first step in overcoming the actions of spiritual evil.

A person might also conclude that since the problems that Job faced were the reason that he repented to God, this should be a pattern that should be followed to get us to do the same. His life was set on a downhill spiral through his own words and through his wife and friends who tried to dissuade him from believing that God is good. He continued in the spiral until God came and revealed Himself to him and explained to Job that making himself acceptable through self-justification was not possible. He fought the good fight of faith in the midst of the negative urgings of his wife and friends, and he came out of the problems in better shape with double what he had when his problems started. That sounds like it should work for us, too.

So when sickness and distress come into our lives, should we accept that God is bringing them upon us so that we will learn something, repent, and come back to him? Has God allowed these situations, not causing them himself, to teach us things? After all, this is what prepared Job to receive the truth, right?

NO!!!!

App #7 Study God's Word. Ignorance of spiritual principles does not relieve us of the consequences of behavior contrary to those principles.

The book of Job has given us a tremendous amount of insight into the spiritual world and the causes of the problems that we face. Application of those insights and principles from Job's experience is crucial to our lives. Thank God that Job declared that a book should be written to help those who came after him! His words were spoken in creative faith that brought the Bible into existence *(see p. 173)*. As a result, we have the ability to search the wisdom of the ages and seek out God's purpose in its pages.

Biblical accounts of other individual lives and actions, with their failures and successes, provide us with still more aspects that are critical to our view and understanding of God and His character.

App #8 ***Seek after God and find out who He says He is. God reveals Himself and His character to those who seek Him.***

If we do not learn about God's promises, we may have great difficulty making it through the challenges of life without turning against Him. Even if we turn to Him, rather than from Him, we still may not come through unscathed. However, we will be stronger if we understand God's character and nature and take active steps to resist evil before we face problems. We do this by using the power of faith that God has provided us with through Jesus. Nevertheless, we do grow in spiritual strength when our faith is tried according to James 1:2-8. It is solidified and focused.

James 1:2-8 *(GWT)*

[2] My brothers and sisters, be very happy when you are tested in different
ways. [3] You know that such testing of your faith produces endurance. [4] En-
dure until your testing is over. Then you will be mature and complete, and
you won't need anything. [5] If any of you needs wisdom to know what you
should do, you should ask God, and he will give it to you. God is generous
to everyone and doesn't find fault with them. [6] When you ask for something,
don't have any doubts. A person who has doubts is like a wave that is blown
by the wind and tossed by the sea. [7] A person who has doubts shouldn't
expect to receive anything from the Lord. [8] A person who has doubts is
thinking about two different things at the same time and can't make up his
mind about anything.

App #9 ***Be mindful of your words. Your words are an active force in your life. They are like a rudder on a ship and direct you in both positive and negative ways. Speaking in faith brings things into physical existence and brings events to pass, both good and bad.***

God does not create or allow these situations. They happen because of the adversary that we harbor within our own character, the influences of Satan, and the evil spiritual influence of the world we live in. We allow bitterness to grow in our lives if we blame God, and this produces a wide variety of personal problems, such as confusion, doubt, anxiety, anger, and depression. These produce a kind of death in our spirit.

We block our own help from the Spirit of God, and we open ourselves up to the influences of evil. We then become fair game and vulnerable to Satan's snares. God is not at fault – we are – and He is not an accomplice to it. He is always there to help us overcome if we exercise faith in Him rather than doubt.

> ***App #10*** ***Pray for those who are against you, whether they are family, friends or true enemies. Job's losses were restored double when he prayed for his errant friends. Be vigilant, however, because in some situations, the ones that are closest to you can give you the worst advice. It comes down to a matter of perspective!***

Jesus makes this final App from Job really come alive. He says this better than anything else that could be written in Matthew 5:43-48, presented here for clarity in the Easy-to-Read Version of the Bible.

Matthew 5:43-48 *(ERV)*

43 You have heard that it was said, 'Love your neighbor, and hate your en-
emy.' 44 But I tell you, love your enemies. Pray for those who treat you badly.
45 If you do this, you will be children who are truly like your Father in
heaven. He lets the sun rise for all people, whether they are good or bad. He
sends rain to those who do right and to those who do wrong. 46 If you love
only those who love you, why should you get a reward for that? Even the
tax collectors do that. 47 And if you are nice only to your friends, you are
no better than anyone else. Even the people who don't know God are nice to
their friends. 48 What I am saying is that you must be perfect, just as your
Father in heaven is perfect.

Job's *lack of agreement* with his friends prevented him from falling into the adversary's trap and being swayed to curse God. Avoiding bad circumstances by not agreeing with them and refusing to take part is very beneficial, but there is an even better way. Let us next explore what can actually be accomplished by *getting into agreement with God* and understanding His covenant with man.

CHAPTER 12

GETTING IN AGREEMENT

Studying God's Word offers personal direction and guidance for our lives. From it, we can learn the principles of spiritual and physical success that God presents to His creation. Covenant is one, if not *the* most important, of these principles. However, we must invest our time to discover and understand how it applies in our individual lives.

A covenant is known by many terms today. Agreement, contract, treaty, promise, pledge, marriage, pact, and alliance all refer to the principle of covenant. Every aspect of life is influenced by covenants. Personal knowledge and understanding of covenant relationships will assure their successful operation in daily life. Knowledge and understanding will also reveal the commitment that a covenant requires, the power it has and the protection that it affords. Covenant concepts are crucial, as humanity is founded on them, specifically the *Blood Covenant*.

A covenant is an agreement between parties.

The Purpose Of Covenant

There are many applications of covenants in our society. They can fulfill a variety of purposes. Some are for businesses to provide product sales or employment contracts. Some are for political purposes, such as treaties. One common usage is found in community CC&R's. The letters CC&R stand for Covenants, Conditions, and Restrictions. They are, in essence, the "Rules of Operation" or documents that govern the actions and responsibilities of those living in a particular community. Other covenants establish or solidify relationships, such as a marriage. Still others involve spiritual relationships. However, the true depth of meaning of the word has become greatly lost over time, and its significance is so profound that it is essential to understand the deeper application of the term. *Wikipedia* offers a historical perspective of the term *covenant*.

> **covenant** *(noun)*
>
> *In historical context, a covenant applies to formal promises that were made under oath, or in less remote history, agreements in which the name actually uses the term 'covenant', implying that they were binding for all time.*[39]

The concept of a covenant that is *binding for all time* is not well understood in today's society. Most contracts, agreements, treaties, or pledges have a timeline associated with them, such as the 99 year lease of Hong Kong by China to the British that expired in 1997. Possession of Honk Kong then reverted to China and Britain relinquished its control, and the agreement ended.[40] These types of agreements are temporary, even though they can extend beyond the lifespan of those who make them. They do not carry the deeper context of a *perpetual* covenant even though they may contain or be described as covenants. Since man, his laws, and his governments are finite, he cannot enforce the true meaning and purpose of a perpetual covenant that has no end.

A covenant that is *binding for all time* can only be made and enforced by the everlasting God and is expressed in biblical terms.[41,42] God's covenants with man are described as everlasting or forever *(see Appendix Chapter 12)*. God is the only one that can offer or enforce such an agreement.

In a Biblical context, a covenant means a compact or a league, which is the definition that comes from the Hebrew word, בְּרִית or *beriyth.*

> ***"covenant"*** - *Strong's* OT:1285 בְּרִית, *beriyth* (ber-eeth')
>
> *from* OT:1262 *(in the sense of cutting [like* OT:1254*]); a compact (because made by passing between pieces of flesh): -confederacy, [con-] feder [-ate], covenant, league.*

This covenant requires cutting and loss of blood since the Hebrew word OT:1285 בְּרִית, *(beriyth)* (ber-eeth') also means *passing between pieces of flesh.* The two parties of the covenant would sacrifice an animal, cut it in half and walk together between the pieces of flesh. This signified unity from within in that the covenant parties are *binding together* as one in their agreement.[43] This is the strongest and most deeply expressed form of covenant as it requires a sacrifice with cutting, blood, and death. This is the type of solemn blood covenant that God first made with Abram (Genesis 15).

The blood covenant from Middle Eastern cultures directly relates to the concept of a covenant contained in the Bible as the Bible is truly a Middle Eastern document. Comparisons can be drawn between other relationships, such as *milk brothers* or *sucking brothers*, who share the breast of a nursing woman while suckling even if they are not related. If a non-related girl and boy share milk from the same breast, they are considered related. They have a *milk kinship*. If they were to marry, it would be considered incest.[44] Likewise, *blood covenants* make the two parties closer than literal familial blood relatives in these cultures.[45]

The Carnal Covenant

A group of farmers might make a blood covenant with a group of warriors. The warriors are not able to plant, cultivate, harvest a crop or raise livestock because they are training, preparing for or doing battle. The farmers may not have the skills or strength to go into battle, but they can plant crops or raise livestock. A perfect covenant between these two groups would be for the farmers to supply food to nourish the warriors, and the warriors would, in turn, protect the farmers from harm.

A typical covenant between men involves an agreement to share the assets of each individual for the betterment of both.

A blood covenant involves sharing of blood between parties through cutting each other's flesh and expressing blood. The exchange occurs by wiping the wounds together, directly ingesting the other's blood, or mixing it in a drink and consuming it. An exchange of gifts of great value is also included along with a written record of the covenant agreement.

History shows us the details of human, carnal covenants. Men commit themselves to one another or represent groups of people in a pact or agreement. Each party brings something to the covenant. The main result of the covenant agreement is that the two parties will become stronger in agreement than they are as individuals. Each party supplies strength to counter the weakness of the other covenant partner.

The gravity of the true blood covenant is that each party commits everything to the other under the penalty of curses, which are pronounced on each other if the covenant is ever broken. All that the farmers have and can supply is now available to the warriors, and everything that the warriors have and can supply is available to the farmers. The enemy of one also becomes the enemy of the other. Each party supplies or supports the other's need. The deeper significance of the true blood covenant is that it is considered binding forever and cannot be broken.

The Spiritual Covenant

In the book of Genesis, God reveals that He actually struck a blood covenant with man, but man broke it. Genesis 2:7 states, "And the Lord God formed man of the dust of the ground, and breathed into his nostrils the breath of life; and man became a living soul." God breathed life, but of necessity, He also infused man with blood. God further set the conditions of the covenant that He made with man in Genesis 2:15-17.

Genesis 2:15-17

> [15] *And the Lord God took the man, and put him into the garden of Eden to dress it and to keep it.* [16] *And the Lord God commanded the man, saying, Of every tree of the garden thou mayest freely eat:* [17] *But of the tree of the knowledge of good and evil, thou shalt not eat of it: for in the day that thou eatest thereof thou shalt surely die.*

The penalty for the breaking of the covenant was death, but it also included a number of other curses that God enumerated in Genesis 3:16-19.

Genesis 3:16-19

16 Unto the woman he said, I will greatly multiply thy sorrow and thy conception; in sorrow thou shalt bring forth children; and thy desire shall be to thy husband, and he shall rule over thee. 17 And unto Adam he said, Because thou hast hearkened unto the voice of thy wife, and hast eaten of the tree, of which I commanded thee, saying, Thou shalt not eat of it: cursed is the ground for thy sake; in sorrow shalt thou eat of it all the days of thy life; 18 Thorns also and thistles shall it bring forth to thee; and thou shalt eat the herb of the field; 19 In the sweat of thy face shalt thou eat bread, till thou return unto the ground; for out of it wast thou taken: for dust thou art, and unto dust shalt thou return.

God's Commitment

The responsibilities of the parties to a solemn, blood covenant agreement go on endlessly or *in perpetuity*. Man has been either unwilling or unable to hold up his side of the covenant. However, even though man broke his side, God continued to honor His part of the covenant. Through other covenants that He made directly with the descendants of Adam, God kept working to restore man to his original position. Noah and Abraham furthered God's covenant plans, proving their willingness and obedience by performing their side of the covenant agreement.

God said to Noah, "But with thee will I establish my covenant; and thou shalt come into the ark, thou, and thy sons, and thy wife, and thy sons' wives with thee" (Genesis 6:18). Again, God said to Noah, "And I, behold, I establish my covenant with you, and with your seed after you." (Genesis 9:9). In like manner, He also spoke with Abram, later renaming him Abraham as a sign of an *everlasting* covenant in Genesis 17:1-2, 5-7.

Genesis 17:1-2

1 And when Abram was ninety years old and nine, the Lord appeared to Abram, and said unto him, I am the Almighty God; walk before me, and be thou perfect. 2 And I will make my covenant between me and thee, and will multiply thee exceedingly.

Genesis 17:5-7

5 Neither shall thy name any more be called Abram, but thy name shall be Abraham; for a father of many nations have I made thee. 6 And I will make thee exceeding fruitful, and I will make nations of thee, and kings shall come out of thee. 7 And I will establish my covenant between me and thee and thy seed after thee in their generations for an everlasting covenant, to be a God unto thee, and to thy seed after thee.

Even though man faltered and at times gave up on the covenant, God was faithful to perform it. God continued to express His nature to rescue man from himself and to forgive and restore him. God honors His Word, regardless of the performance of His covenant partners.

The Power of God's Covenant

The power of covenant only rests in the commitment of the parties involved. That is why a blood covenant is struck. Sharing or co-mingling blood between the parties is a sign of complete and total commitment to the established covenant. If one party or the other is not fully committed, the covenant fails. It is possible, however, for one party to carry the burden of both.

A true blood covenant required the blood of both sides. The original covenant that God made with man involved God supplying man with blood, but man did not commit his blood. That commitment did not come until God renewed the covenant as a blood covenant with Abraham. God discerns "the thoughts and intents of the heart" (Hebrews 4:12). Thus, Abraham's willingness to sacrifice his son Isaac was tantamount to God receiving Abraham's blood to ratify the covenant (Genesis 22:1-19). We will explore the account of Abraham's sacrifice in Genesis 22:3-10 in more detail in the next chapter.

God had provided blood to man for the first covenant relationship with Adam. Abraham was now able to provide blood ratification of the covenant through his obedient willingness to sacrifice the blood of his son Isaac. God is the stronger of the two covenant partners and used his power to uphold the weaker partner. This act goes beyond the comprehension of a man-made blood covenant that one party would honor even after the other failed the covenant. This is the power of the Covenant of God. Whenever man failed to uphold his part of the covenant, God still performed His.

The Protections of Covenant

God knew that man was unable to always keep his end of the covenant, so He put in protections and safeguards to help him. God always sought to preserve the life of His covenant partner, and prosper him in spite of himself. God provided a number of helps and assurances to man, such as protections from fear, oppression, and lack of resources. God also provided a way for man to worship and to serve Him.

Protection From Fear

God repeatedly tells man not to fear because He has his back. That is the job of the covenant partner, to look out for his partner and to commit all of his own personal resources to the job. He models Himself as the protector of His covenant partner. The promise to be a shield in Genesis 15:1 implies the warding off of danger.

Genesis 15:1

> *After these things the word of the Lord came unto Abram in a vision, saying, Fear not, Abram: I am thy shield, and thy exceeding great reward.*

God provides a solid sense and foundation of security, saying that He will strengthen, help, and uphold His covenant partners in Isaiah 41:10.

Isaiah 41:10

> *Fear thou not; for I am with thee: be not dismayed; for I am thy God: I will strengthen thee; yea, I will help thee; yea, I will uphold thee with the right hand of my righteousness.*

In Revelation 1:17-18, God also gives the assurance that He is not going anywhere and that He will always be available to hold up His side of the covenant, no matter what.

Revelation 1:17-18

> 17 *And when I saw him, I fell at his feet as dead. And he laid his right hand upon me, saying unto me, Fear not; I am the first and the last:* 18 *I am he that liveth, and was dead; and, behold, I am alive for evermore, Amen; and have the keys of hell and of death.*

Protection From Oppression

God guarantees that He will establish His partners in righteousness or *right standing*. This means that He will forgive and cover our sins and shortfalls. He assures us of freedom from oppression, fear, and terror in Isaiah 54:14.

Isaiah 54:14

In righteousness shalt thou be established: thou shalt be far from oppression; for thou shalt not fear: and from terror; for it shall not come near thee.

Protection From Lack

God also promises that His partners will not have lack or be without food and that all levels of provision will be supplied according to Philippians 4:19.

Philippians 4:19 *(MSG)*

You can be sure that God will take care of everything you need, his generosity exceeding even yours in the glory that pours from Jesus.

Protection To Serve in Health

God made provision to serve Him with blessings, unity, and honor in Zephaniah 3:9 and John 12:26.

Zephaniah 3:9

For then will I turn to the people a pure language, that they may all call upon the name of the Lord, to serve him with one consent.

John 12:26

If any man serve me, let him follow me; and where I am, there shall also my servant be: if any man serve me, him will my Father honour.

God not only gives us healing for our spirits, He also takes disease away in Exodus 23:25. Jesus took beatings and wounds on his body in 1 Peter 2:24, taking sickness and disease on Himself so we could have *physical healing in our bodies*.

Exodus 23:25 *(BBE)*

And give worship to the Lord your God, who will send his blessing on your bread and on your water; and ***I will take all disease away from among you****.*

1 Peter 2:24 *(GNT)*

Christ himself carried our sins in his body to the cross, so that we might die to sin and live for righteousness. It is ***by his wounds that you have been healed****.*

Some of these promises may not be present in your life. Maybe none of them are. Either way, the validity of the covenant promises are not negated. They are acquired by faith through the understanding of who God is and what He has promised. They are not automatic, but they are guaranteed. However, there is a condition. You must be a covenant partner to receive the promises.

A New Covenant

The blood covenant that God fully instituted with Abraham comes to fruition in Jesus. God asked Abraham for his blood, and he complied with his committed willingness to sacrifice his son. The ratification of the covenant came when God was able to bring His son Jesus to the altar of sacrifice, literally offering His own blood. The completion of the blood covenant through this exchange of God's blood with the *virtual* substitutionary blood of man is designed to unite man with God, to *bind them together into one*, as Jesus said in John 17:21-22.

John 17:21-22 *(BBE)*

21 *May they all be one! Even as you, Father, are in me and I am in you, so let them be in us, so that all men may come to have faith that you sent me.*
22 *And the glory which you have given to me I have given to them, so that they may be one even as we are one. . .*

The exchange of Jesus' blood completed the New Covenant that is now founded on better promises than the first. *"Jesus has been given a priestly work that is superior to the Levitical priests' work. He also brings a better promise from God that is based on better guarantees."* (Hebrews 8:6 *GWT*). God brought His best to the covenant through His power, authority, and grace.

The blood covenant relationship is the strongest relationship known to man. We are born into familial or blood relationships. Man typically considers that blood is thicker than water, holding familial relationships to be supreme. However, we have no influence over them.

Voluntary agreement is the major difference between a covenant relationship and a blood line relationship. The choice to enter the covenant agreement emanates from a heart of commitment. It is a choice. It is not by obligation or birth. God is willing and eager to share all of His assets with man and have him choose to be His covenant partner. He wants man to be successful in every aspect of life, and He supplies everything he needs. We saw this in Philippians 4:19, and we even see God's attitude regarding the prosperity of His servants as described in Psalms 35:27.

Psalms 35:27b

Let the LORD be magnified, which hath pleasure in the prosperity of his servant.

God requires very little of His partner as man brings modest value to the agreement. He brings his sins, disobedience, and rebellion, which God forgives. However, man also brings his love, commitment, and devotion to God. The unity that ensues from the covenant with God through Jesus is the strongest bond that can be experienced in the earth realm. Unlike the man-made blood covenant, this one is very lopsided in favor of the weaker partner. This bond is the melding of God and Man into one as a result of a covenant, and it is eloquently summarized by Jesus as He laid down His life and blood to fulfill His covenant promise in John 15:13-14.

John 15:13-14 *(GWT)*

[13] The greatest love you can show is to give your life for your friends. [14] You are my friends if you obey my commandments.

The covenant "contract" is in place and ready for you. Faith in Jesus and acceptance of His sacrifice is what qualifies you to enter the covenant. Look it over and decide for yourself whether or not you want what God is offering through Jesus. Many have accepted the terms. It began with the Covenant that God declared to Abram which we will explore in more detail in the next chapter. Think about it. The choice is yours alone.

God's Part

Mercy - Grace - Peace - Joy
Physical Healing - Provision
Renewed Youth - Good Things
Spiritual Healing - Prosperity
Repemption - Restoration
Forgiveness - Eternal life
Separation from Your Sin

Man's Part

I Trust You, God
I Believe In Jesus

Entering into the New Covenant with God means that you supply nothing but faith and trust in Jesus and God supplies all the rest!

CHAPTER 13

ABRAM AND THE COVENANT

Every character or personality that is presented in the Bible has a unique place in history. They all have a distinct set of attributes, motivations, experiences, and interactions. Through them, we have insight into what God has provided for His creation, mankind. A study of specific individuals offers personal direction and guidance for our lives if we take the time to learn and understand. All of the characters of the Bible were chosen by the Spirit of God to illustrate God's plans and purposes. Some characters were involved with prophetic events. Some provide discernment into the integrity of God's Word and His commands. Others displayed characteristics and actions which pointed to the fulfillment of God's plan of salvation for all of mankind, which is the coming of Jesus to redeem man from his sins and restore his fellowship and position with God.

The purpose of our study is to further the knowledge, understanding, and awareness of our personal responsibility to act on God's desires and receive His grace. In 2 Timothy 2:15, we see instructions to study God's Word.

2 Timothy 2:15 *(AMP)*

> ***Study and be eager and do your utmost to present yourself to God approved*** *(tested by trial), a workman who has no cause to be ashamed, correctly analyzing and accurately dividing [rightly handling and skillfully teaching] the Word of Truth.*

The study of biblical personalities not only provides great value to the student, but it also reveals the personal consequences of disobedience and the generous benefits of obedience to God. Examples are found throughout the Bible, but one personality that is particularly rich in Godly attributes and provides insightful wisdom is the "father of our faith," Abraham.

Battling "Idol" Influences

Abraham began life as Abram, one of three sons of Terah. Abram's brother Haran had a son named Lot, the nephew of Abram. Abram was 20 generations and 2000 years removed from Adam (Luke 3:34-38) *(see p. 80)*. During this time, the condition of mankind had greatly deteriorated from the intimacy that Adam initially enjoyed with God. Terah and his family had nearly erased the awareness of God, their creator, and had adopted the traditions of pagan worshippers of idols and other gods (Joshua 24:2).[46] They were worshippers of the moon-god, Sin, among others.[47]

The *Midrash*, a Jewish text used as a companion to interpret the Bible, also known as the *Bereshith* or *Genesis Rabba*, provides an interesting narrative of Abram.[48] It details how he resisted the folly of idols that both his father, Terah and Nimrod, a mighty and powerful ruler, engaged in. According to the Midrash, Terah was a maker of idols. Both Nimrod and Terah encountered the wisdom of God through Abram in their exchange with him as revealed in the following passage from the Midrash.

> *"Terah, the father of Abraham and Haran, was a dealer in images as well as a worshiper of them. Once when he was away he gave Abraham his stock of graven images to sell in his absence. In the course of the day an elderly man came to make a purchase. Abraham asked him his age, and the man gave it as between fifty and sixty years. Abraham taunted him with want of sound sense in calling the work of another man's hand, produced perhaps in a few hours, his god; the man laid the words of Abraham to heart and gave up idol-worship. Again, a woman came with a handful of fine flour to offer to Terah's idols, which were now in charge of Abraham. He took a stick and broke all the images except the largest one, in the hand of which he placed the stick which had worked this wholesale destruction.*
> *When his father returned and saw the havoc committed on his "gods" and property he demanded an explanation from his son whom he had left in charge. Abraham mockingly explained that when an offering of fine flour was brought to these divinities they quarreled with one another as to who should be the recipient, when at last the biggest of them, being angry at the altercation, took up a stick to chastise the offenders, and in so doing*

broke them all up. Terah, so far from being satisfied with this explanation, understood it as a piece of mockery, and when he learned also of the customers whom Abraham had lost him during his management he became very incensed, and drove Abraham out of his house and handed him over to Nimrod.

Nimrod suggested to Abraham that, since he had refused to worship his father's idols because of their want of power, he should worship fire, which is very powerful. Abraham pointed out that water has power over fire. "Well," said Nimrod, "let us declare water god." "But," replied Abraham, "the clouds absorb the water; and even they are dispersed by the wind." "Then let us declare the wind our god." "Bear in mind," continued Abraham, "that man is stronger than wind, and can resist it and stand against it." Nimrod, becoming weary of arguing with Abraham, decided to cast him before his god--fire--and challenged Abraham's deliverance by the God of Abraham, but God saved him out of the fiery furnace. [49]

Abram – 1 Idols – 0

Little is known from the Biblical record about Abram's life between his birth and his departure from the city of Haran at age 75. It appears obvious that the Spirit of God did not consider this information crucial to our understanding of the narrative of Abram's life. However, even though Abram and Nimrod were not contemporaries, the passage from the Midrash does provide some interesting insight. Abram became who he was by the choices he made in conducting his life. As a young man he learned through the challenges he encountered in his father's idol-making business and from his interaction with the culture of idol worship surrounding him.

Abram's paradigms of life became quite different from those of his ancestors and contemporaries. His heart was somehow prepared to hear and be obedient to the one true God. God's inspired words brought Abram to complete success over his challenges. As he continued with God, he overcame challenges, displayed faith and trusted in God. God rewarded him with a covenant or agreement and gave him a new prophetic name, Abraham, meaning the "father of many nations." His success brought on harsh persecution, even by fire, but God was with him. God was at work shaping Abram's life even before He established His covenant with him. The influence of the idols in Abram's life lost, and God won.

A Voice From the Sky

The events that shaped Abram's life both during his youth and as an adult in the city of Haran prepared him to hear from God. Nonetheless, it must have come as some shock the first time he actually *heard* from God in Genesis 12:1-4.

> **Genesis 12:1-4** *(ERV)*
> *[1] The Lord said to Abram, "Leave your country and your people. Leave your father's family and go to the country that I will show you. [2] I will build a great nation from you. I will bless you and make your name famous. People will use your name to bless other people. [3] I will bless those who bless you, and I will curse those who curse you. I will use you to bless all the people on earth."*
>
> *[4] So Abram left Haran just like the Lord said, and Lot went with him. Abram was 75 years old when he left Haran.*

The reader might be somewhat nonchalant about the exchange that marked the beginning of Abram's eternal walk with God, but this was a truly monumental experience. Abram had been uprooted by his earthly father Terah and moved from Ur of the Chaldees to the city of Haran in the land of Canaan. In doing this, Abram was being obedient to his father. It is a bit more challenging, however, to understand how Abram at age 75 could just pick up and leave with his family and nephew after hearing a voice from *somewhere*. The Spirit of God must have been dealing with Abram in a deep way all of his life in order for him to be able to hear God's voice and obey.

Abram's Journey

Abram gathered all of his possessions, his wife, his servants and his nephew Lot and set out on a journey. He did this as an act of faith in response to the voice of God. He was rewarded for his step of faith when God actually appeared to him as he went. God declared that the land of Canaan would be given to Abram's seed, meaning his descendants. Abram certainly must have been overwhelmed at hearing God's voice. Awestruck with the prospects and implications of this declaration, Abram immediately built an altar to worship and call upon (pray to) the name of the Lord (Genesis 12:5-8).

Abram and Lot both prospered greatly in the new land to which God had called Abram. In fact, they prospered so much that Abram and Lot could not continue to dwell together. They had outgrown the land and went separate ways. Abram gave preference to Lot and let him choose the region that he desired which was the plain of Jordan. He went into the remaining land, the land of Canaan, and there encountered God yet again. God declared His intent for Abram in Genesis 13:15-17.

Genesis 13:15-17 *(NKJV)*

> [15] *. . . for all the land which you see I give to you and your descendants forever.* [16] *And I will make your descendants as the dust of the earth; so that if a man could number the dust of the earth, then your descendants also could be numbered.* [17] *Arise, walk in the land through its length and its width, for I give it to you."*

It is worth noting that the totality of God's plan was not given to Abram in his first encounter with Him when he entered Canaan. God's direction to Abram was: *"Leave your country and your people. Leave your father's family and go to the country that I will show you"* (Genesis 12:1 *ERV*). Abram was instructed to *leave his family and people,* but he allowed his nephew Lot to go with him. Once he left the company of Lot and they went their separate ways, he was finally in the position that God wanted him to be in. He was alone, dependent upon God, and free of the influence of his family who worshiped idols. When his separation was complete, God was then able to reveal more of His plan for Abram.

This is an important principle to understand. We have a very hard time moving forward if we are anchored in the past. The past may be people, possessions, places, or attitudes. Until we are ready and able to leave our baggage behind, we limit our ability to receive what God has in store for us. God can reach and help us much more easily once we are separated from these influences.

Abram's obedience and faith were accumulating their rewards as God continued to impart His blessings on His servant. His relationship with God was growing through his obedience and faith. This allowed God to bring more and more blessing into Abram's life. He not only established blessings for Abram but also for all of his *seed* or *descendants* (Genesis 13:15). Descendants? Wait a minute! Abram is over 75 years old, and as yet he does not have any children!

Cutting The Covenant

The covenant relationship discussed in the previous chapter has particular importance for Abram. God made a covenant with Abram that was very one-sided. It is described in Genesis 15:1-18.

Genesis 15:1-18 *(ERV)*

[1] After all these things happened, the word of the Lord came to Abram in a vision. God said, "Abram, don't be afraid. I will defend you and give you a great reward."

*[2] But Abram said, "Lord God, there is nothing you can give me that will
make me happy, because I have no son. My slave Eliezer from Damascus
will get everything I own after I die." [3] Abram said, "You have given me no
son, so a slave born in my house will get everything I have."*

[4] Then the Lord spoke to Abram and said, "That slave will not be the one to get what you have. You will have a son who will get everything you own."

[5] Then God led Abram outside and said, "Look at the sky. See the many stars. There are so many you cannot count them. Your family will be like that."

*[6] Abram believed the Lord, and because of this faith the Lord accepted him
as one who has done what is right. [7] He said to Abram, "I am the Lord who
led you from Ur of Babylonia. I did this so that I could give you this land.
You will own this land."*

[8] But Abram said, "Lord God, how can I be sure that I will get this land?"

*[9] God said to Abram, "We will make an agreement. Bring me a three-year-
old cow, a three-year-old goat, a three-year-old ram, a dove, and a young
pigeon." [10] Abram brought all these to God. Abram killed these animals and
cut each of them into two pieces. Then he laid each half across from the
other half. He did not cut the birds into two pieces. [11] Later, large birds flew
down to eat the animals, but Abram chased them away.*

*[12] The sun began to go down and Abram got very sleepy. While he was
asleep, a very terrible darkness came over him. [13] Then the Lord said to
Abram, "You should know this: Your descendants will live in a country that is
not their own. They will be strangers there. The people there will make them
slaves and be cruel to them for 400 years. [14] But then I will punish the nation that made them slaves. Your people will leave that land, and they will
take many good things with them. [15] You yourself will live to be very old. You
will die in peace and be buried with your family. [16] After four generations*

your people will come to this land again and defeat the Amorites. That will happen in the future because the Amorites are not yet guilty enough to lose their land."

17 After the sun went down, it got very dark. The dead animals were still on the ground, each animal cut into two pieces. Then a smoking firepot and a flaming torch passed between the halves of the dead animals.

18 So on that day the Lord made a promise and an agreement with Abram. He said, "I will give this land to your descendants. I will give them the land between the River of Egypt and the great river Euphrates."

God ratified the covenant, a *blood covenant*, which is the strongest kind while Abram was in a deep sleep. The Spirit of God in the form of a smoking furnace and a burning lamp passed between the pieces that Abram had prepared at His instruction. Abram supplied the faith and the sacrifices, and God supplied the promises. These promises included innumerable offspring and land in which they would grow and prosper. The whole weight of the covenant was on God. This is so incredible. God asks so little but gives so much!

Faltering Faith

Abram was willing to be obedient and to follow God's direction, as demonstrated by his actions, even though he did not have any evidence that the promise of his descendants would be realized. It certainly must have been difficult to accept that the promise was for real since all physical evidence pointed to its impossibility. Believing it was an enormous test of faith, but Abram was no stranger to faith in God. After all, he followed God's voice when he left the security of his home and set out into the wilderness.

However, even faith giants falter, and Abram was no exception. Faith and patience go hand in hand as patience is required to act in faith. Some ten years following God's declaration to Abram that he would have a son, his patience failed. Much time had passed with no evidence of the promise getting any closer to being realized. Sarai must have concluded that the promise was given to Abram but not necessarily given to her. She offered Hagar, her handmaiden, to Abram to bear a son and fulfill the promise. Ishmael was born to Abram and Hagar, and it appeared that the promise had been fulfilled. However, the birth of Ismael caused great division in the extended family. In her jealousy about not having a child herself, Sarai wanted to cast Hagar out. Sarai and Abram had both faltered, not realizing that the promise of God was given to both her and Abram together. Nevertheless, God's plan was not to be thwarted.

Establishing The Covenant

This first covenant of God with Abram was just the beginning. On the surface, it was based on a physical or tangible entity, the land. However, underlying the physical was something deeper. God made the declaration that Abram would have children although He did not use these exact words. God said that Abram would have seed or descendants to inherit the land in Genesis 15:18. This original covenant promise was given to Abram when he was about 75 years old. However, the manifestation of that promise was not to occur for another 25 years after God had given him a new name, *Abraham*, in Genesis 17:1-7.

Genesis 17:1-7 *(BBE)*

> [1] *When Abram was ninety-nine years old, the Lord came to him, and said, I am God, Ruler of all; go in my ways and be upright in all things,* [2] *And I will make an agreement between you and me, and your offspring will be greatly increased.*
>
> [3] *And Abram went down on his face on the earth, and the Lord God went on talking with him, and said,* [4] *As for me, my agreement is made with you, and you will be the father of nations without end.*
>
> [5] *No longer will your name be Abram, but Abraham, for I have made you the father of a number of nations.* [6] *I will make you very fertile, so that nations will come from you and kings will be your offspring.*
>
> [7] *And I will make between me and you and your seed after you through all generations, an eternal agreement to be a God to you and to your seed after you.*

What's In A Name

Your name may have been selected by parents who wanted to honor a relative or friend, or maybe it came from a book and just sounded good to them. However, names seem to have had much more significance in ancient days. Children were named according to the hopes of their parents or according to significant events and circumstances. Some names were given to honor promise that the parents had received, and the child was a fulfillment of that promise.

In other times, God actually changed names, reflecting His intended destiny for the child or person according to His plans and purposes. There are many examples occurring in scripture of children who were given one name at birth only to have it changed in adult life. Such is the case with Abram. God made promises to him about the land that he would possess and about the *inheritance of his seed* at a time when Abram and his wife Sarai were childless. God had plans for them, however. He had a purpose and destiny that they were to fulfill, but He needed a way to keep the vision of that destiny in front of their eyes and in their ears at all times.

Changing A Name – Creating A Vision

Thirteen years came and went as Ishmael grew and prospered. God saw the need to bolster Abram's faith relative to His original promise. According to the biblical narrative, it appears that Sarai was the one who first lost patience. God chose to solidify His vision within both Abram and Sarai in a unique way. He spoke to Abram when he was 99 years old and changed his name to *Abraham*, which is interpreted as the *father of many nations* (Genesis 17:5). God also changed Sarai to *Sarah* or *mother of nations.* What better way to instill and remind a person of his or her purpose than to make a name change that reflects that destiny!

God knew that Abram needed a constant reminder of the covenant promise that He had made to him, especially in light of the birth of Ishmael. Every time Abram was addressed as *Abraham* by his family, friends, and servants, it was a reminder of the incredible promise of God. Keeping the promise before him was the best way for Abraham to build his faith. These name changes not only reinforced the promises that God had already made, but He also solidified the promises with a new agreement or *covenant*. This covenant agreement would have eternal consequences that would confirm the new names that God gave to Abram and Sarai.

God established new identities which would spring forth from both Abraham and Sarah. Abraham would not be just a father through a handmaiden, but the father of a son, born of his wife, with whom he had his original marriage relationship. The marriage relationship is man's physical model or example of the concept of a covenant. The marriage covenant is a unique relationship that God had Himself established in Genesis 2:24.

Genesis 2:24 *(CEV)*

> *That's why a man will leave his own father and mother. He marries a woman, and the two of them become like one person.*

The marriage bond is not only a physical one, but more importantly, it is a spiritual one. The man and the woman come together in agreement and begin to act as a single entity. The *King James Version* uses the phrase, "they shall be one flesh" in describing this single entity. When they become one flesh, they not only unite physically, but also in spiritual authority.

When God gave direction to Abram, by inference, He also gave direction to Sarai since they were in a covenant with one another by marriage. The promises that God gave to Abram also extended to Sarai because they were *one flesh*. Changing Sarai's name to Sarah in Genesis 17:15-16 affirmed for her that God had also included her in the promise. This name change made it clear that Sarah also had the opportunity to take part in Abraham's faith and covenant with God. This level of unity is something that Abram and Sarai apparently did not understand. Otherwise Sarai would never have offered her maidservant Hagar to Abram.

Genesis 17:15-16 *(ERV)*

> 15 *God said to Abraham, "I will give Sarai, your wife, a new name. Her new name will be Sarah.* 16 *I will bless her. I will give her a son, and you will be the father. She will be the mother of many new nations. Kings of nations will come from her."*

The act of establishing a covenant requires that each of the parties entering into the agreement commit to performing certain responsibilities. It is not a unilateral contract as each party must bring something to the table. God's part reveals an amazing offer. His promise included abundant offspring through many generations with Abraham being the father nations, a covenant being established through Sarah and kings coming from them. The only thing that Abram and Sarai had to bring was their faith, which was a challenge, since Sarai was without a child at the time. Acceptance of their new names was their *faith ratification* of the covenant. As Abraham and Sarah began to call each other by their new names, they continued to reinforce the promise of God and build their faith.

The Ultimate Challenge

The realization of the birth of Isaac, the promised son through Sarah, came to Abraham just one year after Abraham and Sarah received their name changes. Isaac grew and matured. A physical sign was instituted to commemorate the covenant that God established. It was Abraham's circumcision and the circumcision of Isaac. Then, God gave Abraham the opportunity to really prove his side of the covenant agreement.

Abraham was undeniably thrilled with the birth of Isaac, his covenant son. Some years later, God asked the ultimate of Abraham so that his faith could be thoroughly assured. At the time of this challenge, Abraham was 117-130 years old and Isaac was 17-33 years old. Abraham and Sarah had waited over 25 years to see the culmination of the promise that God had given Abraham when he was 75 years old. Then, God asked something that we would view today as child abuse. It was severe and unthinkable. He was positioning Abraham to bring an extremely important plan to earth, and He needed the faith of His man Abraham to make it happen. God asked Abraham to kill his only son and make him into a sacrificial offering!

The Faith Proving Ground

The relationship that Abraham enjoyed with God is one of the deepest and most precious of all in the Bible, next to that of Jesus. His relationship was based in faith, a willingness to accept God's word as truth, even when circumstances dictated otherwise. The blood line descendants of Abraham inherited his covenant with God. Circumcision was the physical sign that God gave to them as heirs. They would later become known as the Jews. However, Abram was offered God's covenant before he was renamed and circumcised.

In the same manner, those who are not blood line descendants of Abraham (all of them, including you), are offered that same covenant promise because of Abraham received the covenant by faith. All that is required to receive the same covenant promises is the same faith that Abraham modeled for us. He just believed God and because of his faith, he is described as the father of all believers in Romans 4:11-12.

Romans 4:11-12 *(TLB)*

[11] It wasn't until later on, after God had promised to bless him because of his faith, that he was circumcised. The circumcision ceremony was a sign that Abraham already had faith and that God had already accepted him and declared him just and good in his sight-before the ceremony took place. So Abraham is the spiritual father of those who believe and are saved without obeying Jewish laws. We see, then, that those who do not keep these rules are justified by God through faith. [12] And Abraham is also the spiritual father of those Jews who have been circumcised. They can see from his example that it is not this ceremony that saves them, for Abraham found favor with God by faith alone before he was circumcised.

God instructed Abraham to bring his only son, Isaac, to an altar for sacrifice. What an incredible request to make! This is exactly what God asked of him in Genesis 22:1-2. However, God had a mysterious purpose in His request.

Genesis 22:1-2 *(ASV)*

[1] And it came to pass after these things, that God did prove Abraham, and said unto him, Abraham. And he said, Here am I. [2] And he said, Take now thy son, thine only son, whom thou lovest, even Isaac, and get thee into the land of Moriah. And offer him there for a burnt-offering upon one of the mountains which I will tell thee of.

Abraham's response to God's faith challenge proved his faith. Further study of this account reveals even more astounding information and a testimony of faith. Think about this. Abraham was instructed to offer Isaac as a *burnt offering*. This meant that Abraham was to kill his only son, the son of promise, then place him on an altar, light a fire and burn him to a crisp! Examine the activities described in the following narrative of Genesis 22:3-8.

Genesis 22:3-8 *(ASV)*

[3] And Abraham rose early in the morning, and saddled his ass, and took two of his young men with him, and Isaac his son. And he clave the wood for the burnt-offering, and rose up, and went unto the place of which God had told him. [4] On the third day Abraham lifted up his eyes, and saw the place afar off.

[5] And Abraham said unto his young men, Abide ye here with the ass, and I and the lad will go yonder; and we will worship, and come again to you.

[6] And Abraham took the wood of the burnt-offering, and laid it upon Isaac his son. And he took in his hand the fire and the knife. And they went both of them together. [7] And Isaac spake unto Abraham his father, and said, My father. And he said, Here am I, my son. And he said, Behold, the fire and the wood. But where is the lamb for a burnt-offering? And Abraham said, God will provide himself the lamb for a burnt-offering, my son. [8] So they went both of them together.

Abraham obediently gathered everything necessary to accomplish the task. He brought firewood, coals to start the fire, undoubtedly cords to bind and a knife to kill the sacrifice. Isaac was given the task of carrying the wood that would be used to offer him as the burnt offering. Does that sound like anyone else you have heard of? Jesus was forced to carry the wood for the cross on which he would die!

Not only was Isaac carrying one of the instruments of his death as Jesus did, he asked a question similar to one asked by Jesus. Jesus asked God if there was another way. Isaac questioned his father as to the source of the sacrifice (Genesis 22:7). He did not know that it was him!

It was a custom of Abraham to offer sacrifices to God, a lamb being the most likely candidate. Abraham responded to Isaac in a peculiar manner considering the command that he received from God. Abraham said, "God will provide Himself the lamb for a burnt-offering…". That statement has very deep and faith-related prophetic overtones.

Abraham laid claim by faith that Isaac would not actually die or that he would be raised from the dead. He said to his servants, "Abide ye here with the ass, and I and the lad will go yonder; and we will worship, and come again to you" (Genesis 22:5 *ASV*). The account continues in Genesis 22:9-13.

Genesis 22:9-13 *(TLB)*

[9] When they arrived at the place where God had told Abraham to go, he built an altar and placed the wood in order, ready for the fire, and then tied Isaac and laid him on the altar over the wood. [10] And Abraham took the knife and lifted it up to plunge it into his son, to slay him.
[11] At that moment the Angel of God shouted to him from heaven, "Abraham! Abraham!" "Yes, Lord!" he answered.
[12] "Lay down the knife; don't hurt the lad in any way," the Angel said, "for I know that God is first in your life-you have not withheld even your beloved son from me."

[13] Then Abraham noticed a ram caught by its horns in a bush. So he took the ram and sacrificed it, instead of his son, as a burnt offering on the altar.

Faith To The Extreme

Just imagine the scene. Isaac had carried the wood and knew that his father had a knife to slay the sacrificial animal. They probably built the altar together as they worshiped God and prepared themselves to make the offering. Abraham told his son Isaac that God would provide the lamb for the sacrifice. Then, Abraham turned suddenly to Isaac with a cord of some sort and bound Isaac's hands and feet. Remember, Isaac is a young adult and quite capable of putting up a significant defense against a 120 year old man. However, Isaac willingly submitted himself, as Abraham did, to the will of God. He allowed his father to bind him and place him on the wood atop the altar they had built together. We are talking some serious faith here on the part of both Abraham and Isaac!

Not only do we see the demonstration of Abraham's faith as he went to make the sacrifice, but we also see the preparations that he made to do the deed. He told the servants that they would both return, thereby laying claim to the resurrection of his son, should his son actually die in the process. Then, he prophetically uttered that God would provide Himself (as) the Lamb for the sacrifice (Genesis 22:7). Isaac carried the wood on which he would be burned and willingly submitted to what must have inevitably seemed to be his death.

This demonstration and example of faith that Abraham (and Isaac) provided for us was also the act that legally allowed God to fulfill His plan of salvation for mankind through His ultimate sacrifice. Jesus is the Lamb of God that Abraham told Isaac that God would provide. He is the substitutionary sacrifice for the penalty of our sins. He carried His own wooden cross upon which he would be hung to die. Moreover, He did it willingly. He submitted His will to that of His Father, God. The parallels are astounding, except that Jesus actually did give his life.

The faith and obedience of Abraham was rewarded because of his heart posture. He was willing to do what God had instructed, allowing God to bring His plan for man into the earth. The force of faith energized and permeated Abraham and his descendants, but faith also became available to anyone willing to adopt it and receive the grace or *unmerited favor* of God as we see in Romans 4:16.

Romans 4:16 *(ERV)*

So people get what God promised by having faith. This happens so that the promise can be a free gift. And if the promise is a free gift, then all of Abraham's people will get that promise. The promise is not just for those who live under the Law of Moses. It is for all who live with faith as Abraham did. He is the father of us all.

Ushering In God's Plan

Abraham is a multifaceted character study because of the many spiritual truths he lived and represented. One of the most important aspects of his life, however, was the fact that his action was a physical depiction of a spiritual achievement that God had planned from the beginning of creation. God is omniscient, omnipotent, and capable of doing anything that He desires. However, in this earth realm, He has chosen to limit Himself by the words of His own mouth as described in Numbers 23:19.

Numbers 23:19 *(GWT)*

God is not like people. He tells no lies. He is not like humans. He doesn't change his mind. When he says something, he does it. When he makes a promise, he keeps it.

This verse is a pivotal one for our understanding of the relationship that God has established with us. He has declared that He will not *change His mind*. If God were to go against His own word, He would become a liar, which He cannot be. Otherwise, the legal system that He put into place would be hypocritical and implode.

It's All Legal

The concept of legality is very important to the understanding of what transpired during Abraham's act of obedience in sacrificing Isaac. God chose to relinquish some degree of authority and tie His own hands when He gave Adam and Eve dominion and authority over the earth realm. He chose to empower them with free will, giving them personal responsibility for their actions and the outcome in Genesis 1:26-28. As a result of God's choice, He set a legal precedent, preventing Him from directly intervening in any way that would overrule the free-will authority He had given to man.

Genesis 1:26-28

[26] And God said, Let us make man in our image, after our likeness: and let them have dominion over the fish of the sea, and over the fowl of the air, and over the cattle, and over all the earth, and over every creeping thing that creepeth upon the earth. [27] So God created man in his own image, in the image of God created he him; male and female created he them. [28] And God blessed them, and God said unto them, Be fruitful, and multiply, and replenish the earth, and subdue it: and have dominion over the fish of the sea, and over the fowl of the air, and over every living thing that moveth upon the earth.

The word *dominion* means domain such as property or lands, supreme authority such as sovereignty, power, or control as in governance or absolute ownership.[50] There are 11 different Hebrew words that are translated as *dominion* in the *King James Version (see Appendix, Chapter 13)*. The Hebrew word (Strong's OT:7287) found in Genesis 1:26-28 is the most profound and deepest in meaning for mankind. This instance is consistent with the concept of total control and authority over the living things of the earth.

"dominion" - *Strong's* OT:7287 רָדָה *radah* (raw-daw')

a primitive root; to tread down, i.e. subjugate; specifically, to crumble off: ***KJV*** *- (come to, make to) have dominion, prevail against, reign, (bear, make to) rule,- r, over), take.*

Psalms 115:15-16 further describes the extent of man's dominion on the earth.

Psalms 115:15-16 *(GWT)*

[15] You will be blessed by the Lord, the maker of heaven and earth. [16] The highest heaven belongs to the Lord, but he has given the earth to the descendants of Adam.

God made both heaven and earth. He reserved the dominion and authority of the heavens for Himself, but He gave the earth to men. This is a clear reference to man's ownership of the earth. In the garden, God handed this total dominion to Adam and Eve and to all of their offspring. He was entering into a legal contract, witnessed by all of creation, including Satan. In essence, God stated that He would no longer exercise

His authority over the Earth because He passed it on to man. This is why the deception Satan perpetrated upon Adam and Eve was so destructive. Satan probably enjoyed dominion over the earth before the creation of man, but he lost it in his fall. Adam and Eve subjugated themselves to him through his deception and he stole the dominion of Earth back from them. From that point forward, God had to work His plans for man to regain and restore his legal title to the Earth through the power of faith.

Abraham demonstrated his willingness to follow God's direction, not succumbing to doubt and disbelief regarding the sacrifice of his son. This action of faith legally allowed God to do the same with His Son, Jesus. Abraham's faith was the pathway toward ushering in salvation through the man, Jesus. The embodiment of God and the descendant of Adam through Abraham, Jesus is the incarnation or the physical representation of the covenant relationship that God established with Abraham. Without the faith of Abraham, the world might still be expecting salvation rather than enjoying the gift of it through Jesus.

Abraham's example of faith is a key element of the New Testament *faith chapter*, Hebrews 11. Abraham's willingness to offer Isaac is noted, along with his complete confidence that even if Isaac were to die, God would raise him up again.

Hebrews 11:17-19 *(ERV)*

> [17-18] *God tested Abraham's faith. God told him to offer Isaac as a sacrifice. Abraham obeyed because he had faith. He already had the promises from God. And God had already said to him, "It is through Isaac that your descendants will come." But Abraham was ready to offer his only son. He did this because he had faith.* [19] *He believed that God could raise people from death. And really, when God stopped Abraham from killing Isaac, it was as if he got him back from death.*

The virtue of Abraham's faith is evident. He believed according to the manner described in Romans 4:17 *(AMP)* when God "*speaks of the nonexistent things as if they already existed.*"

Romans 4:17 *(AMP)*

> *As it is written, I have made you the father of many nations. [He was appointed our father] in the sight of God in Whom he believed, Who gives life to the dead and* ***speaks of the nonexistent things that [He has foretold and promised] as if they [already] existed****.*

Abraham was not weak in faith. He did not question or second guess the promise of God. He was fully convinced that God would perform His promise and that he would have descendants through Isaac. Abraham's act of faith was counted as righteousness or *right standing* by God. We see the complete picture in the following passage from Romans 4:16-25.

> **Romans 4:16-25** *(ERV)*
>
> *16 So people get what God promised by having faith. This happens so that the promise can be a free gift. And if the promise is a free gift, then all of Abraham's people will get that promise. The promise is not just for those who live under the Law of Moses. It is for all who live with faith as Abraham did. He is the father of us all. 17 As the Scriptures say, "I have made you a father of many nations." This is true before God, the one Abraham believed—the God who gives life to the dead and speaks of things that don't yet exist as if they are real.*
>
> *18 There was no hope that Abraham would have children, but Abraham believed God and continued to hope. And that is why he became the father of many nations. As God told him, "You will have many descendants."*
>
> *19 Abraham was almost a hundred years old, so he was past the age for having children. Also, Sarah could not have children. Abraham was well aware of this, but his faith in God never became weak. 20 He never doubted that God would do what he promised. He never stopped believing. In fact, he grew stronger in his faith and just praised God. 21 Abraham felt sure that God was able to do what he promised. 22 So that's why "he was accepted as one who is right with God." 23 These words ("he was accepted") were written not only for Abraham. 24 They were also written for us. God will also accept us because we believe. We believe in the one who raised Jesus our Lord from death. 25 Jesus was handed over to die for our sins, and he was raised from death to make us right with God.*

Abraham modeled his faith through his words to create and receive God's promise, rather than wait for God to do something and then describe what He had done. The latter is reporting on the news; the former is using faith to create the news! When Abraham asked *Mother of Nations* to get dinner ready, or Sarah asked *Father of Many Nations* to bring her a lamb to prepare, they were speaking God's promise into existence. Abraham also spoke his faith believing that even if Isaac were to die in the sacrifice, he would live and multiply as God promised. They were speaking faith over things that had not yet come into physical existence. God did the same when He spoke creation into existence (Genesis 1).

This *faith talk* is a crucial process for all believers to model. It is through faith that we speak to receive the free gift of God. When we believe Him, set ourselves in agreement with His promises and speak according to our belief, God's promises will manifest in our lives. Therefore, we must *speak* out *before we receive*. Speaking before receiving is faith. That is the requirement for obtaining salvation as we see in Romans 10:8-10.

Romans 10:8-10 *(AMP)*

[8] But what does it say? The Word (God's message in Christ) is near you, on your lips and in your heart; that is, the Word (the message, the basis and object) of faith which we preach, [9] Because if you acknowledge and confess with your lips that Jesus is Lord and in your heart believe (adhere to, trust in, and rely on the truth) that God raised Him from the dead, you will be saved. [10] For with the heart a person believes (adheres to, trusts in, and relies on Christ) and so is justified (declared righteous, acceptable to God), and with the mouth he confesses (declares openly and speaks out freely his faith) and confirms [his] salvation.

Faith speaks things into existence, and this is precisely how the gift of salvation that Jesus provided for us through His sacrifice is obtained. God made the promise to Abraham and to all of his seed, and it was set in motion by Abraham's faithful obedience. This means that not only everyone that came from Abraham's bloodline was included, but also those who would act on their faith and believe the way that Abraham did. God includes us in the blessing even though we might not be the physical descendants of Abraham as we read in Romans 4:23-25. This is awesome!

Romans 4:23-25 *(AMP)*

[23] But [the words], It was credited to him, were written not for his sake alone, [24] But [they were written] for our sakes too. [Righteousness, standing acceptable to God] will be granted and credited to us also who believe in (trust in, adhere to, and rely on) God, Who raised Jesus our Lord from the dead, [25] Who was betrayed and put to death because of our misdeeds and was raised to secure our justification (our acquittal), [making our account balance and absolving us from all guilt before God].

The most important aspect of this narrative of Abraham is the demonstration of God's character that continues to be manifested in the world.

The goodness of God is the common thread that we see in this series of events, along with His desire to keep man from suffering the consequence of his own sins. For our benefit, God prepared the way for a substitute to deliver us from death and destruction when He made His covenant with Abraham. God had to overcome the legal penalty of death for sin in order to do that. He accomplished it in part by confirming where Abraham's heart lay when He asked him to sacrifice his son.

God saved Isaac from death, but He could not have done so without the complete, faithful obedience of Abraham, not only in deed, but more importantly, in his heart. Abraham's declarations of faith that both he and Isaac would return from what appeared to be Isaac's execution was the first step. Convincing his son to believe and submit to both him and God was the next step. The last step was following through to the point of actually performing the action. Abraham proved to God and the rest of creation that he was going to be faithfully obedient no matter what the consequences might be. God has continued to demonstrate His character by offering to save everyone from death and destruction, providing them with a way out of the consequences of their own actions through faith.

Abraham went through a deep transformation as he moved from a culture of idol worship to the worship of the One True God. His life, actions, faith, and descendants have had an immeasurable impact on the world in which we live. We have many things for which to be grateful from a man whose dedication and obedience to our God is nearly without equal. Only Jesus, for whom Abraham paved the way, exceeded his faithfulness. Undoubtedly, God would have found another man to fulfill the mandate of obedience and faith had Abraham been unwilling or unsuccessful. Nevertheless, the fact remains that Abraham accomplished the task that God set before him, and as a result, he set an example to inspire all of those who followed.

The faith of Abraham does not stop here, however, and neither does his influence upon earthly events. More was in store for him as authority over earthly activities was being restored to Abraham, God's covenant man on earth.

CHAPTER 14

THE CRY OF SIN
ABRAHAM'S BARGAIN

Abraham played many key roles over the span of his life. God established a covenant agreement with him. As a result of his faith in God and that covenant, the authority of the earth realm, which was surrendered by Adam and Eve, was re-vested in him. This is evidenced by the following narrative in Genesis 18:17-19.

Genesis 18:17-19

17 And the LORD said, Shall I hide from Abraham that thing which I do;
18 Seeing that Abraham shall surely become a great and mighty nation, and
all the nations of the earth shall be blessed in him? 19 For I know him, that
he will command his children and his household after him, and they shall
keep the way of the LORD, to do justice and judgment; that the LORD may
bring upon Abraham that which he hath spoken of him.

This very illuminating passage reveals God's attitude about the earth He created and the rules under which it operates. The covenant agreement between God and Abraham had much deeper implications than Abraham must have imagined. God was able in this covenant agreement to legally restore to a man the authority over the *Earth Realm* that was lost by Adam and Eve through their disobedience (sin). Also revealing in this passage is God's thought process and reasoning about His relationship with Abraham. God demonstrated His trust and respect for Abraham, His covenant partner, with whom He had declared the covenant. God had done all of the work of the covenant up to this point because Abraham had not yet proven his total faith commitment to God by his willingness to sacrifice his son.

The Visitation

The following conversations in Genesis 18:9-15 immediately followed a visitation by three individuals, one of whom is identified as the *Lord*. The three came to the door of Abraham and Sarah's tent to deliver a message. Abraham hurried to be a good host, offering water to soothe and wash their feet, as well as to provide food to his esteemed guests. Abraham ran to his herd to find a suitable animal and instructed Sarah to prepare a fine meal. After the meal, his guests inquired about Sarah. Abraham said that she was in the tent. The Lord said that Sarah would have a son and that He would return at the time of birth. Sarah was over 90 years old and by then past the time of having normal monthly cycles. As a result, she laughed at the thought of bearing a child, but the Lord replied to her, "Is any thing too hard for the Lord?"The narrative continues and explains that Sarah was afraid and lied about her scoffing doubt. She said, "I did not laugh." But He (the Lord) knowingly said, "Yes, you did laugh."

Genesis 18:9-15 *(NIV)*

> 9 *"Where is your wife Sarah?" they asked him. "There, in the tent," he said.*
> 10 *Then the Lord said, "I will surely return to you about this time next year, and Sarah your wife will have a son." Now Sarah was listening at the entrance to the tent, which was behind him.*
>
> 11 *Abraham and Sarah were already old and well advanced in years, and Sarah was past the age of childbearing.*
> 12 *So Sarah laughed to herself as she thought, "After I am worn out and my master is old, will I now have this pleasure?"*
>
> 13 *Then the Lord said to Abraham, "Why did Sarah laugh and say, 'Will I really have a child, now that I am old?'*
> 14 *Is anything too hard for the Lord, I will return to you at the appointed time next year and Sarah will have a son."*
>
> 15 *Sarah was afraid, so she lied and said, "I did not laugh." But he said, "Yes, you did laugh."*

The group arose to leave following this interchange, but then they stopped to ask the rhetorical question in Genesis 18:17.

Genesis 18:17

> *And the LORD said, Shall I hide from Abraham that thing which I do. . .*

Sarah was just informed that she would have a child very soon but was beyond the "natural" time of this as a possibility. The promise of a son had been given to Abraham 25 years earlier, presumably through his wife, Sarah. However, it seems that the promise had been delayed with Abraham's involvement with Hagar and the birth of Ishmael. Nonetheless, God had not forgotten His promise, in spite of the misdirection by Abraham and Sarah. God reinforced the veracity or reliability of His original promise that was part of the covenant that God had established with Abraham. God's way of doing things is described in Numbers 23:19 and Romans 4:17.

Numbers 23:19

God is not a man, that he should lie; neither the son of man, that he should repent: hath he said, and shall he not do it? or hath he spoken, and shall he not make it good?

Romans 4:17 *(ERV)*

As the Scriptures say, "I have made you a father of many nations." This is true before God, the one Abraham believed—the God who gives life to the dead and speaks of things that don't yet exist as if they are real.

God does not lie. He keeps His word and makes dead things come alive. He also speaks things into existence, considering them done, even before they are seen or manifested. This is why God could speak the way He did regarding Abraham becoming the father of many nations. This is also why God could consider Abraham a person that He should inform and involve regarding situations arising in the Earth Realm. God had declared the *end result* of the covenant that He had made with Abraham, who had become His covenant partner as a result of his faith and trust in His promises to him and Sarah.

The Consultation

God saw the need to inform Abraham of the situation and what was impending in Genesis 18:17-19. A key factor was that God declared that Abraham would "keep the way of the LORD, to do justice and judgment." The authority of the Earth had been stolen from Man by Satan in the garden, but through His covenant, God had reinstated the *Earth Realm Authority* back to Abraham. This narrative revolves around a situation that arose in the cities of Sodom and Gomorrah. God stated, "Shall I hide from

Abraham that thing which I do" in Genesis 18:17. The initial impression upon reading this narrative might be that God is on His way to destroy the cities of Sodom and Gomorrah.

Genesis 18:17

And the LORD said, Shall I hide from Abraham that thing which I do:

However, a careful reading of the subsequent verses reveals something entirely different. Genesis 18:20-21 provides the explanation of what God means when referring to "that thing which I do." The wording in the *King James Version* is awkward, so an alternative version is included for comparison. The *God's Word* translation explains the situation but leaves out an important observation about the "cry" of the sin.

Genesis 18:20-21 *(GWT)*

20 The Lord also said, "Sodom and Gomorrah have many complaints against them, and their sin is very serious. 21 I must go down and see whether these complaints are true. If not, I will know it."

Genesis 18:20-21

20 And the LORD said, Because the cry of Sodom and Gomorrah is great, and because their sin is very grievous; 21 I will go down now, and see whether they have done altogether according to the cry of it, which is come unto me; and if not, I will know.

The Lord does not say that He is on His way to destroy the cities. He is going to discover the truth of what He has heard about the activities there. He was going on a fact-finding mission to find out the severity of the sin according to the "cry of it" in Genesis 18:21*(KJV)*. The "cry" of the cities was great because of the severity of their sin, but where did this cry come from? Is it possible that sin has a *spiritual voice* of its own? This may be what is described in Genesis 18:20 as the "cry of Sodom and Gomorrah." Examining scriptures in Job 1:7 and Revelation 12:10b provides clarification. Sin may indeed have a voice, but when comparing these scriptures, it is not an unreasonable stretch to see Satan as the accuser who spends his time looking for humans to accuse. He cries out to God, demanding accountability for their sins. Abraham thought that the Lord (God) was intent on destroying everyone in the city, but it was the consequence of sin that was actually calling for destruction.

Job 1:7

And the LORD said unto Satan, Whence comest thou? Then Satan answered the LORD, and said, From going to and fro in the earth, and from walking up and down in it.

Revelations 12:10 b

. . . for the accuser of our brethren is cast down, which accused them before our God day and night.

The Lord states that He is going to visit the cities personally to see if the accusations that have come before Him are true or not. He states that if they are not true, He will know. The Lord saw the need to let Abraham in on the intent of the expedition because of the authority God invested in him through the covenant agreement that He made with him. As the trio turned to depart toward Sodom and Gomorrah, Abraham blocked their way and began to plead for the inhabitants of the cities.

Abraham had a nephew named Lot who lived in Sodom along with his wife and four daughters. Their welfare was undoubtedly on Abraham's mind. Believing his family to be righteous before God, Abraham asked in Genesis 18:22-23 if the righteous would be destroyed. This is the first mention of any impending destruction. It must be understood that the Lord did not state that destruction was going to happen. Abraham assumed that destruction was going to happen as he was probably already aware of the sin in the region, and he knew the penalty that their sins would bring.

Genesis 18:22-23 *(NKJV)*

22 Then the men turned away from there and went toward Sodom, but Abraham still stood before the Lord. 23 And Abraham came near and said, "Would you also destroy the righteous with the wicked?"

The Negotiation

Next begins one of the most interesting exchanges between God and a man that is chronicled in the Bible. Abraham enters into a conversation, bargaining for the lives of the inhabitants. His attitude of compassion, care and concern is certainly one of the reasons that God made a covenant with Abraham in the first place. God also knew the character of Abraham and that he would keep the heart of the Lord in his justice and judgment. God knew that He could trust Abraham to be fair and compassionate in his judgment as He previously stated in Genesis 18:19, "For I know him, that he will command his children and his household after him, and they shall keep the way of the LORD, to do justice and judgment...."

Abraham began his negotiation at 50 individuals. Certainly, he must have thought, "Within the two cities, there must be 50 people that are righteous!" Abraham reminded God in Genesis 18:24-26 of His nature that is to save, not to destroy.

Genesis 18:24-26 *(NKJV)*

[24] Suppose there were fifty righteous within the city; would You also destroy the place and not spare it for the fifty righteous that were in it? [25] Far be it from You to do such a thing as this, to slay the righteous with the wicked, so that the righteous should be as the wicked; far be it from You! Shall not the Judge of all the earth do right?"

Abraham now had covenant authority in the earth realm. As a result, he was in a position to negotiate for the salvation of the inhabitants, and this is why the Lord told Abraham that He was going to Sodom and Gomorrah. God is in the business of saving and restoring man. Through his bargaining, Abraham had become the first intercessor of man, and he did so with his faith and the authority that God had invested in him.

Abraham continued his bargaining in Genesis 18:28-33, dropping the number of righteous to 45, and God said that if there were 45 righteous, He would not destroy it. Then, Abraham interceded for 40, then 30, then 20, and finally ten, and the Lord agreed to them all. Being content that there most certainly were ten that were righteous, he abandoned the bargaining. After all, his nephew Lot with his wife, two married daughters, two sons-in-law and two unmarried daughters, accounted for eight people in just Abraham's family alone. Surely, there must have been at least two others that were as righteous as Lot and his family!

Genesis 18:28-33 *(NKJV)*

[28] Suppose there were five less than the fifty righteous; would You destroy all of the city for lack of five?" So He said, "If I find there forty-five, I will not destroy it."

[29] And he spoke to Him yet again and said, "Suppose there should be forty found there?" So He said, "I will not do it for the sake of forty."

[30] Then he said, "Let not the Lord be angry, and I will speak: Suppose thirty

should be found there?" So He said, "I will not do it if I find thirty there."

31 *And he said, "Indeed now, I have taken it upon myself to speak to the Lord: Suppose twenty should be found there?" So He said, "I will not destroy it for the sake of twenty."*

32 *Then he said, "Let not the Lord be angry, and I will speak but once more: Suppose ten should be found there?" And He said, "I will not destroy it for the sake of ten."*

33 *So the Lord went His way as soon as He had finished speaking with Abraham; and Abraham returned to his place.*

Abraham set the parameters of judgment in the situation and declared destruction himself! God had previously declared in Genesis 18:19 that Abraham would administer justice in his judgment. Remember, the Lord told Abraham that He was going to check out the situation, not to destroy the people. Abraham stopped Him, began the process of establishing the level at which judgment would be made and declared the punishment, which was destruction. Abraham decided to stop at ten righteous in the city as he was convinced that this would save his family and the cities. He did not know that two of Lot's daughters and their husbands would seek after sin rather than God's deliverance. Thus, this meant there were only four righteous in the entirety of the two cities!

Abraham, with the authority of the earth realm invested in him through his covenant with God, was the deciding factor of the point at which judgment would be determined and of how justice would be administered. Sin was already in place and had already demanded its penalty and sentence that is death. Abraham was surely aware of this, but in faith toward God, he interceded for both the sinners and the righteous. Abraham stopped at 10. Because of the covenant and his authority, Abraham's words set the terms or parameters for *judgment* and *justice* that was demanded by the sins of the people and ultimately led to the destruction of the cities.

The Evidence Of Sin

The sins of Sodom and Gomorrah were grievous, and that is why their cry came before God. The group that came to Abraham was actually a scouting party, looking for evidence of that sin. After the negotiation or, in truth, the intercession of Abraham, the group left to go into the cities.

Lot found two of the men, angels of the Lord, whose mission was to determine the sin, save the righteous, and exact sin's punishment upon the cities. Lot compelled them to stay with him in his house, rather than on the streets. He prepared a meal for them, and they ate. Then, before they retired for the night, the people of the city proved their sin, as revealed in Genesis 19:4-5. They were all in agreement in their demands to *know* these strangers in their city. They were ready to break down the door of Lot's house to get at them. The angels were new flesh with whom they wanted to have perverted sexual relations.

Genesis 19:4-5 *(ERV)*

4 That evening, just before bedtime, men from every part of town came to Lot's house. They stood around the house and called to Lot. They said,
5 "Where are the two men who came to you tonight? Bring them out to us. We want to have sex with them."

The evidence of their sin was plainly seen by the two angels, who then declared the destruction that Abraham had negotiated in Genesis 19:13. They instructed Lot to gather his family and escape. He went to his two married daughters and their husbands, but they ignored his warning. Ultimately, only Lot, his wife, and two unmarried daughters were left and saved from the destruction.

Genesis 19:13 *(NKJV)*

For we will destroy this place, because the outcry against them has grown great before the face of the Lord, and the Lord has sent us to destroy it.

Setting Limits – The Destruction Of Sin

Sin is the destroyer, not God. God sought out a way to legally save and deliver the righteous from destruction. Destruction came, and God got the credit for it in Genesis 19:29 even though the overwhelming practice of sin by the inhabitants of the cities brought about their own destruction.

Genesis 19:29 *(ERV)*

God destroyed the cities in the valley, but he remembered what Abraham had said. So God sent Lot away from those cities before destroying them.

Abraham, God's covenant partner, determined the conditions. God made provision in his mercy, through the intercession of Abraham, to save the righteous. This was the reason that Abraham even began on this tenuous negotiation with God in the first place.

Abraham was not on a campaign to save the cities. He sought to save the righteous. He knew that there was decadence in the city. His goal was not to allow the destruction of sin to come upon the righteous as well as the sinners. His bargaining with God was to that end. He believed that there were at least eight righteous in the city because those eight people were his family. He obviously thought that there would be at least two more that Lot and his family would have influenced toward righteousness. Unfortunately, for the inhabitants of the cities, Abraham was wrong.

God agreed to every position Abraham took, and the outcome might have been far different had Abraham bargained down to four righteous persons, instead of stopping at ten. Sodom and Gomorrah might still be with us today! This in no way indicts Abraham for the actual destruction. It was just that he set the threshold through his words. Such is the power of words spoken with covenant authority in the earth realm. Abraham missed the actual number of righteous in the city, but God still found a way to bring the righteous out to safety and away from the destruction that was to come upon the sin.

Authority Realized

God's character is further revealed in this account as He is not depicted as a vindictive God, looking for ways to punish or destroy. He is shown to be a merciful and gracious God, willing to let His covenant partner exercise his rightful authority in the earth. It is not a big stretch to see that the permission for the destruction was actually established by Abraham through his bargaining with God.

God gave Adam and Eve the *lease to the planet* in the beginning. As we saw with in the garden, their faith-filled words agreed with the deception of Satan, and they brought about destruction and catastrophe on the world. Conversely, faith-filled words can agree with the guidance of God, through His mercy and grace, and reap great benefits and success. By his faith, this is what Abraham was trying to accomplish but the sin had gone beyond the point of no return for the cities. However, Lot was saved.

Faith is the power upon which God has built His kingdom, and faith is what is being spoken of in the following passage in Mark.

Mark 4:26-29 *(GNT)*

[26] *Jesus went on to say, "The Kingdom of God is like this. A man scatters seed in his field.* [27] *He sleeps at night, is up and about during the day, and all the while the seeds are sprouting and growing. Yet he does not know how it happens.* [28] *The soil itself makes the plants grow and bear fruit; first the tender stalk appears, then the head, and finally the head full of grain.* [29] *When the grain is ripe, the man starts cutting it with his sickle, because harvest time has come."*

This parable is an eloquent description of how the physical and spiritual worlds operate. By faith, man sows or plants a physical seed believing that a crop will grow. In the spiritual world seeds of faith are planted by words. The choice as to where faith seeds are planted is up to each man or woman. They can plant seeds in God or in deceptions that are against God. Either way, he or she will receive a harvest!

Abraham invested his faith in God through his acceptance of the covenant that God offered. He was then vested with the restored authority that Adam and Eve had at the beginning. The activities that occur in the earth realm are determined according to that restored authority. The descendants of Abraham exercise the power of judgment and justice within the earth realm as a result of their inheritance of his covenant either through blood line or through faith. Man is the one that calls for and executes judgment. He can either choose to forgive, restore, and save or to pronounce the parameters of when and how to apply penalties and punishments.

Ultimately, sin will be dealt with, either through having it exacted upon the sinner or applied to Jesus on the cross. The choice of where his bargaining with God takes him is up to man. He can bargain with God to receive the free gifts of grace and mercy, accepting by faith what Jesus did for him, or he can choose to pay the penalty for his own sins himself. The choice is man's alone since he has not only the authority to call for judgment, justice, and penalty, but he also has the privilege to submit to God and accept Jesus by faith. This can be a heavy burden on a person that does not understand or acknowledge this level of personal responsibility. Life happens ***to*** us if we don't take the authority that God has invested ***in*** us.

Chapter 15

TRUTH OR CONSEQUENCES

A superficial understanding of the account of Abraham, his nephew Lot, and the cities of Sodom and Gomorrah gives the impression that God is the destroyer and that He looks for the opportunity to exact punishment. Another example that looks very similar is the one set around the account of Noah and the Flood beginning in Genesis 5:29. There is a tone similar to the account of Sodom and Gomorrah within the narrative account of the flood.

Like Abraham, Noah found favor and grace in the eyes of God, and God sought out a way to preserve him. However, something else sounds similar and interesting when this experience is compared to the Sodom and Gomorrah account. God points out in Genesis 6:13 that *"the end of all flesh is come before me."* This phrasing is the same as the description of the sin in the two cities of Sodom and Gomorrah.

Genesis 6:8-13

[8] But Noah found grace in the eyes of the LORD. [9] These are the generations of Noah: Noah was a just man and perfect in his generations, and Noah walked with God. [10] And Noah begat three sons, Shem, Ham, and Japheth. [11] The earth also was corrupt before God, and the earth was filled with violence. [12] And God looked upon the earth, and, behold, it was corrupt; for all flesh had corrupted his way upon the earth.
[13] And God said unto Noah, ***The end of all flesh is come before me****; for the earth is filled with violence through them; and, behold, I will destroy them with the earth.*

God says in both situations that the cry of the sin had come before him. In Noah's time, the people were full of corruption and violence that was so severe that they were nearly begging for their own destruction. The idea of something "coming before him" gives the impression that someone or something was bringing it to His attention. It was likely that God was trying to overlook and be patient with the people engaged in the sin that was occurring, allowing them time for repentance. The adversary, Satan, undoubtedly brought about the accusations of wrongdoing just like those that were revealed in the case of Job.

The accounts of the flood and Sodom and Gomorrah chronicle faith and obedience contrasted with unrepentant sin and destruction. Both conclude that God was the one who both initiated and carried out the destruction. How then do we know whether or not God is the punisher or the forgiver? Is it simply a matter of how God feels in the morning when He gets up? At what point have you "gone too far" and when is He going to get fed up and destroy you. God is Sovereign, and He can do whatever He wants, but isn't there some way to know what He will do?

There are keys to unlocking this dilemma of understanding and we have studied some of them through the lives of Job and Abraham in the previous chapters. Through the study of Job, we discovered that Satan was the source of his grief even though Job likely opened up the door to the oppression through his words and his actions. Abraham negotiated with God to prevent an impending destruction, but the cities and their inhabitants were still laid waste. In both situations, something was brought before God for Him to make a judgment.

We are all presented with judgments or determinations to make on a daily basis. The challenge that we all face with them is intertwined with the belief system that we use to make those determinations. Belief is a very personal endeavor. As we have seen in our previous discussions, it is based on a variety of factors that may or may not be grounded in truth. If our belief is based on a lie, we are deluded and suffering from a deception of some sort.

Deception & Self-Deception

Deception takes many forms in the human experience and self-deception can be the hardest to overcome. The tangible nature of our physical experience can overwhelm us and prevent us from seeing the reality of our spiritual nature. The experience of some form of abuse or the observation of a traumatic event may deceive us into believing that God was responsible for the injustice. We may believe that God is literally out to get us! We may also have been influenced by others who have ulterior motives of control or domination toward us through *deception*.

deception *(noun)*

The action of causing someone to believe something that is not true, typically in order to gain some personal advantage.[51]

Lies or untruths may be perpetuated by some as self-serving tools to steal, gain control, deprive, or abuse. These purposeful lies are intended to deceive, but some might call them brain-washing. However, misinformation can still be spread without devious, ulterior motives. An untruth may be perpetuated simply out of ignorance of the actual truth, but regardless of motivation, it still plants seeds of deception.

Job's well-intentioned friends were full of partial truths and outright false statements in their conversations with him. None of the misstatements came from God, but He was judged falsely by Job's friends due to their ignorance or lack of understanding and knowledge. Ignorance can lead to assumptions that lead to wrong thinking and create deception, and both have the potential to turn us away from God.

In 2 Thessalonians 2:3-12, these and even more extreme levels of deception are described. The context is end times prophecy, and it speaks of the Man of Evil (the Antichrist) and the return of Jesus to the earth.

2 Thessalonians 2:3b-12 *(ERV)*

3 Don't be fooled by anything they might say. That day of the Lord will not come until the turning away from God happens. And that day will not come until the Man of Evil appears, the one who belongs to hell. 4 He will stand against and put himself above everything that people worship or think is worthy of worship. He will even go into God's Temple and sit there, claiming that he is God.

5 I told you before that all these things would happen. Remember? 6 And you know what is stopping that Man of Evil now. He is being stopped now so that he will appear at the right time. 7 The secret power of evil is already working in the world now. But there is one who is stopping that secret power of evil. And he will continue to stop it until he is taken out of the way. 8 Then that Man of Evil will appear. But the Lord Jesus will kill him with the breath that comes from his mouth. The Lord will come in a way that everyone will see, and that will be the end of the Man of Evil.

9 When that Man of Evil comes, it will be the work of Satan. He will come with great power, and he will do all kinds of false miracles, signs, and wonders. 10 The Man of Evil will use every kind of evil to fool those who are lost. They are lost because they refused to love the truth and be saved.
11 So God will send them something powerful that leads them away from the truth and causes them to believe a lie. 12 They will all be condemned because they did not believe the truth and because they enjoyed doing evil.

The Man of Evil described in these verses is empowered by Satan with the express purpose of deceiving others through spreading falsehoods of all kinds. His intent is to fool or deceive those who have already rejected Jesus and the Truth of God, preventing them from realizing their error and repenting. This man does not come to full power until something that is holding him back or restraining him is removed according to 2 Thessalonians 2:6-7. The restrainer is said to be known already according to 2 Thessalonians 2:5-6. This Restrainer is actually the Holy Spirit of God, Who came to earth as Jesus ascended into heaven.[52]

This and most other versions of the Bible then go on to say that God sent a powerful delusion to these people who were said to be rejecting Him and already lost. This powerful deception attributed to God is one "*that leads them away from the truth and causes them to believe a lie.*" The intent seems to be to assure their condemnation *"because they enjoyed doing evil."* However, as stated in 1 Timothy 2:3-6, this seems very inconsistent with God's desire. He wants everyone to be saved and fully understand the truth.

1 Timothy 2:3-6 *(ERV)*

3 This is good and pleases God our Savior. 4 God wants everyone to be saved and to fully understand the truth. 5 There is only one God, and there is only one way that people can reach God. That way is through Christ Jesus, who as a man 6 gave himself to pay for everyone to be free. This is the message that was given to us at just the right time.

Does God take part in or actively encourage the deceptions that the Man of Evil causes in 2 Thessalonians 2:3-12? If He does, then He seems to be acting against His stated purpose. However, this passage also speaks of the Restrainer, the Holy Spirit of God, being removed and allowing the

Man of Evil to take full control of the world stage, so to speak. Let's look at another translation in *The Bible in Basic English* that offers a slightly different view of God and the deceptive activity.

2 Thessalonians 2:11-12 *(BBE)*

> [11] *And for this cause, God will give them up to the power of deceit and they will put their faith in what is false:* [12] *So that they all may be judged, who had no faith in what is true, but took pleasure in evil.*

This version states God's role in another way with a significant difference in meaning. The impression in the *Easy to Read (ERV)* translation is that God is causing the deception. However, the *BBE* translation indicates that He was giving up trying to influence the people regarding the truth, and He just lets them do whatever they want. These people had gone too far, and as a result, they were beyond being influenced by God.

This view is more consistent with the removal of the Restrainer, the Holy Spirit, whose ministry is to lead us all into the truth as seen in John 14:16-17 and John 16:13-15. This removal is what allows the Man of Evil to have such influence and power to lie and deceive, and why there is no more encouragement to believe the truth.

John 14:16-17 *(ERV)*

> [15] *If you love me, you will do what I command.* [16] *I will ask the Father, and he will give you another Helper to be with you forever.* [17] *The Helper is the Spirit of truth. The people of the world cannot accept him, because they don't see him or know him. But you know him. He lives with you, and he will be in you.*

John 16:13-15 *(ERV)*

> [13] *But when the Spirit of truth comes, he will lead you into all truth. He will not speak his own words. He will speak only what he hears and will tell you what will happen in the future.* [14] *The Spirit of truth will bring glory to me by telling you what he receives from me.* [15] *All that the Father has is mine. That is why I said that the Spirit will tell you what he receives from me.*

Either way, the choice to believe or not believe is in the heart of the individual. However, people are always looking to place the blame on someone else. The deception of evil and deflection of personal accountability are the most insidious detractors from man's ability to receive

God's provision and mercy. The pleasures, distractions, and demands of this world generate intense deceptions for the sake of temporary physical pleasures. When consumed within these worldly endeavors, man thinks that he is living the high life. If man does not believe that he has a problem, then he doesn't need any help.

God did design us to enjoy physical pleasures within specific contexts. However, most of us will freely admit that the pursuit of excess in areas of physical pleasure will ultimately lead to addiction and a great deal of dissatisfaction. These excesses can be found in alcohol, drug, sports, sex, gambling, or the pursuit of wealth at all cost through business or crime. These are all very unhealthy pursuits and in many, if not most cases, actually can become the *god* of the individual. These deceptions and distractions are designed to destroy the fulfillment of our relationship with the one true God.

Deception is a powerful tool that the adversary, Satan, has used from the beginning of human existence. His deceptions are designed to keep people from experiencing the plan of God in their lives. Effective lies combine deception with just enough truth to make them believable. That is why they are so dangerous, especially when a person internalizes the lie and makes it a foundational part of his or her own belief system. This belief is the height of self-deception and the most insidious of all.

Self-deception occurs when a known lie is accepted as truth through denial or ignorance. This kind of deception is summed up in the adage, *"Don't confuse me with the truth, I have already made up my mind!"*

self-deception *(noun)*

> *The action or practice of allowing oneself to believe that a false or unvalidated feeling, idea or situation is true.*[53]

It is very hard, if not impossible, to seek a relationship with God while entrapped by deception and overwhelmed by the world around us. This entrapment is set in motion by rebellion against someone or something and is experienced by every man, woman, and child on the earth. Rebellion is spawned by Satan (also known as Lucifer), the adversary of God, who first lifted himself up in opposition to God as seen in Isaiah 14:12-14 *(see p. 71)*.

He arose to lift up his will in defiance of God, challenging God's authority. This proud, egotistical, arrogant, and self-willed attitude was instilled in all of human kind by the sin of Adam and Eve, and it has corrupted the world's development. It is rebellion against the authority and the very being of God. It is sin, and it ultimately leads to death. Like Satan, humans are created beings. Each had an origin. The God of the Bible is credited with the origin or creation of all as we see in the accounts of Genesis 1:1 - 5:2. He created the heavens and the spiritual beings in the heavenlies. Then, He turned to the earth and created the vegetation and all of the animals and creatures of the earth. Lastly, he created Man.

Can a computer somehow tell the one that built it that it will make itself to be equal with or even superior to its builder? There are certainly aspects of a computer that are superior to the speed and abilities of its creator (man), but a computer does not possess a free will. It functions as a result of specific instructions or programming. However, its creator can still exercise its authority over a potentially rebellious computer by turning it off or pulling the plug!

What can be said for the creation (man or angels) trying to exalt itself against God the Creator? Unlike man with his computer, God does not pull the plug. He is patient, waiting for man to come around. The pulling of man's plug or his destruction is left to his own free will choices. To believe otherwise is to be deceived and to believe a lie.

The Will To Choose Rightly

God has been very careful and precise in explaining the choices, providing numerous examples in His Word for our consideration and benefit. He created mankind to enjoy, not to destroy. Self-deception leads to challenging the authority and power of God in a futile exercise that can only lead to the plug being pulled by the destruction of sin. Free will acknowledgment and submission to God's preeminence and authority overcomes deception inspired rebellion, letting us enjoy the freedom God provides.

As history has unfolded, it is apparent that the adversary's goal has not been to gather companions in his rebellion. He simply wants to come against God by bringing destruction upon as many of His human creations as he can. The adversary, Satan, actually has no power to do physical actions to man. He can only influence him and his decisions. Seeing that the consequence of sin is death, the adversary seeks to have humans destroy themselves before they have the opportunity to encounter the mercy, forgiveness, and provision of God.

Fear, apathy, doubt, deception, and denial are just some of the tools that are used to prevent a person from even discovering the relationship that God offers. Distraction, tradition, rationalization, and complacency are some of the weapons that are employed for the destruction of those who have entered into a covenant relationship with God. Such is the situation in which Lot found himself as he became entangled within the culture of Sodom and Gomorrah. Lot was aware of Abraham's covenant relationship with God. Abraham shared in the promise of that covenant with Lot when he and Lot parted company many years before. Abraham actually gave Lot the preferential treatment and allowed him to choose the region in which he would live. The difference was that Abraham stayed with God, and Lot became intertwined with a decadent society.

Lot seemed to have maintained his righteousness before God in the midst of a great deal of sin as he did not personally partake in the activities of the city. However, Lot apparently did not influence his children in the same way as Abraham did. Some of Lot's children went deeply astray into the sinful world of Sodom and Gomorrah. In Genesis 18:19, God spoke of Abraham in a different light saying, "For I know him, that he will command his children and his household after him, and they shall keep the way of the LORD, to do justice and judgment; that the LORD may bring upon Abraham that which he hath spoken of him". This is just one of the reasons that God made the covenant with Abraham, not Lot.

Two of Lot's daughters were married. Either they or their husbands must have taken some part in the sexual perversion that was prevalent in the city. When given the opportunity to flee the impending penalty of the collective sin of the cities, they and their husbands chose to stay in their lifestyle. The mercies afforded them by a relationship as daughters of Lot were overridden by their free will decision to reject rescue from the impending penalty of sin upon the cities.

Abraham entered into what he thought was a bargaining conversation, and he concluded that there would certainly be ten righteous in the city. However, he was not bargaining or even interceding. He was actually setting the parameters upon which a sentence would be imposed, based on the judgment or determination of sin. The corporate sin demanded to be judged and sentenced, and it was this cry of the sin that had come before God.

Destruction did not come upon the cities because of a whim of God. It came because of the magnitude of the cooperative sin that pervaded the cities. The people were in complete agreement in their sins. They were oblivious to the consequences of their sins. They deceived themselves into believing that if everyone was doing it, it must be okay. This is certainly a dangerous place to be as a society when agreement to commit sin is made acceptable through social attitudes or legislation, and it is still occurring today.

God had set out to determine (or judge) the accuracy of the accusations, but Abraham actually set the threshold for the number upon whom the judgment or determination would be assessed. The judgment of God yielded the determination of the truth that the sin was as it was described. As a result, the penalty for the sin could no longer be withheld. Those who chose to stay voluntarily determined to pit their own will against God's law, authority, and advice just as Lucifer had done. Sin's penalty came due, and they lost.

The character of God is one of patience, longsuffering, mercy, and forgiveness. He actively engages in activity on behalf of man to rescue him from himself. Some will respond to God's call, and His provision for them, and some will reject it in favor of their own will and the pleasures that they can experience on the earth. God set out to bring awareness of the situation of the cities' impending doom to Abraham, His man on the earth. Abraham was a new legal authority by virtue of his faith and the covenant, and his authority would set the boundaries for the legal actions taken against sin.

The consequence of sin, however, had been long before determined. God's desire was to impart mercy, but it was rejected by those in the city, including part of Lot's family. However, God did not *react* to the rejection. He *could no longer hold back* the penalties after the gravity of the sin cried out, and Abraham set the boundaries. God did not destroy the people or the cities. They were in the path of the penalty for sin. In truth, they destroyed themselves as a result of their choices. They were self-deceived, believing that they had nothing about which to worry. They put themselves in the path of the sentence because they refused to *repent* and change direction.

Lot escaped the destruction of the cities with his wife and two of his daughters because of his decision to walk in God's Law and according to His commands. It turned out that Abraham's bargaining should have gone down to three righteous within the cities if the cities were to have been spared the consequence of their grievous sins. Only three were to make it out unscathed. As Lot's wife looked back toward the city, she was undoubtedly looking back with some longing or misgivings in her heart about leaving. Her faltering gaze caused her to be turned into a pillar of salt. She paid the price for her own sin as did the inhabitants of Sodom and Gomorrah. Safety and preservation were offered but refused.

The account of Lot and Sodom and Gomorrah has application in your life. The principles are the same even though the circumstance are different. It is guaranteed that if you do not walk in the *Truth,* you will suffer the *Consequences* of your sins, and the natural penalty for your own sins is death. You are hopelessly unable to walk perfectly in the *Truth* on your own, but God has always endeavored to make a way. Ultimately, He gave Jesus as a sacrifice so that all that believe in Him might be forgiven and freed from the penalty of death. He died your death for you so that your sin penalty would be paid. It is not in your best interest to refuse His gift because He saved you from yourself!

You can follow in the path of God's Truth, accept the gift He has provided through Jesus' sacrifice and be successful, prosperous, blessed, and forgiven. The plan of the God of the Bible is to rescue, forgive, save, deliver, and restore. Is He the God that you know? Or if you prefer, you can blow Him off and enjoy the consequences that your own actions legally demand. Check your motivation, your allegiance, your vision, and your faith. Do not be deceived. Understand the struggle that is going on to take your life from you. Deception is a tactic of the adversary. Be careful what you attribute to God. He is there ***for*** you, not against you.

Truth or consequences, the choice is yours.

And He opened their understanding, that they might comprehend the Scriptures.

Luke 24:45 NKJV

Chapter 16

NO GOOD DEED GOES UNPUNISHED ?

The record of Uzzah provides us with another account of something evil that is attributed to *the anger and the hand of God*. As we have seen in previous chapters, the perspective of the viewer is largely in play, when observations and conclusions are made regarding events. The events that we will now consider are the actions that terminated the life of Uzzah. Therefore, some historical perspective and some understanding of who Uzzah was will be helpful before exploring the specifics of this event.

Uzzah was just trying to do a good deed by preventing the destruction of the Ark of the Covenant. However, things went terribly wrong for him due to *the anger of the Lord*. In 2 Samuel 6:7 we read that "God struck him" and he lost his life.

> **2 Samuel 6:7** *(NKJV)*
> *Then the* ***anger of the Lord was aroused against Uzzah****, and* ***God struck him there for his error****; and he died there by the ark of God.*

So why did he die for his efforts, spent on a good deed, protecting something as valuable as the Ark of the Covenant? As we delve into this account, we will make some discoveries that may give the reader pause in attributing the death of Uzzah to a whim of God's wrath.

The Back Story

Jacob, the grandson of Abraham, had 12 sons, who subsequently established the twelve tribes of Israel. Joseph, one of his sons, was given the honor of representing two half-tribes, through his sons Ephraim and Manasseh. Each of the twelve tribes had been given designated territories, but one tribe, the tribe of Levi, did not have a territory as described in Numbers 1:47-51. The result was still twelve territories since the tribe of Levi was without land, and the half-tribes of Ephraim and Manasseh each had separate territories.

Numbers 1:47-51 *(MSG)*

[47] The Levites, however, were not counted by their ancestral family along with the others. [48] God had told Moses, [49] "The tribe of Levi is an exception: Don't register them. Don't count the tribe of Levi; don't include them in the general census of the People of Israel. [50] Instead, appoint the Levites to be in charge of The Dwelling of The Testimony — over all its furnishings and everything connected with it. Their job is to carry The Dwelling and all its furnishings, maintain it, and camp around it. [51] When it's time to move The Dwelling, the Levites will take it down, and when it's time to set it up, the Levites will do it. Anyone else who even goes near it will be put to death.

Although the tribe of Levi was without land, they had the charge of being priests of the portable tent that was the temple of God. It was also known as the *Dwelling of The Testimony* or the *tabernacle* of God. Their responsibility covered service within the temple, singing of psalms, managing offerings, maintaining the articles of service and worship. Deuteronomy 10:8-9 explains that their duties also included the keeping of the Ark of the Covenant in which were kept the laws of Moses (Ten Commandments written in stone) and a jar of manna, the food that God provided the Israelites in the desert after leaving Egypt (Exodus 16:15). The Ark also included the rod of Aaron, which was used first against Pharaoh's magicians in Egypt (Exodus 7-8) and again following the rebellion of Korah (Numbers 17:8) *(see p. 339 and Appendix Chapter 25)*.

Deuteronomy 10:8-9

[8] At that time the LORD separated the tribe of Levi, to bear the ark of the covenant of the LORD, to stand before the LORD to minister unto him, and to bless in his name, unto this day. [9] Wherefore Levi hath no part nor inheritance with his brethren; the LORD is his inheritance, according as the LORD thy God promised him.

There were specific rules and regulations for the execution of their duties, with great care being given to each activity. The Ark itself was one such article, having a particularly stringent set of regulations and stipulations. The building plans for the Ark are detailed in Exodus 25:10-16.

Exodus 25:10-16 *(GNT)*

10 Make a Box out of acacia wood, 45 inches long, 27 inches wide, and 27 inches high. 11 Cover it with pure gold inside and out and put a gold border all around it. 12 Make four carrying rings of gold for it and attach them to its four legs, with two rings on each side. 13 Make carrying poles of acacia wood and cover them with gold 14 and put them through the rings on each side of the Box. 15 The poles are to be left in the rings and must not be taken out. 16 Then put in the Box the two stone tablets that I will give you, on which the commandments are written.

All of the activities of the temple and the handling of the Ark and the articles of the temple were dedicated to the Levites. Mishandling of these articles would result in death. The sons of Kohath, the grandsons of Levi, could only *transport* the sanctuary and the vessels that were portable, but they *could not touch* any of the Holy things according to Numbers 4:15. The privilege and responsibilities of personal, human contact with these items were reserved only for the high priest at the time.

Numbers 4:15

And when Aaron and his sons have made an end of covering the sanctuary, and all the vessels of the sanctuary, as the camp is to set forward; after that, the sons of Kohath shall come to bear it: but they shall not touch any holy thing, lest they die. These things are the burden of the sons of Kohath in the tabernacle of the congregation.

We now have a little understanding of the requirements that God put in place regarding the holy things of the tabernacle, and there was a consequence attached to mishandling them. The consequence was death. There are at least two ways that this death penalty could be viewed. First, in the traditional sense, God was ready to punish an offender by taking the offender's life. Second, God was issuing a warning that there were forces at work surrounding these *holy things,* and if mishandled, the death of the offender would result.

Other things that we deal with today also require specialized handling. For example, a lack of understanding of the destructive potential of radiation does not prevent injury or death. If proper protocols are not followed due to carelessness or lack of knowledge, a person may be overexposed to a radiation source. Ignorance is no excuse for a breach of protocol when handling a "hazardous" item or situation and could result in the death of the individual. With this in mind, let's take a detailed look at the events that cost Uzzah his life.

The Ark Of The Covenant

The Ark of the Covenant had been lost in battle around 1050 BC and had been carried away by the Philistines when they defeated Israel in battle as described in 1 Samuel 4:10-11. David, the King of Israel, decided some 60 years later that it was time to reclaim the Ark. He gathered together thirty thousand of his chosen men to go out and recover this Holy possession of Israel from its captors. His men were successful and recovered the Ark. He wanted the Ark returned to the City of David, which is Jerusalem, and certainly wanted to treat it with the great respect that it was due. Therefore, he commissioned a new, presumably unused cart on which to set the Ark for transport back to Jerusalem. There is no discussion of the procedure that was used to place the Ark on the cart, but this part of the process most certainly went without incident.

Following its recovery, the Ark had resided in the house of Abinadab for 20 years under the care of Abinadab's son Eleazar (1 Samuel 7:1-2). As Abinadab's house was the caretaker of the Ark, it would be reasonable to assume that his two other sons, Uzzah and Ahio, were also aware of and had probably seen the Ark. David gave instructions for Abinadab's family to transport the Ark. As they set out on the journey, Ahio led the way in front, with Uzzah apparently beside the cart carrying the Ark.

There was a great celebration with fanfare and with music of all sorts and singing. Then, the unthinkable happened in the midst of the celebration. The oxen that were pulling the cart stumbled, apparently shaking the cart and threatening to topple the Ark from the cart. This is where Uzzah made his fatal mistake. He attempted to steady the Ark on the cart with his hand. The full account of this event involving Uzzah is found in two places in the Old Testament: 2 Samuel 6 and 1 Chronicles 13. For the sake of simplicity, only the account found in 2 Samuel is included here.

2 Samuel 6:1-7 *(NKJV)*

> 1 *Again David gathered all the choice men of Israel, thirty thousand.*
> 2 *And David arose and went with all the people who were with him from*
> *Baale Judah to bring up from there the ark of God, whose name is called by*
> *the Name, the Lord of Hosts, who dwells between the cherubim.* 3 *So they*
> *set the ark of God* ***on a new cart****, and brought it out of the* ***house of***
> ***Abinadab****, which was on the hill; and* ***Uzzah and Ahio, the sons***
> ***of Abinadab, drove the new cart****.* 4 *And they brought it out of the*
> *house of Abinadab, which was on the hill, accompanying the ark of God;*
> *and A****hio went before the ark****.* 5 *Then David and all the house of*
> *Israel played music before the Lord on all kinds of instruments of fir wood,*
> *on harps, on stringed instruments, on tambourines, on sistrums, and on*
> *cymbals.* 6 *And when they came to Nachon's threshing floor,* ***Uzzah put***
> ***out his hand to the ark of God and took hold of it, for the oxen***
> ***stumbled****.* 7 *Then the* ***anger of the Lord was aroused against Uz-***
> ***zah****, and* ***God struck him there for his error****; and he died there by*
> *the ark of God.*

Apparently, Uzzah was trying to save the Ark from damage or destruction. All he did was raise his hand to steady the Ark and prevent it from falling from the cart, but in doing so, he touched the Ark. So why did this seemingly insignificant action cost him his life when his intentions were honorable? Uzzah died because the protocols for the handling of the Ark that were established by God were broken in certain areas.

God laid out a list of very specific details that were to be observed for the handling of the Ark. First let's look at the mode of transportation used for the Ark. It was never intended to be placed on a cart of any sort, new, or otherwise. The direction was that it would be carried by men, priests of God, from the tribe of Levi. Putting the Ark on the cart was one mistake or breach of the protocols.

Another breach of protocol was not using the poles to transport the Ark. We saw earlier in Exodus 25 that rings of gold had been placed on the side of the Ark. Staves or poles that were overlaid with gold were to be placed into the rings, and the poles were not to be removed. The Ark was to be lifted by the poles and transported on foot by the Levites.

Another breach occurred, one relative to those who were chosen to transport the Ark. The Levites had the responsibility and charge by God to transport the *Holy Things*. Was Uzzah a descendent of the tribe of Levi?

The Genealogy Of Uzzah

Understanding who is responsible for the death of Uzzah is important. It is revealed through the examination of his lineage. Uzzah and his brother Ahio were the sons of Abinadab, whose father was Jesse. King David was the youngest son of Jesse and Uzzah's father, Abinadab, was David's older brother. Jesus is a descendant of Jesse by way of David. David and Uzzah's lineages are traced back to Judah, a son of Jacob (Israel), one of the twelve tribes in Chronicles Chapter 2. Judah and Levi were brothers, each representing one of the twelve tribes. As we saw in Deuteronomy 10, God separated out Levi and his descendants for service as priests to Him. They alone were given the responsibility of the tabernacle and the Ark. Levi was not provided a physical inheritance among the tribes, so he and his family could dedicate themselves to God's service. As we see in the following chart from 1 Chronicles 2:3-13, neither King David nor his cousin Uzzah were of the lineage of Levi.

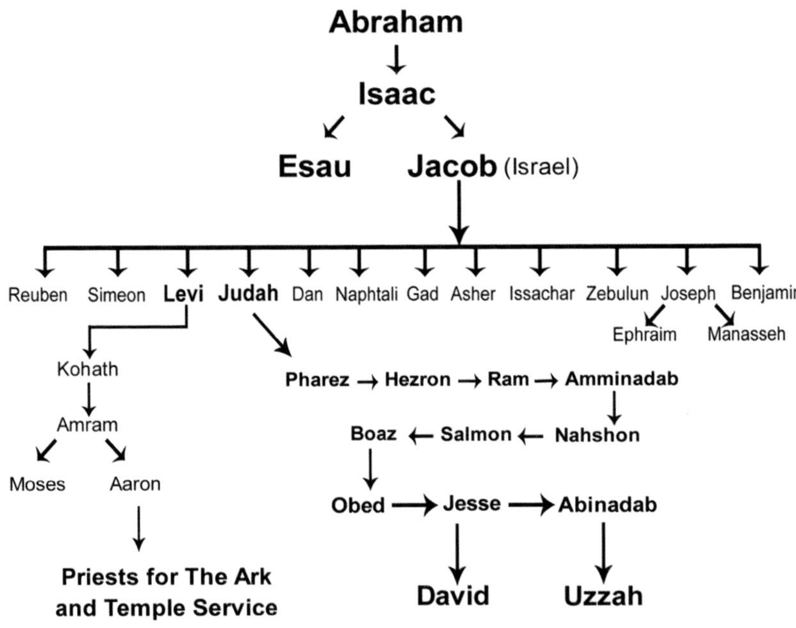

The Genealogy Of Uzzah –1 Chronicles 2:3-13

We now see three things that were not done according to the protocols that God had established for the handling of the Ark. The first was the mode of transport. The Ark was placed on the cart rather than being carried by men on foot. The second was the lack of use of the poles to lift it, and the third was that the transporters were men from the tribe of Judah, not Levi. These were all serious breaches of God's protocols. Uzzah's life was the price that was paid because God's warning was not heeded. King David was the man in charge and was responsible for seeing to it that these protocols were followed. So let's look at David's reaction to the event described in 2 Samuel 6:8-11.

2 Samuel 6:8-11

> [8] *And David was displeased, because the LORD had made a breach upon Uzzah: and he called the name of the place Perezuzzah to this day.*
>
> [9] *And David was afraid of the LORD that day, and said, How shall the*
> *ark of the LORD come to me?* [10] *So David would not remove the ark of the*
> *LORD unto him into the city of David: but David carried it aside into the*
> *house of Obededom the Gittite.* [11] *And the ark of the LORD continued in*
> *the house of Obededom the Gittite three months: and the LORD blessed*
> *Obededom, and all his household.*

David was understandably unhappy about the death of Uzzah and stated that God had *made a breach* upon Uzzah. This attribution of making a breach to God was tantamount to accusing God of making a violation or infraction upon Uzzah. In reality, the infraction or breach was actually one of ignorance or carelessness on the part of David and Uzzah, not God. David recoils from the problem. He sets the Ark aside so that he can assess the situation, placing it into the house of Obededom.

David Recognizes The Problem

David figured out what the problem was and made adjustments to get it right. He moved the Ark to the house of Obededom, a Gittite who likely protected David while he was being pursued by King Saul. Obededom enjoyed great blessings for himself and his household as a result of taking care of the Ark. David then reassembled the transport team according to the protocols that God had established. His efforts are described in 1 Chronicles 15:1-3, 11-28. David called upon the chief priests and the chief fathers of the Levites to sanctify themselves so that they could bring up the Ark. David pointed out that because the protocol was not followed, and they did not seek after God in due order, the breach occurred.

1 Chronicles 15:1-3

[1] And David made him houses in the city of David, and prepared a place for the ark of God, and pitched for it a tent. [2] Then David said, None ought to carry the ark of God but the Levites: for them hath the LORD chosen to carry the ark of God, and to minister unto him for ever. [3] And David gathered all Israel together to Jerusalem, to bring up the ark of the LORD unto his place, which he had prepared for it.

1 Chronicles 15:11-13

[11] And David called for Zadok and Abiathar the priests, and for the Levites, for Uriel, Asaiah, and Joel, Shemaiah, and Eliel, and Amminadab,
[12] And said unto them, Ye are the chief of the fathers of the Levites: sanctify yourselves, both ye and your brethren, that ye may bring up the ark of the LORD God of Israel unto the place that I have prepared for it. [13] For because ye did it not at the first, the LORD our God made a breach upon us, for that we sought him not after the due order.

The new protocol for the second attempt to transport the Ark was according to the instructions given by God. The sanctified priests and Levites carried the Ark upon their shoulders, using the staves as directed by God through Moses, and the event was a success.

1 Chronicles 15:14-15

[14] So the priests and the Levites sanctified themselves to bring up the ark of the LORD God of Israel. [15] And the children of the Levites bare the ark of God upon their shoulders with the staves thereon, as Moses commanded according to the word of the LORD.

Many of those Levites were named for their part in the process, along with those who gave thanks and praised God with music and singing.

1 Chronicles 15:17-24

[17] So the Levites appointed Heman the son of Joel; and of his brethren, Asaph the son of Berechiah; and of the sons of Merari their brethren, Ethan the son of Kushaiah; [18] And with them their brethren of the second degree, Zechariah, Ben, and Jaaziel, and Shemiramoth, and Jehiel, and Unni, Eliab, and Benaiah, and Maaseiah, and Mattithiah, and Elipheleh, and Mikneiah, and Obededom, and Jeiel, the porters. [19] So the singers, Heman, Asaph, and Ethan, were appointed to sound with cymbals of brass; And Zechariah, and Aziel, and Shemiramoth, and Jehiel, and Unni, and Eliab, and Maaseiah, and Benaiah, with psalteries on Alamoth; [20] And Mattithiah, and Elipheleh, and Mikneiah, and Obededom, and Jeiel, and

Azaziah, with harps on the Sheminith to excel. [21] And Chenaniah, chief of the Levites, was for song: he instructed about the song, because he was skilful. [23] And Berechiah and Elkanah were doorkeepers for the ark. [24] And Shebaniah, and Jehoshaphat, and Nethaneel, and Amasai, and Zechariah, and Benaiah, and Eliezer, the priests, did blow with the trumpets before the ark of God: and Obededom and Jehiah were doorkeepers for the ark.

Great celebration ensued with the bringing forth of this vital piece of evidence of the covenant that God had made with His people, Israel. The transport from the house of Obededom was far different than the first attempt that resulted in the death of Uzzah.

1 Chronicles 15:25-28

[25] So David, and the elders of Israel, and the captains over thousands, went to bring up the ark of the covenant of the LORD out of the house of Obededom with joy. [26] And it came to pass, when God helped the Levites that bare the ark of the covenant of the LORD, that they offered seven bullocks and seven rams. [27] And David was clothed with a robe of fine linen, and all the Levites that bare the ark, and the singers, and Chenaniah the master of the song with the singers: David also had upon him an ephod of linen. [28] Thus all Israel brought up the ark of the covenant of the LORD with shouting, and with sound of the cornet, and with trumpets, and with cymbals, making a noise with psalteries and harps.

A "Knowledge" Problem

Uzzah and Ahio grew up with the presence of the Ark of the Covenant in their household since the Ark was present with their father, Abinidab, for 20 years. It is possible that there was a familiarity that they acquired and possibly even a sense of *ownership* of sorts. Obviously, there was a lack of knowledge regarding the handling and protocols that surrounded the Ark, and it is this lack of knowledge that led to Uzzah's destruction. So who actually killed Uzzah? Was it really the *anger* of God that caused a *breach*? Perhaps it was the playing out of the warning of Hosea 4:6, which is very applicable here.

Hosea 4:6

My people are destroyed for lack of knowledge...

Uzzah's lack of knowledge about the consequences of his action made him culpable, but it appears that he was *just following orders*, orders that came down from David, the King. As the King, David had a level of responsibility to God. There was an expectation that he understood the protocols that the handling of the Ark required. He was at very least required to consult with his advisors, the priests, about such matters. It is evident that he did not do so since he freely admitted that the breach had occurred because of a lack of following the *due order*.

It would, therefore, be no stretch of logic or interpretation to see that God was not the culprit in the death of Uzzah. God was not issuing a proclamation of punishment that would occur as a result of an errant activity. He was issuing a warning because He knew what would happen if things were not done according to protocol. Once again, the perspective or prejudice of the observer has attributed an act of violence and destruction to God. However, this was not the case. It was completely in the hands of the individuals involved in the activity. God continually makes warnings to save people from destruction, not to lead them into it.

The way in which you view God determines whether you see Him as your protector or your punisher. A change in your thought process realizing that God is truly "looking out" for you helps you to understand where the responsibility for consequences really lies. Ever since Adam and Eve ate of the "Tree of the Knowledge of Good and Evil," their descendants have been responsible for the consequences of a lack of knowledge. Couple a lack of knowledge with ego or fear, and that deadly combination can lead you to your own destruction as we will see in the next chapter.

CHAPTER 17

THE NUMBERING OF ISRAEL
A THREAT ASSESSMENT

Conflicts of description or narrative occasionally occur in the Bible. These can cause challenges in light of a belief that every word in the Bible is inspired by God and that no error exists. Consider the discussion of Job in Chapter 11 which concluded that everything in the Bible is truly stated, but not necessarily true. One such situation of conflict is found in the record of David's numbering of Israel or the taking of a census. Two accounts of the event are found in the Bible. The first is found in 2 Samuel 24 and the second in 1 Chronicles 21. These two chapters describe the same event, but they provide differing perspectives as to who was involved in instigating the activity.

Every word in the Bible is truly spoken in that it is a true representation of the activities of a particular event and the words spoken. However, those words may not necessarily be an accurate reflection of the truth of the situation. Even when the narrative presents something that is not reflective of the truth, there is a reason for its presence in the Bible. Careful study can reveal hidden truth within the text, and it can also provide a great deal of insight into God and His character and nature. Questions arise when the accounts of 2 Samuel 24 and 1 Chronicles 21 are examined. The answers will provide insight into the apparent contradiction.

- *"Why is there a discrepancy between the two accounts?"*
- *"What is the problem?"*
- *"Moses took a census but was not considered to have sinned, so why was it a sin for David to take a census?"*

Other more basic questions to determine what is going on might be:

- *"Who are the respective authors of these two books?"*
- *"What is the perspective of each writer?"*

There is speculation among scholars regarding the authorship of these books. Two likely co-authors of 2 Samuel are identified as contemporaries of David. The first was Gad the Seer, one of the prophets of David, and the second was Nathan, another prophet, who played some notable roles during the reign of David. The book of 1 Chronicles is attributed to the prophet Ezra and was written about 400 years after this event.

Who Did It?

The account in 2 Samuel 24:1 begins by stating that God's anger was directed against Israel. It attributes the prompting to take the census to the Lord or Yahweh (Strong's OT:3068).

"Jehovah" - *Strong's* OT:3068 יְהֹוָה, Yehovah (yeh-ho-vaw');
from OT:1961; (the) self-Existent or Eternal; Jehovah, Jewish national name of God: KJV - Jehovah, the Lord.

Although they were written 400 years apart, the narrative of the two accounts is consistent except in one crucial point. The motivation for David's census is different and the source is noted at the beginning of each account. A comparison of the texts beginning with 2 Samuel 24:1-4 reveals that both perspectives cannot be correct because they clearly attribute the causation to two greatly differing sources.

2 Samuel 24:1-4 (*Author probably Gad or Nathan)*
[1] And again ***the anger of the LORD was kindled against Israel,***
and he moved David against them to say, Go, number Israel and Judah.
[2] For the king said to Joab the captain of the host, which was with him,
Go now through all the tribes of Israel, from Dan even to Beersheba, and
number ye the people, that I may know the number of the people. [3] And
Joab said unto the king, Now the LORD thy God add unto the people,
how many soever they be, an hundredfold, and that the eyes of my lord the
king may see it: but why doth my lord the king delight in this thing? [4]
Notwithstanding the king's word prevailed against Joab, and against the
captains of the host. And Joab and the captains of the host went out from
the presence of the king, to number the people of Israel.

In stark contrast to 2 Samuel, the 1 Chronicles account attributes the provocation to Satan (Strong's OT:7854). Satan, sometimes translated adversary, is always associated with evil while God (the Lord or Yahweh) is sometimes associated with both good and evil.

"satan", - *Strong's* OT:7854 שָׂטָן, *satan* (saw-tawn'), from OT:7853;
an opponent; especially (with the article prefixed) Satan, the arch-enemy of good: KJV-- adversary, Satan, withstand.

The apparent conflict between these two accounts clearly produces some serious confusion. In the 2 Samuel account, God was considered the adversary of David and Israel. Understanding who prompted David's action is essential since in 1 Chronicles 21:1-4 Ezra describes a very different scenario, casting Satan as the adversary.

1 Chronicles 21:1-4 *(Likely author is the Prophet Ezra)*
1 ***And Satan stood up against Israel, and provoked David*** *to*
number Israel. 2 And David said to Joab and to the rulers of the people, Go,
number Israel from Beersheba even to Dan; and bring the number of them
to me, that I may know it. 3 And Joab answered, The LORD make his people
an hundred times so many more as they be: but, my lord the king, are
they not all my lord's servants? why then doth my lord require this thing?
why will he be a cause of trespass to Israel? 4 Nevertheless the king's word
prevailed against Joab. Wherefore Joab departed, and went throughout all
Israel, and came to Jerusalem.

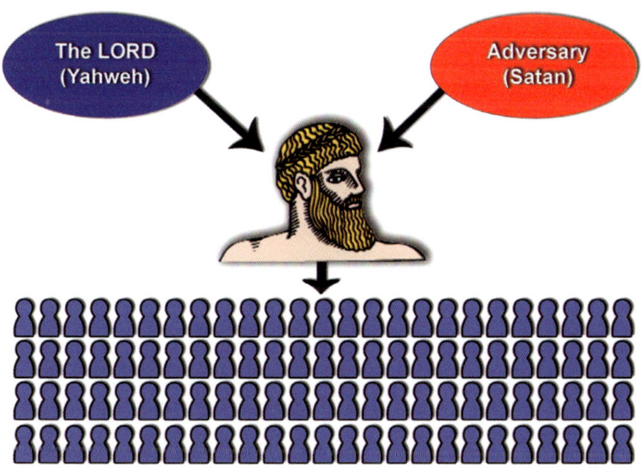

Who prompted David to take a census to count his fighting forces?
Did God want to make him sin or was it a deception of Satan?

Some might say that God is responsible either way since He created everything, including Satan. However, God is not just playing a cosmic chess game with the lives of mankind. If God is viewed through that lens, man is just a puppet for God's amusement. One account portrays God as both good and evil, and the other clearly shows evil in the camp of the adversary, Satan. Where then, does the responsibility for the prompting of David lie? With God or with Satan? Examination of these two accounts certainly generates some concerns. These concerns might be answered by studying the observational context of the writers as we did in the discussions of relativity, the ping pong players, the cars and the stationary observers in Chapter 6 *(see p. 47)*.

The Authors

The perspective and understanding of the authors of 2 Samuel and 1 Chronicles differed greatly. Gad and Nathan were part of the court of David, sharing the experiences of the events that took place. They were direct observers or eyewitnesses of the events. Gad was very much involved in the activities as he later brought choices of punishment to David for his sin. Either Gad or Nathan, as potential reporters of the event, brought a very close, experiential perspective of the events. Their eyewitness descriptions lend credence to the accuracy of the 2 Samuel account that attributes the instigation of the sinful event to God. There are times, however, when being close to a situation is actually a detriment to the understanding of it as with the saying, "You can't see the forest for the trees." This paradigm was seen in the discussion of the events in Job's life earlier in this book. However, the veracity or accuracy of either account may even cause doubts in the mind of the reader because of the discrepancy.

Ezra was removed from the events by some 400+ years. He was undoubtedly familiar with the eyewitness account of 2 Samuel but was not influenced by emotions or the relationships that Gad and Nathan had with David. Ezra viewed the events more objectively as he rewrote the account from a historical perspective, through the magnifying glass of time which made the underlying motivation for David's action clear.

Faith vs. Fear

It is important to understand why the numbering or census of Israel in 1 Chronicles was a trespass or sin before delving deeper into the matter of perspective. Even though there is a clear conflict in motivation depicted in the two narratives, why is there even a problem with David calling for a census? In the book of Genesis, Moses initiated the taking of a census, but his census was not considered evil or sinful. Moses was living under the covenant God established with Abraham, but he was also in direct contact with God. David was also living and operating under the promise made to Abraham as well as the Law that Moses brought from God. Genesis 13:14-16 and 15:5 describe some of the conditions of the covenant with Abraham under which both David and Moses were living.

Genesis 13:14-16

[14] And the LORD said unto Abram, after that Lot was separated from him, Lift up now thine eyes, and look from the place where thou art northward, and southward, and eastward, and westward: [15] For all the land which thou seest, to thee will I give it, and to thy seed for ever. [16] ***And I will make thy seed as the dust of the earth: so that if a man can number the dust of the earth, then shall thy seed also be numbered*****.**

Genesis 15:5 *(NIV)*

He took him outside and said, "Look up at the heavens and count the stars-- ***if indeed you can count them****." Then he said to him, "So shall your offspring be."*

Both Moses and David were living under the same law and promise, but there were differences between these two censuses. An examination of the underlying conditions and covenants will provide a more comprehensive understanding of David's problem as we see that the *motivations* for the two census actions were actually quite different.

David's faith in God guided his actions and began long before his reign. He had an encounter with a bear and a lion that were attacking his father's sheep. The young shepherd boy relied on his faith in God and killed both of the attackers with his bare hands. He honored his father and took the job he had as a sheepherder very seriously. He gave God credit for empowering him to prevail against his enemy. He told King Saul that because of his faith and the success that God gave him, he would have no problem defeating a foe of Israel, Goliath the Philistine. He declared his confidence in 1 Samuel 17:32-37 because God would be with him.

1 Samuel 17:32-37 *(TLB)*

[32] "Don't worry about a thing," David told him. "I'll take care of this Philistine!" [33] "Don't be ridiculous!" Saul replied. "How can a kid like you fight with a man like him? You are only a boy, and he has been in the army since he was a boy!" [34] But David persisted. "When I am taking care of my

> *father's sheep," he said, "and a lion or a bear comes and grabs a lamb from the flock, [35] I go after it with a club and take the lamb from its mouth. If it turns on me, I catch it by the jaw and club it to death. [36] I have done this to both lions and bears, and I'll do it to this heathen Philistine too, for he has defied the armies of the living God! [37] The Lord who saved me from the claws and teeth of the lion and the bear will save me from this Philistine!" Saul finally consented, "All right, go ahead," he said, "and may the Lord be with you!"*

David was ultimately victorious against Goliath, a trained soldier, because he relied upon the Lord for his strength. He rose to become the King of Israel as he demonstrated his faith, living in the covenant he had with God through Abraham. However, David was not perfect and encountered several faith "speed bumps" along the way. One of them likely created the reason that the census detailed in 1 Chronicles and 2 Samuel was an offense to God and considered to be a sin.

David's Verdict

Before to the incident of the numbering of Israel, David decided to steal another man's wife (2 Samuel 11-12). He saw a woman bathing herself on a rooftop and was immediately overcome with lust. He inquired as to her identity. He was told that her name was Bath-sheba and that she was the wife of Uriah, one of David's soldiers currently in battle and waging war on his behalf. David sent for her immediately in spite of the fact that his messengers identified the woman as being married. He had her brought to his chambers and had sexual relations with her. Shortly after that, Bath-sheba informed David that she was pregnant.

David panicked knowing that he had done wrong and sent word for Uriah to be brought back to the city from the battle. David's plan was for Uriah to take a rest and lay with his wife so that David could cover up his involvement in the pregnancy. However, Uriah was a man of intense honor and integrity and would not allow himself to enjoy the comforts of home while his brothers-in-arms were doing battle. He even refused to enter into his home though David had gotten him drunk in an attempt to facilitate his deception. David decided that there were no options left to him, so he sent Uriah back to the war. Uriah carried David's orders instructing Joab, his commander, to put him into a battle situation in which he would surely be in mortal danger. Uriah was killed shortly afterward.

Some who knew Uriah might have ascribed his death to the will of God. They might have thought that God in His wisdom had decided to take Uriah home to be with Him. However, this is the furthest thing from the truth. God had nothing to do with Uriah's death. His death came about because David was trying to cover up his sin. David was solely responsible as he sent Uriah to his death at the hand of the enemy soldiers.

Nathan, David's seer, told him a story of a poor man, who had no flocks, but only a single lamb. He loved the lamb as it played with his children, shared his food, drank from his own cup and was like a daughter to him. This lamb was suddenly taken for a feast by a rich man with abundant flocks and wealth, unjustly depriving the man of his well-loved lamb. David was enraged at the injustice. In 2 Samuel 12:5-6, he inadvertently declared the punishment for his sin of murder out of his own mouth!

> **2 Samuel 12:5-6** *(GNT)*
> *[5] David became very angry at the rich man and said, "I swear by the living Lord that the man who did this ought to die! [6] For having done such a cruel thing, he must pay back four times as much as he took."*

David's Declaration

The story that Nathan told was an analogy or parable illustrating David stealing Bath-sheba from Uriah. David made a judgment and declared his verdict of guilt upon the imaginary man and then determined a sentence of death. He just didn't realize that he was convicting himself of his own injustice. His own words brought his punishment upon him!

The narrative in 2 Samuel 12:13-15 tells us that God spared David from the punishment demanded by his own declaration, but he was informed through Nathan that his illegitimate child would not survive.

> **2 Samuel 12:13-15** *(BBE)*
> *[13] And David said to Nathan, Great is my sin against the Lord. And Nathan said to David, The Lord has put away your sin; death will not come on you. [14] But still, because you have had no respect for the Lord, death will certainly overtake the child who has newly come to birth. [15] Then Nathan went back to his house. And the hand of the Lord was on David's son, the child of Uriah's wife, and it became very ill.*

David pled, wept, and fasted for the life of the child, but his declaration of death was visited upon his own child. God "put away" or forgave

David's sin, yet David's decree demanded a price. The price was the death of his child, and David's intercession for the life of his child was to no avail. God got the blame for causing a sickness to come upon the child. However, David declared the penalty of death out of his own mouth. Man has authority in the earth realm, and his declaration is what will bring things to pass even if he brings them on himself.

Even though God gets the blame, He does not look for occasions to punish unjustly and destroy the innocent as in the case of this innocent child. He actually looks for opportunities to forgive and overlook transgressions. Destruction is the realm of the evil one, Satan, and sometimes even man himself. The union of Bath-sheba and David was eventually restored, and they became the parents of the wisest man of all time. Their second son, Solomon, found great favor with God, became a king of Israel and built the first temple of God.

David demanded punishment for his own sin through his assessment (judgment) of the injustice in the hypothetical example posed by Nathan. He demanded death, but God restored him and blessed him in spite of his sin. Let's keep this situation in mind while we continue to explore the rest of the description of David's census.

Why Was Numbering Israel A Sin?

The *eyewitness* account of Gad or Nathan in 2 Samuel 24:9-10 tells us that David had a revelation of his error in taking the census. However, it wasn't until David was already given a partial account of the census that he became aware of the problem that he now faced. He realized that he had lapsed in his faith toward God and made a grievous error in judgment. He also understood that there would be consequences. There is no revelation to the reader of why David's action was considered to be a sin. This determination is left to the contextual and historical knowledge of the reader. However, David immediately sought forgiveness for this misstep and admitted his awareness of the sinful nature of the action.

2 Samuel 24:9-10 *(BBE)*

> [9] *And Joab gave the king the number of all the people: there were in Israel eight hundred thousand fighting men able to take up arms; and the men of Judah were five hundred thousand.* [10] *And after the people had been numbered,* **David's heart was troubled.** *And David said to the Lord, "Great*

has been my sin in doing this; but now, O Lord, be pleased to take away the sin of your servant, for I have done very foolishly."

Joab, his commander, warned him of his error as soon as David issued the order for the census, but David would not listen. David was seemingly blinded by his own ambition or fear. God made a promise to Abraham in Genesis 15:5 when He said *"Look now toward heaven, and tell the stars, if thou be able to number them: and he said unto him, So shall thy seed be."* The parallel account of Ezra in 1 Chronicles 27:23-24 clearly restates this promise that God *"would increase Israel like to the stars of the heavens."* It is given as the reason that David did not number those under 20 years old. However, the promise is not mentioned in the 2 Samuel account of the eyewitnesses.

1 Chronicles 27:23-24 *(Ezra)*

[23] But David took not the number of them from twenty years old and under: because the LORD had said he would increase Israel like to the stars of the heavens. [24] Joab the son of Zeruiah began to number, but he finished not, because there fell wrath for it against Israel; neither was the number put in the account of the chronicles of king David.

The promise of innumerable seed was plainly given, which would logically infer the inability to obtain a count. Thus, there was no rationale or justification for a census. However, this is not the complete issue. David's strength in battle and as a ruler was established from the beginning, based on trust in the strength of his God, Jehovah, as described in Psalms 44:3. As David prepared for further conflict, he left that trust and faith behind and began to look to his own prowess and strength.

Psalms 44:3 *(NIV) (Speaking of God)*

It was not by their sword that they won the land, nor did their arm bring them victory; it was your right hand, your arm, and the light of your face, for you loved them.

David left his faith and trust in God and began trusting in the strength of his own *right hand*, rather than trusting in God. He was relying upon his own abilities and the strength of his armies. This change of heart was a measure of either arrogance or fear.

There is no discussion of this possibility, but David might have felt more than a little unsure of his relationship with God immediately following the Bath-sheba/Uriah situation. Following the story that Nathan told him, David had just been faced with the gravity of his sin and his declaration of punishment that ultimately landed on his son. He had just endured the death of a child and most certainly had been plagued with some doubts regarding whether God would support him in battle. These thoughts may have led him to verify that he had enough physical strength in his army, just in case God was no longer helping him.

Sin has a way of distracting us from our faith in God even when He has forgiven and restored us. Our adversary is always ready to remind us of our failings. David's fear is what led him to count his troops to determine the strength of his fighting force. Once he gave the order, David realized the error of his ways. He acted with a lack of trust, denying the promise of God that the children of Israel would be innumerable and began to rely on his own abilities. Rather than trusting in God, David departed from the faith that he had displayed as a youth when he came against Goliath *in the name of the Lord* in 1 Samuel 17:45. His lack of faith and trust is why David's census was a sin.

1 Samuel 17:45 *(NKJV)*

Then David said to the Philistine, "You come to me with a sword, with a spear, and with a javelin. But I come to you in the name of the Lord of hosts, the God of the armies of Israel, whom you have defied."

Eyewitness Bias

In the 2 Samuel narrative, Gad's frame of reference for evaluating the situation assumed that God did both good and evil. He may have been swayed by his emotional closeness to the situation, and he was undoubtedly aware of David's recent sin of adultery with Bath-sheba. He may have concluded that David was out of favor with God and that God was still looking for ways to punish him. He faced the same problem as Job did in that he may not have been aware that there was another force working against David and Israel. He was unaware that Satan was the force that influenced David's decision. Gad's *situational* or *relative* truth is what led him to conclude that God was against David and Israel.

Awareness of evil was certainly a revelation in the Old Testament, but there was very little knowledge of the central, evil personage, Satan. The book of Job exemplifies this problem and shows what resulted from a lack of understanding *(see Chapter 11, p. 119)*. It is no wonder that there is confusion when God, the one that they looked to for blessings, was also the one whom they expected would bring evil upon them! The reality of the situation is evidenced in Numbers 23:19. God does not change.

Numbers 23:19 *(ERV)*

God is not a man; he will not lie. God is not a human being; his decisions will not change. If he says he will do something, then he will do it. If he makes a promise, then he will do what he promised.

David's situation was clearly a temptation. Satan did have some information on recent sinful activity with which to remind and convict David. If this did occur, David failed to overcome the challenge. The narrative of 2 Samuel says that God *moved* David to take the census and number the people. The Hebrew word translated *moved* is סוּת. It is referenced in Strong's as OT:5496. It is the same word encountered in Job 2:3 when Satan *moved* God to come against Job without cause *(see p. 131)*.

"moved" - *Strong's* OT:5496 **סוּת,** *cuwth* **(sooth);**

perhaps denominative from 7898; properly, to prick, i.e. (figuratively) stimulate; by implication, to seduce: (Translated in the KJV as - entice, move, persuade, provoke, remove, set on, stir up, take away.)

This word in the Hebrew clearly implies a condition of provocation or temptation. For something to be a temptation, a wrong choice must lead to disobedience or sin. However, the New Testament book of James concludes that God cannot be tempted, nor does He tempt any man. James 1:13-16 provides us a good understanding of how God operates.

James 1:13-16 *(NIV)*

[13] When tempted, no one should say, "God is tempting me." For God cannot be tempted by evil, nor does he tempt anyone; [14] but each one is tempted when, by his own evil desire, he is dragged away and enticed. [15] Then, after desire has conceived, it gives birth to sin; and sin, when it is full-grown, gives birth to death. [16] Don't be deceived, my dear brothers.

James 1:13-16 *(CEV)*

[13] Don't blame God when you are tempted! God cannot be tempted by evil, and he doesn't use evil to tempt others. [14] We are tempted by our own desires that drag us off and trap us. [15] Our desires make us sin, and when sin is finished with us, it leaves us dead. [16] Don't be fooled, my dear friends.

David faltered in his actions and from his dedication to God's direction and leading. He was tempted and drawn away from God simply because of fear and doubt. David was tempted, just like Eve was when the serpent spoke to her in the garden *(see p. 94)*. His temptation from Satan may have sounded something like this:

> *Come on David, you don't really think that God is going to come through for you with that huge Philistine army, do you? Don't you remember that sin with Bath-sheba. Certainly you will have to do this on your own, and you don't even have the manpower to pull it off, do you?*

David may have thought, "That's right, God is not going to give me the victory. I had better be sure that I can manage this situation on my own with the strength of my army. I don't have faith in God to come through for me." He could have thought that either because of his sin or because of the way the odds appeared to be set against him.

Unlike David and the rest of humanity, God is always the same. He does not falter. He seeks to bless, save, and give life, rather than to curse, reject, and kill. The problem with mankind is that it views the actions and heart of God the same way it sees itself, very fickle and untrustworthy and with questionable motives. However, even with this understanding, sometimes it is difficult to hang on to what God has promised by faith. It is easy to fall into doubt and question the covenant assurances that God has provided especially in light of very severe circumstances.

God is certainly not trying to get us to trip up so that He can punish us. We must be careful not to lay blame upon God when we exercise our free will choice to doubt or not believe. The motivations for disobedience and disbelief originate in fear, doubt, conceit, pride, vanity, ego, and arrogant self-will. None of these come from God. They originate within our own spirit and are self-deceptive and encouraged by our adversary, Satan.

Regardless of the motivation, all of these impulses lead straight to sin. Regardless of the degree or reasons for the sin, the penalty for that sin is destruction and death. However, forgiveness is available from God. To think that God tempts a person to sin so that He can punish that person for that sin is absurd. This is akin to an abusive parent goading a child into failure of some sort so that the parent can justify beating the child. This is blatant child abuse and will put the parent in jail. God should be locked up as a child abuser if we follow that line of reasoning!

The narratives in 2 Chronicles and 2 Samuel affix provocation or "blame" to vastly different sources, God and Satan. David was a devout man, a man after God's own heart, who might have assumed that God was against him at times due to little understanding of the influence of Satan as the accusing adversary. As a result, both good and evil are easily attributed to God. The observational, eyewitness bias of Gad and Nathan may have influenced their view of the reasons for the actions of David and wrongly attributed the temptation to God.

David realizes the problem and comes to the full realization of his rebellious and sinful action against God and His covenant. He actually knows in his spirit that God is his savior. He immediately seeks forgiveness for his sin and asks God to relieve his burden. Both narratives record his reaction to the recognition of his sin and his request to God for forgiveness in 2 Samuel 24:10 and 1 Chronicles 21:8.

2 Samuel 24:10

> ***And David's heart smote him*** *after that he had numbered the people. And David said unto the LORD, I have sinned greatly in that I have done: and now, I beseech thee, O LORD, take away the iniquity of thy servant; for I have done very foolishly.*

1 Chronicles 21:8

> *8 And David said unto God, I have sinned greatly, because I have done this thing: but now, I beseech thee, do away the iniquity of thy servant; for I have done very foolishly.*

David's reaction is further substantiation that his motivation and temptation to take the census and to determine his physical power and strength of his armies did not originate with God. God does not attempt to coerce man to disobey His commands and instructions to cause him to fail. God did not do it with Adam and Eve, and He did not do it with Job. He did not do it in the midst of David's lustful and adulterous affair with Bath-sheba, and He will not do it to you!

Gad's Demand

In response to David's request for forgiveness of his sin, Gad instructs David to choose one of three acts of corporate punishment against all of Israel. The very serious transgression of David with Bath-sheba deprived Uriah, a loyal and innocent man, of his life. David basically committed murder to cover his adulterous affair. Even though the true legal penalty was his death, his life was spared. However, David personally suffered the consequence. It was not directed against all of Israel. In contrast, the penalty for the sin of numbering Israel was much more severe, based on the choices Gad offers in the name of the Lord. The punishments were directed at all of Israel according to 2 Samuel 24:11-14 and 1 Chronicles 21:9-13.

2 Samuel 24:11-14

> [11] *For when David was up in the morning, the word of the Lord came unto the prophet Gad, David's seer, saying,* [12] *Go and say unto David, Thus saith the Lord , I offer thee three things; choose thee one of them, that I may do it unto thee.* [13] *So Gad came to David, and told him, and said unto him, Shall seven years of famine come unto thee in thy land? or wilt thou flee three months before thine enemies, while they pursue thee? or that there be three days' pestilence in thy land? now advise, and see what answer I shall return to him that sent me.*
> [14] *And David said unto Gad, I am in a great strait: let us fall now into the hand of the Lord ; for his mercies are great: and let me not fall into the hand of man.*

1 Chronicles 21:9-13

> [9] *And the Lord spake unto Gad, David's seer, saying,* [10] *Go and tell David, saying, Thus saith the Lord, I offer thee three things: choose thee one of them, that I may do it unto thee.* [11] *So Gad came to David, and said unto him, Thus saith the Lord, Choose thee* [12] *Either three years' famine; or three months to be destroyed before thy foes, while that the sword of thine enemies overtaketh thee; or else three days the sword of the Lord, even the pestilence, in the land, and the angel of the Lord destroying throughout all the coasts of Israel. Now therefore advise thyself what word I shall bring again to him that sent me.*
> [13] *And David said unto Gad, I am in a great strait: let me fall now into the hand of the Lord; for very great are his mercies: but let me not fall into the hand of man.*

Previously, David's pleas for forgiveness had always been met favorably by God with a response of mercy, but apparently not in this case. Gad attributed both the initial temptation and the penalties for the sin to God. Rather than instructions to repent and make an offering to atone for his sin, he brought the choice of three corporate punishments to David.

He went on to insist that David make a choice so that he could report to "*him that sent me*" (2 Samuel 24:13 and 1 Chronicles 21:12). Based on Ezra's observations in 1 Chronicles 21:1, Gad wrongly attributed the initial temptation to God *(see p. 211)*. Was he also wrong in the origin of the instructions for the punishment? Any one of the three choices was designed to punish all of Israel, not David personally.

David decreed that a punishment be assigned as a result of his affair with Bath-sheba, and he also spoke out and decreed the punishment to be inflicted for the numbering of Israel when he selected one of Gad's choices. His choice was not to be subject to the ravages of his enemies. Instead, he chose the pestilence as the punishment that is described as the sword of the Lord. It caused more than 70,000 men to lose their lives in payment for his sin. The Lord repented (or changed His mind) of the evil destruction upon Israel and stopped the destruction according to the observation of Gad written in 1 Chronicles 21:14-15 and 2 Samuel 24:15-16.

2 Samuel 24:15-16

[15] So the Lord sent a pestilence upon Israel from the morning even to the time appointed: and there died of the people from Dan even to Beer-sheba seventy thousand men. [16] And when the angel stretched out his hand upon Jerusalem to destroy it, the Lord repented him of the evil, and said to the angel that destroyed the people, It is enough: stay now thine hand. And the angel of the Lord was by the threshingplace of Araunah the Jebusite.

1 Chronicles 21:14-15

[14] So the Lord sent pestilence upon Israel: and there fell of Israel seventy thousand men. [15] And God sent an angel unto Jerusalem to destroy it: and as he was destroying, the Lord beheld, and he repented him of the evil, and said to the angel that destroyed, It is enough, stay now thine hand. And the angel of the Lord stood by the threshingfloor of Ornan the Jebusite.

In 2 Samuel 1:1, Gad accepted as fact the notion that God had tempted David to sin so that he could inflict an evil punishment upon him and all of Israel. However, Satan is the one who tempts according to the spiritual understanding revealed in Genesis 3:1-13 *(see p. 95)*, and he is the accuser and the one who wants to punish and enact evil activity according to Job 1:6-11 *(see p. 122)*. The 1 Chronicles 21 account of Ezra *(see p. 211)* attributes the temptation of David to Satan. This suggests that Gad's point of reference or view of God as the tempter and the punisher described in 2 Samuel 24:1 may be errant *(see p. 210)*, just like Job was incorrect in his perspective.

However, regardless of who instigated the temptation, David sinned when he did not resist, and a punishment was required for his act of disobedience. Unless it was commuted through atonement or mercy, his sin against God carried the sentence of death. Instead of offering to put away David's sin through forgiveness and mercy, Gad brings David three choices of severe corporate or national punishment. These choices which Gad attributes to the Lord in 1 Chronicles 21:10 and 2 Samuel 24:12 were considered evil as indicated in 1 Chronicles 21:15 and 2 Samuel 24:16 and are consistent with identifying God as the one who tempted David.

The evil destruction occurred as a result of David's actions and his choice of the pestilence. The account continues in 1 Chronicles 21:16-27 as David observed an angel with a sword outstretched over Jerusalem *(v. 16)* and assumed that the angel was the destroyer. He pleaded for the people *(v. 17)*, was instructed to set up an altar *(v. 18)*, and make an offering for his sin to the Lord. The offering was accepted as evidenced by fire coming from heaven to consume it *(v. 26)*, and the angel withdrew and sheathed its sword *(v. 27)*.

1 Chronicles 21:16-18, 26-27

[16] *And David lifted up his eyes, and saw the angel of the Lord stand between the earth and the heaven, having a drawn sword in his hand stretched out over Jerusalem. Then David and the elders of Israel, who were clothed in sackcloth, fell upon their faces.*

[17] *And David said unto God, Is it not I that commanded the people to be numbered? even I it is that have sinned and done evil indeed; but as for these sheep, what have they done? let thine hand, I pray thee, O Lord my God, be on me, and on my father's house; but not on thy people, that they should be plagued.*

[18] *Then the angel of the Lord commanded Gad to say to David, that David should go up, and set up an altar unto the Lord in the threshingfloor of Ornan the Jebusite.*

[26] *And David built there an altar unto the Lord, and offered burnt offerings and peace offerings, and called upon the Lord; and he answered him from heaven by fire upon the altar of burnt offering.*

[27] *And the Lord commanded the angel; and he put up his sword again into the sheath thereof.*

David sinned and he realized that his sin carried a penalty. His guilt for his sin led him to accept that the punishments that Gad offered were from the Lord. He knew the principles of atonement and knew that sacrifice would atone for the sin and restore him to right standing before God. When he was offered three evil choices, he did not resist and say that he would make a sacrifice to atone for that sin. Instead, he chose from one of the three evil options offered to him. He concluded in his judgment or determination that the sin was worthy of a verdict of punishment not forgiveness. He later asked for mercy, but still skipped the part of atonement for that sin. In essence, he declared the penalty or sentence in his judgment that he had sinned because he selected from the choice of punishments offered to him. He brought upon himself and all of Israel the pestilence that took more than 70,000 lives.

Satan tempted David to sin against God while he was weak in faith. Gad was wrong in blaming God for David's temptation, and it is not unreasonable to conclude that the punishments that he offered to David originated with Satan similar to the way he accused and attacked Job in Job 1:19-22 *(see p. 122)*. David gave the opening for Satan to act because he was in doubt and decided to trust in his own strength by counting his army rather than trust in God. He decreed the judgment and punishment from his own mouth as he selected a choice offered by Gad. It is possible that the evil destruction would not have occurred had David taken a fourth option of trusting God rather than choosing one of the three options of punishment because the destruction did not stop until David repented and made a sacrifice of atonement for his sin.

God's Protection

In 1 Chronicles 21:14-15, David observed what he considered to be a destroying angel of the Lord. This prompted him to intercede for the people of Israel in 1 Chronicles 21:17 saying, *"Is it not I that commanded the people to be numbered? even I it is that have sinned and done evil indeed ..."* He asked God to visit the punishment upon him rather than all of Israel. The problem is that David had already accepted and declared the punishment upon all of Israel. He did not refuse the choices and personally accept the responsibility. He chose to have the pestilence come upon the land. However, after David plead for Israel before God, the angel then spoke to Gad and relayed instructions to David to make an altar and offer a sacrifice for his sin.

The angel that David saw was not a destroying angel, but a protecting one. The angel was standing guard over Jerusalem, actually protecting Jerusalem from the destruction of the pestilence, accepted by David, and enacted by Satan. The angel would not allow the destruction to go beyond a certain point, in the same way that destruction was limited in Job's situation in Job 1:12 *(see p. 125)*. The angel also gave David instruction as to how to stop the destruction that David himself had begun. The angel put his sword of protection over Jerusalem away only after David repented and offered the sacrifice for the forgiveness and atonement of his sin. Once David atoned for the sin, he removed the permission that he had granted Satan to act against him and Israel.

David was possibly reeling from guilt over his adulterous affair with Bath-sheba, his murder of her husband, Uriah and the death of his infant son because the events had taken place so recently. He may not have been thinking clearly during the entire census taking situation since he had turned his trust away from God. If David had immediately remedied the situation with an attitude of repentance and a sacrifice for atonement, the pestilence might not have come and killed 70,000 of his people.

God is neither the tempter nor the punisher. The apparent conflict between the accounts of Samuel and Chronicles is easily resolved by understanding the perspective of the observers, or in this case, the writers. Satan both tempts and demands that man be punished when he falls into his temptations. Since Satan does not have the authority to act arbitrarily against man, he must coerce a man to speak against himself as Job had done or distrust God as David did. Satan overwhelms with temptation and then taunts with guilt. He leaves a man to self-judge, self-condemn, and proclaim punishment upon himself or other men. Man and mankind are the proclaimers of their own judgment and destruction, not God.

God is also consistent and unwavering in His dealing with man and the declarations of His Word. He does not change His mind, nor does He act in an arbitrary fashion. His Word is absolute in its Truth and Integrity. God offers us an explanation through human interaction of how His Word and His Law works which we will explore in the next chapter.

Chapter 18

UNWAVERING INTEGRITY THE UNCHANGEABLE LAW

Everything in the Bible points in one direction, toward a successful life that establishes a relationship between God and Man. Nothing is in the Bible by mere chance. God has a purpose for every account, narrative, record, teaching, description, or character revealed in it. The principles and truths that are established, revealed, and expounded upon in the Bible are essential for our lives. Everything that has any degree of lasting benefit is based on them.

Many in contemporary business, spiritual, and motivational roles seem to have taken credit for inventing or creating some of these concepts. They may seem to be ground-breaking new paradigms. However, a student of the Bible can see that they are simply one or more of God's eternal principles re-applied to a contemporary problem or challenge making it appear fresh and new. The truth and stability of God's Word never changes because it is universal and absolute. Living according to His truth produces a fulfilled life that overcomes the challenges it faces.

A thorough comprehension of the provisions that God has established for man leads to deeper insight into God's character. This understanding also reveals the plans that God has for us, plans that are always for good, giving mankind every opportunity for success. The precious God—Man relationship is set out for us in the text and the spirit of the Bible. The pitfalls, distractions, and challenges are laid out for the reader along with the physical and spiritual activities that support, extend, or cut short a successful life. Each account reveals information to the student of God's Word that can deepen his or her understanding of the spiritual nature of the world. They also reveal the principles and order upon which God has chosen to operate the world system.

The God of the Bible is sovereign. Although the word *sovereign* does not appear in the *King James Version* of the Bible, it is used in many other versions. It is generally agreed that this characteristic is perfectly descriptive of God. However, what is the understanding that people have when God is described as being sovereign? The word *sovereign* has several meanings all of which point to the concept of supremacy. In human terms, the noun form of the word more commonly refers to a head of state, monarch, or king.

sovereign *(noun)*

> *1) a monarch; a king, queen, or other supreme ruler. 2) a person who has supreme power or authority. 3) a group or body of persons or a state having sovereign authority.*[54]

When describing God, the definition from *Easton's Bible Dictionary* probably sums it up the best.

sovereignty *(adjective)*

> *Of God, His absolute right to do all things according to His own good pleasure.*[55]

Many scriptures lend credence to this definition and support the "all-powerful, do anything He wants to" nature of God *(see Appendix Chapter 18)*. However, this definition makes God sound more like a dictator than a sovereign. Is this truly the way God operates?

Traditional views of God and His character did not just begin in the last few generations. Knowledge of God's Word had been largely separated from the common man for centuries. As a result, the perspectives of a relatively few individuals were expanded upon and evolved into the widespread traditional views we hold today. One such perspective is the *sovereignty* of God. In the human mind, there is an unpredictable element when the concept that "God can do whatever He wants, whenever He wants to" is considered. There is certainly no doubt that He can do whatever He wants. After all, He did make everything. The question is: Does He actually act that way, or does His character and nature provide some predictability to His methods?

For Such A Time As This

The book of Esther offers some interesting insight into this question of God's way of doing things. It provides excellent examples of some of the general principles and operation of God's universe even though this book does not directly mention God or the Lord.

The events of the book of Esther took place about the time of Ezra and Nehemiah, circa 492-460 BC.[56] Esther reveals principles of God's character and Law and also reveals the differences between the two Covenants. These are the agreements that God established with man, the Old Covenant or Old Testament and the New Covenant or New Testament *(see Chapter 12, p. 147)*. There is a clear change in the manner that God interacts with man after the establishment of the New Covenant. The book of Esther is provided to help us understand the Old Covenant operation, the need for a New Covenant, and the results that the New Covenant brings.

The book of Esther also explains throne room etiquette and provides an allegory to the unchangeable nature of the established law of God. Much respect for authority and protocol is lost in everyday, contemporary society. The result is a lack of understanding and appreciation of the authority of God and the respect that He should command in our lives. The book opens by revealing the cast of characters in the drama and the struggle that is about to unfold. Several key individuals are introduced as the narrative begins.

King Xerxes of Persia, a pagan (non-Jewish) King, also known as Ahasuerus, reigned from 486-465 BC. in the city of Shushan, together with his queen, Vashti. Mordecai was the chief minister of Ahasuerus. He was the son of Jair, a Benjamite, one of the twelve tribes of Israel. Mordecai had previously been carried into captivity by Nebuchadnezzar, King of Babylon. He constantly sat at the gate of the king's palace, observing and listening. Esther was his cousin, and after her parents had died, he took her in as his daughter. Haman is the final key character. He was chief of the princes of the court of King Ahasuerus. He was like a Prime Minister, bestowed with honor and authority before the king.

Order In The Court

The narrative begins with a royal drama, the disobedience of Queen Vashti. She was summoned by the King to make an appearance during a celebration at his court, but she refused the command of the King. This action caused her to pay dearly as it was considered to be an act of rebelliousness and defiance. Had her defiance against his sovereignty as king been allowed to stand, it would have established an unacceptable precedent, potentially encouraging other wives of the princes and rulers to rebel against their husbands. They decided to make a "royal example" of her for the sake of order in the kingdom and petitioned the King to expel her. He made a law that stripped of her position and privilege, and a search for a replacement queen was begun in Esther 1:12, 15, 19-22.

Esther 1:12, 15, 19-22

*12 **But the queen Vashti refused to come at the king's commandment** by his chamberlains: therefore was the king very wroth, and his anger burned in him.*

*15 What shall we do unto the queen Vashti according to law, **because she hath not performed the commandment of the king** Ahasuerus by the chamberlains?*

19 If it please the king, let there go a royal commandment from him,
***and let it be written among the laws of the Persians and the Medes, that it be not altered,** That Vashti come no more before king Ahasuerus; and let the king give her royal estate unto another that is better than she.*
20 And when the king's decree which he shall make shall be published throughout all his empire, (for it is great,) all the wives shall give to their husbands honour, both to great and small.
21 And the saying pleased the king and the princes; and the king did according to the word of Memucan:
22 For he sent letters into all the king's provinces, into every province according to the writing thereof, and to every people after their language, that every man should bear rule in his own house, and that it should be published according to the language of every people.

The fairness of the King's action, not to be compared to God's actions, is not the subject of this discussion, as it could be hotly debated. The important aspect of this situation is the understanding of law and obedience, in that, once a decree is spoken or written by the authority or law-giver, it is absolute and unchangeable. There was an existing protocol for activity within the court of the King and Vashti disobeyed it. The result was the formation of a law that was unalterable, even by the King himself. This concept is a direct correlation to the authority and unalterable nature of the Word of God. We will see how important this is as the events continue to unfold, revealing a serious problem that arises and the ingenious way in which it is overcome.

Taking Offence

Some select, notable passages will be examined. However, the reader can study the entire narrative if desired. There are many key issues that should be understood. The book's namesake, Esther, enters the scene by way of Mordecai, her cousin and adoptive father. He was aware of the search for a new queen because of his proximity to the palace of the king. At Mordecai's encouragement, Esther became a candidate. She was brought before the king and in Esther 2:17, we see that *"she obtained grace and favour in his sight,"* and the King *"made her queen instead of Vashti."* It is also key to note that at the instruction of Mordecai, Esther did not reveal her Jewish heritage.

Mordecai continued to play a prominent role in the activities as he stayed in contact with Esther. He was privy to an incident of insurrection and an attempted assassination of the king. He relayed the information to Esther, who told the king. The culprits were apprehended, punished with hanging, and the incident, along with Mordecai's contribution, was recorded in the *Book of the Chronicles of the Kings of Media and Persia*.

Later, Mordecai had a run-in with the chief prince, Haman. He had refused to bow and reverence Haman, who then became *full of wrath*. When Haman discovered that Mordecai was a Jew, he was not satisfied to just punish Mordecai alone for his actions. He sought to destroy all of Mordecai's people, the entire nation of the Jews throughout the kingdom! We see the struggle between good and evil as described in Proverbs 29:27 and learn how Haman's evil expanded its reach in Esther 3:6.

Proverbs 29:27 *(NIV)*
The righteous detest the dishonest; the wicked detest the upright.

Esther 3:6 *(GNT)*
. . . . when he learned that Mordecai was a Jew, he decided to do more than punish Mordecai alone. He made plans to kill every Jew in the whole Persian Empire.

Haman was in a position to exact his revenge and satisfy his anger because he had the ear of the king. Armed with his vengeance and a plan, he approached the king with the injustice done to him. Haman was overcome with his own wickedness as described in Proverbs 4:19 and 6:18.

Proverbs 4:19 *(NKJV)*
The way of the wicked is like darkness; They do not know what makes them stumble.

Proverbs 6:18
An heart that deviseth wicked imaginations, feet that be swift in running to mischief.

Making It Official

Haman made his distorted case against the Jews before the King and set a date for the execution of his plan. He offered 10,000 talents of silver *(approximately 335 tons of silver or $150 billion today!)* to pay for the costs of his destructive vendetta![57, 58] Perhaps this was a real bounty that Haman was able to pay, or perhaps it was a wild, exaggerated promise to show the king the fervor of his hatred of Mordecai and the Jews. It might also have been a portion of a bounty that he expected to gather from the Jews he was planning to kill. Nonetheless, Haman wanted to have the king write a new law in Esther 3:7-9, giving him the authority to carry out his plan.

Esther 3:7-9 *(NKJV)*
7 In the first month, which is the month of Nisan, in the twelfth year of
King Ahasuerus, they cast Pur (that is, the lot), before Haman to determine
the day and the month, until it fell on the twelfth month, which is the
month of Adar. 8 Then Haman said to King Ahasuerus, "There is a certain
people scattered and dispersed among the people in all the provinces of
your kingdom; their laws are different from all other people's, and they do
not keep the king's laws. Therefore it is not fitting for the king to let them
remain. 9 If it pleases the king, ***let a decree be written that they be***
destroyed*, and I will pay ten thousand talents of silver into the hands of*
those who do the work, to bring it into the king's treasuries."

The sovereign King was persuaded by Haman's arguments and approved the slaughter of the Jews at the hand of Haman. He gave his ring to Haman, saying he could do as he wished to the people. The King told Haman that he would provide the money to carry out the hostilities. The official stamp of the authority of the King and his sovereignty was his ring.

Once the imprint of the ring was affixed to a decree, it became law, an unchangeable law, unable to be repealed. The King had obviously entrusted nearly all of his power in Haman because he removed the ring from his finger and gave it to him. At that point, Haman possessed the power and authority of the kingdom embodied in the King's ring.

Haman immediately set out to craft a decree calling for the annihilation of the Jews. He dictated the terms to the King's scribes. They then wrote the law in every language that was represented by the people and addressed it to all of the lieutenants, governors, and rulers over all of the King's realm. The decree was written in the name of the King, and Haman made it law by sealing it with the King's ring in Esther 3:10-12.

Esther 3:10-12 *(NKJV)*

[10] So the king took his signet ring from his hand and gave it to Haman, the son of Hammedatha the Agagite, the enemy of the Jews. [11] And the king said to Haman, "The money and the people are given to you, to do with them as seems good to you." [12] Then the king's scribes were called on the thirteenth day of the first month, and a decree was written according to all that Haman commanded — to the king's satraps, to the governors who were over each province, to the officials of all people, to every province according to its script, and to every people in their language. In the name of King Ahasuerus it was written, and sealed with the king's signet ring.

The decree was copied and circulated throughout the kingdom, and the day of destruction was fixed at eleven months later. The decree, understandably, caused a great deal of concern within the Jewish and general populations alike. People would have to choose sides while confusion reigned in the land because of this impending massacre. In contrast, Haman sat down to relax in his new found power and anticipated victory.

Esther 3:13-15 *(NKJV)*

[13] And the letters were sent by couriers into all the king's provinces, to destroy, to kill, and to annihilate all the Jews, both young and old, little children and women, in one day, on the thirteenth day of the twelfth month, which is the month of Adar, and to plunder their possessions.
[14] A copy of the document was to be issued as law in every province, being published for all people, that they should be ready for that day. [15] The couriers went out, hastened by the king's command; and the decree was proclaimed in Shushan the citadel. So the king and Haman sat down to drink, but the city of Shushan was perplexed.

Born To A Purpose

Mordecai learned of the decree and immediately humbled himself and cried out in grief. News of his public display of grief was brought to Esther, and she sent messengers to find out the reason. The messengers brought Esther news of Haman's decree from Mordecai along with his request that she go before the king to plead the case of the Jews. Esther replied to Mordecai with a statement regarding the current law of the King's court. She indicated that she was not at liberty to speak to the king whenever she pleased, but only at the King's bidding. She said that she had no power to intercede and would be subject to death herself if she tried.

> **Esther 4:11-14** *(NKJV)*
> *[11] "All the king's servants and the people of the king's provinces know that any man or woman who goes into the inner court to the king, who has not been called,* ***he has but one law: put all to death, except the one to whom the king holds out the golden scepter, that he may live.*** *Yet I myself have not been called to go in to the king these thirty days."[12] So they told Mordecai Esther's words. [13] And Mordecai told them to answer Esther: "Do not think in your heart that you will escape in the king's palace any more than all the other Jews. [14] For if you remain completely silent at this time, relief and deliverance will arise for the Jews from another place, but you and your father's house will perish.* ***Yet who knows whether you have come to the kingdom for such a time as this?"***

Mordecai made it clear to Esther that it was her destiny to intercede for her people. In verse 4:14, he said, *"who knows whether you are come to the kingdom for such a time as this?"* Esther knew that fulfilling Mordecai's request could likely end in her death because of the conditions outlined in the law. She was well aware that the etiquette of the throne room for those in the presence of the king was not something to be taken lightly.

The Sceptre Of Grace

Esther was also aware that the King could grant her *grace* and signal that he would allow her to enter his presence through a simple move of his golden sceptre. She proceeded with faith and confidence in her calling. The scepter represented power, but it could be used to provide grace given from a position of authority. It is also a prophetic reference to the future grace that is applied to mankind through the sacrifice that Jesus made for sin. References to the sceptre occur in many places in scripture.

Genesis 49:10 *(MSG)*
The ***scepter*** *shall not leave Judah; he'll keep a firm grip on the command staff Until the ultimate ruler comes and the nations obey him.*

Numbers 24:17 *(GWT)*
I see someone who is not here now. I look at someone who is not nearby. A star will come from Jacob. A ***scepter*** *will rise from Israel. He will crush the heads of the Moabites and destroy all the people of Sheth.*

Psalms 45:6 *(NIV)*
Your throne, O God, will last for ever and ever; a ***scepter*** *of justice will be the* ***scepter*** *of your kingdom.*

Hebrews 1:8
But unto the Son he saith, Thy throne, O God, is for ever and ever: a ***sceptre*** *of righteousness is the* ***sceptre*** *of thy kingdom.*

These scripture references point to the longevity of the sceptre and to the scepter (or authority) that will arise out of Israel and overcome evil. They further state that the sceptre represents the justice and righteousness of the kingdom of God. The sceptre of King Ahasuerus is a physical example of these spiritual truths as well as the authority of the law of the kingdom of God. Esther decided to take a step of faith according to the principle of Proverbs 15:29. She did not challenge the authority of the King but implored him for mercy and grace because of the gravity of the situation that she and her people were facing.

Proverbs 15:29 *(NIV)*
The LORD is far from the wicked but he hears the prayer of the righteous.

The Confidence Of Faith

Esther found her faith through an extreme need, coupled with a sense of destiny. This example of the faith of Esther plainly describes what true faith is. It is a confident expectation, an undoubting certainty or determination to proceed, regardless of the possible consequences. Faith is not a hope that "maybe it will work, maybe it won't." It is an attitude of certainty. Faith can be found through many different avenues of motivation. As a result of her faith, Esther approached the king without being summoned.

She had confidence, fully expecting that he would accept her presence by putting forth his scepter and offering his grace to her. We see this interaction in Esther 5:1-2, 8.

Esther 5:1-2, 8 *(NKJV)*

[1] Now it happened on the third day that Esther put on her royal robes and stood in the inner court of the king's palace, across from the king's house, while the king sat on his royal throne in the royal house, facing the entrance of the house. [2] So it was, when the king saw Queen Esther standing in the court, that she found favor in his sight, and the king held out to Esther the golden scepter that was in his hand. Then Esther went near and touched the top of the scepter.

[8] If I have found favor in the sight of the king, and if it pleases the king to grant my petition and fulfill my request, then let the king and Haman come to the banquet which I will prepare for them, and tomorrow I will do as the king has said."

The book of Hebrews in the New Testament speaks directly regarding *throne room etiquette*. It explains that the rules changed with the advent of Jesus. There is an expectation set in the New Covenant that believers will be heard at the throne without the accompanying fear that Esther had to overcome. This privilege is granted through the same kind of faith that Esther acted on in Esther 5:1-2. It is not blind faith or hope, but confidence placed in a relationship with Jesus Christ in Hebrews 4:14-16.

Hebrews 4:14-16 *(GNT)*

[14] Let us, then, hold firmly to the faith we profess. For we have a great High Priest who has gone into the very presence of God — Jesus, the Son of God. [15] Our High Priest is not one who cannot feel sympathy for our weaknesses. On the contrary, we have a High Priest who was tempted in every way that we are, but did not sin. [16] Let us have confidence, then, and approach God's throne, where there is grace. There we will receive mercy and find grace to help us just when we need it.

Esther is an example that God provides to show what true faith can accomplish. The *process* of acting in faith is also revealed. Faith is defined in Hebrews 11:1 in the New Testament as a surety or certainty of what is hoped for, but not yet experienced or seen manifested.

Hebrews 11:1 *(NIV)*

Now faith is being sure of what we hope for and certain of what we do not see.

The result of Esther's faith was the favor or *grace* of the King. However, even though Esther obtained the favor of the King, she exercised wisdom. She did not immediately reveal her ultimate desire but waited for just the right moment to make her request. This could be considered to be a calculated act, but as the narrative continues, the hand of the Spirit of God moving upon mankind can be seen. The king had a restless night and desired what amounted to a "bedtime story" as he requested that the *Book of the Chronicles of the Kings of Media and Persia* be read to him.

As it so happens, the section that was read to him was one about the actions of Mordecai when he revealed a plot that was being planned to assassinate him. He had been unaware of the plot and did not know that Mordecai had been involved in thwarting it. It is possible that he did not even knew who Mordecai was. The king then inquired as to what reward was given to Mordecai for his service to him, and he was told in Esther 6:2-3 that nothing had been done.

Esther 6:2-3 *(GWT)*

[2] The records showed how Mordecai had informed him that Bigthan and Teresh, two of the king's eunuchs who guarded the entrance, had plotted a rebellion against King Xerxes. [3] The king asked, "How did I reward and promote Mordecai for this?"

Honor Given – Humiliation Received

Haman was coming in to speak to the king about hanging Mordecai for his lack of honor to him. Just then, the king asked him what should be done to honor a man that saved the life of the king. In his arrogance, Haman assumed that the king was speaking about him. Haman proceeded to outline a series of extravagant blessings and honors to be performed, not realizing that the king was inquiring for the sake of Mordecai. The king then directed Haman to perform personally all of the acts to honor Mordecai. This further enraged Haman against him as the narrative in Esther 6:6-10 reveals.

Esther 6:6-10 *(GWT)*

[6] So Haman came in. The king then asked him, "What should be done for the man whom the king wishes to reward?" Haman thought to himself, "Whom would the king wish to reward more than me?"

[7] So Haman told the king, "This is what should be done: [8] The servants should bring a royal robe that the king has worn and a horse that the king has ridden, one that has a royal crest on its head. [9] Give the robe and the horse to one of the king's officials, who is a noble. Put the robe on the man whom the king wishes to reward and have him ride on the horse in the city square. The king's servants are also to shout ahead of him, 'This is what is done for the man whom the king wishes to reward.'"

[10] The king told Haman, "Hurry, take the robe and the horse as you said. Do this for Mordecai the Jew who sits at the king's gate. Do not omit anything you have said."

Immediately after being humbled by having to honor Mordecai, and with this anger against Mordecai still eating at him, Haman was summoned to a banquet with Queen Esther and the king. Esther then presented her request to the king in the presence of Haman as she revealed Haman's plot against the Jews in Esther 7:3-6.

Esther 7:3-6 *(GNT)*

[3] Queen Esther answered, "If it please Your Majesty to grant my humble request, my wish is that I may live and that my people may live. [4] My people and I have been sold for slaughter. If it were nothing more serious than being sold into slavery, I would have kept quiet and not bothered you about it; but we are about to be destroyed — exterminated!"

[5] Then King Xerxes asked Queen Esther, "Who dares to do such a thing? Where is this man?"

[6] Esther answered, "Our enemy, our persecutor, is this evil man Haman!"

The Destruction Of Evil

Esther's faith was rewarded, and she continued to find favor in the sight of the king. Favor is defined as kindness, goodwill, preferential treatment or grace. Grace is *unmerited favor*.[59] This favor is an example of the grace that God bestows upon us as a result of our faith. Through the grace of the king, Esther was able to explain her situation and plead her case before him. Haman made the fatal mistake of pleading before Queen Esther. He did so in such a way that his actions were badly misinterpreted. He appeared to be forcing himself upon the Queen in her bed in Esther 7:8-10.

Esther 7:8-10 *(NIV)*

8 Just as the king returned from the palace garden to the banquet hall, Haman was falling on the couch where Esther was reclining. The king exclaimed, "Will he even molest the queen while she is with me in the house?" As soon as the word left the king's mouth, they covered Haman's face.

9 Then Harbona, one of the eunuchs attending the king, said, "A gallows seventy-five feet high stands by Haman's house. He had it made for Mordecai, who spoke up to help the king." The king said, "Hang him on it!"

10 So they hanged Haman on the gallows he had prepared for Mordecai. Then the king's fury subsided.

The price that Haman paid seemed appropriate for the evil that he sought to bring upon the Jews. However, the act that sealed his fate was actually innocent. The book of 1 Thessalonians warns us against the "appearance of evil," which in this case cost Haman his life.

1 Thessalonians 5:20

Abstain from all appearance of evil.

It is evident that trouble came upon Haman although the method of enactment was surprising and seemingly unrelated. Nevertheless, the wickedness that Haman devised came back upon him and his family. Proverbs 11:8 offers an explanation.

Proverbs 11:8 *(NIV)*

The righteous man is rescued from trouble, and it comes on the wicked instead.

The Law Still Stands

Although Haman met his end, the evil that he had devised against the Jews was still in place. The slaughter of the entire Jewish population was still a matter of law and could not be changed! Something needed to be done that would mitigate the effect of this law. Even though the King was sovereign, he was still bound by the law that was written in his name and with his consent. The law needed to be superseded in some way.

This is a very poignant example of God's grace toward man. God made a law against sin that resulted in death. In His sovereignty, God did not just "do anything He wanted" but rather chose to limit Himself by His Word and His Law. His desire was to redeem man from his sin-filled deeds. God needed to find a way to satisfy the Law and to still realize His desire for mankind. He accomplished this through the exercise of mankind's faith. The example of the Kings' decree in Esther is a corollary of God's Law, in that God's Law (His Word), once decreed or spoken, cannot be altered.

Esther continued to plead her case before the king, asking that the actions of the law crafted by Haman be reversed. The king declared that he had taken the life of Haman and given control of Haman's household to Esther. However, those actions could not alleviate the effects of the law that Haman wrote in the king's name. The only thing that could prevent the enactment of that law was to write a new law that would successfully negate the effects of the first one. Making a new law is an allegory of the grace that God offers to man and is exemplified in the King's words in Esther 8:5-8.

Esther 8:5-8 *(NKJV)*

> [5] *"If it pleases the king, and if I have found favor in his sight and the thing seems right to the king and I am pleasing in his eyes, let it be written to revoke the letters devised by Haman, the son of Hammedatha the Agagite, which he wrote to annihilate the Jews who are in all the king's provinces.*
> [6] *For how can I endure to see the evil that will come to my people? Or how can I endure to see the destruction of my countrymen?"*
>
> [7] *Then King Ahasuerus said to Queen Esther and Mordecai the Jew, "Indeed, I have given Esther the house of Haman, and they have hanged him on the gallows because he tried to lay his hand on the Jews.* [8] *You yourselves write a decree concerning the Jews, as you please, in the king's name, and seal it with the king's signet ring; for whatever is written in the king's name and sealed with the king's signet ring* ***no one can revoke****."*

A New Law

This example of legally overcoming the negative effects of an existing law is a corollary to the actions that God would take by bringing Jesus into the world. The Law of the Old Testament resulted in death, but the law of the New Testament results in LIFE for all those who believe! The new law was written through the life, the shed blood, the death, and the resurrection of Jesus and negates the effects of the first Law without changing it. God made this possible through the faith of the believer. The first Law would still remain in effect, but the new law made a new decree in Romans 8:2.

Romans 8:2 *(NKJV)*

> *For the law of the Spirit of life in Christ Jesus has made me free from the law of sin and death.*

This new law of the *Spirit of life in Christ Jesus* was written to overcome the effects of the first Law because the first Law could not be changed. The law that Esther and Mordecai wrote to overcome the law of Haman is described in Esther 8:11-12.

Esther 8:11-12 *(NKJV)*

> *[11] By these letters the king permitted the Jews who were in every city to gather together and protect their lives — to destroy, kill, and annihilate all the forces of any people or province that would assault them, both little children and women, and to plunder their possessions, [12] on one day in all the provinces of King Ahasuerus, on the thirteenth day of the twelfth month, which is the month of Adar.*

The new law that Esther and Mordecai wrote with the blessing of the King gave the Jews power against their enemies. The law exacted the same kind of destruction that Haman had called for against the Jews. It allowed them to defend themselves against the aggression from their enemies. Haman, the leader and author of the first law, had been destroyed. However, Mordecai grew in great favor in the sight of the king. The confidence of the enemies of the Jews was replaced with fear. This new law took effect on the same day as the first decree, but the advantage went to the Jews in Esther 9:3-4.

Esther 9:3-4 *(BBE)*

> *[3] And all the chiefs and the captains and the rulers and those who did the king's business gave support to the Jews; because the fear of Mordecai had come on them. [4] For Mordecai was great in the king's house, and word of him went out through every part of the kingdom: for the man Mordecai became greater and greater.*

The Jews had prepared to defend themselves and defeat their enemies when the time of the decree of Haman came to pass. Because of the new law that Mordecai and Esther had written, a great fear had fallen upon the king's administrators, and they helped the Jews. The favor of the king toward Ester and Mordecai prevailed in Esther 9:19-22.

Esther 9:19-22 *(BBE)*
19 So the Jews of the country places living in unwalled towns make the fourteenth day of the month Adar a day of feasting and joy and a good day, a day for sending offerings one to another.
20 And Mordecai sent letters to all the Jews in every division of the kingdom of Ahasuerus, near and far,
21 Ordering them to keep the fourteenth day of the month Adar and the fifteenth day of the same month, every year,
22 As days on which the Jews had rest from their haters, and the month which for them was turned from sorrow to joy, and from weeping to a good day: and that they were to keep them as days of feasting and joy, of sending offerings to one another and good things to the poor.

What Goes Around, Comes Around

Haman and all of his sons were hung at the command of the king. The destruction planned by the wicked came back upon them. The Jews overtook their enemies even though they still tried to destroy them. It is important to note a few things when examining these events.

1. The first law from Haman was one of aggression prompted by jealousy and offense.
2. The second law, written by Esther and Mordecai, was one of defense and protection. Had there been no aggressors, there would have been no battles.
3. Even though the new law went into effect, the enemies empowered by the first law did not relent. They still took up arms against the Jews hoping to destroy them.
4. The Jews fought valiantly against their aggressors in defense of their lives according to the new law of Esther and Mordecai.

The Integrity of the Law

Our faith in the New Covenant that is in place today through Jesus will be challenged even though the new law has been written for our success. We will still have to resist the attacks of the aggressor, Satan. Victory won't always come easily, but it is assured.

The success of the Jews in Esther was celebrated in the feast of Purim and is still celebrated today.

Esther 9:23-27 *(BBE)*

[23] And the Jews gave their word to go on as they had been doing and as Mordecai had given them orders in writing; [24] Because Haman, the son of Hammedatha the Agagite, the hater of all the Jews, had made designs for their destruction, attempting to get a decision by Pur (that is, chance) with a view to putting an end to them and cutting them off; [25] But when the business was put before the king, he gave orders by letters that the evil design which he had made against the Jews was to be turned against himself; and that he and his sons were to be put to death by hanging.

[26] So these days were named Purim, after the name of Pur. And so, because of the words of this letter, and of what they had seen in connection with this business, and what had come to them, [27] The Jews made a rule and gave an undertaking, causing their seed and all those who were joined to them to do the same, so that it might be in force for ever, that they would keep those two days, as ordered in the letter, at the fixed time every year.

This book of Esther is extremely important to the New Testament believer, and anyone who searches out the true character and nature of God. The unchangeable nature of God's Word is aptly portrayed. Understanding this characteristic of the laws of God is crucial to our understanding of the New Covenant. God's desire has always been to save mankind from his sins.

This eloquent example of how death and destruction were averted through a new law is exactly what God accomplished through Jesus with the New Testament Covenant. The gift of God through Jesus is available to all, However, make no mistake about it, destruction will come upon those that oppose Him, God's Law and His people. Faith is the key issue exemplified by Esther, who acted on her beliefs in spite of her fear and the threat of death. There are many references in Proverbs that certainly are proven out in the record of Esther, but Proverbs 10:24 has especially shown to be true.

Proverbs 10:24

The fear of the wicked, it shall come upon him: but the desire of the righteous shall be granted.

Once God has made a decree or declaration of a truth, it does not change, nor can it be altered even by God Himself! Words that have come from God's mouth have become His laws. He chose to bind Himself by those words. This is why the Laws of God that were delivered to man through Moses are still in effect today. Most civil law finds its foundation in God's Word, whether or not the world establishment, bureaucrats, or politicians want to acknowledge it. These laws from God cannot be repealed. They are the only absolutes in a world of relativism and situational ethics.

The account of Esther punctuates these concepts as it describes the unalterable nature of the laws of the Medes and the Persians. The etiquette of the throne room points directly to Jesus as the Sceptre that provides for grace and enables our audience before God. This example of the legal system of the earth is presented in the book of Esther to give insight into the unchangeable nature of God's Word. When God says it, it is established, and He does not change His mind. However, like Esther and Mordecai, God provided a remedy to overcome the detrimental effects of an earlier law. The first Law of God was based on performance or works, but the remedy of the new law is based on faith in Jesus and is freely available to all who want it.

God's Word can be counted on as a constant in this world. He does not exercise His sovereignty by changing His mind when it suits Him. He cannot go against His own Word or His own Law. Trusting in His Word, combined with faithful adherence, will keep you safe through all sorts of harrowing circumstances as it did with Daniel in the next chapter.

CHAPTER 19

DECEPTION, DESTRUCTION AND DELIVERANCE

God has chosen to bind himself legally by His own Word. In other words, God is accountable to and bound by His Law. We saw an example of this principle in the book of Esther, but two additional examples in the book of Daniel lend additional insight into this concept. The first example centers on three of Daniel's friends, through whom God finds a way to overcome a sentence of death through the faith of believers.

Daniel was a Hebrew, who along with his companions Shadrach, Meshach, and Abed-nego, was highly favored by Nebuchadnezzar, the non-Hebrew king of the pagan Babylonian Empire. This favor came about as a result of Daniel's correct interpretation of a very troubling dream of the king. The king was upset because his seers could not interpret the dream. However, he was impressed that God enabled Daniel to correctly interpret the dream. As a result, he declared that the God of Daniel was the God of gods and the Lord of kings, in Daniel 2:47-49. This declaration is quite an important in light of the events yet to unfold.

Daniel 2:47-49 *(NKJV)*

> [47] *The king answered Daniel, and said, "Truly your God is the God of gods, the Lord of kings, and a revealer of secrets, since you could reveal this secret."* [48] *Then the king promoted Daniel and gave him many great gifts; and he made him ruler over the whole province of Babylon, and chief administrator over all the wise men of Babylon.* [49] *Also Daniel petitioned the king, and he set Shadrach, Meshach, and Abed-Nego over the affairs of the province of Babylon; but Daniel sat in the gate of the king.*

Honored By God

Daniel and his companions enjoyed honor among the king and his court, but they were also the object of the jealousy and resentment of others. Because of their sudden rise to authority, power, and favor with the king, they acquired some very influential enemies. These enemies had undoubtedly lost their positions and some of their influence as they were displaced by Daniel, Shadrach, Meshach, and Abed-nego. Daniel and his friends may or may not have been aware of their enemies as they continued their duties and the worship of their God. Nebuchadnezzar may also have not been aware of the growing animosity within his court, but he was most certainly aware that Daniel and his friends worshiped God, based on the declaration that he made in Daniel 2:47.

Nebuchadnezzar gave a nod to God, but he still worshiped idols. Sometime after the elevation of Daniel and his friends to their new positions, Nebuchadnezzar made a very large idol of gold which he set up in Babylon. He was certainly very proud of it as it stood threescore cubits in height and six cubits in width. A cubit is generally considered to be 18-21 inches. Threescore means three units of twenty or a total of 60 cubits. Taking an average of 20 inches as a cubit, the idol was 60 cubits x 20 inches, which is 1200 inches or 100 feet in height. It was 6 cubits x 20 inches, which is 120 inches or 10 feet in width. It was not only a big idol at 100 feet tall by 10 feet wide, but that is a lot of gold as well!

Nebuchadnezzar was very happy with his new idol, which was probably a statue of himself. When it was finished, he made a kingdom-wide decree regarding the idol. He declared a state-sponsored dedication ceremony in which attendance by "the princes, the governors, and the captains, the judges, the treasurers, the counsellors, the sheriffs, and all the rulers of the provinces" (Daniel 3:2), was certainly mandatory. An edict also went forth regarding mandatory worship of this idol in Daniel 3:4-6.

Daniel 3:4-6 *(NKJV)*

> [4] *Then a herald cried aloud: "To you it is commanded, O peoples, nations, and languages,* [5] *that at the time you hear the sound of the horn, flute, harp, lyre, and psaltery, in symphony with all kinds of music, you shall fall down and worship the gold image that King Nebuchadnezzar has set up;* [6] *and whoever does not fall down and worship shall be cast immediately into the midst of a burning fiery furnace."*

The edict was a decree that demanded that everyone worship the idol daily and at a particular time. The penalty for disobedience was death. However, the king did not consider the relationship that Daniel and his friends had with God since he only recognized for Him a moment. He did not commit his own thoughts and spirit to God. He had only acknowledged God through Daniel's dream interpretation. As a result, he did not fully consider the effect that his decree would have on Daniel and his friends.

Evil men, corrupted by greed and privilege, corrupt power to accomplish their own agendas. The decree made a way for the enemies of Daniel and his friends to trap them. These evil men seized the opportunity to "take down" the Hebrews to whom the king had given favor. They sought to further their own success at the expense of others. An accusation was then brought against Shadrach, Meshach, and Abed-nego because they refused to dishonor God, obey the lawful decree of the king and worship the idol (Daniel 3:6).

A Fiery End?

Even though they had been previously favored by the king, the king's wrath was brought upon them because of his decree, and they were thrown into a furnace. Why was this punishment chosen? Where did the fiery furnace originate? There is no scriptural indication of its origin. However, the fiery furnace of Daniel 3:15 would have already been in place because of the construction of the idol. After all, to construct a 100 foot tall and 10 foot wide idol, there had to be a lot of molten gold! Not only was the furnace the chosen form of execution due to its terrifying consequences, but most likely it was also the birthplace of the idol. Executing the three Hebrews in the fires of this furnace would be tantamount to sacrificing them to the very idol that they refused to worship!

Daniel 3:15 *(NKJV)*

Now if you are ready at the time you hear the sound of the horn, flute, harp, lyre, and psaltery, in symphony with all kinds of music, and you fall down and worship the image which I have made, good! But if you do not worship, you shall be cast immediately into the midst of a burning fiery furnace. And who is the god who will deliver you from my hands?

Faith In The Midst Of The Fire

Shadrach, Meshach, and Abed-nego reveal the great power that faith in God expresses on the behalf of believers. The faith of these three Hebrew men is exemplified by their reply to the king's direct orders to them in Daniel 3:16-18. The king was unrelenting in his demand that they worship his idol, but they refused and responded with words of faith.

Daniel 3:16-18 *(NKJV)*

> *16 Shadrach, Meshach, and Abed-Nego answered and said to the king, "O Nebuchadnezzar, we have no need to answer you in this matter. 17 If that is the case, our God whom we serve is able to deliver us from the burning fiery furnace, and He will deliver us from your hand, O king. 18 But if not, let it be known to you, O king, that we do not serve your gods, nor will we worship the gold image which you have set up."*

Literally, "they were without need" to even answer the king's demand. Another way to put it might be this, *"King, there is really no need for us to even discuss this with you."* They went on to explain their faith in God by saying, *"Our God whom we serve is able to deliver us from the burning fiery furnace, and He will deliver us out of thine hand, O king."* This is a statement affirming that not only is God *able*, but He *will* deliver them. However, before they made that statement, they said, *"If that is the case,"* meaning that if the king were to carry out his punishment of throwing them into the furnace, God would deliver them.

They continued by saying, "*But if not....*" Many people take this to mean that they were expressing doubt as to whether or not God would deliver them. Their statement at the end of the sentence has a completely opposite meaning, however. If they were expressing doubt in God, the logical conclusion would be that they would die in the furnace. However, if they died in the furnace, their defiant statement in verse 18 that they would still not serve the king's gods or worship the image is ridiculous because they would already be dead! In reality, what they were saying was something like this:

> *King, we don't even need to discuss this with you. If you want to throw us into the furnace, go right ahead. Our God is not only able to save us, but he will deliver us out of your control. And just so you know, if you change your mind and decide not to throw us into the furnace, we are still not going to follow your law and worship your gods or your idol!*

The king was so enraged by the disobedience of Shadrach, Meshach, and Abed-nego that he commanded that they be executed in the furnace. He ordered the furnace to be heated to seven times its normal temperature. Then, he commanded that the most mighty men of his army bind them and throw them into the furnace in Daniel 3:19-23.

Daniel 3:19-23 *(NKJV)*

19Then Nebuchadnezzar was full of fury, and the expression on his face changed toward Shadrach, Meshach, and Abed-Nego. He spoke and commanded that they heat the furnace seven times more than it was usually heated. 20 And he commanded certain mighty men of valor who were in his army to bind Shadrach, Meshach, and Abed-Nego, and cast them into the burning fiery furnace. 21 Then these men were bound in their coats, their trousers, their turbans, and their other garments, and were cast into the midst of the burning fiery furnace. 22 Therefore, because the king's command was urgent, and the furnace exceedingly hot, the flame of the fire killed those men who took up Shadrach, Meshach, and Abed-Nego. 23 And these three men, Shadrach, Meshach, and Abed-Nego, fell down bound into the midst of the burning fiery furnace.

The furnace was so hot that the king's guards were themselves consumed by the fire at the opening. However, the fire was not to consume the three Hebrews. God honored their commitment to Him not to worship the idol and was with them in the furnace as described by Nebuchadnezzar. However, there was a fourth individual that Nebuchadnezzar saw with them in the furnace. They were all without any injury. The fourth person in the furnace was identified in Daniel 3:24-25 as having the form of the Son God, which would be Jesus! They were saved from death without even a trace of the smell of smoke upon them.

Daniel 3:24-25 *(NKJV)*

24 Then King Nebuchadnezzar was astonished; and he rose in haste and spoke, saying to his counselors, "Did we not cast three men bound into the midst of the fire?" They answered and said to the king, "True, O king."
25 "Look!" he answered, "I see four men loose, walking in the midst of the fire; and they are not hurt, and the form of the fourth is like the Son of God."

The king was astonished at what he saw. It was also witnessed by all the dignitaries that were called to the dedication ceremony for the idol. They saw the protection that God provided to Shadrach, Meshach, and Abed-nego. The king made a decree that if anyone spoke against the God of Shadrach, Meshach, and Abed-nego, they would be destroyed. He acknowledged that only the God of Shadrach, Meshach, and Abed-nego could deliver in this way because they would not submit to the law to worship the idol. Nebuchadnezzar did not turn from his idol worship or the worship of his gods, but he acknowledged that this demonstration changed his word, the word of the king. Unlike those we discussed in Chapter 5, this was a real *act of God,* in which God protected and delivered His servants, ultimately raising them to even higher honor as the king called them out of the furnace in Daniel 3:26-30.

Daniel 3:26-30 *(NKJV)*

> 26 *Then Nebuchadnezzar went near the mouth of the burning fiery furnace and spoke, saying, "Shadrach, Meshach, and Abed-Nego, servants of the Most High God, come out, and come here." Then Shadrach, Meshach, and Abed-Nego came from the midst of the fire.*
> 27 *And the satraps, administrators, governors, and the king's counselors gathered together, and they saw these men on whose bodies the fire had no power; the hair of their head was not singed nor were their garments affected, and the smell of fire was not on them.*
>
> 28 *Nebuchadnezzar spoke, saying, "Blessed be the God of Shadrach, Meshach, and Abed-Nego, who sent His Angel and delivered His servants who trusted in Him, and they have frustrated the king's word, and yielded their bodies, that they should not serve nor worship any god except their own God!*
> 29 *Therefore I make a decree that any people, nation, or language which speaks anything amiss against the God of Shadrach, Meshach, and Abed-Nego shall be cut in pieces, and their houses shall be made an ash heap; because there is no other God who can deliver like this."*
>
> 30 *Then the king promoted Shadrach, Meshach, and Abed-Nego in the province of Babylon.*

The actions of hateful and jealous people were overcome, and God's people were delivered from harm by their faith. The motivations of the enemies were to destroy the three Hebrew men because they were in a position of authority that they had lost. Shadrach, Meshach, and Abed-nego stood their ground, using their faith in God to resist and overcome the adversity that they faced. They had confidence in God and declared the end result of their faith. They stayed true to God, were unharmed by the fires of the furnace, brought honor to God and were promoted. Their faith even caused the king to *change his word* and issue a new decree that superseded the first and called for people throughout the land to exalt the God of Shadrach, Meshach, and Abed-nego!

Bound By The Word

The second example of being bound by law is found in Daniel, chapters 5 and 6. It involves Daniel himself and the overcoming of an existing law. Throughout his reign, Nebuchadnezzar had made alliances and conquered many peoples. One of the empires with which he made alliance and joined forces was the Median Empire (the Medes), which was part of Persia. He did so through his marriage to Amytus of Media, the daughter of the Median king. It appears that this alliance brought a form of structure to the legal system that continued in the reign of Nebuchadnezzar. It probably played a part in the decree that the king made following the promotions of Shadrach, Meshach, and Abed-nego and the king's decree concerning their God.

Nebuchadnezzar passed the kingdom to his son Belshazzar, who was murdered and replaced by Darius, a Mede. However, the principles of the law continued when as the kingdom was taken by Darius. Daniel maintained his favored status through both transitions as he accurately interpreted the dreams of the kings. When Darius took the kingdom, he also favored Daniel, recognizing him by putting him in charge of the whole realm in Daniel 5:31 - 6:3.

Daniel 5:31 - 6:3

31 And Darius the Median took the kingdom, being about threescore and two years old.

1 It pleased Darius to set over the kingdom an hundred and twenty princes, which should be over the whole kingdom; 2 And over these three presidents; of whom Daniel was first: that the princes might give accounts unto them, and the king should have no damage.

3 Then this Daniel was preferred above the presidents and princes, because an excellent spirit was in him; and the king thought to set him over the whole realm.

Daniel had great favor in the eyes of King Darius, so much so that the king's advisors were very jealous of him and his relationship with the king. The devious action of these advisors is documented in Daniel 6: 4-7, as they convinced the king to make a decree that would allow them to destroy Daniel.

Daniel 6:4-7 *(GNT)*

[4] Then the other supervisors and the governors tried to find something wrong with the way Daniel administered the empire, but they couldn't, because Daniel was reliable and did not do anything wrong or dishonest. [5] They said to each other, "We are not going to find anything of which to accuse Daniel unless it is something in connection with his religion."

[6] So they went to see the king and said, "King Darius, may Your Majesty live forever! [7] All of us who administer your empire — the supervisors, the governors, the lieutenant governors, and the other officials — have agreed that Your Majesty should issue an order and enforce it strictly. Give orders that for thirty days no one be permitted to request anything from any god or from any human being except from Your Majesty. Anyone who violates this order is to be thrown into a pit filled with lions.

They wrote a decree that made it illegal to pray to any God or make a request of any man except the king for 30 days or be thrown into a den of lions. They knew that Daniel was devoted to God and would continue to pray to God regardless of the decree. The continuation of legal protocols is evidenced in Daniel 6:8-9 when the decree was made attempting to destroy Daniel. The King signed it into law according to the same principle that we explored in Esther 1:19 *(see p. 230)*.

Daniel 6:8-9 *(GNT)*

[8] So let Your Majesty issue this order and sign it, and it will be in force, a law of the Medes and Persians, ***which cannot be changed****." [9] And so king Darius signed the order.*

It was clearly stated that the law would be established according to the laws of the Medes and Persians. Consequently, once put in place it could not be changed even by the King that made the decree. They planned to force the King into a position of requiring Daniel to be put to death in the lion's den. They encouraged the King to sign the 30-day decree that they wrote, knowing that Daniel would obey God rather than the decree.

Evil men again set out to destroy someone for the sake of their own power and influence. They corrupted the law to accomplish their own desires. They seized the opportunity to coerce the King to sign a law for which he did not fully appreciate the consequences. They sought to further their own success at the expense of others. This action was the height of was corrupt manipulation that has gone on since Cain killed Able. Doesn't this also sound familiar in the world today?

As anticipated, Daniel did not obey the decree, even under penalty of death, but continued to worship his God. The King was very grieved, in Daniel 6:18-28 when he realized that he had been manipulated to pass a sentence of death upon Daniel. The penalty for disobedience was demanded and had to be fulfilled. The King labored to find somehow a way to save Daniel from the sentence of death. The jealous advisors reminded the king of the decree and the fact that it was unchangeable in any way. The King was trapped, bound by his own decree because it was written according to the principles of the laws of the Medes and Persians (Daniel 6:15). No matter how much it grieved him, he could not change it.

Daniel 6:18-28 *(GNT)*

18 Then the king returned to the palace and spent a sleepless night, without
food or any form of entertainment. 19 At dawn the king got up and hurried
to the pit. 20 When he got there, he called out anxiously, "Daniel, servant of
the living God! Was the God you serve so loyally able to save you from the
lions?"

21 Daniel answered, "May Your Majesty live forever! 22 God sent his angel
to shut the mouths of the lions so that they would not hurt me. He did this
because he knew that I was innocent and because I have not wronged you,
Your Majesty."

23 The king was overjoyed and gave orders for Daniel to be pulled up out of the pit. So they pulled him up and saw that he had not been hurt at all, for he trusted God.

24 Then the king gave orders to arrest all those who had accused Daniel, and he had them thrown, together with their wives and children, into the pit filled with lions. Before they even reached the bottom of the pit, the lions pounced on them and broke all their bones.

25 Then King Darius wrote to the people of all nations, races, and languag-
es on earth: "Greetings! 26 I command that throughout my empire everyone
should fear and respect Daniel's God. He is a living God, and he will rule
forever. His kingdom will never be destroyed, and his power will never come
to an end. 27 He saves and rescues; he performs wonders and miracles in

heaven and on earth. He saved Daniel from being killed by the lions."

[28] *Daniel prospered during the reign of Darius and the reign of Cyrus the Persian.*

Darius did not write a new law concerning Daniel as we saw in the book of Esther. Instead, he interceded for Daniel by declaring that God would deliver him. King Darius spoke faith over Daniel! He fasted throughout the night and did not sleep as he labored over the deliverance of Daniel from the lions. The next morning, King Darius found Daniel unharmed and gave glory to God. The King took vengeance upon the conspirators and their families and sent them to their deaths in the lion's den. He then made a decree that throughout his kingdom, all would tremble and fear the God of Daniel because He was a God of deliverance.

The Law Of Intended Consequence

This physical example of King Darius, being bound by his decree, gives us a way to understand how God is similarly bound by His Word. Just like the allegory of the laws of the Medes and Persians, God's Word cannot be changed. Unfortunately, the king discovered that there was an unintended consequence of his decree. He did not realize that the decree could be used to create a situation potentially leading to the death of Daniel. Daniel was being forced to choose to sin against God and live, or to obey God and die. Daniel chose to obey God and trust in Him by faith. Daniel trusted, Darius spoke in agreement, and God delivered him.

The laws of God state that the penalty for sin (disobedience) is death. The advisors tricked the King into making a law to affect Daniel that was just the opposite. Their decree was designed to reward sin with life or, more accurately, punish obedience to God with death. However, God rewards obedience.

The king did not think through his law as to its unintended consequences. Vanity and ego most likely got the best of him as his advisors manipulated him. God's Law does not have any unintended consequences, however. There is no ego or vanity involved in the *intended* consequences of God's Law, which are to destroy the sin and save the individual. God does not decree the penalty against you but against the sin in which you might participate. His Law reveals sin but offers compassion and mercy, knowing that we are all weak and incapable of avoiding sin entirely. It is your choice whether or not to engage in sin, but if you do without atonement, your penalty is death.

God could not remove His law, but He was able to establish new provisions, legally circumventing the effects of the law, just as we saw in Esther *(see p. 240)*. He made a way in the Old Testament for a substitute to pay the penalty of death for man's sins. On a yearly basis, the priests offered the blood from animal sacrifices to atone for the sins of the people.

However, God's ultimate plan for atonement was to supply a one-time, permanent substitute for all sins to those who would act on faith and believe. He would do this without altering the original law. He brought His Son, Jesus, into the world to be that substitute and offer His blood once to pay the price for all of our sins. Daniel lived by acting on his faith in God, and in the same way, you can live by placing your faith in God's gift of His Son, Jesus. Jesus paid the price for your sins so that by faith you can have eternal life with Him. This is the Mystery of the Gospel.

Plan To Win

The unwavering integrity and constancy of the Word of God carries a uniform thread throughout. It is a thread that binds together all of mankind. This common thread is God's love, His provision, His care and His desire to provide a way back to eternal fellowship in His presence for all of mankind. God created man to enjoy this eternal fellowship with Him. Evil is always around because we live in a fallen world in which Satan has a tremendous influence upon the spirit of man. However, God has a way to deal with that evil as stated in Romans 12:17-21.

Romans 12:17-21 *(GNT)*

> [17] *If someone has done you wrong, do not repay him with a wrong. Try to do what everyone considers to be good.* [18] *Do everything possible on your part to live in peace with everybody.*
>
> [19] *Never take revenge, my friends, but instead let God's anger do it. For the scripture says, "I will take revenge, I will pay back, says the Lord."* [20] *Instead, as the scripture says: "If your enemies are hungry, feed them; if they are thirsty, give them a drink; for by doing this you will make them burn with shame."* [21] *Do not let evil defeat you; instead, conquer evil with good.*

Evil manifests itself in many ways through the sins of mankind. We can see it all around us. Sometimes it is obvious, but sometimes it is cloaked behind social attitudes or political correctness. Adam and Eve were kind enough to be sure that we all have the knowledge of good and evil *(see p. 99)*. Regardless of the way that people choose to believe or legislate, right is right and wrong is wrong. Wrong is sin, and when it has been verified through the righteous judgment of God, it has a predetermined sentence of eternal death. Haman was unrepentant in his evil conspiracy and received the death sentence when he and his family were destroyed. Haman's allies chose the social and legislative approval of his evil law. They died at the hands of the Jews rather than siding with the righteous law that Esther and Mordecai created when Esther acted on her faith *(see p. 255)*. Along with their families, the jealous advisors of Darius received death in the den of lions for their sin against Daniel as they conspired to make him dishonor God (Daniel 6:24).

God interacts with mankind through His Word and His Law. His principles are unchangeable. They are the bedrock of the universe and our world. Once He has made a declaration, it cannot be changed. Death and destruction will come upon sin. However, God has an eloquent means of handling sin in the earth realm using the principles that He described in Esther. He made a new law to supersede the first one through which He offers forgiveness with a commuted sentence and penalties if there is genuine repentance. This is the essence of the New Covenant through Jesus. It is a new law that does not change the old one but instead provides a way to overcome its penalties.

Just like a two-year-old begins to challenge the world that he is waking up in, man continues to challenge the boundaries that are set before him. Changing the rules to fit the situation never works in the long haul. At some point, payment will be required. Understanding the character of God and His nature provides insight into His heart and His willingness to save us from ourselves. This crucial step leads to fulfilled and harmonious living on this earth. Understanding that in His love for us He provided the way to overcome the penalties of our error and give us the opportunity to accept His gift and enjoy eternal life through Jesus Christ.

Sin and evil are both insidious and rampant in the world. However, since God created the whole universe, some might say that He also created evil and sin and is ultimately responsible for all of it. So logically, God must be at fault for the sin in the world, right? Let's see if that is true and take a look at where the fault really lies.

Chapter 20

IT'S NOT MY FAULT !

Isn't that what you hear so much of these days? It's not my fault. It was my mother's, my father's, my teacher's, my friend's, the drugs, the alcohol, the economy, whatever, or whoever's fault. I'm not guilty! Someone else is to blame. The devil made me do it, or maybe it was even God's fault. But it certainly wasn't my fault!

Some people think they can do anything they want whenever they want. This is actually true. It is called *free will,* and God gave it to us. The problem is that these people also do not want to be held responsible for their choices. They try to divert the unpleasant effects of their actions away from themselves onto something or someone else. The Bible plainly states in 1 Corinthians 6:12 and 10:23 that while all things may be lawful or allowable, some things may not be good for the individual.

1 Corinthians 6:12 *(AMP)*

> *Everything is permissible (allowable and lawful) for me; but not all things are helpful (good for me to do, expedient and profitable when considered with other things). Everything is lawful for me, but I will not become the slave of anything or be brought under its power.*

1 Corinthians 10:23 *(AMP)*

> *All things are legitimate [permissible — and we are free to do anything we please], but not all things are helpful (expedient, profitable, and wholesome). All things are legitimate, but not all things are constructive [to character] and edifying [to spiritual life].*

The nature of man is to be self-justifying. "I want to do it. Therefore, it is OK." Or in other words, "If it feels good, do it." Man alters social values and God's law to *normalize* and endorse his desired behaviors and make himself acceptable. Certain groups of like-minded individuals lobby to have laws written or changed to fit their lifestyles. They want to permit or even encourage behaviors that are contrary to God's law and universally considered to be immoral, illegal, or otherwise *sinful* by the vast majority of society. Getting aberrant or sinful activity accepted by society does not make it right. Free will *permits* you to do what you want, but you will still face the consequences and a reckoning for your actions.

God endowed man with enormous ability, talent, skill, understanding, comprehension, and ingenuity. After all, according to the Biblical account in Genesis 1:26-27, God created man in His image.

Genesis 1:26-27

26 And God said, Let us make man in our image, after our likeness: and let them have dominion over the fish of the sea, and over the fowl of the air, and over the cattle, and over all the earth, and over every creeping thing that creepeth upon the earth. 27 So God created man in his own image, in the image of God created he him; male and female created he them.

However, God knew the significance of the gifts that He *built into man,* the potential for abuse of those gifts and man's need for guidance. He constructed the Old Testament Law to point out the things that were conducive to life, health, community, and peace and in stark contrast to the activities that would destroy both the individual and the community. God stated His purpose by encouraging man to make correct choices in Jeremiah 21:8 as well as in Deuteronomy 4:8, 11:26-28 and 30:19.

Jeremiah 21:8

And unto this people thou shalt say, Thus saith the Lord, Behold, I set before you the way of life, and the way of death.

Deuteronomy 4:8

And what nation is there so great, that hath statutes and judgments so righteous as all this law, which I set before you this day?

Deuteronomy 11:26-28 *(ERV)*

26 Today I am giving you a choice. You may choose the blessing or the curse. 27 You will get the blessing if you listen and obey the commands of the Lord your God that I have told you today. 28 But you will get the curse if you refuse to listen and obey the commands of the Lord your God. So don't stop living the way I command you today, and don't follow other gods that you don't know.

Deuteronomy 30:19 *(GWT)*

I call on heaven and earth as witnesses today that I have offered you life or death, blessings or curses. Choose life so that you and your descendants will live.

Who Is Responsible?

This simple question brings forth a myriad of complications, and the implications of the answer are far reaching, many times difficult to live with and sometimes hard to accept. The mores of society seem to create new sets of rules as they change and evolve. The ultimate expression of the *ideolatry* of man's spiritually un-renewed mind is his arrogance in legislating into acceptability things that are in opposition to the natural order of God's universe. However, the key to understanding the role that mankind plays in the earth realm is found in the *spiritually renewed* mind.

The Renewed Mind

A *renewing* of the mind is essential to fully understand the answer to the question, "Who is Responsible?" Ephesians 4:17-24 speaks about *renewing* the mind through the Spirit of God. This renewal comes by embracing God's life in you and not holding on to a corrupt lifestyle and thought process. It is a purposeful, personal, quality decision that you must make for yourself. The Spirit provides you with help, but you must "put on" your new nature and renew your mind to God's way of thinking.

Ephesians 4:17-24 *(NLT)*

17 With the Lord's authority I say this: Live no longer as the Gentiles do,
for they are hopelessly confused. 18 Their minds are full of darkness; they
wander far from the life God gives because they have closed their minds and
hardened their hearts against him. 19 They have no sense of shame. They
live for lustful pleasure and eagerly practice every kind of impurity. 20 But
that isn't what you learned about Christ. 21 Since you have heard about
Jesus and have learned the truth that comes from him, 22 throw off your old
sinful nature and your former way of life, which is corrupted by lust and
deception. 23 Instead, let the Spirit renew your thoughts and attitudes.
24 Put on your new nature, created to be like God–truly righteous and holy.

You are encouraged to change your lifestyle and avoid giving too much heed to the understanding of your mind. This lifestyle change occurs as you demonstrate the *new creature* that you have become through acceptance of Christ in 2 Corinthians 5:17 and reorganize your mind to the spiritual perspectives of God through His Word *(see p. 20)*. You must *release your personal ideolatry* as described in Ephesians 4:22-24 *(AMP)*.

Ephesians 4:22-24 *(AMP)*

[22] Strip yourselves of your former nature [put off and discard your old unrenewed self] which characterized your previous manner of life and becomes corrupt through lusts and desires that spring from delusion; [23] And be constantly renewed in the spirit of your mind [having a fresh mental and spiritual attitude], [24] And put on the new nature (the regenerate self) created in God's image, [Godlike] in true righteousness and holiness.

The spiritually un-renewed mind is subject to *ideolatry* because it views itself as superior or even supreme. It does not acknowledge the fact that there is a higher level of truth or understanding that exceeds its own ability to comprehend. Human understanding comes from the mind, and it is carnal. *Carnal mind reasoning* is based on experience, education, culture, tradition, and many other factors. It operates under the premise that everything can be conquered or mastered by the human intellect. This level of understanding makes truth a relative concept since everyone sees things differently and judgment depends upon the perspective of the individual *(see p. 41)*. In Isaiah 55:8-9, we see that God thinks and acts far differently than we do.

Isaiah 55:8-9

[8] For my thoughts are not your thoughts, neither are your ways my ways, saith the Lord. [9] For as the heavens are higher than the earth, so are my ways higher than your ways, and my thoughts than your thoughts.

A new thought process that comes from a spiritually renewed mind is essential for understanding the real truth of God. Real truth is not situational. It is absolute. It is up to us individually to find it. The tools have been provided for us, the evidence is all around us, and the desire for it is implanted in our beings. The problem is that the influence of the world system of lust, greed, and selfishness clouds that spiritual yearning.

Man has created many ways and even organizations which are also based on *carnal mind reasoning* to satisfy his worldly yearning. These can further confuse the truth. The truth is that we are all responsible for our own spiritual well-being and growth. However, relying upon a man-conceived religion, institution, or rules set by an organization simply serves to pass off that responsibility to someone or something else. The relationship with God that we need is not through an intermediary of some sort. We need a direct, one-on-one relationship with our Creator.

Personal Responsibility

Deflection of responsibility seems to be the new normal, and the concept of personal responsibility does not seem to be in vogue much anymore. It pervades society from children acting out violently in school with no repercussions to the highest levels of politicians and leaders who accept no accountability for their actions. Personal responsibility for individual actions seems to be eroding on a daily basis in our society.

Responsibility is frequently reasoned away by the carnal mind of the individual when there are significant consequences for a specific action. The rejection of responsibility allows us to avoid guilt and punishment. However, judgment (determination) establishes accountability and assigns responsibility. A judge or a jury uses evidence to discern truth and liability. Consequences then ensue from that determination. The killing of Abel by his brother Cain was the first murder *(see p. 63)* and is described in Genesis 4:2-8. However, what prompted Cain to act out in such anger?

Genesis 4:2b-8 *(NIV)*

> [2] *Now Abel kept flocks, and Cain worked the soil.* [3] *In the course of time Cain brought some of the fruits of the soil as an offering to the Lord .* [4] *But Abel brought fat portions from some of the firstborn of his flock. The Lord looked with favor on Abel and his offering,* [5] *but on Cain and his offering he did not look with favor. So Cain was very angry, and his face was downcast.*
>
> [6] *Then the Lord said to Cain, "Why are you angry? Why is your face downcast?* [7] *If you do what is right, will you not be accepted? But if you do not do what is right, sin is crouching at your door; it desires to have you, but you must master it."*
>
> [8] *Now Cain said to his brother Abel, "Let's go out to the field." And while they were in the field, Cain attacked his brother Abel and killed him.*

Cain and Abel both made offerings to the Lord. The offering of Abel was accepted, but Cain's was not. There is much speculation about why Cain's offering was rejected by God as there is no clear indication in the text. It may have been that Cain offered inferior crops rather than the best first fruits. He may have disobeyed previous instruction about what and how to offer, or he may have just had a grudging attitude about making the offering. We have no clues, but according to Psalms 44:20-21, God knows the innermost thoughts and motivations of our hearts.

Psalms 44:20-21 *(NLT)*
[20] *If we had forgotten the name of our God or spread our hands in prayer to foreign gods,* [21] *God would surely have known it, for he knows the secrets of every heart.*

The appearance of Cain changed as he became angered at the rejection of his offering. Confronting his anger, God asked a very important question and made a very revealing statement in Genesis 4:7. He asked, *"If you do right, will you not be accepted?"* This question clearly implies that there was some defect in Cain's offering, actions, or heart posture. Then, God said, *"But if you do not do what is right, sin is crouching at your door; it desires to have you, but you must master it."* This statement explains the struggle of personal responsibility and what to do about it that has engaged all of mankind throughout the ages. Cain sinned. He knew it, and God knew it. God confronted him by saying that he could do right, fix the problem and be accepted. Cain chose not to follow that advice, but instead became angry and developed a jealous, envious attitude toward Abel. Instead of repenting of his sin and setting things right, Cain defied God and expressed his rebellion by lashing out at someone that was doing the right thing.

Isn't that what we see every day in the world around us? Those who are actively engaged in sin and doing wrong set out to destroy those who are doing right. They do this to cover their sins and further their own agenda. Rather than face their sins and repent, these people rebel against the law, whether it is civil, moral, or spiritual. Then, they become activists to get those around them to accept and normalize their sins, so they can justify themselves and feel good about engaging and living in their sins.

However, God offered Cain a warning, a way out that applies to all of us. He said, "*sin desires to have you,*" meaning that sin waits at the door of your life, looking for opportunities to pounce on you and consume you, and it will if you let it. You *can* overcome or master it. You don't have to let it consume you. This struggle is one of personal responsibility, acknowledging your failings (sin) and resisting the tendency to repeat them while seeking to do what is right. Cain chose the path of sin, denied his personal responsibility for his actions and refused to change. What will you do?

Responsibility for actions and the consequences of those actions lies squarely upon the shoulders of the individual. Choices and actions are subject to the individual's free will. The gift of free will does not mean that there is an exemption from the consequence of a decision to express that free will wrongly. Every decision that we make carries an effect that is placed into action by that decision. Bad decisions also carry costs that we do not want to pay. God knows our innermost thoughts, and there is no hiding. He holds us accountable as stated in Hebrews 4:12-13.

Hebrews 4:12-13 *(ERV)*

*12 God's word is alive and working. It is sharper than the sharpest sword
and cuts all the way into us. It cuts deep to the place where the soul and
the spirit are joined. God's word cuts to the center of our joints and our
bones. It judges the thoughts and feelings in our hearts. 13 Nothing in all
the world can be hidden from God. He can clearly see all things. Everything
is open before him. And to him we must explain the way we have lived.*

God also plainly explains the benefits of positive decisions and the detrimental effects of poor ones. The following passage was written specifically to the Israelites after God brought them out from slavery in Egypt. They had been wandering for forty years in the desert. There are several principles upon which God builds an expectation for His people. These are universal truths that apply to every person today as much as they did to the Israelites. The choice of the path and ultimately the outcome always lies in the hands of individual people. God made them aware of the consequences of their choices in Deuteronomy 30:15-18.

Deuteronomy 30:15-18 *(NLT)*

*15 Now listen! Today I am giving you a choice between life and death,
between prosperity and disaster. 16 For I command you this day to love the
Lord your God and to keep his commands, decrees, and regulations by walking in his ways. If you do this, you will live and multiply, and the Lord your
God will bless you and the land you are about to enter and occupy.*

*17 But if your heart turns away and you refuse to listen, and if you are
drawn away to serve and worship other gods, 18 then I warn you now that
you will certainly be destroyed. You will not live a long, good life in the
land you are crossing the Jordan to occupy.*

God laid out a clear choice. He offered good and life as well as evil and death. The choice was theirs, and the same choice is ours. It is the essence of our free will to follow our own path. God's statement of what was needed for prolonged life, success, and prosperity is valid for us as well. He also stated what would happen if they or we chose another path. It is spelled it out in no uncertain terms in Deuteronomy 30:19-20.

Deuteronomy 30:19-20 *(NKJV)*

> [19] *I call heaven and earth as witnesses today against you, that I have set before you life and death, blessing and cursing; therefore choose life, that both you and your descendants may live;* [20] *that you may love the Lord your God, that you may obey His voice, and that you may cling to Him, for He is your life and the length of your days. . . .*

The instruction in this verse is very clear. There is a choice available to us. This opportunity to choose is the definition of *free will*. Life and death as well as blessing and cursing are choices subject to the desires of the individual. Actually, choice is not only *available* to us, it is *demanded* of us. We are required to make choices throughout our lives. The Word of God is full of encouragements not only to exercise choice but also to make use of wisdom and good judgment when making choices.

God is not responsible for bad decisions on the part of an individual. His counsel to us is always to make the right choice. Judgment, wisdom and understanding are essential for making good decisions, but the lack of them is not an excuse for making poor ones because God provides these essentials within our spirits and in His Word. Romans 1:18-32 explains the degradation that occurs when we turn against the evidence of God that is all around us. He has revealed it to us through His creation, and we the have intrinsic knowledge that He built into our human spirit.

Romans 1:18-32 *(CEV)*

> [18] *From heaven God shows how angry he is with all the wicked and evil things that sinful people do to crush the truth.* [19] *They know everything that can be known about God, because God has shown it all to them.* [20] *God's eternal power and character cannot be seen. But from the beginning of creation, God has shown what these are like by all he has made. That's why those people don't have any excuse.* [21] *They know about God, but they don't honor him or even thank him. Their thoughts are useless, and their stupid minds are in the dark.* [22] *They claim to be wise, but they are fools.* [23] *They don't worship the glorious and eternal God. Instead, they worship idols that are made to look like humans who cannot live forever, and like birds, animals, and reptiles.*

[24] So God let these people go their own way. They did what they wanted to do, and their filthy thoughts made them do shameful things with their bodies. [25] They gave up the truth about God for a lie, and they worshiped God's creation instead of God, who will be praised forever. Amen.
[26] God let them follow their own evil desires. Women no longer wanted to have sex in a natural way, and they did things with each other that were
not natural. [27] Men behaved in the same way. They stopped wanting to have sex with women and had strong desires for sex with other men. They did shameful things with each other, and what has happened to them is punishment for their foolish deeds.
[28] Since these people refused even to think about God, he let their useless minds rule over them. That's why they do all sorts of indecent things.
[29] They are evil, wicked, and greedy, as well as mean in every possible way. They want what others have, and they murder, argue, cheat, and are hard
to get along with. They gossip, [30] say cruel things about others, and hate God. They are proud, conceited, and boastful, always thinking up new ways to do evil.
These people don't respect their parents. [31] They are stupid, unreliable, and
don't have any love or pity for others. [32] They know God has said that anyone who acts this way deserves to die. But they keep on doing evil things, and they even encourage others to do them.

A person who *chooses* to deny God's guidance and instruction does so by his or her own free will and will engage in some or all of the evil activities outlined in this passage of Romans. It is in His character to warn, lead, and guide us into the choices that will result in life and blessing. God did not create us to live lifestyles that are contrary to His will. We are not born *"that way"*. We *choose* lifestyles by letting our minds and our bodies control our spirits. We are tempted to follow the evil desires of our flesh and our mind as we act on the lust of our desires. It is our responsibility to become educated and acquire understanding, judgment, and wisdom. James 1:13-17 plainly explains the struggles that we face, the role God does not play and our responsibility as we encounter the struggles of life.

James 1:13-17 *(NKJV)*

[13] Let no one say when he is tempted, "I am tempted by God"; for God cannot be tempted by evil, nor does He Himself tempt anyone. [14] But each one
is tempted when he is drawn away by his own desires and enticed. [15] Then, when desire has conceived, it gives birth to sin; and sin, when it is full-grown, brings forth death.

> [16] *Do not be deceived, my beloved brethren.* [17] *Every good gift and every perfect gift is from above, and comes down from the Father of lights, with whom there is no variation or shadow of turning.*

Temptations are born from the lustful pursuits of Romans 1:18-32, and we engage in activities and make choices that reflect our own desires. Fundamental errors with long reaching, detrimental effects can be avoided by seeking the counsel of God's Word from which we receive understanding, judgment, and wisdom to apply to any decision-making process. The servant in Luke 12:48 was punished lightly for his misdeeds because he did not know the expectations of his master and some people do prefer to stay ignorant and slide by rather than get educated and have something required of them. However, it is so much better to receive the knowledge and the responsibilities and subsequent authority that goes with it.

Luke 12:48 *(ERV)*

> *But what about the servant who does not know what his master wants? He also does things that deserve punishment. But he will get less punishment than the servant who knew what he should do. Whoever has been given much will be responsible for much. Much more will be expected from the one who has been given more.*

When the believer fully appreciates the magnitude of the blessings that God has provided, he or she will have an attitude of gratitude and be happy to do whatever He asks. Choices carry responsibilities that are rooted in the *investment of authority* that God made in Adam and Eve. They lost it to Satan in the garden *(see p. 99)*, but by His sacrifice, Jesus won it back for the believer. He speaks of it in Mark 11:22-24 and Psalms 8:4-6.

Mark 11:22-24 *(NLT)*

> [22] *Then Jesus said to the disciples, "Have faith in God.* [23] *I tell you the truth, you can say to this mountain, 'May you be lifted up and thrown into the sea,' and it will happen. But you must really believe it will happen and have no doubt in your heart.* [24] *I tell you, you can pray for anything, and if you believe that you've received it, it will be yours."*

Psalms 8:4-6 *(GNT)*

> [4] *What are human beings, that you think of them; mere mortals, that you care for them?* [5] *Yet you made them inferior only to yourself; you crowned them with glory and honor.* [6] *You appointed them rulers over everything you made; you placed them over all creation.*

Having authority is a far different than being responsible for mistaken activities like the servant in Luke 12:48. A new freedom with a new thought process comes when a person exercises their proactive authority as a believer. However, we might struggle to use and live in this authority because of a lack of knowledge, understanding or faith. Jesus detailed the extent of the believer's authority in Mark 16:15-18 and John 16:23.

Mark 16:15-18

15 And he said unto them, "Go ye into all the world, and preach the gospel to every creature. 16 He that believeth and is baptized shall be saved; but he that believeth not shall be damned. 17 And these signs shall follow them that believe; In my name shall they cast out devils; they shall speak with new tongues; 18 They shall take up serpents; and if they drink any deadly thing, it shall not hurt them; they shall lay hands on the sick, and they shall recover."

John 16:23

And in that day ye shall ask me nothing. Verily, verily, I say unto you, Whatsoever ye shall ask the Father in my name, he will give it you.

God has also freed us from guilt and the penalty of wrongdoing through belief in and acceptance of Jesus Christ. However, we must still accept personal responsibility for our own free will choices. Poor choices that are at odds with or in disobedience to God's direction and absolute law are defined as sin. Even though the eternal penalty of sin is paid for through Jesus Christ, the temporal effects can still take their toll. It is unknown who first said it, but "*sin will take you farther than you want to go, keep you longer than you want to stay and cost you more than you want to pay.*" Exercising wisdom is the way to avoid the problems that sin causes. Proverbs 4:5-7 tells us that "*Wisdom is the principle thing.*"

Proverbs 4:5-7

5 Get wisdom, get understanding: forget it not; neither decline from the words of my mouth. 6 Forsake her not, and she shall preserve thee: love her, and she shall keep thee. 7 Wisdom is the principal thing; therefore get wisdom: and with all thy getting get understanding.

God's instruction to "*get wisdom*" is the foundation that establishes the basis for understanding and in turn provides the ability to execute judgment. There is no standard upon which to make decisions without wisdom that is rooted in the everlasting and absolute nature of God's Word and His Law. Good choices enhance life, promote personal success, and provide contentment. Embrace responsibility rather than shrinking from it. You will then be ready for the empowerment that arises from a life populated with decisions that are guided by wisdom-inspired judgment.

Who Is The Real Problem?

Many human interactions involve significant demands to conform to another's way of thinking. This imposition of man's will with his demands to conform is at least a source, if not *the* source, of the personal conflict and even war that we see occurring globally. Man's will is individual and subject to wide variance because it is based on relativity and has no absolute foundation. Man frequently makes up his own rules to suit himself as he goes through his life and finds it unacceptable to simply allow others to have their own differing opinions or views. When taken to the extreme, the imposition of man's will is designed to dominate and control through manipulation, aggression, conflict, and wars. The wills of individuals or groups have created beliefs and customs that have given rise to the many different community forms observed within our world. Differing opinions are reasonable. However, standards of behavior that embrace some level of agreement and cooperation must be established to create and maintain a cohesive, civilized society.

When Things Go Wrong

Rules or laws of social interaction and behavior did not develop in a vacuum or simply at a whim. The most basic standards and rules that develop into laws governing the activities and behaviors of a populace are not based on man's opinions. They can actually trace their fundamental origins and their legal structure back to God's Law that was given through Moses. The laws that God established are the underpinning of nearly all humanly established laws and govern most social conduct. However, each society seems to pick and choose which ones they wish to emphasize or diminish. As rules develop into codified laws, they are assigned consequences or punishments that are handed down when they are disobeyed.

Some questions come to mind in this discussion. "Who is at fault when a punishment is assigned to an individual for disobeying a particular law?" Are the police responsible because they arrest a person for breaking a law? Is the judge responsible because he or she presides over the determination of guilt or innocence and decides the punishment? Or perhaps the government is responsible because it enacted the law? Certainly, the individual cannot be held responsible because his circumstances made him do it! The only one that is left is God, so he must be responsible since He established the original law!

This type of reasoning is totally absurd, but this is the way that our western world is going. There is a growing tendency to be more and more *politically correct*, blaming the environment, circumstances, a lack of opportunity, education, etc. The net effect is the shifting of responsibility away from an individual and onto someone or something else. Parents, extended family, co-workers, employers, the government and who knows who or what else are blamed for an individual's failings, rather than the individual being held accountable for his or her own choices.

God created us with the freedom of choice. The individual chooses his or her course of action and is responsible for his or her own choices and their consequences. Impaired judgment based on upbringing, circumstance, ignorance, and other influences are factors, but they do not exonerate a person from responsibility. Freedom comes with responsibility. The two cannot be separated.

Another question is this, "Who allows bad things to happen?" This is probably one of the most important questions that any of us will ever ask. Many people end with the same answer. God must be responsible because He is in charge of everything. On the contrary, neither God nor anyone else is responsible for the actions of an individual who exercises his or her free will. Choices may indeed be limited by circumstance, but we still face daily decisions between good and bad. Therefore, since God does not make the choices, the answer to the question is that *we* allow bad things to happen by the *choices we make*. Lack of acceptance of this responsibility leads to denial and deflection. The Bible records the first and second instances in Genesis 3:12-13.

Genesis 3:12-13 *(NKJV)*

> [12] *Then the man said, "The woman whom You gave to be with me, she gave*
> *me of the tree, and I ate."* [13] *And the Lord God said to the woman, "What is*
> *this you have done?" The woman said, "The serpent deceived me, and I ate.*

When Adam ate of the fruit of the tree of the knowledge of good and evil, he basically said that he was just doing what his wife told him to do. However, Adam implied that it was God's fault because He is the one who gave Eve to him. Then, Eve claimed that the devil made her do it. The third instance came in Genesis 4:8-9 when Cain was caught in his wrongdoing. He denied his responsibility for murdering Abel.

Genesis 4:8-9 *(NKJV)*

[8] Now Cain talked with Abel his brother; and it came to pass, when they were in the field, that Cain rose up against Abel his brother and killed him.
[9] Then the Lord said to Cain, "Where is Abel your brother?" He said, "I do not know. Am I my brother's keeper?"

There is always someone or something that you can point to so you can deflect blame away from yourself. However, "It's not my fault" does not help you. Certain elements also seek to justify or excuse actions based on environmental conditions, circumstances, family, religious upbringing, peer influence, drug or alcohol influence, or a whole host of other factors. However, in the end, even if society chooses not to require it, the individual will be held accountable.

Who Do You Blame?

God is the ultimate scapegoat for blame when all else fails. After all, He isn't around to defend Himself, and the Bible says that He kills and destroys! Is this the God that you know? Is God the one to whom you divert personal responsibility for your life? Do you first look to blame someone else, or do you look to find where human error may have contributed to or caused a problem? Sin is defined as disobedience. Disobedience demands a guilty verdict and a sentence that includes punishment. You are the only one that is responsible for the consequences of your sins. Fortunately, God provided a way for you through His Son, Jesus Christ, to enjoy freedom from the guilt and punishment that result from your poor choices. It is up to you to search out the truth and welcome Jesus into your heart. This simple choice is where your responsibility lies. God is not your problem. You are your own problem.

Actions require determinations to evaluate them. These determinations are called judgments. A guilty verdict is assigned if the judgment determines that a law has been broken or a sin committed. A sentence is declared according to the penalties associated with the law that has been broken. However, who determines where the authority to judge resides?

Chapter 21

WHO IS JUDGING YOU ?

Descriptions of praise, acknowledgments of pleasing actions, high moral or ethical values, uplifting conversation, pleasant attitudes or rewards are never described as being judgmental. However, a person is frequently described as being judgmental if he or she talks bad about another person. It is also considered judgmental to look down upon another person's values, behaviors, or attitudes or to actively condemn another person with the intent of shame or punishment. Negative comments or descriptions may have some truth, but they are still considered prejudicial attitudes or remarks. Judging or being judgmental nearly always carries a negative connotation. So when the question in the title of this chapter is asked, the natural inclination is to assume that the one that is judging is casting condemnation and calling for punishment. However, this is not necessarily the case.

Word Interpretation vs. Intent

Most of our thinking is formed in pictures. When we see or hear words, those words produce a mental picture. The words apple, orange, and banana do not seem to require much description once we have knowledge of what these objects are. One might think that the mental picture formed of these three fruits would probably be fairly consistent. The orange would be a round, stippled object of the same color; the banana would most likely be long and yellow; and the apple would likely be a stemmed red sphere. However, the orange might be smooth-skinned instead of deeply stippled. The banana might be green or yellow with brown-black splotches or streaks, and the apple could have striations or even be yellow or green in color.

Sometimes a word such as "apple," "banana," or "orange" can create significant variations in multiple images or thoughts.

So we can see that even simple, commonplace words can create some degree of ambiguity in meaning, and as a result, the mental pictures formed could vary. How much more difficult is the interpretation of less concrete words like *judge* and *judgment*, which must be filtered through the sieves of tradition, culture, experience, education, emotion, time, and more. An interpretation, created though our filters, can lead to a personal definition of a word that may or may not agree with reality or an absolute truth. An individual might apply his or her own distorted definition whenever they encounter that particular word.

We briefly examined terminology or *semantics* in Chapter 9 *(see p. 82)*, and it is again required to explore the meanings of these words, *judge* and *judgment*. Semantics is extremely important because of the variety of impressions, opinions, and emotions that words evoke. As a result, words can be interpreted with *relative* meanings that may or may not be accurate.

Words form impressions and convey meaning, thought, and intent based on our own personal definitions. Therefore, it is extremely important to understand the true meanings and intents of the words we use so that communication can be accurate and convey the correct information. Although some words do have intrinsic, even universal meanings, an individual may sometimes base their entire life on an errant definition. It may be drawn from misunderstanding, incorrect teaching, faulty education or a distorted and incorrect interpretation, based on personal experience.

Sometimes, the true meaning of a word is at odds with the way that the word is being used in its application. When words are poured through the *funnel of time*, they can also become distorted or diluted and even assume totally opposite meanings. Certain colloquialisms may alter the original meaning of a word altogether. This distortion can be seen in many instances of slang terminology such as with the slang expression of the word *bad* which in some contexts means *good*.

Over time, words can take on new meanings that can be confusing and different from their original intents.

Consider the terms *judge, judgment, condemn,* and *sentence*. Regardless of their accuracy, our personal definitions of these words are at the core of our individually perceived reality and understanding of God's character and nature. Therefore, a common understanding of the true meaning of these terms is needed in order to fully understand the true character and nature of God.

judge *(verb)*

From Middle English juggen, from Anglo-French juger, from Latin judicare, from judic-, judex judge, from jus right, law + dicere to decide, say, to form an opinion about through careful weighing of evidence and testing of premises; to determine or pronounce after inquiry and deliberation.[60]

judgment *(noun)*

A formal utterance of an authoritative opinion; an opinion so pronounced.[61]

condemn *(verb)*

To declare to be reprehensible, wrong, or evil usually after weighing evidence and without reservation; to pronounce guilty.[62]

sentence *(verb)*

Judgment; specifically: one formally pronounced by a court or judge in a criminal proceeding and specifying the punishment to be inflicted upon the convict; the punishment so imposed.[63]

The meanings of these words are intertwined and can cause confusion when not properly understood. The words *judge* and *judgment* do not mean the same as *to condemn* or *to sentence*. Judge and judgment are truly descriptive not of punishment, but of a conclusion based on inquiry, facts, testing, and evidence. A determination is then passed on to the next phase.

A determination or judgment can go either way. Freedom comes with a *judgment of innocence,* but once a determination of wrongdoing is established, a *judgment of guilt* is declared. When guilt is determined, a declaration of the imposed punishment is handed down, and a sentence is imposed upon the one *judged* to be guilty. The degree of punishment depends on the penalty affixed to the offense. However, many people use the words *judge* and *judgment* as declarations of only guilt and punishment.

The word *judgment* is found many times in the Old Testament. The following passages in Isaiah 1:17 and 1:21 are a small sampling of context in which *judgment* is used with a positive meaning. Isaiah 1:17 indicates that the purpose of judgment is to determine good through discernment and to pronounce positive blessings.

Isaiah 1:17

Learn to do well; seek judgment, relieve the oppressed, judge the fatherless, plead for the widow.

Exploration of some uses and context of *judgment* will illustrate the point. Isaiah 1:21 indicates that the righteous inhabited the city and that it was *full of judgment*. It is evident in this passage that a lack of right judgment caused an influx of evil, in this case, murderers.

Isaiah 1:21

How is the faithful city become an harlot! it was full of judgment; righteousness lodged in it; but now murderers.

By contrast, Isaiah 54:17 illustrates a negative connotation of judgment. In this situation, there is a promise offered to the *servants of the Lord*. It is one of protection from a negative judgment that is accusing and attempting to condemn.

Isaiah 54:17

No weapon that is formed against thee shall prosper; and every tongue that shall rise against thee in judgment thou shalt condemn. This is the heritage of the servants of the Lord, and their righteousness is of me, saith the Lord.

The original Hebrew word that is translated *judgment* in the *King James Version* of Isaiah 54:17, is מִשְׁפָּט or *mishpat*, identified in the *Strong's Hebrew Dictionary* as OT:4941. It is found in either a favorable/unfavorable or right/wrong context and is translated as such according to the context of the verse.

"judgment" - *Strong's* OT:4941 מִשְׁפָּט, *mishpat* (mish-pawt') from OT:8199;

properly, a verdict (favorable or unfavorable) pronounced judicially, especially a sentence or formal decree (human or [participant's] divine law, individual or collective), including the act, the place, the suit, the crime, and the penalty; abstractly, justice, including a participant's right or privilege (statutory or customary), or even a style:

Rendered in the KJV as adversary, ceremony, charge, crime, custom, desert, determination, discretion, disposing, due, fashion, form, to be judged, judgment, just (-ice, -ly), (manner of) law (-ful), manner, measure, (due) order, ordinance, right, sentence, usest, worthy, + wrong.

God is very precise with His words. Therefore, it is essential for man to understand their meanings. Sometimes, there can be a wide discrepancy between what the sender (God) means and what the receiver (man) hears. Consequently, there is great potential for misunderstanding that can completely alter one's life due to inaccurate, unique personal definitions that are based on *life filters and perspective*. This is why understanding the meanings of relevant terms is so important.

Correct thinking is one of the first steps to understanding the character of God. The proper meaning of the word *judgment* is decision or determination. It does not mean condemnation. Frequently, the word is used in the sense of making a righteous judgment or discernment to know the difference between right and wrong and to choose right. It can be difficult to determine what side God is on unless the truth of His character is revealed. However, with the right understanding, scriptures can take on completely different meanings than those upheld by some religious or traditional views that assume that God is the enemy and a friend at the same time.

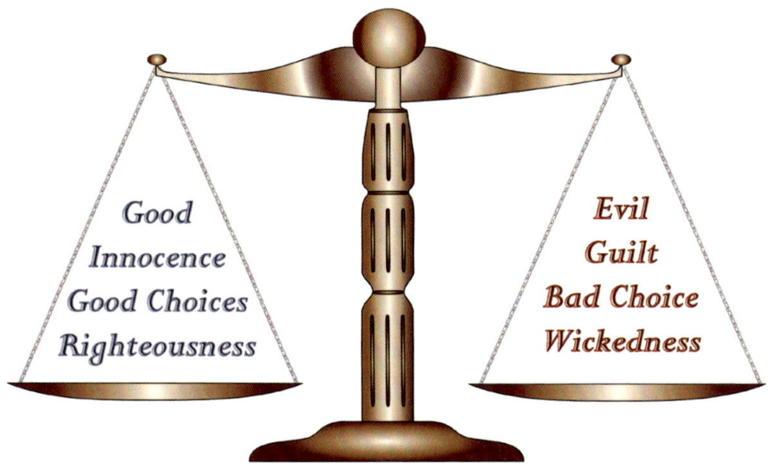

The Balance of Judgment is used to make a determination.

Judgment vs. Sentence

Someone must bring about an accusation to produce a situation in which a judgment must take place. No one brings an accusation of innocence and demands a judgment. Remember, the word judgment refers to an act of determination as opposed to a declaration of guilt or innocence. However, the accuser that requires judgment or determination does so by bringing an allegation of guilt. The act of judgment weighs the evidence that is presented and applies wisdom to make a determination of the truth of a matter. Man does not always get it right because the evidence may be lacking, and the full extent of the circumstance and the heart motives are not necessarily known. However, through His Word, God never gets it wrong. He knows the thoughts and intents of the heart (Hebrews 4:12).

The process of accusation of guilt originates in various ways. Certainly, accusations come about from observation of someone disobeying some civil or criminal statute or law. Other accusations come about from investigation of a crime as following clues and evidence may lead to a suspicion of guilt, resulting in an accusation against someone. These two examples result in a situation where a judgment is made based on established human law. Still other accusations come from those who may feel that they have been wronged emotionally or through some relationship. This type of judgment comes out of a perceived breach of a personal code of conduct.

There is still a more basic source of accusation that demands judgment. It is a source that originates in the spiritual world. It is of a higher order and has greater significance than human law because this source affects the entire world. This source is one that we investigated in an earlier chapter when discussing Job. However, the book of Job is not the only place that discusses this source. It is also seen in Revelation 12:10.

Revelation 12:10

And I heard a loud voice saying in heaven, Now is come salvation, and strength, and the kingdom of our God, and the power of his Christ: for the accuser of our brethren is cast down, which accused them before our God day and night.

The accuser spoken of here is Satan (Lucifer, the Devil). His pervasive nature is evident in the text as it explains that his accusations come day and night, implying that they are continuous and unceasing. He is active until he is cast down by God in the final confrontation. However, this verse in Revelation also tells us before whom the accusation is brought. The human system of law requires that the accusation be brought before a judge to render a judgment. Then, a determination of guilt or innocence is made. If guilt is determined, a verdict is rendered and a sentence proclaimed. The spiritual realm differs in that the end point of all accusations is God. In the Old Testament, He is considered the judge of everything, *the One who determines guilt and innocence.*

However, the course of judgment changed with the arrival of Jesus on earth and was sealed with His death, burial, and resurrection. The Gospel of John provides the evidence that God, the Father, has passed the responsibility of judgment to His Son, Jesus Christ as described in John 5:18-23.

John 5:18-23 *(NKJV)*

[18] Therefore the Jews sought all the more to kill Him, because He not only broke the Sabbath, but also said that God was His Father, making Himself equal with God. [19] Then Jesus answered and said to them, "Most assuredly, I say to you, the Son can do nothing of Himself, but what He sees the Father do; for whatever He does, the Son also does in like manner. [20] For the Father loves the Son, and shows Him all things that He Himself does; and He will show Him greater works than these, that you may marvel. [21] For as the Father raises the dead and gives life to them, even so the Son gives life to whom He will. [22] For the Father judges no one, but has committed all judgment to the Son, [23] that all should honor the Son just as they honor the Father. He who does not honor the Son does not honor the Father who sent Him."

Spiritually speaking, the responsibility to judge sin has been delegated to Jesus, undoubtedly because He paid the penalty for every sin. However, sin is still the core issue for breaking human law since the laws of man share their foundation with the laws of God. Sin breeds the conditions that call for judgment because it results in accusations of guilt. Following His resurrection, Jesus came to the disciples, passed the Holy Spirit to them and told them that they were invested with the authority to hold or release a person from sin. This process of determination or judgment was given to Jesus, and He passed to men the authority to judge or determine sin as is stated in John 20:19-23. However, Jesus added something to the authority for making a judgment regarding sin. He authorized men to have the power to forgive and overlook sin as well.

John 20:19-23 *(NKJV)*

[19] Then, the same day at evening, being the first day of the week, when the doors were shut where the disciples were assembled, for fear of the Jews, Jesus came and stood in the midst, and said to them, "Peace be with you."
[20] When He had said this, He showed them His hands and His side. Then the disciples were glad when they saw the Lord.

[21] So Jesus said to them again, "Peace to you! As the Father has sent Me, I also send you." [22] And when He had said this, He breathed on them, and said to them, "Receive the Holy Spirit. [23] If you forgive the sins of any, they are forgiven them; if you retain the sins of any, they are retained."

An extreme example of this transference of authority is evident in the account of a husband and wife who owned property and sold it for the common benefit of their fellow believers. This couple had the authority and power to do what they wished with their property, but they made a private agreement between themselves to lie to the disciples and to God. Together, they planned the deception. The event unfolds in Acts 5:1-4.

Acts 5:1-4 *(NKJV)*

1 But a certain man named Ananias, with Sapphira his wife, sold a possession. 2 And he kept back part of the proceeds, his wife also being aware of it, and brought a certain part and laid it at the apostles' feet. 3 But Peter said, "Ananias, why has Satan filled your heart to lie to the Holy Spirit and keep back part of the price of the land for yourself? 4 While it remained, was it not your own? And after it was sold, was it not in your own control? Why have you conceived this thing in your heart? You have not lied to men but to God."

Peter had discernment from the Holy Spirit concerning the depth of the deception of Ananias and Sapphira. He also had the choice and the responsibility to deal with the deception once it was revealed to him *(see Appendix Chapter 21)*.[64] He *judged* the situation and made the determination that Ananias and Sapphira were both guilty of deception and lying to God. Peter took the responsibility that was given to him by Jesus in John 20:23 and made the choice that he would neither overlook nor forgive the sin of Ananias and Sapphira.

The sin of Ananias and Sapphira was directed straight at God, and Peter knew it through wise discernment and the counsel of the Holy Spirit. He uncovered the sin and held them accountable for it. Jesus said in Matthew 12:30-32 that there is a lot that man can do and be forgiven for, but there is a point of no return.

Matthew 12:30-32

30 He that is not with me is against me; and he that gathereth not with me scattereth abroad.

31 Wherefore I say unto you, All manner of sin and blasphemy shall be forgiven unto men: but the blasphemy against the Holy Ghost shall not be forgiven unto men.

32 And whosoever speaketh a word against the Son of man, it shall be forgiven him: but whosoever speaketh against the Holy Ghost, it shall not be forgiven him, neither in this world, neither in the world to come.

Peter probably knew that the severity of the sin of Ananias and Sapphira involved the one *unforgivable sin*, a point of no return, which is blasphemy (Strong's NT:988) against the Holy Spirit. It qualified because it was a unified lie of conspiracy and deception against the Holy Spirit.

> ***"blasphemy"*** - *Strong's* NT:988, *blasfhmi/a blasphemia* (blas-fay-me'-ah); *from* NT:989; *vilification (especially against God): KJV - blasphemy, evil speaking, railing.*

The resulting death of Ananias may seem a bit harsh, especially in light of the grace that is given to us through Jesus, but some actions harden men's hearts from receiving forgiveness. Peter did not pronounce a sentence of any sort upon Ananias. He only confronted him with the deception and told him that he had lied to God, not to men. The physical cause of the sudden death of Ananias could have easily been from a heart attack as he was overwhelmed with the weight of his own sin. We can only suppose that the callousness of the sin and the conspiracy with his wife left Ananias in a state where there was no repentance as seen in Acts 5:5-6.

Acts 5:5-6

5 And Ananias hearing these words fell down, and gave up the ghost: and great fear came on all them that heard these things. 6 And the young men arose, wound him up, and carried him out, and buried him.

Perhaps Peter might have had a moment of compassion for Ananias that would have led him to forgive the sin. However, there is no evidence that Ananias even asked for forgiveness. He knew his sin, and he knew that he was found out. He was likely aware of other situations in which evil befell those who tried to deceive God. In 2 Kings 5:20-27 *(see Appendix Chapter 21)*, the greed of a man named Gehazi led him to lie to God and a prophet, and he was turned into a leper. Maybe he remembered the account of Esau relayed in Hebrews 12:14-17 and was overcome with hopelessness in his situation.

Hebrews 12:14-17 *(NLT)*

14 Work at living in peace with everyone, and work at living a holy life, for those who are not holy will not see the Lord. 15 Look after each other so that none of you fails to receive the grace of God. Watch out that no poisonous root of bitterness grows up to trouble you, corrupting many. 16 Make sure that no one is immoral or godless like Esau, who traded his birthright as the firstborn son for a single meal. [17]You know that afterward, when he wanted his father's blessing, he was rejected. It was too late for repentance, even though he begged with bitter tears.

Peter handled the confrontation with Sapphira differently in Acts 5:7-10. He simply asked her a question to confirm what he already knew about the conspiracy. He chastised her for her part in the deception and informed her that her life would be immediately required. Neither Ananias nor Sapphira is recorded as seeking any repentance.

Acts 5:7-10

[7] And it was about the space of three hours after, when his wife, not knowing what was done, came in.

[8] And Peter answered unto her, Tell me whether ye sold the land for so much? And she said, Yea, for so much. [9] Then Peter said unto her, How is it that ye have agreed together to tempt the Spirit of the Lord? behold, the feet of them which have buried thy husband are at the door, and shall carry thee out.

[10] Then fell she down straightway at his feet, and yielded up the ghost: and the young men came in, and found her dead, and, carrying her forth, buried her by her husband.

Sin cannot stand in the presence of the Holy Spirit whom Peter states is equal with God in Acts 5:3-4. The shock of the discovery of their deception directed toward God was too much for them to survive. Neither Ananias nor Sapphira could stand in the presence of the Holy Spirit and Peter with the weight of their sins of deception and blasphemy.

This action by Peter was that of a judge. Peter, a mere man, was responsible for the determination of innocence or guilt. He pronounced the verdict after the evidence was made known and then imposed the sentence. Ananias died spontaneously, but Peter pronounced the sentence of death on Sapphira. He did not kill them, and neither did God. It was their sins of deception and blasphemy, directly in the face of the Holy Spirit of God, which took their lives from them.

The Responsibility of Judgment

Jesus authorized Peter and the disciples to exercise judgment and sentence over sin in John 20:23, but before He told them this, Jesus spoke extensively about judgment. Jesus used the word *judgment* in Matthew 5:21 and 7:1-2. The definition in both instances is *decision*. The translators infer that the decision referenced here will go badly for the one involved. Therefore, the impression that most readers get is that of condemnation, not decision.

Matthew 5:21 *(NKJV)*

You have heard that it was said to those of old, You shall not murder, and whoever murders will be in danger of the judgment.

"judgment" - *Strong's* NT:2920, κρίσις, *krisis* (kree'-sis);

decision (subjectively or objectively, for or against); by extension, a tribunal; by implication, justice (especially, divine law) KJV - accusation, condemnation, damnation, judgment.

Matthew 7:1-2 *(NKJV)*

1 Judge not, that you be not judged. 2 For with what judgment you judge, you will be judged; and with the measure you use, it will be measured back to you.

"judgment" - *Strong's* NT:2919, κρίνω, *krino* (kree'-no);

properly, to distinguish, i.e. decide (mentally or judicially); by implication, to try, condemn, punish KJV - avenge, conclude, condemn, damn, decree, determine, esteem, judge, go to (sue at the) law, ordain, call in question, sentence to, think.

The word *judgment* used in Matthew 5:21 states that the offender would be in danger, implying or inferring guilt. However, it could be read, "in danger of an unfavorable decision regarding the charges of murder." Matthew 7:2 could be read "for what decisions you make to decide guilt or innocence will be applied to your own life." This warning is articulated by Jesus because man is nearly incapable of rendering true or unbiased judgment. Unlike God, man does not have all of the facts, and Jesus is clear about this distinction in John 8:15-16.

John 8:15-16

15 Ye judge after the flesh; I judge no man. 16 And yet if I judge, my judgment is true: for I am not alone, but I and the Father that sent me.

Man spends his time in the physical world. Consequently, his senses are tuned to it and are incapable of discerning or judging the difference between good and evil. This discernment has to be taught or learned through spiritual or Godly wisdom. Man judges the physical realm according to appearance, not truth. Jesus spoke about judging and judgment in the spiritual world, not the physical world. The senses of man must be realigned to not only discern the physical world but the spiritual world as well. The *knowledge* of the presence of good and evil that Adam and Eve brought upon mankind is not enough. Exercise of spiritual senses is required to properly discern good from evil.

The book of Hebrews presents a contrast between "milk" and "strong meat" as it relates to spiritual principles and understanding. Milk is for babies who are not mature because they are still developing and growing. Strong meat, on the other hand, is meant for the mature body that is developed and needs fuel to replenish and sustain its activities. This contrast relates to spiritual activity and maturity in the same way.

Discernment of good and evil is considered to be an activity of depth, much like strong meat is a complex nutrient. It only comes with the exercise or repeated use of spiritual senses as explained in Hebrews 5:12-14.

Hebrews 5:12-14 *(NKJV)*

*12 For though by this time you ought to be teachers, you need someone to
teach you again the first principles of the oracles of God; and you have
come to need milk and not solid food. 13 For everyone who partakes only of
milk is unskilled in the word of righteousness, for he is a babe. 14 But solid
food belongs to those who are of full age, that is, those who by reason of use
have their senses exercised to discern both good and evil.*

This passage in Hebrews makes a point to discuss the *spiritual skill* of the individual. The Greek word translated as *unskilful* in Hebrews 5:13 means inexperienced or ignorant.

"unskilful" - *Strong's* NT:552, ἄπειρος, *apeiros* (ap'-i-ros);
inexperienced, i.e. - ignorant.

The way to overcome being unskillful is to apply oneself to education and training. In spiritual things, this comes from studying the words that God gave to us in the Bible. Understanding the application of these words is how man's senses are exercised to discern both good and evil. The spiritual baby can only use the milk of God's word, the basic spiritual precepts of God's kingdom. To the non-spiritual person, these are really big things, but God considers them just to be milk for babies. They are identified in Hebrews 6:1-2 as repentance, salvation through Christ, faith in God, baptism, praying for people, the resurrection of the dead, and an eternal hell.

Hebrews 6:1-2 *(NKJV)*

[1] Therefore, leaving the discussion of the elementary principles of Christ, let us go on to perfection, not laying again the foundation of repentance from dead works and of faith toward God, [2] of the doctrine of baptisms, of laying on of hands, of resurrection of the dead, and of eternal judgment.

Understanding also allows the individual to move on to *perfection* in Hebrews 6:1-2, which is rendered from the Greek word meaning mental or moral completeness.

"perfection" - *Strong's* NT:5047, τελειότης, *teleiotes* (tel-i-ot'-ace); *completeness (mentally or morally)*

The words that are contained within the Bible are very important as spiritual growth depends upon them. Jesus was very specific about the words that He used. He clearly stated in John 12:47-50 that He did not speak His own words but spoke the words of the Father that sent Him.

John 12:47-50 *(NKJV)*

[47] And if anyone hears My words and does not believe, I do not judge him; for I did not come to judge the world but to save the world. [48] He who rejects Me, and does not receive My words, has that which judges him — the word that I have spoken will judge him in the last day. [49] For I have not spoken on My own authority; but the Father who sent Me gave Me a command, what I should say and what I should speak. [50] And I know that His command is everlasting life. Therefore, whatever I speak, just as the Father has told Me, so I speak.

Jesus was saying that He is a conduit through whom God speaks to man. He specifically stated that He did not come to judge or make determinations on the world but to save the world. He further declared that if a man rejected Him and His words, he would be rejecting the words of His Father, God. Jesus further stated that neither He nor God will judge. He said that the way a man acts upon the words that Jesus spoke will judge or make a determination upon each man's heart in the last day. In other words, a person's own actions will serve as his or her judge.

Judgment regarding how each person deals with Jesus is not up to religions or other men. The responsibility for that judgment, which is a determination and weighing of evidence based on the Words of Jesus, resides only with God. This is why Jesus said that even He would not judge those who rejected Him. The words that He spoke do the judging because they are the parameters and foundation of truth.

Jesus did, however, tell us to look at the way people conduct themselves. He said that we should be "fruit inspectors" in Matthew 7:15-20. We are not to make decisions or evaluations related to the *hearts* of men because only God knows their innermost thoughts toward God and Jesus.

Jesus did, nevertheless, instruct us to beware of those who produce no fruit or evil fruit. It is evident that Jesus was speaking about the *actions* of people. In Matthew 7:15-20, it appears that if there is any good fruit, the tree is not completely corrupt. If there is only corrupt fruit or no good fruit, then the tree is corrupt and will be destroyed by fire.

Matthew 7:15-20 *(ERV)*

15 Be careful of false prophets. They come to you and look gentle like sheep.
But they are really dangerous like wolves. 16 You will know these people
because of what they do. Good things don't come from people who are
bad, just as grapes don't come from thornbushes, and figs don't come from
thorny weeds. 17 In the same way, every good tree produces good fruit, and
bad trees produce bad fruit. 18 A good tree cannot produce bad fruit, and
a bad tree cannot produce good fruit. 19 Every tree that does not produce
good fruit is cut down and thrown into the fire. 20 You will know these false
people by what they do.

This parable is obviously comparing the tree to men, and the fruit to the actions of men so that those with understanding and discernment will not allow themselves to be influenced and led astray by deceivers.

Jesus took these same warnings in Matthew 12:35-37 and applied them directly to men. He made the concept very clear indeed but then took it to a new level. He stated that men will be judged based on their own words. Another way to say it is that we will condemn ourselves with our evil words, but we will be justified or made righteous by our words of agreement and acceptance of God's Word and of Jesus.

Matthew 12:35-37

[35] A good man out of the good treasure of the heart bringeth forth good things: and an evil man out of the evil treasure bringeth forth evil things.
[36] But I say unto you, That every idle word that men shall speak, they shall give account thereof in the day of judgment. [37] For by thy words thou shalt be justified, and by thy words thou shalt be condemned.

Matthew 12:35-37 *(ERV)*

[35] Those who are good have good things saved in their hearts. That's why they say good things. But those who are evil have hearts full of evil, and that's why they say things that are evil. [36] I tell you that everyone will have to answer for all the careless things they have said. This will happen on the day of judgment. [37] Your words will be used to judge you. What you have said will show whether you are right or whether you are guilty.

Armed with this perspective and the neutral interpretation of the words *judge* and *judgment*, this passage can be seen more clearly and lead to a more thorough understanding. The context of the words used, coupled with the character of the one issuing the words, removes preconceptions and allows the Word of God to reveal the intent behind its words. This approach will yield a more thorough understanding of the words in use.

God is not judging you or pronouncing a sentence upon you. Sin does that. Your own sin judges you and demands a verdict. However, God in His wisdom and mercy has provided a way through Jesus to avoid eternal jail time. A deeper understanding of the terms *judge* and *judgment, condemn,* and *sentence* may put the question posed in this chapter regarding "Who Is Judging You?" in a much different light.

Chapter 22

THE TWO LAWS OF GOD
FREEDOM OR DEATH

There are many sources of power in the world today. Nuclear, petroleum, coal, solar, steam, geothermal, and hydroelectric are some examples of naturally occurring or man facilitated power. All have a degree of danger when they are misapplied or mishandled. Consider a nuclear reactor, chemical plants, oil refineries or even a reservoir or dam. Mishaps with any of these can have very widespread, negative consequences. One power source that we come into contact with regularity is electricity that is generated by a variety of sources.

Electricity has very positive attributes when handled and controlled according to the laws that govern and contain it. Microwave ovens, televisions, computers, air conditioning and other devices provide us with great benefits because they operate within the laws governing electricity.

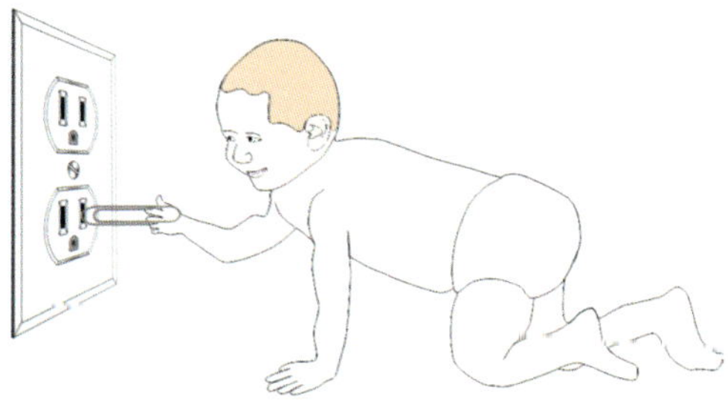

Improper interaction with something like electricity is an example of poor judgment and can be very dangerous.

If a child were to place a paper clip or metal utensil into an electrical outlet, there would be a significant chance that a catastrophe would occur. If the parents of the child had taken steps to *childproof* the outlets and warned the child of this danger, they would have exercised wisdom as would the child if their warning was understood and heeded. If the child ignored the warnings and actually placed the metal into the outlet, there is a significant possibility that he or she would be injured or killed.

Should a storm or an accident topple a power line, the dangerous live wire is not contained or controlled, but it still behaves according to the laws of electricity. It becomes a very dangerous force indeed. Misapplications or loss of control can occur in other situations as well, such as overloading an electrical outlet and causing a fire. Another misuse might be an electrical cord that has become frayed or a plug that is broken and exposes bare wires. You can imagine the results of this improper handling of the *laws of electricity*. A severe burn or even death might occur from a sudden and massive release of uncontrolled energy that was previously kept in check by following the law.

Do we blame electricity for the damages, injuries, or death when this sort of misapplication occurs? Do we point the finger at the power company and say that they caused the injury? Of course not!

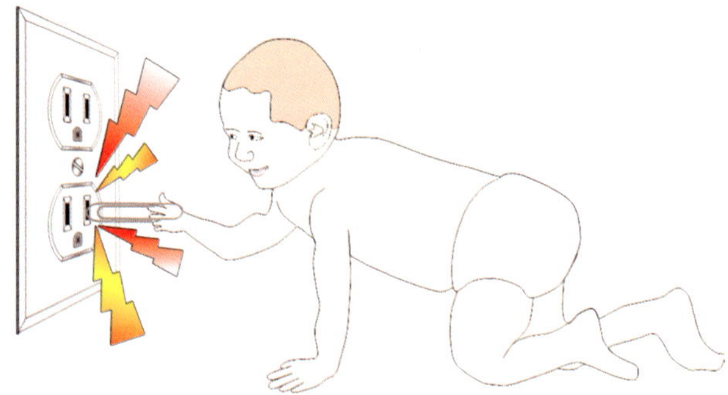

Poor judgment can be catastrophic, but who is responsible for the disaster? Is it the child, the parent, the electric company, the home builder or perhaps God?

Still, some might actually point to God if a child were to be electrocuted while playing with an electrical outlet. They might ask, "God, how could you take my child?" They might say that God needed another angel, implying that He was responsible or was an *accomplice* who allowed it to happen. However, where does the real problem lie? It lies with the lack of adult supervision to protect the child from harm. It lies in a lack of diligence and shirking of personal responsibility for the safety of the child. God had nothing to do with it!

The problem was the misapplication of the laws of electricity, either through ignorance or callous disregard of the consequences. The laws of electricity are established. There are rules for the manner in which it must be handled to be safe and productive rather than dangerous and deadly. God's Law operates in the same way in that not observing it has severe consequences.

We all have a tendency to look elsewhere when tragedy occurs and affix blame somewhere besides ourselves. God's Law (over 600 individual laws in all) points out the inadequacies and failings inherent in our human condition. The law teaches us that we cannot perform to the standard of perfection that God describes for us, and therefore, bad things will happen for which we are responsible. The law points to the fact that we need a relationship with Him to observe the law and not mess everything up. His plea to us is to make the right choices, follow His guidance through the law and seek after Him. However, God is aware that we are fundamentally unable to fulfill and perform all of the law. Is this some cruel joke, to tell us to do something when there is certain failure waiting? It might be if He did not give us a way out!

Choices

Life is a series of choices. Hopefully, the choices we make are based on a deep knowledge of the ramifications of those choices. Some of our choices affect only us, some affect strangers, and some affect those that are closest to us. The circumstances with which we are presented, and the ensuing decisions we make are governed by two basic, general principles or laws that surround both. These two laws rule what we do in our lives, and they apply universally to everyone. Romans 8:1-2 reveals these two laws that have such tremendous power and influence upon us.

Romans 8:1-2

> [1] *There is therefore now no condemnation to them which are in Christ Jesus, who walk not after the flesh, but after the Spirit.* [2] *For the law of the Spirit of life in Christ Jesus hath made me free from the law of sin and death.*

The choice to observe either *the law of the Spirit of life* or *the law of sin and death* will determine what happens to us. Let's get more information about these two laws and what they really mean. First, let us look into *the law of sin and death*.

God established the complete statutes of the law, and we see them spelled out throughout Leviticus and Deuteronomy. Deuteronomy 28 provides an expansive treatise on both the blessings of following the law and the negative consequences or cursings for rejecting the law. Rejection or disobedience to God's Word or His decrees, mandates, or laws is referred to as sin.

Consider the first command or law that God gave man in Genesis 2:16, which we discussed previously *(see Chapter 7, p. 56)*. It describes how the results of disobedience or sin would ultimately infect all of humanity.

Genesis 2:16-17

> [16] *And the LORD God commanded the man, saying, Of every tree of the garden thou mayest freely eat:* [17] *But of the tree of the knowledge of good and evil, thou shalt not eat of it: for in the day that thou eatest thereof thou shalt surely die.*

This scripture identifies the beginning of the law of sin and death. There is one reason that this scenario resulted in death. That reason is sin, which is disobedience to the commands of God. All of the law of sin and death is wrapped in willful disobedience. It is willful because we have free will to choose to obey or disobey. The more than 600 statutes that God established are truly overwhelming in their scope, but they were instituted to guide man into a successful life, not to trip him up and have cause for punishment. Unfortunately for man, rejection or transgression of even one of these laws results in eventual physical death, but more importantly it results in spiritual death.

It is clear that Adam and Eve did not instantaneously die a physical death on the day in which they ate of the fruit of the forbidden tree. However, they did die an immediate spiritual death. This spiritual death is the most important aspect of the *law of sin and death*. Spiritual death is the condition that was passed on to all of mankind. However, God did not view this as an acceptable situation. It required a solution that He had already planned, but it was wrapped in a mystery and kept secret from the rest of His creation.

Man multiplied and spread over generations, and his world became much more complex. Many hundreds of years later, God established a more detailed framework to help man through his complicated existence. The Law is the framework that provided more structure and guidance, but it was still punctuated with death if it was broken. Still, God encouraged the choice of life in Deuteronomy 30:14-19.

Deuteronomy 30:14-19 *(NKJV)*

> [14] *But the word is very near you, in your mouth and in your heart, that you may do it.*
>
> [15] *See, I have set before you today life and good, death and evil,*
>
> [16] *in that I command you today to love the LORD your God, to walk in His ways, and to keep His commandments, His statutes, and His judgments, that you may live and multiply; and the LORD your God will bless you in the land which you go to possess.*
>
> [17] *But if your heart turns away so that you do not hear, and are drawn away, and worship other gods and serve them,* [18] *I announce to you today that you shall surely perish; you shall not prolong your days in the land which you cross over the Jordan to go in and possess.*
>
> [19] *I call heaven and earth as witnesses today against you, that I have set before you life and death, blessing and cursing;* ***therefore choose life****, that both you and your descendants may live.*

According to verse 19, God sets *life and death, blessing, and cursing* before us. He further explains that we have a choice in the matter when He stated, *"therefore choose life, that both you and your descendants may live."* We have the privilege of exercising our free will in order to make a choice. God neither says that *He* will punish those who are disobedient, nor does He say that *He* will take any action against them. God simply states that if they make the wrong choice, they will perish (prematurely) and not have prolonged life in the land He promised to them.

This passage is specifically referring to the children of Israel escaping the rule of the Egyptians and crossing the Jordan River into the *promised land*. The reference to perishing is clear as it refers to their specific, personal lives. The reference to prolonged days pointed to the length of time that they would enjoy or possess the promised land as a people. The principle revealed in this scripture is still applicable to each and every person today, however. Obedience is defined as *choosing life,* and the effects of the choice are passed down through descendants or generations. Premature death is clearly implied for those who choose disobedience.

The Blessings of Obedience

The book of Deuteronomy provides a written account of the blessings and cursings that God was speaking of when He recommended that we choose life and blessings. Deuteronomy 28 is 66 verses long. The first 14 verses are filled with the joy, prosperity, and life that come with the choice of obedience to God's laws. Every aspect of life overflows with the success that is said to even *overtake* those who choose obedience.

Deuteronomy 28:1-14 *(NKJV)*

1 Now it shall come to pass, if you diligently obey the voice of the LORD your God, to observe carefully all His commandments which I command you today, that the LORD your God will set you high above all nations of the earth.
2 And all these blessings shall come upon you and overtake you, because you obey the voice of the LORD your God:

3 Blessed shall you be in the city, and blessed shall you be in the country.

4 Blessed shall be the fruit of your body, the produce of your ground and the increase of your herds, the increase of your cattle and the offspring of your flocks.

5 Blessed shall be your basket and your kneading bowl.

6 Blessed shall you be when you come in, and blessed shall you be when you go out.

7 The LORD will cause your enemies who rise against you to be defeated before your face; they shall come out against you one way and flee before you seven ways.

8 The LORD will command the blessing on you in your storehouses and in all to which you set your hand, and He will bless you in the land which the LORD your God is giving you.

9 The LORD will establish you as a holy people to Himself, just as He has sworn to you, if you keep the commandments of the LORD your God and walk in His ways.
10 Then all peoples of the earth shall see that you are

called by the name of the LORD, and they shall be afraid of you.

[11] *And the LORD will grant you plenty of goods, in the fruit of your body, in the increase of your livestock, and in the produce of your ground, in the land of which the LORD swore to your fathers to give you.*

[12] *The LORD will open to you His good treasure, the heavens, to give the rain to your land in its season, and to bless all the work of your hand. You shall lend to many nations, but you shall not borrow.*

[13] *And the LORD will make you the head and not the tail; you shall be above only, and not be beneath, if you heed the commandments of the LORD your God, which I command you today, and are careful to observe them.*

[14] *So you shall not turn aside from any of the words which I command you this day, to the right or the left, to go after other gods to serve them.*

Curses of Disobedience

The opposite is true for those who choose disobedience and cursing that leads to death. The last 52 verses of Deuteronomy 28 describes the implementation of the curses that will come as a result of really bad choices. There are 52 verses of curses compared to 14 verses of blessings. In other words, 20% are devoted to blessings, and 80% are devoted to cursings. The entire 52 verses of cursings are not presented here, but let's look at the introduction to the curses in Deuteronomy 28:15.

Deuteronomy 28:15 *(NKJV)*

But it shall come to pass, if you do not obey the voice of the LORD your God, to observe carefully all His commandments and His statutes which I command you today, that all these curses will come upon you and overtake you.

Notice that just as the blessings would *come upon and overtake* those who are obedient, the same is true for the curses. They will also *come upon and overtake* the disobedient (Deuteronomy 28:2). The next 51 verses outline just how bad the curses will be. Although no numerological implications are inferred, there is a nearly 4:1 ratio of cursing to blessing. From this ratio, it would appear at first glance that God is far more interested in punishment than reward!

The list of curses is quite onerous. They appear in a few categories that are directed at the individual, the land, livestock, buildings, agriculture as well as corporate curses directed at the entire population. Individual curses included thirst, hunger, nakedness, blindness, terror, and madness. Their children would die, and their livestock would produce stillborn offspring. Crops would be consumed by locusts and grapes by worms. Olive trees would lose their fruit until the land yielded virtually nothing. Property and food supplies would be stolen, destroyed, and overtaken by strangers and conquerors. The people would be defeated by their enemies, becoming poor, indebted slaves. They would lose their identity and heritage and be scattered. Pestilence, long plagues and long sicknesses of every known and unknown type would come upon them. They would be against each other to do evil. Brother would be against brother, mother against child and husband against wife. Children would be taken into slavery, and in desperation, a mother would eat her own child. They would be in constant need with no rest, praying in the morning for the night to come quickly and in the night for morning to come quickly, not knowing whether they would live or die.

This is some seriously bad stuff! God must be a really bad guy to put all of this on people. How could He possibly be a good and loving God in light of all of this? However, take note that Deuteronomy 28:15 does not say that *God* will *punish* the disobedience. It infers that the curses come as a natural course of the acts of disobedience. God lists all of these really bad things as a warning about the effects of sin and what it will produce. He is making it very clear to man so that he will fully understand what is at stake and just how important obedience is.

Let's just think a bit about what God is dealing with here. It is mankind, you and me! We have a very stubborn and rebellious streak in us that was probably manifested at a very early age. This is why the expression the *terrible twos* is so widely understood and seen in child raising. Why is there such weight placed on the negative consequences of disobedience rather than the positive rewards to obedient behavior? In His love for man, God is pointing out what can happen and how to avoid it.

However, man does not *want* to submit to anything. Following his rebellious, stiff-necked nature he exerts his own will and constantly looks for ways to circumvent God's direction. He wants to rule his own universe. This is one of the reasons that there is corruption in politics and political power. Someone always wants to control everyone else by pushing them down and creating a ruling class and a ruled class. The rulers feed their need for power and domination at the expense of the ruled class.

This is why communism and socialism do not work long term. These rulers believe and act as if they are the supreme authority and do not submit to God's rule and authority.

The general masses of people are treated in one manner as they are held under the authority of a single individual or a small group of individuals. They are kept in check by the imposition of force, the distortion of philosophy or religion, oppression in their financial lives and threats of punishment for dissent. The ruling group in any of these scenarios enjoys a much different lifestyle. Their lifestyle is free of the constraints of the common man. They can easily run amok, with severe overindulgence and increased lust for power but without the restraints of accountability. This ultimately leads to civil unrest and wars of rebellion.

God, on the other hand, has put laws in place to protect and prosper His creation, not oppress it. However, man still operates as if he can do whatever he wants. He simply assumes that all of his actions are acceptable and good because he has deceived himself into believing this lie. He leans to his own understanding and not to that of his creator, God. He simply considers that whatever he does is good. He assumes that he can take what he needs from others or achieve the rewards of the righteous just because he is who he is. Unfortunately for man, the world just does not work that way!

The disproportionate emphasis on the negative consequences of disobedience seen in Deuteronomy 28:15-66 is written because man constantly challenges God's authority. He needs to have nearly every possible scenario pointed out to him in which he might suffer as a result of his rebellion. However, humans are also prone to comparative standards, morals, ethics, and situational truth. Imagine the attitude that goes with this statement, "Everyone else does it, so it must be OK!" This attitude also challenges the absolute authority and truth of God.

A news story on television or the radio or in a newspaper might bring us the worst activities of the day. Most will be repulsed by these stories, but along with the repulsion, comes a sense that we must be doing OK because we are not doing anything as bad as that. We feel better because someone else is doing worse than we are. We can judge ourselves to be OK, or we self-justify because we are not doing what the bad people are doing. *However, the standard of discernment or judgment is not within us or among the rest of humankind.* Truth and standards are not situational. They truly come from God, and He wants to provide the path to the realization of the blessings through those standards. This is why He made laws and the Ten Commandments, which might be referred to as *The Ten Strongly Recommended Behaviors If You Want To Avoid Problems.*

We get a vivid description of what will happen either way in Deuteronomy 30:19.

Deuteronomy 30:19

I call heaven and earth to record this day against you, that I have set before you life and death, blessing and cursing: therefore choose life, that both thou and thy seed may live.

There are two basic spiritual laws that govern the human condition. The choice described in Deuteronomy 30:19 is actually a choice between them. One leads to life; the other, not so much. We also see the effects of our choices explained in the New Testament in Romans 8:1-14. Here, in great detail, we find out how things work in the spiritual realm.

Romans 8:1-14

[1] *There is therefore now no condemnation to them which are in Christ Jesus, who walk not after the flesh, but after the Spirit.*

[2] *For the* ***law of the Spirit of life in Christ Jesus*** *hath made me free from the* ***law of sin and death****.*

[3] *For what the law could not do, in that it was weak through the flesh, God sending his own Son in the likeness of sinful flesh, and for sin, condemned sin in the flesh:*

[4] *That the righteousness of the law might be fulfilled in us, who walk not after the flesh, but after the Spirit.*

[5] *For they that are after the flesh do mind the things of the flesh; but they that are after the Spirit the things of the Spirit.*

[6] *For to be carnally minded is death; but to be spiritually minded is life and peace.*

[7] *Because the carnal mind is enmity against God: for it is not subject to the law of God, neither indeed can be.*

[8] *So then they that are in the flesh cannot please God.*

> [9] *But ye are not in the flesh, but in the Spirit, if so be that the Spirit of God dwell in you. Now if any man have not the Spirit of Christ, he is none of his.* [10] *And if Christ be in you, the body is dead because of sin; but the Spirit is life because of righteousness.*
>
> [11] *But if the Spirit of him that raised up Jesus from the dead dwell in you, he that raised up Christ from the dead shall also quicken your mortal bodies by his Spirit that dwelleth in you.*
>
> [12] *Therefore, brethren, we are debtors, not to the flesh, to live after the flesh.*
>
> [13] *For if ye live after the flesh, ye shall die: but if ye through the Spirit do mortify the deeds of the body, ye shall live.*
>
> [14] *For as many as are led by the Spirit of God, they are the sons of God.*

The *law of the Spirit of life in Christ Jesus* provides liberty and freedom from the penalties that come from disobedience to the Law. The reason for this liberty and freedom is that Jesus paid the price for you. If you follow Jesus and trust by faith in what He did for you, you will not continue to try to make yourself acceptable or *self-justify* as Job did. Self-justification comes from following the other law, the *law of sin and death*. Choosing this course brings just the opposite of liberty. It brings death and destruction.

Life and peace come through the law of the Spirit of Life in Christ Jesus when you become a son or daughter of God and no longer chase the things and justifications of the flesh. The *law of the Spirit of life* sets us free. It relieves us of the burden of sin in our lives. This law comes about from the grace of God that flows from His nature. It is His character and nature to save us from our own destruction, and He accomplishes it through the shed blood of Jesus. How can the blood of Jesus accomplish this for us? For that, we must fully understand what the *law of sin and death* really means.

The "Undo" Button Or Words Eternal?

When God speaks, it becomes truth, and there is no way to dismiss it or change it. We can understand this because of the examples that we found in Esther 1:19 *(see p. 230)* and Daniel 6:8-9 *(see p. 252)* regarding the laws of the Medes and Persians. There is nothing that He can say that does not become truth because His word by its very nature is truth. Once declared by God, His words are eternal and He cannot and will not take them back. God is vastly different from us in that He does not lie as we have previously seen in Numbers 23:19.

Numbers 23:19

God is not a man, That he should lie; neither the son of man, that he should repent: hath he said, and shall he not do it? Or hath he spoken, and shall he not make it good?

In the world of humans, this is not the case. Although one may be described as "a man (woman) of his (her) word," the truth is that we are all guilty in some way of falling short of that description. We have all said something that we later regretted. We wanted to take back the words or more correctly, the effects of those words. We can be forgiven, but the damage has been done and cannot be reset or undone. This concept is becoming increasingly difficult to appreciate fully in today's world.

We live in a computer generation where mistakes can easily be *undone*. Video games may result in the death of your character, but it can easily be brought back to life. If you do not win the game, you can *undo* the steps and start again. If you make a mistake typing or drawing on the computer, you can easily go back a few steps. If your hard drive crashes, you can restore it from a backup copy if you took the time to make one. However, in real life you cannot *un-break* something or get a *do-over* whenever you want. As technology becomes more and more ingrained in our lives, the realities of life can become distorted.

We cannot press the *undo* button in real life and *undo* our words, choices, or actions. Neither can God. *His words become truth* and affect the entirety of creation ***forever***. His words are absolute and unchangeable. This is why His words carry such gravity. Your words and choices determine your fate in a similar manner.

Job's friend, Eliphaz, caught a glimpse of this principle of the absolute nature of words when he was speaking with Job during his problems. Eliphaz seemed to understand the power of words as described in Job 22:28.

Job 22:28

Thou shalt also decree a thing, and it shall be established unto thee: and the light shall shine upon thy ways.

This same principle is reiterated in the book of Romans 4:17 and is seen in slightly different ways in these two translations.

Romans 4:17b *(MSG)*

...trust God to do what only God could do: raise the dead to life, with a word make something out of nothing.

Romans 4:17b *(ERV)*

...the God who gives life to the dead and speaks of things that don't yet exist as if they are real.

When God speaks, whatever He says becomes truth and is eternal. When He makes a decree, it happens, and the universe is held responsible for its implications. Therefore, when God spoke the world into existence in Genesis, it came into existence. When God spoke life into Man, he became alive. God said that the dominion of the earth belonged to Adam, and it was his until Adam relinquished it to Satan through sin. God warned that the penalty for sin is death and that death will follow when sin is committed. Thus, Adam died.

This concept of the power and absolute nature of words is critical to our understanding. We will stand accountable for our words. We shape our lives by our choice of words because the words that we use are a reflection of what we believe, what we think and how we act. The words of man either agree or disagree with God's words. Our words guide us and will also lay a foundation for what we will become.

The sin of Adam put the world into a tailspin because of the decree of the *law of sin and death* that God spoke at the beginning. The entire human race was doomed because of sin. However, God had a plan to bring in the *law of the Spirit of life in Christ Jesus* to set things back on course. God *could not repeal* His first Law. However, He found a way to make a new law that would satisfy the requirements of the first Law, just like in the events of Esther. God did it by sacrificing Himself through Jesus for the benefit of all of Mankind. According to Ephesians 2:8-9, He did it by grace through the faith exercised by each human spirit that chooses Him!

Ephesians 2:8-9

[8] *For by grace are ye saved through faith; and that not of yourselves: it is the gift of God:*

[9] *Not of works, lest any man should boast.*

God's character and nature is to bring good news, release and heal, make the blind see, deliver the oppressed, and provide grace and free favor. We do not have to work or perform some ritual to receive His grace and favor, we must only believe.

In Luke 4:18-19 Jesus quoted the words of the prophet in Isaiah 61:1-2 which were written about Him 700 years before.

Luke 4:18-19 *(AMP)*

> [18] *The Spirit of the Lord [is] upon Me, because He has anointed Me [the Anointed One, the Messiah] to preach the good news (the Gospel) to the poor; He has sent Me to announce release to the captives and recovery of sight to the blind, to send forth as delivered those who are oppressed [who are downtrodden, bruised, crushed, and broken down by calamity],* [19] *To proclaim the accepted and acceptable year of the Lord [the day when salvation and the free favors of God profusely abound.]*

Jesus fulfilled this prophecy, and the character and nature of God is to provide all of this for you freely. However, you still must choose between the *law of sin and death* and the *law of the Spirit of life in Christ Jesus*. You see, it is *fair* that you should pay the price of your own sin. However, God is very *unfair* in His approach to you through His grace that we will explore in the next chapter.

Chapter 23

IT'S JUST NOT FAIR!

Wait a minute! There are lots of scriptures that say that God is responsible for all kinds of curses of evil, sickness, disease, and destruction. There are also many scriptures that say that God is blessing us, taking care of us and rescuing us from our misery and self-destruction. Which is it then? It doesn't seem right or fair that with one hand God does good and with the other He does evil! It seems so indiscriminate, so how can I believe that God is good and just when *His* Bible says that *He* does all of this bad stuff too? Here are some examples in Deuteronomy 28:61, Isaiah 45:7 and Amos 3:6 where God appears to be doing evil.

Deuteronomy 28:61

Also every sickness, and every plague, which is not written in the book of this law, ***them will the Lord bring upon thee, until thou be destroyed.***

Isaiah 45:7

I form the light, and create darkness: I make peace, and ***create evil****: I the Lord do all these things.*

Amos 3:6

Shall a trumpet be blown in the city, and the people not be afraid? ***shall there be evil in a city, and the Lord hath not done it****?*

These examples certainly give the impression that God has an evil side to His character. Some scriptures provide character examples of God that are only good and supportive in nature and appear to refute the possibility of an evil side. However, the scriptures above seem to paint a clear picture of a very different character, one of both good and evil, they suggest that God is responsible for all of it. Which is it then, good or evil, blessing or cursing? Does God do both? Faced with this dilemma, let's examine James 3:8-12, which poses an interesting truth.

James 3:8-12 *(NKJV)*

*[8] But no man can tame the tongue. It is an unruly evil, full of deadly poi-
son. [9] With it we bless our God and Father, and with it we curse men, who
have been made in the similitude of God. [10] Out of the same mouth proceed
blessing and cursing. My brethren, these things ought not to be so. [11] Does
a spring send forth fresh water and bitter from the same opening? [12] Can
a fig tree, my brethren, bear olives, or a grapevine bear figs? Thus no spring
yields both salt water and fresh.*

The Natural Order

This scripture compares natural, physical impossibilities with words that are both good and evil that come from the same source. It concludes that something is wrong with this picture. Words are clearly given a higher importance in the comparison. There is no doubt that this scripture poses a serious question as to the understanding or character of an individual who *claims* to be one way speaking blessings but *speaks* in another way to be proclaiming curses. This comparison clearly implies corruption. The conclusion is that the source of such ambiguity is not trustworthy or reliable.

Therefore, if it appears that both blessing and cursing come from the mouth of God, then God is either in conflict with His own creation and natural order, or He is a liar. Does God operate in conflict with Himself? Is He inconsistent in His own character? Is our life with God just like picking petals off of a daisy? He loves me? He loves me not? Does God bless out of one side of His mouth and speak evil curses out of the other side?

If He did, there would be utter confusion and God's system would not be fair or just at all! James said that this type of conflict should not be. However, there is another possibility as we saw in the earlier discussion of relativity*(see p. 46)*. There might be an incorrect conclusion, attribution, or understanding on the part of the writer or observer of what God does and says.

Faith vs. The Law – It's Your Choice

In the opening scriptures of this chapter, it appears that two diametrically opposed views and actions are being attributed to the same source, God. However, is this really what is happening? Look closely at the following scripture in Galatians 3:11-14 and make a determination for yourself.

Galatians 3:11-14

[11] *But that no man is justified by the law in the sight of God, it is evident:*
for, ***The just shall live by faith****.* [12] *And the law is not of faith: but,*
The man that doeth them shall live in them*.* [13] *Christ* ***hath re-***
deemed us from the curse of the law*, being made a curse for us: for*
it is written, Cursed is every one that hangeth on a tree: [14] *That* ***the bless-***
ing of Abraham might come on the Gentiles *through Jesus Christ;*
that we might receive the promise of the Spirit through faith.

There is a great distinction between personal *faith* and the *law*. The law carries with it blessings for obedience and curses for disobedience. What we might interpret as evil is actually a manifestation of the curse of disobedience to the law. *The responsibility for that manifestation rests on the one who is disobedient, not the one who established the law.*

This concept is extremely important to understand. It is not a matter of semantics. It is a matter of personal responsibility. The order of the universe is one of cause and effect. There is no effect without a cause. Subsequently, when an effect is observed, there must be a cause. Identification of the cause can be extremely difficult or very painful in many situations. Effects follow causes (actions or decisions on the part of individuals). An entirely different view of one's life and surroundings ensures from a full realization of the truth of this principle. Suddenly, things are actually fair and just even though they are not always so pleasant to accept or fully understand!

Some of the biggest problems of humankind come when we try to protect ourselves from a cause and effect relationship. We may not have any concerns with being the cause of something, but we don't want to suffer any of the effects. While trying to obscure the truth that may reveal that our own actions caused a situation that hurt us or someone else, we have a tendency to deflect our responsibility and condemn or blame others. This is called lying! No place is more evident than the world of politics whether it be in public office or the corporate business world. When discovered, these deflections or cover-ups manifest in very public ways as they come to light. Companies, employees, and even entire populations can suffer from the consequences of the lies of one or a few individuals trying to protect themselves from something they caused. It is much the same in our own personal and private lives.

Punishment or Consequence?

For many, it is difficult to accept that circumstances of life, health, economics, and even death are subject to and dependent upon the decisions we make. The things that occur in our lives have causes. However, it is much more convenient and emotionally comfortable to place blame and responsibility on someone else rather than ourselves. It is even *politically correct* to affix blame for actions away from individuals. And who better to blame than an ethereal, unseen, can-do-anything-He-wants *sovereign* God!

However, was it God that caused your grandfather to destroy his body with alcohol and drugs, potentially altering the genetics of his sperm? Did God force your grandmother to smoke and drink causing damage during her pregnancy with your parent? Did God cause those genetic or health mutations to occur which manifested as a disease in your body in your generation? Did God instill hatred, bigotry, racism, or rejection of Him into you or your ancestry? NO, to all of them!

Did God force you to abuse your own body through drugs, alcohol, tobacco, poor nutrition or overwork? Poor personal choices result in physical, emotional, and spiritual manifestations that come from those abuses and problems. They are both personal and shared curses that manifest as a result of poor decisions, which are sometimes referred to as transgressions or sins. Deuteronomy 5:9-10, Exodus 20:5-6, Exodus 34:5-7 and Numbers 14:17-18 all refer to these curses. Let's look at the explanation found in Exodus 34:5-7.

Exodus 34:5-7 *(NLV)*

> [5] *Then the Lord came down in a cloud and stood there with him; and he called out his own name, Yahweh.* [6] *The Lord passed in front of Moses, calling out, "Yahweh! The Lord! The God of compassion and mercy! I am slow to anger and filled with unfailing love and faithfulness.* [7] *I lavish unfailing*

love to a thousand generations. I forgive iniquity, rebellion, and sin. But I do not excuse the guilty. I lay the sins of the parents upon their children and grandchildren; the entire family is affected— even children in the third and fourth generations.

Generational Curses

This passage does not make it sound at all like God would punish the innocent generations after sin took place. It sounds as if God is talking out of both sides of His mouth and is contradicting Himself! However, punishment of sons and grandsons is promised as a result of the sins of the father, the grandfather and the great-grandfather. This type of punishment could be called a *generational curse*. It is definitely a real phenomenon, but the matter of perspective still plays a role. Is God actually punishing the innocent generations of a sinful, rebellious person, or is the actual mechanism of punishment emanating from a cause and effect relationship? Does God unfairly punish the innocent? Or, do the habits, decisions, rebellion, and sin create destructive effects that last through four generations? Does God do the punishing, or is God warning that it just takes that long to clear the slate of the physical, mental, and emotional abuses that sin creates?

Much of who we are is passed from generation to generation through attitudes, moral perspectives and faith. What does it take to *break the mold*? What causes the *unfailing love and faithfulness and forgiveness of iniquity, rebellion, and sin* mentioned in Exodus 34:6-7 to change into generations of punishment for those very sins? God does not want sin to divert your attention from Him, and Deuteronomy 5:8-10 provides insight.

Deuteronomy 5:8-10 *(NKJV)*
8 *You shall not make for yourself a carved image — any likeness of anything that is in heaven above, or that is in the earth beneath, or that is in the water under the earth;* 9 *you shall not bow down to them nor serve them. For I, the Lord your God, am a jealous God, visiting the iniquity of the fathers upon the children to the third and fourth generations of those who hate Me,* 10 *but showing mercy to thousands, to those who love Me and keep My commandments.*

It is important to note the word that is translated as *visiting* in the *King James Version*. It appears in Deuteronomy 5:9, Exodus 20:5 and 34:7, and

Numbers 14:18. It is the same Hebrew word, פָּקַד, *paqad* (paw-kad'), Strong's OT:6485, in all four of the verses.

> ***"visiting"*** - *Strong's* OT:6485 פָּקַד, paqad (paw-kad')
>
> *a primitive root; to visit (with friendly or hostile intent); by analogy, to oversee, muster, charge, care for, miss, deposit, etc.*

The obvious inference in the text of these verses is that *God* is *visiting* or causing the curse to manifest through four generations. This Hebrew word is similar to those we examined previously. The verb, *to visit* in Hebrew has the Qal stem that is not causative in nature. This means that it does not specifically refer to an individual, in this case, God, as the causative factor.

Once again, God appears to be getting the blame for something that is against His nature. He was simply warning that the evil, rebellion, iniquity, and sin will repeat throughout four generations before it dissipates unless it is stopped by the descendants repenting and coming to Him. He is not able to overlook active rebellious sin because the breaking of His Law carries its own inherent penalties. However, if anyone puts away their sins and repents, He will *forgive iniquity, rebellion, and sin.* His forgiveness is how the generational curse can be broken. However, if it is left alone, it is destined to be repeated.

The American Idol

The path to destruction in the generational curse occurred with the rejection of God and the worship of other things of this world. Idol worship was common during this time as man was easily overawed by unexplained phenomenon. There were many *gods* that seemed to demand attention as we read earlier regarding Abraham *(see p. 158).* It might seem that 21st-century man is far too sophisticated to fall for worshipping the hand crafted idols or *gods* of Abraham's father, Terah.

However, there is still a strong draw to these types of objects in the tenets of *New Age* theology. Nevertheless, for the more mainstream individual, the objects of worship, especially in America, have become less obvious and more insidious. The distractive and destructive force behind present-day worship still remains the same. The new *gods* could be money, fame, work, attention, sex, drugs, alcohol, physical pleasures, the internet, hobbies, or even reality television to name a few. An insatiable thirst for knowledge and the demand for *scientific proof* of everything before believing are just a few of the plethora of distractions that could be classified as idols as seen in the previous discussion on religion *(see p. 31)*.

So the question still remains, "Does God make these bad, destructive, punishing things occur as a penalty for disobedience and sin?" The discussion about Job sheds light on some possible answers, as does Genesis 6:12-13 *(see p. 119)*.

Genesis 6:12-13

> [12] *And God looked upon the earth, and, behold, it was corrupt; for all flesh had corrupted his way upon the earth.* [13] *And God said unto Noah, The end of all flesh is come before me; for the earth is filled with violence through them; and, behold, I will destroy them with the earth.*

The statement, *"The end of all flesh is come before me,"* was powerful and terrifying, especially for those who were not among Noah's family members! Corruption on the earth had hit an all-time high. Violence and perversion ruled the entire globe, but even so, God did not say, "I have had it with you people. I am going to kill you all!" God said the end of all flesh *is come before me,* meaning that this is a legal issue, not one of preference.

God established the order of things back in the garden with Adam and Eve when He told them that the consequence of sin was death. He sought to forgive and overlook their sins and the sins of their generations. He desired to have His free-will-instilled creation make a quality decision to worship and imitate Him. The insight from the book of Job pointed out that there is an accuser, one who takes every opportunity to accuse man of his sins and demands that the penalty be enforced. This is what occurred when, *the end of all flesh*, came before God. A justifiable, legal demand on God's word and a declaration that the penalty for sin is death was made. There was no way to overlook it or delay the consequences because of the severity and pervasiveness of the sin.

Wait a minute! God is Sovereign. He can do whatever He wants! He did not have to give in to the legal demand. He could have simply changed the rules to fit the circumstances. Many humans do that every day in their lives, but that is what the whole concept of situational ethics and relativism is all about. We do not like to live by absolutes. We want to make up the rules as we go along. However, in God's world (of which you are a part, whether or not you like it or believe it), there are absolutes. The greatest absolute is the integrity of God's own words. If He were to renege on His Word, He would become a liar, and His entire universe would collapse upon His sin!

God being sovereign, He decided to play by His own rules and chose to be bound by them. He did not have a choice about the destruction of all flesh since the rules were in place from the time of Adam and Eve. Corruption on the of the earth had grown to epic proportions before the time of the flood. All flesh had called for its own destruction according to its own actions. God spent generations holding back the destruction that the sins of all flesh demanded until the sin had become so great that destruction could no longer be restrained. The only redemptive part of the entire scenario was that Noah and his family did listen to God and did act in obedience to Him. Their flesh (and that of mankind) was saved from the destruction of *all flesh* as a result of their rejection of the sins of their time and their choice to follow and worship God.

Corruption Continues

Noah was about 600 years old at the time of the flood (c. 2300 BC). He lived about 950 years (c. 2902-1952 BC) and could have witnessed Abram's birth (c. 1950 BC). Abraham (Abram) only lived 175 years as life spans decreased dramatically following the flood. The corruption that prevailed on the earth had abated since Noah, and his family were the only survivors. However, over the remaining 350 years of his life, Noah began to see corruption seep back into the earth. His great-great-grandson, Nimrod, was born about 100 years after the flood. He was a great hunter and founded the kingdom of Babel (Genesis 10:8-10) which became known as Babylon. The unity of mankind in corruption came to a head again in Genesis 11:1-9 with the tower that he built there.

Genesis 11:1-9

11 And the whole earth was of one language, and of one speech. 2 And it
came to pass, as they journeyed from the east, that they found a plain in
the land of Shinar; and they dwelt there. 3 And they said one to another,
Go to, let us make brick, and burn them throughly. And they had brick for
stone, and slime had they for morter. 4 And they said, Go to, let us build us
a city and a tower, whose top may reach unto heaven; and let us make us a
name, lest we be scattered abroad upon the face of the whole earth.

[5] And the Lord came down to see the city and the tower, which the children of men builded. [6] And the Lord said, Behold, the people is one, and they have all one language; and this they begin to do: and now nothing will be restrained from them, which they have imagined to do.

[7] Go to, let us go down, and there confound their language, that they may not understand one another's speech. [8] So the Lord scattered them abroad from thence upon the face of all the earth: and they left off to build the city. [9] Therefore is the name of it called Babel; because the Lord did there confound the language of all the earth: and from thence did the Lord scatter them abroad upon the face of all the earth.

The tower was an act of cooperative arrogance and self-will similar to Satan challenging God's authority in Isaiah 14:12-14 *(see p. 71)*. The people of the earth spoke a single language in cooperation with one another. However, they sought to exalt themselves above God and make themselves supreme. The result was not death or a flood but a disruption of their communication. Cooperative sin once again met its match. The people were scattered because they could no longer understand one another and abandoned the Tower of Babel project (c. 2242 BC).[65]

The decay of man continued with the scattering and the worship of other gods became prevalent. However, God searched for a man that would be obedient to Him, and He found Abram. God spoke to him even before He established His covenant with him. He gave Abram a glimpse into the fact that He did not bring the destruction, but man brought it upon himself through sin. The narrative presented here is from Genesis 15:13-16. It is presented in two different translations for clarity.

Genesis 15:13-16 *(MSG)*

[13] GOD said to Abram, "Know this: your descendants will live as outsiders in a land not theirs; they'll be enslaved and beaten down for 400 years.
[14] Then I'll punish their slave masters; your offspring will march out of there loaded with plunder. [15] But not you; you'll have a long and full life and die a good and peaceful death. [16] Not until the fourth generation will your descendants return here; ***sin is still a thriving business among the Amorites****."*

Genesis 15:13-16 *(AMP)*

[13] And [God] said to Abram, "Know positively that your descendants will be strangers dwelling as temporary residents in a land that is not theirs

> *[Egypt], and they will be slaves there and will be afflicted and oppressed for 400 years.* [14] *But I will bring judgment on that nation whom they will serve, and afterward they will come out with great possessions.* [15] *And you shall go to your fathers in peace; you shall be buried at a good old (hoary) age.* [16] *And in the fourth generation they [your descendants] shall come back here [to Canaan] again,* ***for the iniquity of the Amorites is not yet full and complete****."*

The narrative in both these and other versions speaks about the iniquity or sin of the Amorites, and the fact that it had not fully played out to its conclusion. God did not step in and destroy the people because of their sins. Their sins were a polluting and corruptive influence that was eating away at the fabric of their lives on a daily basis. God is patient and hopeful that all people will turn from their ways, acknowledge Him, and change the direction of their sinful ways. However, there comes a point when the heart of the individual, or in this case, the Amorite people, will not turn from sinful ways. This refusal to repent is what occurred in the time of Noah. It also occurred with Pharaoh and Moses, and it seems to be happening in America and other places in the world today!

The Greek word NT:3340 is translated as *repent* in several King James New Testament verses.

> ***"repent"*** - *Strong's* NT:3340 μετανοέω, *metanoeo* (met-an-o-eh'-o); from NT:3326 and NT:3539; to think differently or afterwards, i.e. reconsider (morally, feel compunction).

Simply stated, repentance means to realize that you are going the wrong way, and you voluntarily change your direction. Willingness to change direction is essential to repentance. However, if in his heart of hearts a man knows that he will not leave his sinful ways and submit to God's love and mercy, he is truly lost and will pay the entire penalty of death for his sins.

God has put forth a great deal of effort to get the point across to mankind. He has given great detail regarding the provisions of the Law and the expectations placed on us. He identified the blessings for obedience and the curses attached to disobedience of the Law in Deuteronomy 28.

What's The Curse?

Our study of Deuteronomy Chapter 28 revealed that only 25% of the verses (1-14) are spent outlining the blessings, whereas 75% of the verses (15-68) are devoted to a description of the curses *(see p. 291)*. God is making His expectations very clear to a very self-willed, stubborn, and headstrong human race. He knows that it takes a lot to get through to us and get us to avoid disobedience and overcome our complacency. It seems that Man likes to find *loopholes* to get around the intent of the law with technicalities. God closed the door on those loopholes in His extensive discussion of the curses for various acts of disobedience. He knows that we understand and learn best when we are given physical examples to which we can relate. This is one of the reasons why Jesus taught in parables, which are physical examples of spiritual principles.

God had another reason for listing the extreme detail in Deuteronomy 28. It was to state clearly the reasons that curses come. These scriptures tell us that curses come from disobedience. They do not come from God; they come from breaking the Law. God set in motion a *self-regulating* law. The Law has everything it needs within it to run on its own, much the way a seed has within it what it needs to grow and bring forth its fruit. Accordingly, blessings will come if a person obeys the Law, but curses come when a person's actions and behaviors are contrary to the instruction of the Law. Proverbs 26:2 gives some insight into curses in general.

Proverbs 26:2 *(BBE)*

. . . .so the curse does not come without a cause.

God is not responsible for curses that may manifest in your life. They only come when there is a cause. You and your ancestors are responsible for your choices and actions, and they will result in blessings or curses. It is sometimes very painful to come face to face with this reality. It also seems to be ingrained into human nature to deflect that responsibility away from ourselves. Curses are not arbitrary, and when we realize that there actually are causes and that our choices are at the core, we can take the first step toward *reversing the curse*.

Curses can come from a variety of sources and result in a variety of undesired and unpleasant circumstances. We live in a *fallen* and corrupt world. The authority of the Earth realm was transferred from God's creation, Adam, to Satan through deception *(see p. 128)*. The book of Job tells us who enacts the curses, and it is not God *(see p. 126)*.

In light of the understanding that we glean from the account of Job, how do we reconcile the clear attribution of evil to God in the following verses in Deuteronomy 28:61, 1 Samuel 16:14-15, Isaiah 45:6-7 and Amos 3:1-7?

Deuteronomy 28:61

> *Also every sickness, and every plague, which is not written in the book of this law,* ***them will the Lord bring upon thee, until thou be destroyed.***

1 Samuel 16:14-15

> [14] *But the Spirit of the LORD departed from Saul, and an evil spirit from the LORD troubled him.* [15] *And Saul's servants said unto him, Behold now, an evil spirit from God troubleth thee.*

Isaiah 45:6-7

> [6] *That they may know from the rising of the sun, and from the west, that there is none beside me. I am the Lord, and there is none else.* [7] *I form the light, and create darkness: I make peace, and* ***create evil****: I the Lord do all these things.*

Amos 3:1-7

> [1] *Hear this word that the Lord hath spoken against you, O children of Israel, against the whole family which I brought up from the land of Egypt, saying,* [2] *You only have I known of all the families of the earth: therefore I will punish you for all your iniquities.*
>
> [3] *Can two walk together, except they be agreed?* [4] *Will a lion roar in the forest, when he hath no prey? will a young lion cry out of his den, if he have taken nothing?* [5] *Can a bird fall in a snare upon the earth, where no gin is for him? shall one take up a snare from the earth, and have taken nothing at all?* [6] *Shall a trumpet be blown in the city, and the people not be afraid?* ***shall there be evil in a city, and the Lord hath not done it?***
>
> [7] *Surely the Lord God will do nothing, but he revealeth his secret unto his servants the prophets.*

According to these verses, God appears to be an accomplice to the negative actions at best, and at worst, He actually does the evil. However, there is a difference between *permitting* and not *preventing* a particular action as discussed earlier *(see Chapter 9, p. 81) and Chapter 14, p. 177)*. The sense of permission suggests an active agreement with the action (as an accomplice). Prevention requires intervention, for which there is no legal foundation. Legally, the consequences of the actions of an individual have been determined in advance.

Being Double-Minded

There is a paradox that is very difficult to reconcile if we believe that God does both the blessing and cursing. James 3:10-12 appears to say that both blessing and cursing (by inference – good and evil) cannot exist in the same place, person, or thing at the same time.

James 3:10-12 *(NKJV)*

> [10] *Out of the same mouth proceed blessing and cursing. My brethren, these*
> *things ought not to be so.* [11] *Does a spring send forth fresh water and bitter*
> *from the same opening?* [12] *Can a fig tree, my brethren, bear olives, or a*
> *grapevine bear figs? Thus no spring yields both salt water and fresh.*

This passage plainly states that God cannot both bless and curse. However, it can be said that God is ultimately responsible for the creation of evil, as seen in the previous scriptures, because He is responsible for all of creation. He is also responsible for creating the Law and the penalties for ignoring it. However, there is a difference between God being purposefully evil and Him allowing Man or Satan to exercise free will that might lead to evil and sin.

Sometimes, it appears that mankind is actually held to a standard that is higher than the standard that God holds himself! This cannot possibly be true, but the appearance is there just the same. However, God is not *double-minded* which is what James 3:10 is illustrating. He is consistent throughout His dealings with mankind. He makes it clear in James 1:5-8 that being *double-minded* is an unstable condition.

James 1:5-8 *(NKJV)*

> [5] *If any of you lacks wisdom, let him ask of God, who gives to all liberally*
> *and without reproach, and it will be given to him.* [6] *But let him ask in*
> *faith, with no doubting, for he who doubts is like a wave of the sea driven*
> *and tossed by the wind.* [7] *For let not that man suppose that he will receive*
> *anything from the Lord;* [8] *he is a double-minded man, unstable in all his*
> *ways.*

Jesus also spoke of a *double-minded* situation when He responded to being accused of casting out demons from people by the power of the devil in Mark 3:24-26.

Mark 3:24-26

*24 And if a kingdom be divided against itself, that kingdom cannot stand.
25 And if a house be divided against itself, that house cannot stand. 26 And
if Satan rise up against himself, and be divided, he cannot stand, but hath an end.*

Only unified, consistent actions with corresponding fruit or results can survive according to this verse in Mark. This applies to God, Satan, and Man. God's kingdom would fall if He were at odds with His own purpose of restoring Man's relationship with Him. It is not legal, and it is neither right nor true that God would act against His own word. A system that would allow such inconsistencies while demanding man's adherence to a higher standard of behaviors would be hypocritical. It would be erratic on God's part and not be right or fair at all. Since being *double-minded* is a guaranteed failure, God recommends that we avoid it in James 4:7-10.

James 4:7-10 *(MSG)*

*7 So let God work his will in you. Yell a loud no to the Devil and watch
him scamper. 8 Say a quiet yes to God and he'll be there in no time. Quit dabbling in sin. Purify your inner life. Quit playing the field.
9 Hit bottom, and cry your eyes out. The fun and games are over. Get serious, really serious.
10 Get down on your knees before the Master; it's the only way you'll get on your feet.*

James 4:7-10 *(ERV)*

*7 So give yourselves to God. Stand against the devil, and he will run away
from you. 8 Come near to God and he will come near to you. You are sinners, so clean sin out of your lives. You are trying to follow God and the world at the same time. Make your thinking pure.
9 Be sad, be sorry, and cry! Change your laughter into crying. Change your joy into sadness.
10 Be humble before the Lord, and he will make you great.*

These two translations explain things a little differently, but the message is the same. Do not try to live in sin and follow God at the same time. It is a *double-minded* endeavor and is doomed to failure.

So What is Fair?

When men speak, they do so out of their own understanding and thought process. Man's process is far different than God's. In Isaiah 55:8-9, we see that He operates in a completely different realm.

Isaiah 55:8-9

> [8] *For my thoughts are not your thoughts, neither are your ways my ways, saith the* Lord. [9] *For as the heavens are higher than the earth, so are my ways higher than your ways, and my thoughts than your thoughts.*

God thinks with a different mind than the mind of humans *(see p. 259)*. Man thinks inside the box of his observations, perspectives, and understanding or according to his ideolatry. God has no such box and is not limited by anything but His own Word. He sees things differently, and He does things differently.

Man thinks inside the box of his observations, perspectives and understanding according to his own Ideolatry.

Some situations in the Bible are related from experience by eyewitnesses. Others are presented from the perspective of historical hindsight from a distant observer. Still others are attributed as direct quotes from the mouth of God. The words used in the original writings may also be altered in meaning in some situations by the translators. They used the best words available according to their understanding of the events, but a different perspective can sometimes be more revealing.

The Bible expresses the totality of God's purpose for man. Ultimately, He is in the business of saving, delivering, rescuing, redeeming, blessing, and guiding him. Everything that He has done and that He has provided is toward one goal, restoring man back to the status that he had when he was first created. He wants to separate him from his sins and bring him back into fellowship with Him. Therefore, if we observe an inconsistency in an account of God's actions or words, our understanding of the situation must be flawed.

Unfavorable circumstances are viewed as God's active punishment or correction, but the concept of punishment is very simply stated as *a penalty imposed for wrongdoing.*[66] The actual reality is this: God's Word is His correction. He does not punish. It is sin that does the punishing. His Word reveals our sins as we see in Hebrews 4:12-13, and He offers forgiveness through Jesus.

Hebrews 4:12-13 *(ERV)*

> 12 *God's word is alive and working. It is sharper than the sharpest sword and cuts all the way into us. It cuts deep to the place where the soul and the spirit are joined. God's word cuts to the center of our joints and our bones. It judges the thoughts and feelings in our hearts.*
>
> 13 *Nothing in all the world can be hidden from God. He can clearly see all things. Everything is open before him. And to him we must explain the way we have lived.*

A penalty is not a proactive act of vengeance that is seen with vindictive human nature. It is a predetermined result activated by disobedience. Lying or cheating on your taxes will bring financial penalties or possibly worse. It is disobedience to the law, and the law carries a punishment for disobedience. Excessive use of alcohol, smoking, or using illegal drugs might lead to injury, sickness, or death. Overeating and gluttony may do the same or lead to poverty. None of these are wise, and God recommends against these kinds of activities in Proverbs 23:15-21.

Proverbs 23:15-21 *(ERV)*

[15] My son, it makes me happy when you make a wise decision. [16] It makes me feel good inside when you say the right things.

[17] Never envy evil people, but always respect the Lord. [18] This will give you something to hope for that will not disappoint you.

[19] So listen, my son, and be wise. Always be careful to follow the right path.

[20] Don't make friends with people who drink too much wine and eat too much food.

[21] Those who eat and drink too much become poor. They sleep too much and end up wearing rags.

God does know what is best for us. However, from our perspective, "no" is a bad thing, and it forms a longing for that which is denied, making it something to be desired.

Fortunately, God provided a way out of the hopelessness of our own sins. He gave the Law to point out to us that we really cannot do it on our own. We need Him, His grace, and His mercy. It is impossible for a sinful man to live up to the Law. Blood (death) was required to satisfy the penalty (punishment) of sin. The penalty for sin is death, and this is the reason why God provided substitutionary animal sacrifice within the Law as a way to temporarily pay for sin. There were detailed procedures and yearly ceremonies set up to atone for sins through those sacrifices. However, God also had a better plan that would no longer require periodic animal sacrifices.

God brought His Son into the world to be the substitutionary, blood sacrifice for all of the sins of all mankind. Because Jesus Christ lived a sinless life according to the Law, there was no legal precedent for Him to die. Jesus had no penalty for sin upon himself. He voluntarily offered Himself to be the blood sacrifice for all of our sins.

There is only one requirement that God places on you to be covered by Jesus' substitutionary sacrifice. You must believe and receive by faith that Jesus Christ is the Son of God and that He died in place of you, assuming the penalty for your own personal sins. Jesus Christ has redeemed the believer from the curses of the Law. He paid the penalty of the curse for the believer. God extends Grace through Jesus Christ to the believer, and that grace overcomes the curses that the Law contains!

Do not let yourself get hung up on what you do not understand. God works differently than you do. Faith and trust in Him are what is required to do the right things and make the right decisions. In Proverbs 3:5-8, we see that His wisdom and counsel will refresh you and act like a medicine for your body.

Proverbs 3:5-8 *(ERV)*

> [5] *Trust the Lord completely, and don't depend on your own knowledge.*
>
> [6] *With every step you take, think about what the Lord wants, and he will help you go the right way.*
>
> [7] *Don't trust in your own wisdom, but fear and respect the Lord and stay away from evil.*
>
> [8] *If you do this, it will be like a refreshing drink and medicine for your body.*

So you see, you may have had a different idea as to what the title of this chapter meant. It is fair and just for man to suffer for his own sins, but in His love for mankind God did something that is not fair. He made a way that offers you an opportunity not to bear the responsibility for your own personal sins! To be fair, you should have to die for your own sins, but not so with God. God extends His grace and mercy to you through Jesus Christ. He does not require you to pay the penalty for your own actions and sins. He allows Jesus to pay it for you. He only requires that you change your direction (repent), have faith in what Jesus did for you and follow Him.

Just how ***fair*** is that? Through the sacrifice of Jesus, God does not have to give you what you deserve. He doesn't have to be ***fair*** at all!

Chapter 24

WHEN DID GOD CHANGE HIS MIND?

After discussing the premise and content of this book and reading an early draft copy, a friend posed the interesting question that is the title of this chapter. My first response to him was that I thought that everything that I had already written would have answered that question. Then, I looked back and realized that this was a truly pivotal question that demanded specific treatment.

The question draws upon two schools of thought related to the interactions that God has with His creation, mankind. The first and probably the most universal and widely held viewpoint is that the God of the Old Testament is angry, hostile, punishing, unforgiving, and maybe even cruel. The Old Testament seems to depict God as a very rigid, demanding entity that tolerates nothing other than perfect obedience and complete submission. God appears to be using the Law or the short version, better known as the Ten Commandments, to beat mankind into submission.

The New Testament, on the other hand, provides the framework for the second viewpoint which depicts God as loving, compassionate, forgiving, and abundant in grace toward His wayward creation. Some of the scriptures in the New Testament seem to say that everything is now OK, such as this verse in 1 Corinthians 10:23.

1 Corinthians 10:23

All things are lawful for me, but all things are not expedient: all things are lawful for me, but all things edify not.

There appears to be a conflict between these two positions, and many people cannot fully accept the apparent change in God's dealings with mankind that is portrayed in the New Testament. Some who are steeped in traditional views have been taught that God is looking over their shoulder, and they had better not mess up because He is always looking for ways to punish them and send them to Hell. Their conditioning might not allow them to accept or understand the forgiving and loving God that is revealed through Jesus. Trying to weave this traditional understanding of God into the fabric of the New Testament presents some challenges.

Jesus is equated with God in the New Testament. Therefore, by extension, Jesus and God are the same throughout time. This is supported by the description of Jesus found in Hebrew 13:8. This would also imply that Jesus would display the same attributes God displayed in the Old Testament. Therefore, the God that is found in the Old Testament, with all of the apparent negative baggage, must still be that same in the New Testament as expressed through Jesus.

Hebrews 13:8

Jesus Christ the same yesterday, and to day, and for ever.

Traditional *"hell, fire, and brimstone"* preaching leads us to believe that God was not so nice in the Old Testament. It looks like God is going to get you for your evil ways. However, Jesus (God) offers peace, love, and salvation in the New Testament. This apparent contradiction presents an interesting conflict to the reader and student of the Bible, giving rise to the question posed in the title of this chapter, "When did God change His mind?"

What Just Happened?

The logical answer is that God changed His mind at the inception of the New Testament, coinciding with the Gospel accounts of Matthew, Mark, Luke, and John. However, the New Testament did not begin until the very end of the Gospels and the beginning of the Book of Acts. Jesus actually walked the earth under the laws of the Old Testament, not the grace of the New Testament. Jesus was the founder of the New Testament, not during His life, but following His death and resurrection.

A definition might be in order at this point to help clarify this situation. What exactly is meant by the word, *testament*, whether new or old? Simply stated, a testament is a covenant or the formalization of an agreement. A more detailed examination of the word *covenant* will help us better understand the use of the word testament. Pertinent aspects of the definition are that a testament has tangible proof, is formal and binding. It is based on performance, and there are provisions for damages due to a breach of the contract.

testament *(noun)*

> *1a) archaic: a covenant between God and the human race, 1b) capitalized: either of two main divisions of the Bible. 2a) a tangible proof or tribute, 2b) an expression of conviction: creed.*[67]

covenant *(noun)*

> *1a) usually formal, solemn, and binding agreement: compact, 2a) a written agreement or promise usually under seal between two or more parties especially for the performance of some action. 2b) the common-law action to recover damages for breach of such a contract.*
>
> *(Concise Encyclopedia) In the Hebrew scriptures, an agreement or treaty among peoples or nations, but most memorably the promises that God extended to humankind (e.g., the promise to Noah never again to destroy the earth by flood or the promise to Abraham that his descendants would multiply and inherit the land of Israel). God's revelation of the law to Moses on Mount Sinai created a pact between God and Israel known as the Sinai covenant. In Christianity, Jesus' death established a new covenant between God and humanity.*[68]

The Ten Commandments and the entire Law were an offshoot from the first Covenant between God and Man that is described in the Old Testament. Some men such as those listed above (Noah, Abraham, and Moses) were party to the covenants. The only thing that they had to offer on their side of the agreement was their faith and obedience. It is important to note that these agreements entered into by God were somewhat, if not totally, unilateral in scope. All of the commitment to perform was on His part and was only conditioned on man's performance of faith, trust, and obedience.

The issue of man's performance is the reason for the implementation of the Law. We are a bit on the stubborn and self-willed side as you will certainly agree just based on your own life and personal experience. Since we have problems figuring out what to do in many situations, we need a little bit of guidance about the truth and what is right, hence the Law. You see, the Law was not instituted to find reasons to punish us. It was established to guide us into making right and truthful decisions and acting in the appropriate manner. Making right decisions and taking right actions puts us into the position of being able to take part in the benefits that God had outlined in His agreement or Covenant with Abraham.

The results of rebellion against God have been evident throughout the existence of man. However, it was not until a law was put in place that man became fully responsible for disobedience and rebellion. The book of Romans provides that explanation in Chapter 5:13.

Romans 5:13 *(ERV)*

Sin was in the world before the Law of Moses. But God does not consider people guilty of sin if there is no law.

Sin has been present since the fall of Adam and Eve. Adam and Eve brought the beginning of the curse of death upon themselves and their descendants. However, without a law, man was not held accountable for that sin. The Law made man personally responsible for his sinful individual and corporate actions. The actions of Adam, the first man, brought down the curse of sin upon all of mankind. However, until the Law, the breadth and scope of the requirements upon man were not completely evident. The totality of the Law plainly illustrated that man was not able to achieve the expectations of God all on his own. He needed the help that Adam rejected by following after sin.

Examination of this passage in Romans 5:12-21 provides a very clear picture of God's plan to restore man to his original condition before the sin of Adam.

Romans 5:12-21 *(CEV)*

12 Adam sinned, and that sin brought death into the world. Now everyone has sinned, and so everyone must die. 13 Sin was in the world before the Law came. But no record of sin was kept, because there was no Law. 14 Yet death still had power over all who lived from the time of Adam to the time of Moses. This happened, though not everyone disobeyed a direct command from God, as Adam did.

In some ways Adam is like Christ who came later. 15 But the gift that God was kind enough to give was very different from Adam's sin. That one sin brought death to many others. Yet in an even greater way, Jesus Christ alone brought God's gift of kindness to many people.

[16] There is a lot of difference between Adam's sin and God's gift. That one sin led to punishment. But God's gift made it possible for us to be acceptable to him, even though we have sinned many times. [17] Death ruled like a king because Adam had sinned. But that cannot compare with what Jesus Christ has done. God has been so kind to us, and he has accepted us because of Jesus. And so we will live and rule like kings.

[18] Everyone was going to be punished because Adam sinned. But because of the good thing that Christ has done, God accepts us and gives us the gift of life. [19] Adam disobeyed God and caused many others to be sinners. But Jesus obeyed him and will make many people acceptable to God.

[20] The Law came, so that the full power of sin could be seen. Yet where sin was powerful, God's kindness was even more powerful. [21] Sin ruled by means of death. But God's kindness now rules, and God has accepted us because of Jesus Christ our Lord. This means that we will have eternal life.

Actions that were not right and true put man into a position of *breach of contract* for which there were consequences. Unfortunately for Man, the remedy for a breach of contract was death. This death was not an imposed death because God wanted to punish man for his disobedience. Death was the natural course of events that man would be destined to follow if he did not observe God's recommendations. God instituted the Covenant through Abraham to show man the possibilities of a life that was lived in obedience to God. God wanted Man to have a life that would be bursting with fulfillment and reward. The Law was put in place with Moses to show Man what was right and wrong and to provide a framework and path to follow so he would not *breach* the contract.

The Law was not to be worshiped. Although many people received punishment for willful disobedience, it's purpose was not to punish. The Law was not created to be used as a weapon to control people as many use it even today. The Law was designed to show man where he was falling short so that God's will and desire could be accomplished in each life that He created.

The Law was a stepping stone to show the totality of mankind that it needed help, help that God wanted to provide. The Law joined with the Covenant He made with Abraham to provide a path upon which the sacrifice of Jesus could be revealed. It is upon that revelation that God enacted the totality of the plan that He had for Man from the beginning. His plan was that man would desire to have a relationship with Him, his creator and that by faith man would trust God to provide for his every need.

A Single Focus

The truth is that God never did change His mind. He has always been on the same path, singularly focused on the success of man, His ultimate creation. He has consistently sought to deliver man from his own corrupted nature, to reveal and *save him* from his own destructive behaviors and to provide him with everlasting life. Armed with the understanding provided by the book of Esther we see that *God cannot breach (break) His own Word or take any actions that would be illegal.*

There is not much left to say on this matter in light of the following scripture in John 8:23-29.

> **John 8:23-32** *(TLB)*
> *23 Then he said to them, "You are from below; I am from above. You are of*
> *this world; I am not. 24 That is why I said that you will die in your sins;*
> *for unless you believe that I am the Messiah, the Son of God, you will die*
> *in your sins." 25 "Tell us who you are," they demanded. He replied, "I am the*
> *one I have always claimed to be. 26 I could condemn you for much and teach*
> *you much, but I won't, for I say only what I am told to by the one who sent*
> *me; and he is Truth." 27 But they still didn't understand that he was talking*
> *to them about God.*
>
> *28 So Jesus said, "When you have killed the Messiah, then you will realize*
> *that I am he and that I have not been telling you my own ideas, but have*
> *spoken what the Father taught me. 29 And he who sent me is with me - he*
> *has not deserted me - for I always do those things that are pleasing to him."*
>
> *30-31 Then many of the Jewish leaders who heard him say these things*
> *began believing him to be the Messiah. Jesus said to them, "You are truly my*
> *disciples if you live as I tell you to, 32 and you will know the truth, and the*
> *truth will set you free."*

God altered His method of interaction with Man in the New Testament, but not His character and nature. He is still the same now as He was in the Old Testament, and Jesus is a reflection of God embodying the truth of who He is. Since Jesus paid the ultimate price for our breach of contract, we now live in a time of Grace, not law. Through Jesus, God Himself not only made the New Covenant for our benefit, but He paid the price Himself to be certain that we could enjoy the benefits of that covenant! God did not change His mind. He has always had your best interests in His mind. This is His character and nature.

God chose to implement a specific system in this existence that we call home. His Word is the legal precedence and standard upon which everything in this system is based. He also chose to bind Himself to that system and its legal principles and will not override them. For a time throughout the Old Testament, it appears that God was being forced into a corner by His own system. The appearance is that His wrath was being unleashed upon the precious creation of man that was being destroyed through sin. However, from the beginning God had a proverbial *ace up his sleeve*, a mystery that he had planned to reveal when the time was right. It is through this mystery that God expresses His wrath.

CHAPTER 25

THE WRATH OF GOD

What is the Wrath of God? Where the word *wrath* appears in scripture, it seems to point to a manifestation of destruction, death, pain, disease, or maybe even financial calamity. This impression would seem to be reasonable in light of all of the destruction described in the Old Testament. The word *wrath* is found in many places in the King James Bible and is translated from a variety of Hebrew words *(see Appendix Chapter 25)*. Most of the meanings of the various Hebrew words refer to anger, rage, displeasure, fury, and indignation.

It is interesting to note that none of these Hebrew words seem to speak to any action. They describe an emotion or feeling. This sense is quite contrary to the sense that many people take the word *wrath* to mean. *Merriam-Webster.com* offers two definitions. The preferred or most common definition refers to the attitudinal or emotional component of the word. The second definition of the word refers to an action. It is this meaning of the word *wrath* that is most commonly associated with God.

wrath *(noun)*
1) strong vengeful anger or indignation
2) retributory punishment for an offense or a crime: divine chastisement.[69]

Semantics is very important in this discussion. The meaning that most attach to the word *wrath* in scripture is the secondary definition, which is the acting out of the anger described in the first sense of the definition. However, none of the Hebrew words translated as *wrath* carries the action of punishment in its definition. It is possible to be angry and have rage or to experience displeasure, fury, or indignation without a corresponding action of punishment or chastisement. Even as children, we are taught to control our anger and not lash out. It is not unreasonable to experience these feelings and emotions but not act on them.

How frustrated and angry do you feel when you see evil taking place around you? Sometimes you may want to take action, but you cannot because you either have no authority or do not have the ability to act. You still experience the painful emotions regardless of your ability to take action against the evil. If it is your young child that is causing the issue, you may step in to try and correct the behavior. However, with an adult child, you may have a tendency to try to *overlook, forgive, or cover up* the issue.

God is understandably *wrathful* because His prize creation, mankind, disappoints Him through sin. The disobedient and rebellious actions of man surely cause deep wounds and emotional responses in God such as sorrow and anger. However, God does not act on them by punishing man because the actions of wrath are directed toward sin, not people. The actions associated with His wrath against sin have already been determined by the Law. Thankfully, because of His love for man, God's character and nature is to make a way to forgive and cover the sin. The sacrificial observances in the Old Testament were short-term solutions that were designed to satisfy the penalties of sin. However, through the New Testament, He created a new and permanent way to deal with sin.

The effects of sin sometimes flow over on to those who may not have been directly involved with it. Those hanging around the sin can be sucked up into the penalties that are prescribed for it. This is the situation that Abraham was facing when he interceded for Sodom and Gomorrah. He did not want anyone to perish, and he especially did not want to see the righteous perish alongside the wicked when the penalties for the sin were fully realized. He thought that he understood what was happening, and he began to bargain for the lives of both the wicked and the righteous. He was trying to prevent the actions that were about to be played out. However, God was working on a different plan through Abraham, one to deal with the effects of sin, one that was suitable for His wrath.

Do You Hear What I Hear?

God wrapped His way of acting on His wrath in a mystery. It was a secret plan that would apply action to His wrath. This plan is the mystery of the kingdom that Jesus spoke of in Mark 4:9-12.

Mark 4:9-12

9 And he said unto them, "He that hath ears to hear, let him hear." 10 And
when he was alone, they that were about him with the twelve asked of him
the parable. 11 And he said unto them, "Unto you it is given to know the
mystery of the kingdom of God: but unto them that are without, all these
things are done in parables: 12 That seeing they may see, and not perceive;
and hearing they may hear, and not understand; lest at any time they
should be converted, and their sins should be forgiven them."

Everyone who hears or is capable of hearing sound is not always capable of actually hearing with understanding. The filters through which we observe and understand our existence may prevent us from actually hearing with the necessary understanding. There are some who live by this motto, "Don't confuse me with the facts, I have already made up my mind!" These are people who cannot "hear" what Jesus is teaching through the parables. They have been steeped in tradition, religion, or any other prejudice that *blocks their ability to hear with understanding*.

Jesus was a storyteller. However, His stories were not ordinary. On the surface, they sounded like anecdotes about life, but they were parables or "comparables" which drew moral or spiritual truths from everyday activities and situations. He never told a parable without a specific purpose. Through them, Jesus revealed aspects of the mystery of the kingdom of God. However, some listeners lacked the discernment or spiritual insight needed to understand.

The revealing of this mystery would not fully occur until an appointed time. God had been working behind the scenes throughout the ages with men and women who would listen to Him and act on their faith in Him to bring about the mystery at the right time. God revealed parts of the mystery to them through His Spirit as a result of their faith and obedience. However, the arrival of Jesus on the earth marked the time for the fullness of the revelation as described in Ephesians 3:3-6.

Ephesians 3:3-6 *(MSG)*

3 I got the inside story on this from God himself, as I just wrote you in brief.
4 As you read over what I have written to you, you'll be able to see for your-
selves into the mystery of Christ. 5 None of our ancestors understood this.
Only in our time has it been made clear by God's Spirit through his holy
apostles and prophets of this new order. 6 The mystery is that people who
have never heard of God and those who have heard of him all their lives

(what I've been calling outsiders and insiders) stand on the same ground before God. They get the same offer, same help, same promises in Christ Jesus. The Message is accessible and welcoming to everyone, across the board.

Ephesians 3:6 *(NIV)*

6 This mystery is that through the gospel the Gentiles are heirs together with Israel, members together of one body, and sharers together in the promise in Christ Jesus.

These two translations differ only in that the *New International Version (NIV)* identifies the *insiders* and *outsiders* who are mentioned in *The Message (MSG)* translation as Jews and Gentiles. Through this passage, the apostle Paul states that the mystery is that the Gentiles or all non-Jews also share with the Jews in the offer to inherit God's promise to Abraham.

Also, there are many other references to "things that have been kept secret" and "the mystery." The secret has been kept for a long time, actually from the foundation of the world according to a prophecy in Psalms 78:2, which is restated in Matthew 13:35. This prophecy also describes Jesus as speaking in parables and states that Jesus will utter secrets through these parables.

Matthew 13:35 *(From Psalms 78:2)*

That it might be fulfilled which was spoken by the prophet, saying, I will open my mouth in parables; I will utter things which have been kept secret from the foundation of the world.

Thus, we see that Jesus revealed the mystery through His preaching, much of which was done through parables. The same mystery and secret was made manifest or evident in Jesus as described in Romans 16:25-27.

Romans 16:25-27 *(CEV)*

25 Praise God! He can make you strong by means of my good news, which is the message about Jesus Christ. For ages and ages this message was kept secret, 26 but now at last it has been told. The eternal God commanded his prophets to write about the good news, so that all nations would obey and have faith. 27 And now, because of Jesus Christ, we can praise the only wise God forever! Amen.

We now have more information about the mystery, but what is being said in these verses about the *mystery of Christ*? Does this mean that Jesus spoke of mysteries or that He was the Mystery?

The Secret Place

To understand this "mystery of Christ," we must first examine the word *Christ*. The literal word translated as *Christ* in the New Testament is the Greek word, Χριστός ***(Christos)***, meaning "anointed" or "Messiah." Jesus is known as Jesus of Nazareth, Jesus Christ or Christ. Christ is not Jesus' last name, nor is it a swear word. It is a reference to His title as the Messiah, the Anointed One or the Saviour. More properly, He should be referred to as Jesus, the Christ, or Jesus, the Messiah.

> ***"Christ"*** - *Strong's* NT:5547 from NT:5548 Χριστο, Christos (khris-tos'); *anointed, i.e. the Messiah, an epithet of Jesus:* ***KJV*** *- Christ.*

This mystery of Christ was kept from the ancestors according to Ephesians 3:5 *(MSG)*. The same verse in the *King James Version (KJV)* refers to them as the *"sons of men"* or the common man. Many were idol worshippers and had little to no understanding of the One True God. The mystery was kept secret from the rest of the *spiritual* world because God did not want His plan discovered until it was fully implemented. His plan was a very special way to carry out His wrath against sin, and the mystery was designed to put it into action.

Revelation of the mystery was given to the prophets of the Old Testament by the Spirit of God, but it was obscured in the text of scripture. The prophets preached the parts of it that were entrusted to them. Isaiah 53:1-7 is an eloquent prophecy that describes the life, suffering, and purpose of Jesus, the Christ. It is veiled or hidden to those who are not spiritually in tune. However, it reveals part of the mystery and makes known some of God's plan. Later, when the time was right, Jesus revealed the plan to His disciples and subsequently to the rest of the world. However, it still remains a mystery to those who are not ready to hear and do not seek to understand.

Isaiah 53:1-7

> [1] *Who hath believed our report? and to whom is the arm of the Lord revealed?*
>
> [2] *For he shall grow up before him as a tender plant, and as a root out of a dry ground: he hath no form nor comeliness; and when we shall see him, there is no beauty that we should desire him.*
>
> [3] *He is despised and rejected of men; a man of sorrows, and acquainted*

with grief: and we hid as it were our faces from him; he was despised, and we esteemed him not.

4 *Surely he hath borne our griefs, and carried our sorrows: yet we did esteem him stricken, smitten of God, and afflicted.*

5 *But he was wounded for our transgressions, he was bruised for our iniquities: the chastisement of our peace was upon him; and with his stripes we are healed.*

6 *All we like sheep have gone astray; we have turned every one to his own way; and the Lord hath laid on him the iniquity of us all.*

7 *He was oppressed, and he was afflicted, yet he opened not his mouth: he is brought as a lamb to the slaughter, and as a sheep before her shearers is dumb, so he openeth not his mouth.*

This passage of prophecy was written about 700 years before Jesus was born. It gives a very precise description of the life and person of Jesus. He was tender and grew up in a general void of spiritual understanding. He was not a beautiful or handsome man. He was rejected by most and despised by the ruling religious authorities. He suffered rejection and oppression from the people to whom He preached and was considered by many to be afflicted by God. He was beaten and bruised for the sins of all men and suffered for our physical healing over sickness as described in verse 5. He did not speak in His own defense. Rather, His purpose was to offer His sinless blood as a sacrifice to pay the price of our sins.

Simeon was paying attention to the prophets with the heart of God on his mind and understood these revelations. He understood the secret mystery and knew what it was from the words of the prophets which he had studied. He looked forward to the coming of God's promise of salvation and knew it was Jesus, the Christ. He was satisfied because when Simeon saw Jesus, he knew that he had seen the prophecy of Isaiah and the promise of God made to Abraham in the covenant in Luke 2:25-32.

Luke 2:25-32

25 *And, behold, there was a man in Jerusalem, whose name was Simeon; and the same man was just and devout, waiting for the consolation of Israel: and the Holy Ghost was upon him.*

26 *And it was revealed unto him by the Holy Ghost, that he should not see death, before he had seen the Lord's Christ.*

27 *And he came by the Spirit into the temple: and when the parents brought*

in the child Jesus, to do for him after the custom of the law, [28] Then took he him up in his arms, and blessed God, and said, [29] Lord, now lettest thou thy servant depart in peace, according to thy word: [30] For mine eyes have seen thy salvation, [31] Which thou hast prepared before the face of all people; [32] A light to lighten the Gentiles, and the glory of thy people Israel.

Simeon waited for the promise of God and saw it in Jesus because he studied the Words of God with spiritual rather than intellectual understanding. The Holy Spirit (Ghost) was upon him as a result of his faith. Many others witnessed the same event and saw nothing. The *wisdom* of the world did not understand the significance of this world-altering event.

wisdom *(noun)*

1) knowledge that is gained by having many experiences in life.

2) the natural ability to understand things that most other people cannot understand.

3) knowledge of what is proper or reasonable : good sense or judgment.

Worldly wisdom is defined by things that come out of the human mind. It does not acknowledge the spiritual world of the true God. The event that Simeon was waiting for and witnessed completely escaped the awareness of the world's wisdom and the rulers of this world according to 1 Corinthians 2:4-10.

1 Corinthians 2:4-10 *(CEV)*

[4] When I talked with you or preached, I didn't try to prove anything by sounding wise. I simply let God's Spirit show his power. [5] That way you would have faith because of God's power and not because of human wisdom.

[6] We do use wisdom when speaking to people who are mature in their faith. But it isn't the wisdom of this world or of its rulers, who will soon disappear. [7] We speak of God's hidden and mysterious wisdom that God decided to use for our glory long before the world began.

[8] The rulers of this world didn't know anything about this wisdom. If they had known about it, they would not have nailed the glorious Lord to a cross.

[9] But it is just as the Scriptures say, "What God has planned for people who love him is more than eyes have seen or ears have heard. It has never even entered our minds!"

[10] God's Spirit has shown you everything. His Spirit finds out everything, even what is deep in the mind of God.

These verses state that the worldly wisdom of the *rulers* who were in control of the world system came to nothing, and they died in their sins. They were lacking in spiritual wisdom and had they been aware of the truth of the mystery of God, they never would have crucified Jesus. In the *King James Version (KJV),* deeper meaning is provided by using the phrase *princes of this world* rather than *rulers* to describe those who crucified Jesus.

1 Corinthians 2:8 *(KJV)*

> *Which none of the princes of this world knew: for had they known it, they would not have crucified the Lord of glory.*

The phrase *princes of this world* refers to both the demonic spirits that influence the world as well as the physical men who were in positions of authority in the government and Jewish religious society. They had no idea what God had designed to destroy the power of sin and death. As a result, they played right into God's plan. This is why God kept the mystery hidden from the spiritual as well as the physical world and why the mystery was kept obscure from worldly wisdom.

The wisdom of the world only acknowledges what man can understand with his intellect. However, wisdom that is from God, which was in place before the earthly or carnal world began, is on a much higher level than worldly wisdom. This Godly wisdom was hidden and mysterious to the world and was only revealed through the Holy Spirit to those who sought after God. The sacrifice of Jesus was the undoing of the worldly system, the defeat of sin, death, and Satan. These verses tell us that if the princes of this world had any insight into the Mystery of God, they never would have crucified Jesus because that act led to their defeat. For this reason, God kept His *mystery of Christ* hidden from the ages.

The Mystery Revealed

The *mystery of Christ*, the *mystery of the Gospel,* and the *mystery of God* are one and the same. Gospel means *good news.* It is the sacrifice of Jesus that takes away sins for those who would accept Him by faith. This is what the preaching of the Gospel reveals. The mystery is to be made known because it no longer needs to be a secret. It only had to be a secret to hide it from the destructive influences of Satan that began in the Garden of Eden.

The evil influences that led to Jesus being killed played right into God's plan. God has always loved man. His love has been continually expressed throughout time by His instruction, guidance, forgiveness, and grace. In His love, He had planned to provide man with an eternal sacrifice from the beginning, one that would atone for (forgive and cover) all of his sins. Jesus did not sin and, therefore, did not carry the sentence of death as a penalty for sin as we do. This is why His sinless blood can satisfy the penalty of sins for all of mankind. The blood of Jesus is the expression of God's wrath against sin. Just as light expels darkness, His love drives out sin through grace and forgiveness!

God's love for us, openly proclaimed, is the Gospel of the Good News. The mystery is no longer a mystery to those who embrace the message in faith. The verses in Ephesians 3:9, 6:19 and Colossians 2:2-3 speak to the preaching of the mystery and having the "fellowship of the mystery."

Ephesians 3:9

And to make all men see what is the fellowship of the mystery, which from the beginning of the world hath been hid in God, who created all things by Jesus Christ.

Ephesians 6:19

And for me, that utterance may be given unto me, that I may open my mouth boldly, to make known the mystery of the gospel.

Colossians 2:2-3

[2] That their hearts might be comforted, being knit together in love, and unto all riches of the full assurance of understanding, to the acknowledgement of the mystery of God, and of the Father, and of Christ; [3] In whom are hid all the treasures of wisdom and knowledge.

Colossians 4:3 and 1 Timothy 3:16 plainly state that the mystery is Christ. 1 Timothy also states that Jesus Christ is God in the flesh.

Colossians 4:3 *(GWT)*

At the same time also pray for us. Pray that God will give us an opportunity to speak the word so that we may tell the mystery about Christ. It is because of this mystery that I am a prisoner.

1 Timothy 3:16

And without controversy great is the mystery of godliness: God was manifest in the flesh, justified in the Spirit, seen of angels, preached unto the Gentiles, believed on in the world, received up into glory.

1 Timothy 3:16 is a clear reference to the fact that Jesus Christ is part of the Godhead, which is God the Father, God the Son (Jesus) and God the Holy Spirit. After His death and resurrection, Jesus was received into glory. There are many places in the Old Testament that provide insight into the benefits and realization of the mystery of God. Psalms 91:1-2 is a forward-looking description of the "secret place of the most High," within which there is refuge, protection, and trust.

Psalms 91:1-2

[1] He that dwelleth in the secret place of the most High shall abide under the shadow of the Almighty. [2] I will say of the Lord, He is my refuge and my fortress: my God; in him will I trust.

Psalms 107 says that God sent His Word to save, heal, and deliver.

Psalms 107:19-21 *(NKJV)*

[19] Then they cried out to the Lord in their trouble, And He saved them out of their distresses. [20] He sent His word and healed them, And delivered them from their destructions. [21] Oh, that men would give thanks to the Lord for His goodness, And for His wonderful works to the children of men!

Jesus is the Word of God in the flesh according to John 1:14. He is the personification of every word that God has spoken, the expression of His will, and the embodiment of His love and forgiveness freely given to man.

John 1:14

And the Word was made flesh, and dwelt among us, (and we beheld his glory, the glory as of the only begotten of the Father,) full of grace and truth.

The verses of Psalms 103:1-13 provide a detailed list of the incredible benefits that come from worshipping the One True God. Some of these benefits were available under the Old Covenant through annual sacrifice. Through Jesus and the New Covenant, each of these benefits is fully realized in the sacrifice that Jesus provided on our behalf. The benefits are forgiveness, healing, redemption, satisfaction, renewed youth, mercy, grace, separation from our sins and God's compassionate love.

Psalms 103:1-13

[1] Bless the Lord, O my soul: and all that is within me, bless his holy name.

[2] Bless the Lord, O my soul, and forget not all his benefits:

[3]Who forgiveth all thine iniquities; who healeth all thy diseases;

[4]Who redeemeth thy life from destruction; who crowneth thee with lovingkindness and tender mercies;

[5]Who satisfieth thy mouth with good things; so that ***thy youth is renewed like the eagle's.*** *[6]The Lord executeth righteousness and judgment for all that are oppressed. [7] He made known his ways unto Moses, his acts unto the children of Israel. [8]The Lord is merciful and gracious, slow to anger, and plenteous in mercy. [9] He will not always chide: neither will he keep his anger for ever.*

[10] He hath not dealt with us after our sins; nor rewarded us according to our iniquities. [11] For as the heaven is high above the earth, so great is his mercy toward them that fear him.

[12] As far as the east is from the west, so far hath he removed our transgressions from us.

[13] Like as a father pitieth his children, so the Lord pitieth them that fear him.

These blessings of God on the faithful believer are amazing. All of His goodness and provision for man is well described. One of particular interest is the description in verse 4, *thy youth is renewed like the eagle's.* The eagle has a particularly long life span of up to 30 years or more.[70] This verse probably refers to the yearly molting process during which all of its feathers are replaced.[71, 72] As a result the eagle essentially *renews* its youth. God's blessings similarly renew the believer.

God compares His love for those that fear or are morally reverent toward him to the love that a human father has toward his children. The word *pitieth* in verse 13 is translated from the Hebrew word רָחַם *racham* (raw-kham'). This word principally means *compassionate love.*

"pitieth" - *Strong's* OT:7355 רָחַם *racham* (raw-kham')

a primitive root; to fondle; by implication, to love, especially to compassionate: ***KJV*** *- have compassion (on, upon), love, (find, have, obtain, shew) mercy (-iful, on, upon), (have) pity, Ruhamah,* X *surely.*

This passage of Psalms also speaks about judgment being executed for all who are oppressed, with the clear implication from verse 1 that it is speaking of those who both believe and trust in God. This judgment is not punishment, but determination *(see p. 275, 282)*. His mercy and grace are provided for those who are oppressed and trust in Him.

King David wrote Psalm 103 and lived from about 1040-970 BC. This was a time in which prevailing thought held the earth to be flat. This thought did not begin to change for another 700 years until Eratosthenes (c 276 to 195 BC) calculated a round earth from angles that shadows cast.[73] At the time of David, it would not have been known that north and south would meet on a round earth and that east and west would never meet. Is it possible that God revealed something quite profound to David about the earth that science would not discover for 700 years?

The Hebrew words that are translated *east* and *west* mean the regions of the rising and setting sun from which the words are translated east and west. In Psalms 103:10, God does not reward the believer's sin according to what it deserves but separates sin from them as far as east is from west. Think about this for a moment. If you travel around the world in a north-south direction, north eventually becomes south, and south eventually becomes north. However, this is not the case with east and west. East is always going east, and west is always going west. THEY NEVER MEET!!! East from west is just how far God wants your sins to be removed from you, and He has accomplished that for you through Jesus, the Christ!

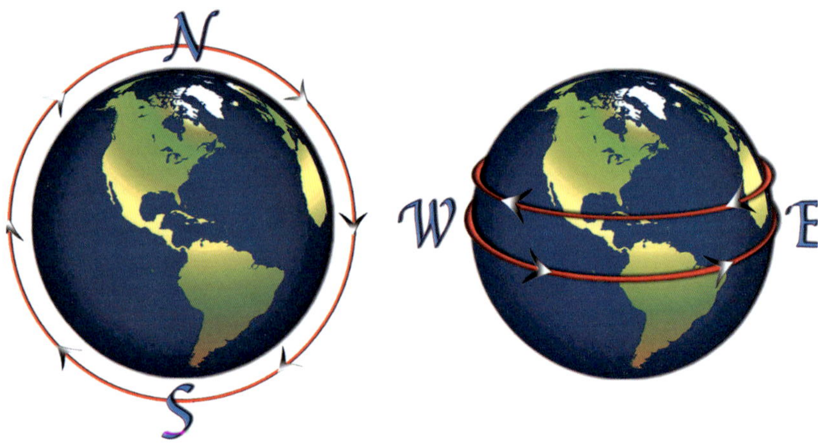

If you keep traveling North, you will eventually switch directions and begin to travel South. However, if you travel East, you will never find West. If you travel West, you will never find East. East from West is how far God separates us from our sins through Jesus.

Jesus and Judgment

We have seen that there is a lot of discussion about judgment in the Old Testament, but how is Jesus involved with judgment? He had a lot to say about it in the New Testament and offered a perspective on judgment that is different from the way things appeared in the Old Testament. The position that Jesus holds relative to judgment and why is explained in John 5:21-23. God, the Father, gave the responsibility of judgment to His Son, Jesus, so that all men would honor Jesus as they honor the Father. It is up to Jesus to give life to whomever He chooses. This is a very big deal, so it is very important to understand how Jesus judges and the results of His judgments.

John 5:21-23 *(NKJV)*

> [21] *For as the Father raises the dead and gives life to them, even so the Son gives life to whom He will.* [22] *For the Father judges no one, but has committed all judgment to the Son,* [23] *that all should honor the Son just as they honor the Father. He who does not honor the Son does not honor the Father who sent Him.*

As we enter into this discussion of Jesus and judgment, it is important to note the covenant under which Jesus lived his life. The New Testament or New Covenant did not begin until Jesus was crucified, died, and resurrected. The change in God's New Covenant did not fully take place until Jesus had ascended into heaven. Jesus walked the earth living under the Old Covenant. The rules of the covenant and the Law of Moses governed His actions. He lived under the Law, and His life is the bridge between the Old Covenant *law* and New Covenant *grace*. This awareness is crucial to our understanding of how Jesus accomplished what He did on our behalf.

Old vs. New

Let's look at some comparisons of how Jesus talked about judgment versus what we observe in the Old Testament. One example is the account of Korah, the son of Kohath, found in Numbers 16:1-50 *(see Appendix Chapter 25)*. It is a startling event describing a rebellion against Moses and God's instructions. It occurred after the children of Israel came out of Egypt and were wandering in the desert. The following is a synopsis of the event.

Korah and his family were members of the tribe of the Levites. It was their duty as Levites to exercise authority over the temple, and they had the responsibility of service to the Lord in worship. However, God had given Moses authority over the entire congregation. God put him in charge when He delivered the Law and gave instructions to him. Korah and his group challenged Moses' authority, stating that he should not be the boss, so to speak. They refused to acknowledge that God put Moses in charge because they wanted to preserve their power, influence, and authority. They rebelled against Moses and God.

This challenge to God's direction enraged Moses. He was not a stranger to rebellion against God as he had faced this similar attitude with Pharaoh in Egypt as described in Exodus 7-12. Moses made a judgment regarding the rebellion of Korah and his company. He did not choose to overlook this sin against God. The sin was going to consume the entire congregation, so Moses called them out on it. He was looking out for the well-being of His people and interceded for them. God told Moses that he should separate himself and the congregation from Korah and his clan, so they would not be destroyed along with Korah's sin as detailed in Numbers 16:21-26.

Numbers 16:21-26

[21] *Separate yourselves from among this congregation, that I may consume them in a moment.*

[22] *And they fell upon their faces, and said, O God, the God of the spirits of all flesh, shall one man sin, and wilt thou be wroth with all the congregation?*

[23] *And the Lord spake unto Moses, saying,*

[24] *Speak unto the congregation, saying, Get you up from about the tabernacle of Korah, Dathan, and Abiram.*

[25] *And Moses rose up and went unto Dathan and Abiram; and the elders of Israel followed him.*

[26] *And he spake unto the congregation, saying, Depart, I pray you, from the tents of these wicked men, and touch nothing of theirs, lest ye be consumed in all their sins.*

Moses decreed a spectacular sentence, saying that the earth would swallow up Korah, his friends, their families and their possessions, to prove God's choice of Moses as the leader. The execution of the sentence was swift and complete. They were all destroyed. Moses made the decree in much the same way that Peter made the decree over Ananias and Sapphira, and with the same result, death. Moses had the authority, and he decreed a harsh sentence with his guilty verdict. God did not make the judgment, decree the verdict, or declare the sentence, but He did declare that they would be *consumed in all their sins*. It was Moses who judged the situation, decreed the verdict and carried out the sentence. Judgment was made to discern the situation; the verdict was decreed, and the sentence was carried out. Sin against the Law of God was subject to the death penalty. This penalty was carried out because Moses enforced it under his authority. This account provides a stark contrast to Jesus, who brought in a new way of dealing with sin through His judgment.

Separated from Sin

Jesus provided a way for the individual to be separated from his sins through forgiveness and grace and not only survive, but prosper. Matthew 12:15-21 is drawn from a prophecy spoken in Isaiah 42:1-6 hundreds of years before.

Isaiah 42:1-6 *(TLB)*

[1] *"See my servant, whom I uphold; my Chosen One in whom I delight. I have*
put my Spirit upon him; he will reveal justice to the nations of the world.
[2] *He will be gentle-he will not shout nor quarrel in the streets.* [3] *He will*
not break the bruised reed, nor quench the dimly burning flame. He will
encourage the fainthearted, those tempted to despair. He will see full justice
given to all who have been wronged. [4] *He won't be satisfied until truth and*
righteousness prevail throughout the earth, nor until even distant lands
beyond the seas have put their trust in him."

[5] *The Lord God who created the heavens and stretched them out, who cre-*
ated the earth and everything in it, who gives life and breath and spirit
to everyone in all the world, he is the one who says [to his Servant, the Mes-
siah], [6] *"I the Lord have called you to demonstrate my righteousness. I will*
guard and support you, for I have given you to my people as the personal
confirmation of my covenant with them.You shall also be a light to guide
the nations unto me.

Matthew 12:15-21 *(NKJV)*

[15] *But when Jesus knew it, He withdrew from there. And great multitudes*
followed Him, and He healed them all. [16] *Yet He warned them not to make*

Him known, [17] *that it might be fulfilled which was spoken by Isaiah the prophet, saying:*

[18] *"Behold! My Servant whom I have chosen, My Beloved in whom My soul is well pleased! I will put My Spirit upon Him, And He will declare justice to the Gentiles.*

[19] *He will not quarrel nor cry out, Nor will anyone hear His voice in the streets.* [20] *A bruised reed He will not break, And smoking flax He will not quench, Till He sends forth justice to victory;* [21] *And in His name Gentiles will trust."*

As a man, Jesus was God's chosen servant, with whom He was well pleased. He had the Holy Spirit of God upon Him as He walked the earth as a human. He was to show judgment to the Gentiles, which sounds ominous, in light of the way judgment is portrayed in the Old Testament. However, through the prophet Isaiah, God said that Jesus would not fight, nor yell, nor raise His voice in the streets. Jesus was not going to be obvious. He would need to be sought out, much like at the time of His birth. He would be gentle, but His judgment would be victorious, and the Gentiles would trust *in His name*. Jesus' way of dealing with sin was different, but not everyone understood it. He explains this in Mark 4:11-12.

Mark 4:11-12
[11] *And he said unto them, "Unto you it is given to know the mystery of the kingdom of God: but unto them that are without, all these things are done in parables:* [12] *That seeing they may see, and not perceive; and hearing they may hear, and not understand; lest at any time they should be converted, and their sins should be forgiven them."*

The revelation in Mark 4:11-12 begins to unlock the secret mystery of God. Those who were spiritually blind who had unteachable hearts would see what Jesus was doing, but they would not understand it. They would hear what Jesus said, but not comprehend or grasp the meaning because he spoke in parables.

Setting Your Standard

Only individuals who would see and hear with the heart of God could perceive the mystery and understand Jesus' message. They believed, were converted and their sins were forgiven. However, the hard of heart, those who rejected the true nature of God that was revealed in Jesus, were left in their sins. In Matthew 7:1-2, they are referred to as those who *would receive the measure of their own judgment and condemnation*.

Matthew 7:1-2 *(NKJV)*

> [1] *Judge not, that you be not judged.* [2] *For with what judgment you judge, you will be judged; and with the measure you use, it will be measured back to you.*

Jesus dealt with sin and judgment differently than what we see in the Law. His way was to love and forgive. He demonstrated this in John 8:3-11 when the Jewish rulers brought a woman to Him who was caught in adultery. They told Jesus that the Law demanded that she be stoned to death. Jesus spoke to the crowd in John 8:7 and told them, "He that is without sin among you let him first cast a stone at her." None of them were without sin, and they all left the scene. Jesus was left alone with her and with no accusers. Jesus told her that He did not condemn her and that she should go and sin no more. He conquered the sin with forgiveness.

John 8:3-11

> [3] *And the scribes and Pharisees brought unto him a woman taken in adultery; and when they had set her in the midst,* [4] *They say unto him, Master, this woman was taken in adultery, in the very act.* [5] *Now Moses in the law commanded us, that such should be stoned: but what sayest thou?*
>
> [6] *This they said, tempting him, that they might have to accuse him. But Jesus stooped down, and with his finger wrote on the ground, as though he heard them not.*
>
> [7] *So when they continued asking him, he lifted up himself, and said unto them, "He that is without sin among you, let him first cast a stone at her."*
>
> [8] *And again he stooped down, and wrote on the ground.* [9] *And they which heard it, being convicted by their own conscience, went out one by one, beginning at the eldest, even unto the last: and Jesus was left alone, and the woman standing in the midst.*
>
> [10] *When Jesus had lifted up himself, and saw none but the woman, he said unto her, "Woman, where are those thine accusers? hath no man condemned thee?"* [11] *She said, No man, Lord. And Jesus said unto her, "Neither do I condemn thee: go, and sin no more."*

Jesus conveyed the point about "casting the first stone" when He gave us clear instruction about our actions in Luke 6:35-38.

Luke 6:35-38

[35] But love ye your enemies, and do good, and lend, hoping for nothing again; and your reward shall be great, and ye shall be the children of the Highest: for he is kind unto the unthankful and to the evil. [36] Be ye therefore merciful, as your Father also is merciful. [37] Judge not, and ye shall not be judged: condemn not, and ye shall not be condemned: forgive, and ye shall be forgiven: [38] Give, and it shall be given unto you; good measure, pressed down, and shaken together, and running over, shall men give into your bosom. For with the same measure that ye mete withal it shall be measured to you again.

He instructed us to love our enemies, to give and expect nothing in return, to be merciful as God is and to not judge or condemn but to forgive. He said that we would receive according to the way we acted when applying our measure (assessment or judgment) to a situation. He said that we would receive according to what we give. This principal is the same that He applied when He challenged the rulers to "cast the first stone" (John 8:7).

Jesus provided another example of His love and forgiveness in a situation involving a man who was sick with a paralytic, convulsive disease and could not walk. When presented with the man, Jesus declared that the man should be happy because He forgave his sins. The rulers were irate at this action, but Jesus proved His point by telling the man to stand up, take his stretcher and go home, which he did. Jesus provided a startling, physical sign by healing the man to prove that He also had the power and the will to forgive sins in Matthew 9:2-6.

Matthew 9:2-6 *(NKJV)*

[2] Then behold, they brought to Him a paralytic lying on a bed. When Jesus saw their faith, He said to the paralytic, "Son, be of good cheer; your sins are forgiven you." [3] And at once some of the scribes said within themselves, "This Man blasphemes!" [4] But Jesus, knowing their thoughts, said, "Why do you think evil in your hearts? [5] For which is easier, to say, 'Your sins are forgiven you,' or to say, 'Arise and walk'? [6] But that you may know that the Son of Man has power on earth to forgive sins"— then He said to the paralytic, "Arise, take up your bed, and go to your house."

Jesus encountered a woman known to be a sinner as He came to visit a *Pharisee* or Jewish ruler at his home in Luke 7:36-50. The ruler thought within himself that Jesus should have known that the woman was a sinner and shunned her because of her sins. Jesus proceeded to tell the ruler a parable about forgiveness. Then, He turned His attention to the woman.

Luke 7:36-50 *(MSG)*

37 Just then a woman of the village, the town harlot, having learned that Jesus was a guest in the home of the Pharisee, came with a bottle of very expensive perfume 38 and stood at his feet, weeping, raining tears on his feet. Letting down her hair, she dried his feet, kissed them, and anointed them with the perfume. 39 When the Pharisee who had invited him saw this, he said to himself, "If this man was the prophet I thought he was, he would have known what kind of woman this is who is falling all over him."

40 Jesus said to him, "Simon, I have something to tell you." "Oh? Tell me."

41 "Two men were in debt to a banker. One owed five hundred silver pieces, the other fifty. 42 Neither of them could pay up, and so the banker canceled both debts. Which of the two would be more grateful?"

43 Simon answered, "I suppose the one who was forgiven the most." "That's right," said Jesus. 44 Then turning to the woman, but speaking to Simon, he said, "Do you see this woman? I came to your home; you provided no water for my feet, but she rained tears on my feet and dried them with her hair.

45 You gave me no greeting, but from the time I arrived she hasn't quit kissing my feet. 46 You provided nothing for freshening up, but she has soothed my feet with perfume. 47 Impressive, isn't it? She was forgiven many, many sins, and so she is very, very grateful. If the forgiveness is minimal, the gratitude is minimal."

48 Then he spoke to her: "I forgive your sins."

49 That set the dinner guests talking behind his back: "Who does he think he is, forgiving sins!" 50 He ignored them and said to the woman, "Your faith has saved you. Go in peace."

The ruler considered a sinner to be below him in stature, but Jesus pointed out the actions of the woman. She had washed His feet with her tears, wiped them with her hair and then kissed His feet. Jesus explained that He did not condemn or shun her, but rather He forgave her many sins and that, in turn, her love would be great. He told her that her faith (in Him) had saved her.

It is easy to fall prey to the very dangerous attitude that this account highlights. It is an attitude of superiority and self-justification. One sin is not more severe than another in the eyes of God, and no one except Jesus was sinless. Everyone either pays for his or her own sins or receives the sacrifice of Jesus to pay the penalty. There is no other way.

Another challenge that this ruler and others face is one of complacency. Forgiveness may be taken for granted by a person who is basically good and infrequently succumbs to sin. However, forgiveness for the person who has lived his or her life in the bowels of sin creates almost overwhelming gratitude and joy. This is what the woman in this account was expressing by her actions toward Jesus. This contrast is what Jesus was pointing out when He said in *"She was forgiven many, many sins, and so she is very, very grateful. If the forgiveness is minimal, the gratitude is minimal."* (Luke 7:47). However, those without the spiritual ears to hear and understand muttered against Jesus behind his back.

Every situation that Jesus encountered involving the sins of people who sought the heart of God ended with Him forgiving, restoring, and physically healing the individual if needed. At no time did Jesus condemn anyone. He did point out that the hypocritical rulers would die in their own sins because of their pride and rejection of the grace of God. However, He did not condemn them. He only told them where their path was leading. Jesus did warn about an *unforgivable sin*, however. That sin is blasphemy against the Holy Spirit. Matthew 12:31-32 and Mark 3:28-30 provide the narrative about this sin.

Matthew 12:31-32

> 31 *Wherefore I say unto you, All manner of sin and blasphemy shall be forgiven unto men: but the blasphemy against the Holy Ghost shall not be forgiven unto men.* 32 *And whosoever speaketh a word against the Son of man, it shall be forgiven him: but whosoever speaketh against the Holy Ghost, it shall not be forgiven him, neither in this world, neither in the world to come.*

Mark 3:28-30 *(MSG)*

> 28 *"Listen to this carefully. I'm warning you. There's nothing done or said that can't be forgiven.* 29 *But if you persist in your slanders against God's Holy Spirit, you are repudiating the very One who forgives, sawing off the branch on which you're sitting, severing by your own perversity all connection with the One who forgives."* 30 *He gave this warning because they were accusing him of being in league with Evil.*

Except for one specific sin, every sinful thing that man does can be forgiven. Mark 3:30 reveals what the sin is. It states that it was because they said that Jesus, who was filled with the Holy Spirit, had an unclean spirit. They rejected Jesus and equated the Holy Spirit of God with the spirit of Satan. This rejection is what is unforgivable. It comes from the hardness of their hearts, and their unwillingness to repent.

Jesus spoke concerning the judgment of the *world* in John 12:30-32. However, what He said might not refer to what initially comes to mind. When Jesus speaks here of the *world*, He is speaking not of the physical world but of the spiritual world that operates in the earthly realm. This system is controlled by Satan because he stole the authority away from Adam in the garden.

John 12:30-32 *(NKJV)*

> [30] *Jesus answered and said, "This voice did not come because of Me, but for your sake.* [31] *Now is the judgment of this world; now the ruler of this world will be cast out.* [32] *And I, if I am lifted up from the earth, will draw all peoples to Myself."*

Jesus said that the judgment or the determinate evaluation of the world (system) was happening at that point in time because the *"ruler of this world will be cast out"* (John 12:31). The ruler is Satan, and Jesus is the reason that the ruler was displaced. Satan used his authority and deception against the inhabitants of the world, but he was about to be fully revealed and defeated by Jesus through a spiritual and legal confrontation. Jesus would offer His Life and Blood to atone (pay for) the sins of the world, specifically for all those who would accept His sacrifice for them by faith. Jesus being "lifted up" (John 12:32) referred to His death on the cross as well as His resurrection and ascension into heaven. Through these acts, Jesus draws all people to Himself and His work will be preached among all nations according to Luke 24:46-47.

Luke 24:46-47

> [46] *And said unto them, "Thus it is written, and thus it behoved Christ to suffer, and to rise from the dead the third day:* [47] *And that repentance and remission of sins should be preached in his name among all nations, beginning at Jerusalem."*

True Colors

God showed His true character and nature in John 3:16 when Jesus explained His role. Jesus said that His life was being offered to *save*, not to condemn. God's words offer us the same choice of choosing life or death that He presented to man in the Old Testament. We still have free will and can choose Jesus and have everlasting life or reject Jesus and suffer the condemnation for our sins that was established in the beginning.

John 3:16-18 *(NKJV)*

[16] For God so loved the world that He gave His only begotten Son, that whoever believes in Him should not perish but have everlasting life. [17] For God did not send His Son into the world to condemn the world, but that the world through Him might be saved.

[18] He who believes in Him is not condemned; but he who does not believe is condemned already, because he has not believed in the name of the only begotten Son of God.

Acceptance of God's gift through Jesus requires an expression of faith through words spoken by the individual. Words are extremely important and powerful. Jesus points out just how important our words are in Matthew 12:36-37 when He says that we are either justified or condemned by our words. They are the difference between life and death. Faith-filled words, based on God's Word, bring life, righteousness, and salvation as described in Romans 10:8-11.

Matthew 12:35-37 *(NKJV)*

[35] A good man out of the good treasure of his heart brings forth good things, and an evil man out of the evil treasure brings forth evil things.
[36] But I say to you that for every idle word men may speak, they will give account of it in the day of judgment. [37] For by your words you will be justified, and by your words you will be condemned.

Romans 10:8-10 *(NKJV)*

[8] But what does it say? "The word is near you, in your mouth and in your heart" (that is, the word of faith which we preach): [9] that if you confess with your mouth the Lord Jesus and believe in your heart that God has raised Him from the dead, you will be saved. [10] For with the heart one believes unto righteousness, and with the mouth confession is made unto salvation.

The preaching of God's good news is the proclamation of what Jesus did for us. Your spoken faith is your agreement with and your belief in the fact that God sent Jesus and raised Him from the dead. Speaking out that faith with our words justifies us and speaking by faith brings salvation. In this case, *confession* does not mean exposing and asking forgiveness for your sins. It means to proclaim your heartfelt faith with your mouth.

Jesus commemorated His sacrifice in advance with His disciples at the "last supper." Knowing what was about to take place, He plainly stated the purpose of His impending sacrifice. He gave them a physical example of His body and His blood by comparing it to the bread they ate and the wine they drank at the meal. He told them that eating His body and drinking of His blood would cover all of their sins (Matthew 26:27-28). Jesus was telling them to spiritually consume His entire being making Him one with them. This observance is known as communion and was to be repeated so that they and future generations would remember and understand the sacrifice that He made for every individual on the earth.

Matthew 26:26-28 *(NKJV)*

> [26] *And as they were eating, Jesus took bread, blessed and broke it, and gave it to the disciples and said, "Take, eat; this is My body."* [27] *Then He took the cup, and gave thanks, and gave it to them, saying, "Drink from it, all of you.*
> [28] *For this is My blood of the new covenant, which is shed for many for the remission of sins."*

The apostle Paul, a devout and learned Jew, was a persecutor of the new Christian believers following the resurrection of Jesus. He actively sought them out to kill and destroy them, but God had other plans for him. He wanted Paul to be His voice to the Gentiles. Jesus appeared to him and gave him a challenge in Acts 26:14-18, much like God did with Abram in the Old Testament. His challenge was to accept Jesus as God's salvation, abandon his persecution of the Christians and proclaim the goodness of God through Jesus to the entire world. His mission was to open their eyes and take them from darkness into the light of truth. By doing so, they would be removed from the power of Satan and turn to God. He was to accomplish this by preaching the forgiveness of sins through Jesus and teaching them about the inheritance that God had provided for them by faith.

Acts 26:14-18 *(GNT)*

> [14] *All of us fell to the ground, and I heard a voice say to me in Hebrew, "Saul, Saul! Why are you persecuting me? You are hurting yourself by hitting back, like an ox kicking against its owner's stick."*
>
> [15] *"Who are you, Lord?" I asked. And the Lord answered, "I am Jesus, whom you persecute.*
>
> [16] *But get up and stand on your feet. I have appeared to you to appoint you as my servant. You are to tell others what you have seen of me today and what I will show you in the future.*
>
> [17] *I will rescue you from the people of Israel and from the Gentiles to whom I will send you.*
>
> [18] *You are to open their eyes and turn them from the darkness to the light and from the power of Satan to God, so that through their faith in me they will have their sins forgiven and receive their place among God's chosen people."*

For those who will believe, a verdict of innocence, grace, and forgiveness is the result of the judgment that Jesus has made regarding their sins. His sentence is not condemnation. In the Old Testament, sin was able to bring condemnation on all, but now Jesus brings mercy, restoration, and healing. The character and nature of God is to open His arms and provide the gift of forgiveness. He wants to restore, heal, and provide everlasting life to repair the damage that sin has done in the world. He continues to do this through Jesus because of His love for man.

Jesus In the Wilderness

The tactics that Satan uses have not changed even though God removed us from his power through faith in Jesus. He attacks us with deception at our lowest point to tempt us to turn away from the truth of God. His powerful deceptions come in the form of spiritual attacks that are based on partial truth and mixed with blatant lies. He attacked Jesus with temptations when He was at a point of severe physical weakness when He went out into the wilderness and fasted for 40 days. We see accounts of this interaction in Matthew 4:1-11, Mark 1:11-13 and Luke 4:1-13. Mark provides little detail, but Matthew and Luke are quite descriptive. Matthew and Luke are virtually the same except for the order of the events, so we will look at the account in Luke, which is slightly more detailed.

The First Temptation

Luke 4:1-4

[1] And Jesus being full of the Holy Ghost returned from Jordan, and was led by the Spirit into the wilderness, [2] Being forty days tempted of the devil. And in those days he did eat nothing: and when they were ended, he afterward hungered. [3] And the devil said unto him, If thou be the Son of God, command this stone that it be made bread.

[4] And Jesus answered him, saying, "It is written, That man shall not live by bread alone, but by every word of God."

The first confrontation came from the tempter, the devil (Satan) when Jesus had fasted 40 days and was very hungry. The devil taunted Him to turn stones into bread. Although this act would have been a completely self-centered miracle, it was not the real temptation. The temptation came out of the challenge that the devil posed to Jesus. The devil presented his challenge as an "If. . ., then. . ." statement in Luke 4:3. He said, "If thou be the Son of God, then..." This challenge is one of the devil's favorite ploys. He posed a question and offered a selection of bad decisions, which did not require a reply or a choice. King David experienced this ploy through the words of Gad, one of his advisors *(see p. 221)*. We encounter this ploy almost daily in our lives. Just because someone tells you to make a choice, it doesn't mean you have to!

Jesus responded to this first challenge from the devil without making a choice by quoting God's word. The devil did not have the authority to pose his demanding choice. He did not have authority over Jesus because He was sinless. Jesus dispatched the challenge. He said, *"It is written, That man shall not live by bread alone, but by every word of God"* which a clear reference to Deuteronomy 8:3.

Deuteronomy 8:3

And he humbled thee, and suffered thee to hunger, and fed thee with manna, which thou knewest not, neither did thy fathers know; that he might make thee know that ***man doth not live by bread only, but by every word that proceedeth out of the mouth of the Lord doth man live.***

This challenge to Jesus to prove Himself through a demonstration was also tempting God. The clear implication was that if Jesus did not perform the miracle, the devil would say that Jesus was, therefore, not the Son of God. When the devil made his challenge, he was plainly questioning the position and authority of Jesus which Jesus dealt with later.

The Second Temptation

Adam gave up his authority in the earth in much the same way that Esau gave up his birthright to Jacob in Genesis 25:29-34. Esau made the choice to relinquish his firstborn rights in exchange for food because he was hungry. This play on the desires of the flesh is the same tactic that Satan used on Jesus in the wilderness, but it failed because Jesus replied with the Word of God. Esau considered that satisfying his hunger for a moment was more important than the lifetime gift of being the firstborn with all of its rights and privileges.

Genesis 25:29-34

> 29 *One day Esau came back from hunting. He was tired and weak from hunger. Jacob was boiling a pot of beans.* 30 *So Esau said to Jacob, "I am weak with hunger. Let me have some of that red soup." (That is why people call him "Red.")* 31 *But Jacob said, "You must sell me your rights as the firstborn son."* 32 *Esau said, "I am almost dead with hunger, so what good are these rights to me now?"*
>
> 33 *But Jacob said, "First, promise me that you will give them to me." So Esau made an oath to him and sold his rights as the firstborn son to Jacob.*
>
> 34 *Then Jacob gave Esau bread and lentil soup. Esau ate the food, had something to drink, and then left. So Esau showed that he did not care about his rights as the firstborn son.*

What probably started as innocent banter between competitive brothers ended up very badly for Esau. Certainly, he could have overpowered Jacob and taken the food. After all, he was the firstborn and a hunter. He did not have to take the choice that Jacob offered to him. However, he casually fell to the desires of his flesh without giving much thought to the consequences.

Adam did the same thing when he disobeyed God. However, the stakes were much higher. He gave up his birthright to the authority of the earth and relinquished it to Satan because he rejected God's instruction. This action is very important to understand because it demonstrates the authority that the devil does have as a result of his deception of Adam and Eve in the Garden.

The second temptation involved the ownership of authority in the earth as described in Luke 4:5-8. This situation could not have been a temptation to Jesus if the devil was not able to deliver on his promise. He did have the authority. Jesus did not question or challenge that fact.

Luke 4:5-8

[5] And the devil, taking him up into an high mountain, shewed unto him all the kingdoms of the world in a moment of time. [6] And the devil said unto him, All this power will I give thee, and the glory of them: for that is delivered unto me; and to whomsoever I will I give it. [7] If thou therefore wilt worship me, all shall be thine.

[8] And Jesus answered and said unto him, "Get thee behind me, Satan: for it is written, Thou shalt worship the Lord thy God, and him only shalt thou serve."

The devil demanded that Jesus worship him in exchange for power over the earth through its kingdoms. He certainly knew who Jesus was and that He represented God on the earth. From his perspective, Satan must have thought that Jesus wanted the same kind of influence over the earth that he had. However, in this proposition, Satan was attempting to redefine who would worship whom.

He was using the authority that he had stolen from Adam and Eve as a bargaining chip to get Jesus to serve him! Jesus knew the implications and the deceptive trick that the devil was trying to pull. It was just like Jacob stealing the birthright from his brother Esau and the role reversal that ensued. Once again, Jesus replied with God's word on the subject, taken from Deuteronomy 6:13-14. He said, *"Thou shalt worship the Lord thy God, and him only shalt thou serve"*(Luke 4:5-8).

Deuteronomy 6:13-14 *(ERV)*

[13] Respect the Lord your God and serve only him. You must use only his name to make promises. [14] You must not follow other gods. You must not follow the gods of the people who live around you.

The Third Temptation

Luke 4:9-13

[9] And he brought him to Jerusalem, and set him on a pinnacle of the temple, and said unto him, If thou be the Son of God, cast thyself down from hence: [10] For it is written, He shall give his angels charge over thee, to keep thee: [11] And in their hands they shall bear thee up, lest at any time thou dash thy foot against a stone.

[12] And Jesus answering said unto him, "It is said, Thou shalt not tempt the Lord thy God." [13] And when the devil had ended all the temptation, he departed from him for a season.

Once again, the devil tried to get Jesus to do something that was unnecessary to prove something that did not need to be proved. Do you remember when you were *dared* to do something when you were a child? It was an attack on your self-worth or your ego. You may have been bullied in this way. There was no real reason to respond to the challenge, but you may have felt that you had no choice because of the taunting.

Jesus knew better because He knew the Word of God. He knew who He was. This challenge to His position and authority fell to defeat when Jesus again responded with God's Word. Jesus quoted Deuteronomy 6:16 when He said, *"Thou shalt not tempt the Lord thy God."*

Deuteronomy 6:16a

Ye shall not tempt the Lord your God....

Overcoming Through The Word

The devil retreated from his assault on Jesus with this blow from the Word of God. We see more insight in 2 Timothy 2:26 about the truth and mechanics of what Jesus accomplished in facing down the devil. He did not argue with the deception, ponder the possibilities or engage with the lie. He knew that the Word of God was (and is today) the ultimate authority on everything in this earth realm. He was not taken in by the devil because He knew the truth of His Word.

2 Timothy 2:23-26 *(NKJV)*

[23] But avoid foolish and ignorant disputes, knowing that they generate strife. [24] And a servant of the Lord must not quarrel but be gentle to all, able to teach, patient, [25] in humility correcting those who are in opposi-

tion, if God perhaps will grant them repentance, so that they may know the truth, [26] *and that they may come to their senses and escape the snare of the devil, having been taken captive by him to do his will.*

Jesus left the temptations behind and proceeded to go out to the people with His message of hope, deliverance, and salvation. The apostle Peter, who walked with Jesus, spoke of Him in Acts 10:38.

Acts 10:38

God anointed Jesus of Nazareth with the Holy Ghost and with power: who went about doing good, and healing all that were oppressed of the devil; for God was with him.

He said that Jesus was anointed with the Holy Spirit and power. In addition to doing good, Jesus healed all who were oppressed of the devil. It is important to note that Peter associated sickness and disease with oppression of the devil. However, many people believe that God puts sickness upon them or others to teach them something or punish some sinful act. If God were using sickness as a way to instruct or punish, Jesus would not have gone about healing them. He would have been working against God when He overcame all of the oppression of sickness and disease. However, Jesus healed all of the sick that came to him in faith because sickness and disease are one of the manifestations of the oppression of the devil. Sickness and disease are not brought about by God!

Satan left Jesus alone for a while, but he was not yet done with his temptations. He would try again to make Him fall. His conceit and self-deception made him think that he was still going to conquer Jesus and even God Himself! He did not know the mystery of the Gospel described in 1 Corinthians 2:7-8 that had been hidden from him and the rest of the world that did not seek after God. He incited many others as false witnesses against Jesus. These false accusations ultimately led to His crucifixion. Had he known what was going on, he would not have pursued the path that he did. The devil thought he had finally won the battle when Jesus died, but he ultimately lost the war!

1 Corinthians 2:7-8 *(NKJV)*

[7] *But we speak the wisdom of God in a mystery, the hidden wisdom which God ordained before the ages for our glory,* [8] *which none of the rulers of this age knew; for had they known, they would not have crucified the Lord of glory.*

The struggle for the authority that Satan stole from Adam continues in the earth realm. The *Earth Realm Authority* belongs to believers in Jesus since He took the authority back from the devil by His victory over sin. However, on the earth today, there are those who do not believe and do not accept, understand, or exercise the authority that Jesus has provided them through His victory over Satan. Consequently, they are still under the authority and rule of Satan.

This is why there is so much evil in the world today. Satan still spiritually controls the earth realm and influences humans to do His will. The generational curse started with Adam and continued through to Jacob and Esau. Esau despised and rejected his birthright, as non-believers reject the gift of Jesus. He did not value the gift that he was given. He was more interested in feeding his flesh rather than his spirit, which is also the prevalent attitude in much of the world today. Jesus broke the generational curse by invoking God's Word, denying the authority of Satan and restoring that authority to the believer. Will you choose to walk in that authority in your life?

The Ways Of God

God knew that man was incapable of living a righteous life after the fall of Adam. He immediately put His plan in motion to create a legal framework upon which to build His case for the redemption of man. This plan was later expressed through the Law. God was not willing to let man, His precious creation, destroy himself through sin like Satan did. God began to reach out to men in an effort to find someone who would listen and be obedient in the midst of increasing sin and rejection of Him. He found Noah, who believed and acted upon His instructions at a time when the intensity of sin grew to such great proportions that the destruction of the world was imminent. Noah was obedient, and God expressed His love by saving Noah and subsequently preserving Mankind from the destruction that sin legally demanded.

The corrupted nature of man was temporarily stayed after the Flood. However, it began to grow again with disregard and active rebellion against God. God found Abram during this time when there was extensive worship of idols and other gods. He spoke to Abram and made promises to him in the Covenant. He changed his name to Abraham and told him that he would be the father of many nations and have a son through his covenant wife, Sarah. Then, God asked something unthinkable of Abraham. He asked him to sacrifice this very son, Isaac, which He had promised to Abraham, this precious son through whom God had promised fruitfulness, possession of land and a lineage of kings.

Abraham, a man who was also corrupted through the sin of Adam, responded to God in faith and prepared to sacrifice his son of promise. Abraham was intent on being obedient to God and was ready to plunge his knife into Isaac when God stopped him. According to 1 Peter 5:8, by this act Abraham's unwavering faith in God was proven to all of creation, including Satan, who roams the earth searching for men that he can devour.

1 Peter 5:8

Be sober, be vigilant; because your adversary the devil, as a roaring lion, walketh about, seeking whom he may devour:

Abraham had faith and was ready and willing to sacrifice his son for God. Because of his faith, God was now legally able to reciprocate Abraham's sacrificial intentions by bringing His own Son, Jesus, as the Christ, to become a permanent sacrifice for all of the sins of mankind. This is the foundation of the Mystery of the Gospel and the expression of the Wrath of God toward sin. Because one man was willing to sacrifice his only son for God, He was able to sacrifice His only Son for all men (and women).

This love that God has expressed to mankind did not require the death of Abraham's son. It only required Abraham's faith in God. We can also express our faith in God by accepting the sacrifice that God made for us through Jesus in the same way that Abraham expressed his faith in God when he was prepared to sacrifice Isaac. God took a part of himself, turned Himself into Flesh (Jesus) that walked among men. Jesus preached deliverance, offered forgiveness of sins, supplied spiritual and physical healing and offered eternal life with Him. It is this compassionate love of a father described in Psalms 103:13 that God expresses for us by the sacrifice of Himself (through Jesus) on our behalf.

Psalms 103:13 *(NIV)*

As a father has compassion on his children, so the Lord has compassion on those who fear him;

God planned from the beginning that He would offer Himself as a sacrifice to cover and overcome the effects of sin upon mankind. All it takes to receive this incredible gift is to accept by faith that Jesus died on the cross to pay the price for your sins, was buried and rose again from the dead and is alive with God today. Consider Isaiah 53:4 *(see p. 331).*

Isaiah 53:4

> *Surely he hath borne our griefs, and carried our sorrows: yet we did esteem him stricken, smitten of God, and afflicted.*

This passage clearly states that the impression that *worldly wisdom* has regarding the oppression, beatings, scourgings, mockings, suffering, and death of Jesus was that God was doing this to Him. However, the world is wrong. In the same manner, many attribute the sufferings and destructions of the Old Testament to God, but they are also wrong. It is clear that it was not God that was taking out His wrath or prescribing punishment upon Jesus. It was the full weight of the sins of the entire world that came crashing down on Jesus as He took them upon Himself for you and me.

God's plan does not make sense to the human intellect because the ***Ideolatry*** of the human mind demands vengeance, payback, and penalties. The mystery that He kept hidden was that His wrath against your sins is forgiveness through Jesus. Forgiveness is God's act of wrath and vengeance, to destroy sin and death through the power of His love and provide restoration to every individual that believes Him. However, make no mistake, without Jesus, sin will still take its toll and demand its payment.

The character and nature of God is to reach out to man in love and forgive his sins and to restore him to fellowship with Himself. God said, "This one is on me, I will pay the bill!" Forgiveness is an exacting and everlasting blow to the deceptive nature of sin that Satan wrought upon mankind in the Garden of Eden. Lack of understanding, lack of knowledge of His provision and unwillingness to accept His free gift by faith is the problem.

God is *not* your problem!

CHAPTER 26

HOW IS YOUR DECEIVER ?

As we explored in chapter 3, *How Is Your Receiver?*, having the right *receiver* makes it possible to hear what God is saying. It is the first step to determining the truth of His will. Tuning in your spirit to receive His truth also makes it much easier to detect deception when it acts against you. There are various versions of truth in many situations, but there is only one absolute truth of God as we explored in chapter 6, *Our Universe–Relative Or Absolute* and chapter 7, *It's Nothing Personal*. Deception is a powerful tool. It can be brought on us by an outside agent or be self-imposed by an unwillingness to accept God's truth. Deception can also result when human reasoning and carnal mind thinking are used to try to discern His truth. Discernment based on Godly wisdom is the key to overcoming deception and His will is understood by using a mind that is renewed to the spiritual wisdom of His Word. This combination reveals His true character and nature.

We tend to look at God and His will in the same way that we look at human authority figures, through tainted experiences and distorted thinking as we explored in chapter 4, *How Do You See God?*. Sometimes, the will of those authority figures can be confusing. It may be difficult to respect and adhere to when it is fluid and unpredictable. It may be wavering and change based on circumstances, or cruel and arbitrarily imposed according to their self-interest.

Personal experience with the will of authority figures in our lives can color our understanding and expectations of God and His will. Many people believe that God has two different expressions of His will, a ***permissive will*** and a ***perfect will***. His perfect will is said to be what He really wants to happen, while His permissive will explains why God ***allows*** things to go wrong when someone falls into some dire circumstance, sickness or other problem. This is what Romans 8:28 is seems to be saying.

Romans 8:28

And we know that all things work together for good to them that love God, to them who are the called according to his purpose.

As a result, some people might say something like this regarding God and His "permissive will":

God ***allowed*** *that to happen so that person would respond to Him and get things right.*

This sounds spiritual since God is at the top of the "food chain" so to speak and can do whatever He wants. However, we explored this concept in Chapter 9, *God–The Accomplice?* and Chapter 11, *Trials and Testing–What's Up With Job?* and it is totally wrong! ***God has a single, perfect will.*** He does not have a permissive will, a tolerant will, a situational will, or an arbitrary will. When something other than His will occurs, it does not happen because He allows or permits it, but because someone (a human with authority in the earth realm) has either demanded or permitted it by their sin, their words or their direct or indirect actions. *His will is His will.*

Some might say that bad things occur as teaching opportunities so that we will learn something, but this is not true, even though we actually might learn something! God will reveal a way to work around our stubbornness and disobedience (sin) in the midst of a situation, but this is not His "permissive will" as some may see in Romans 8:28. His character and nature is to help us in spite of ourselves and regardless of our choices, but it would be so much better for us to use our free will to follow His will in the first place! However, there is still some evidence that God sends trials (pain, suffering and bad circumstances) into our lives to toughen up our faith and make it strong. This viewpoint is revealed in some translations, such as the *New International Version* of 1 Peter 1:6-7.

1 Peter 1:6-7 *(NIV)*

[6] *In this you greatly rejoice, though now for a little while you may have had to suffer grief in all kinds of trials.* [7] ***These have come so that your faith*** *— of greater worth than gold, which perishes even though refined by fire —* ***may be proved genuine*** *and may result in praise, glory and honor when Jesus Christ is revealed.*

This translation states, "*These have come so that your faith.*" Trials are by nature difficult, bad, or possibly evil circumstances. This phrasing clearly implies that the trials that we all face in this spiritually corrupt world are designed by and purposely come from God to refine and prove our faith. An action of this sort might be compared to you teaching your five-year-old daughter to ride a bicycle, and as soon as she got going, you pushed her over and made her crash. Would you really do that so that you could prove how tough she is? Do you truly think that God does that?

The Message Bible provides a different perspective by which there is no indication that the trials come for such a purpose, but they do come.

> **1 Peter 1:6-7** *(MSG)*
> [6] *I know how great this makes you feel, even though* ***you have to put up with every kind of aggravation in the meantime.*** [7] *Pure gold put in the fire comes out of it proved pure;* ***genuine faith put through this suffering comes out proved genuine.*** *When Jesus wraps this all up, it's your faith, not your gold, that God will have on display as evidence of his victory.*

There is a very, very big difference between these two views. One states that difficulties and challenges come from God. The other states that things happen. Bad things happen every day regardless of whether we cause them personally or whether they come because of someone else's fallout. Regardless, they are all opportunities for us to exercise and strengthen our faith and trust in God. What matters is how we use our faith to deal with and overcome them.

The reality of the situation is this: God has given man freedom of choice through his free will. He does not control the choices, as that would override our free will. Choices form a path that man follows, much like the switches that provide choices of which direction a train will go on a track. When coming to an intersection of roads, we can choose to turn right, left, or go straight ahead. The choice is ours and ours alone. He does not create evil circumstances to get a man or woman to change his or her ways. However, in an attempt to deflect responsibility for poor choices, man tries to deflect to someone or something else, and many times he points to God as the problem.

The character of God is one of grace, mercy, salvation, and inclusion. He wants us to make choices that are right and consistent with His guidance or His Will. When we make wrong choices, they are not at His prompting. They are a result of our willful disobedience, ignorance, stubbornness, or deception. God finds ways to alert us in the midst of a poor choice and to help prevent an impending destruction from occurring. He does this because He wants to save us from ourselves and restore us. He works on our behalf to keep us alive long enough for us to make the right choices. We cannot be truly successful until we make the decision to leave the bad choices behind and come around to making the right choices that follow the guidance of His will.

However, our choices can initiate circumstances that are beyond correction. The adversary wins, and the results are destruction and death. It is not God's will that leads to reaping destruction. It is man's choices that place him in harm's way. God does not have a "permissive will" that takes a person's life just because He wants them to be in heaven with Him. God only has one will, His way. The cold, hard fact is that destruction comes upon us in much the same way as the flood of Noah's time and the destruction of Sodom and Gomorrah came upon the inhabitants who rejected God and His truth. Destruction and death are the payment and penalty for sin that is demanded by our spiritual adversary. They are a result of poor personal choices. However, according to Deuteronomy 30:19, we do the choosing!

Deuteronomy 30:19 *(NIV)*

This day I call heaven and earth as witnesses against you that I have set before you life and death, blessings and curses. Now choose life, so that you and your children may live.

God offers a whole host of promises that are His will for you. Here are just a few that are found in Isaiah 54:14-17, Proverbs 24:16, Psalms 35:27; 1:1-3 and 84:11-12, and Galatians 3:10-14. These are just some of the promises that are the expression of His will for your life.

Protection

Isaiah 54:14-17

14 *In righteousness shalt thou be established: thou shalt be* ***far from oppression****; for thou* ***shalt not fear: and from terror; for it shall not come near thee****.*

15 *Behold, they shall surely gather together, but not by me:* ***whosoever***

shall gather together against thee shall fall for thy sake.

[16] *Behold, I have created the smith that bloweth the coals in the fire, and that bringeth forth an instrument for his work; and I have created the waster to destroy.*

[17] ***No weapon that is formed against thee shall prosper;*** *and* ***every tongue that shall rise against thee in judgment thou shalt condemn. This is the heritage of the servants of the Lord,*** *and their righteousness is of me, saith the Lord .*

Success

Proverbs 24:16

For a just man falleth seven times, and riseth up again: *but the wicked shall fall into mischief.*

Prosperity

Psalms 35:27

Let them shout for joy, and be glad, that favour my righteous cause: yea, let them say continually, ***Let the Lord be magnified, which hath pleasure in the prosperity of his servant.***

Psalms 1:1-3

[1] ***Blessed is the man that walketh not in the counsel of the ungodly, nor standeth in the way of sinners, nor sitteth in the seat of the scornful.***

[2] *But his delight is in the law of the Lord, and in his law doth he meditate day and night.*

[3] *And* ***he shall be like a tree planted by the rivers of water, that bringeth forth his fruit in his season; his leaf also shall not wither; and whatsoever he doeth shall prosper.***

Blessings

Psalms 84:11-12

[11] *For the Lord God is a sun and shield:* ***the Lord will give grace and glory: no good thing will he withhold from them that walk uprightly.***

[12] *O Lord of hosts,* ***blessed is the man that trusteth in thee.***

Galatians 3:10-14

> [10] *For as many as are of the works of the law are under the curse: for it is written, Cursed is every one that continueth not in all things which are written in the book of the law to do them.*
>
> [11] *But that no man is justified by the law in the sight of God, it is evident: for, The just shall live by faith.*
>
> [12] *And the law is not of faith: but, The man that doeth them shall live in them.*
>
> [13] ***Christ hath redeemed us from the curse of the law**, being made a curse for us: for it is written, Cursed is every one that hangeth on a tree:*
>
> [14] ***That the blessing of Abraham might come on the Gentiles through Jesus Christ; that we might receive the promise of the Spirit through faith**.*

If these promises are not operating in your life, it is not because God is against you with a "permissive will." His only will is to provide you with everything that is needed for this life on earth and the eternal life to come. You have either been unaware of the promises, or you are working against yourself by rejecting what God has provided for you.

Activate your *receiver* and deactivate your *deceiver*. Don't let yourself be deceived by anyone – especially yourself. God implores us to *choose life* so that we can enjoy His promises and provision. The choices of your life lead you to a myriad of potential outcomes, both good and bad. You are ultimately responsible, and no one else. Blame shifting will not do you any good. You should be looking at yourself first and not blaming anyone else, especially God. He is there for you at every turn. He has provided you with a way of escape from the sin, destruction, and death that are a result of poor choices in your life. He has provided Jesus and His life, death, blood, and resurrection for your benefit. *This is His Will*. However, the *free will choice* to accept Him and His will is still in your hands.

Choose wisely!

Chapter 27

WALKING IN GOD'S PLANS

You may acknowledge a god as a supreme authority. However, who is the god that you recognize and follow? Is your God the God of the Bible, or have you designed your own god through your ***Ideolatry***? It is certainly more comfortable to serve a god that you create in your own mind because you can make that god in your image. Your god can then conform to your own desires and prejudices and approve of your direction and standard of conduct. However, this kind of thinking could produce chaos. Each individual on the planet would have a different god to suit their specific needs, and they could do whatever they wanted!

There is a problem with this approach, however, and that is the absolute nature of the true God. He reveals Himself in the pages of His Word, the Bible. You are made in His image. He is not made in your image or your imagination. He does not conform to you. He is not subject to being redesigned according to your needs. The reality is just the opposite. You need to redesign yourself according to His plans.

Embracing this reality is the first obstacle to be overcome in order to live in submission to God's plan for your life. However, there just may be some things that you don't know, and your version of God may not be accurate. To accomplish your redesign, you must extend your faith to accept the God of the Bible as He is. You may already understand this and have mentors and teachers in your life who are helping you grow and from whom you draw wisdom and understanding. However, you must find out who God is by exploring His instruction manual, the Bible, for yourself.

When these principles are accepted and acted upon, many misunderstandings and misconceptions can be overcome and explained. As you seek to learn about God, He will reveal Himself to you through His Spirit. The ongoing challenge for your life is to walk with God being armed with the re-created spirit that Jesus bought for you, submitted to His "divine guidance" and being truly "led of His Spirit."

Being led of the Spirit is required if we are to experience the completeness of God's Will in our lives. However, it is not a requirement of the Law, as evidenced in Galatians 5:18.

Galatians 5:18 *(NKJV*

But if you are led by the Spirit, you are not under the law.

Experiencing God's guidance through the leading of the Spirit does nevertheless require an understanding of who God is. It also requires an understanding of the covenant agreement that He established with man, His purposes and plans for man, and the nature of man as a *new creature* after accepting Jesus in 2 Corinthians 5:17.

2 Corinthians 5:17

Therefore if any man be in Christ, he is a new creature: old things are passed away; behold, all things are become new.

Who Is The God That We Serve?

Discernment is a key factor in being led of the Spirit. However, many influences vie for our attention. The temptation to follow after them can be powerful and deceptive. Therefore, it is imperative that the *new creature*, the believer, understand the voice of the Spirit of God. Discernment can be learned through studying the Bible or "operator's manual" that God has provided for us. However, the temptation, especially in the modern day in which we live, is to seek instant results and shortcuts along the way.

The age in which we live has many advantages and disadvantages as compared to previous ages. Disadvantages come in the form of the incredible number of distractions that we are faced with moment by moment that fill our minds and demand our time leaving little room for God. The world is also becoming more and more ungodly with each passing decade and generation. However, there is a major advantage of our age. We have the ability to look back into the events of history, in many cases with a more complete "world view" than those who lived through them. Spiritually speaking, we are also privy to centuries of evidence that reveals the way God has dealt with His people and gives us a great deal of insight into His character.

God spoke through His Spirit in a variety of ways throughout the ages, but all were consistent in purpose. The details are well documented in the Bible. There is no shortcut to learning these details, however. It takes time to study the Bible and glean from its pages. The Spirit leads us to observe and discern God's previous interactions with man when we become a student and invest our time in study. Many individuals have had encounters with the Spirit of God and have been led in a variety of ways. We can look at these people and see some general as well as situation-dependent examples of the Spirit's leading. However, Jesus is truly our prime example. He is the embodiment of God's Word as described in John 1:1-4 and 14. It is not easily understood, but is the bedrock of faith.

John 1:1-4, 14

> [4] *In the beginning was the Word, and the Word was with God, and the Word was God. The same was in the beginning with God. All things were made by him; and without him was not any thing made that was made. In him was life; and the life was the light of men.*
>
> [14] *And the Word was made flesh, and dwelt among us, (and we beheld his glory, the glory as of the only begotten of the Father,) full of grace and truth.*

Jesus is the Word that was with God in the beginning. He is God. He became flesh and walked upon the earth. God kept hidden the mystery that He existed in three distinct yet unified entities, God the Father, God the Son (Jesus, the Word), and God the Holy Spirit. It was Jesus, the Word or voice of God, who spoke in Genesis 1:1 and created the universe. When He spoke, things came into existence. The voice of God manifested itself in the flesh as Jesus who faithfully followed the Holy Spirit as described in Luke 4:18-19.

Luke 4:18-19

> [18] *The Spirit of the Lord is upon me, because he hath anointed me to preach the gospel to the poor; he hath sent me to heal the brokenhearted, to preach deliverance to the captives, and recovering of sight to the blind, to set at liberty them that are bruised,* [19] *To preach the acceptable year of the Lord.*

Jesus acted according to the true character and nature of God. He brought the good news or the Gospel to heal, restore, deliver, and free all who were oppressed. He preached *"the acceptable year of the Lord,"* basically saying, "The time is now" (Luke 4:19). The words that Jesus spoke and the actions that He took were specific to His time on the earth, but fortunately for us, His message is also applicable to us and is unchanging throughout time according to Hebrews 13:8.

Hebrews 13:8 *(NKJV)*
Jesus Christ is the same yesterday, today, and forever.

To witness Jesus is to know God – His character, His nature, His purpose and His will. Discernment through the Spirit is much less complicated than we might think. Jesus provided consistent and dependable examples as He operated under the first covenant, the Old Covenant, founded under the Law. Because Jesus fulfilled that covenant and made Himself a permanent sacrifice for all of mankind, He ushered in a New and better Covenant that provided us with the Holy Spirit as our teacher and guide.

God's Covenant Agreement With You

The word *covenant* simply means an agreement between two parties. It can be in the form of a contract, promise, pledge, or agreement. Every covenant has provisions that apply to both sides. In our society today, a good covenant between parties is considered to be a "win-win" with both parties having equal responsibilities, equal participation and equal reward. Fortunately for us, God does not operate this way. He prefers an unequal agreement, one in which He gives far more than He receives!

The Old Covenant

Before The Law

God's initial covenant was established with Adam in the Garden of Eden. God gave Adam everything, simply everything, except one thing, the awareness of two opposing forces – the knowledge of good and evil. He created a covenant with Adam and Eve in their innocence with His only condition being obedience. Needless to say, the covenant did not work out well for man because he chose not to comply, and the penalty for not complying with the agreement was death *(see p. 56)*. From the beginning, God was not taker, but a giver of life. However, the act of disobedience on the part of Adam was *his choice,* and through it, *he chose* death rather than life.

The close relationship that man had with God in the garden had badly deteriorated up to the time of the Flood. God was not to be deterred, however. He made another covenant with Noah to preserve the creation of mankind from its own sins. Again, this was based simply on the obedience of one man. Noah was obedient to the leading of the Holy Spirit. The limited covenant was successful. He heard the Spirit of God in the midst of great adversity *(see p. 307)*. He and his family survived the Flood. However, the same decay soon spiraled down again. This happened because of the carnality of man's flesh which refused to honor God as we see explained in Romans 8:5-8.

Romans 8:5-8

> [5] *For they that are after the flesh do mind the things of the flesh; but they that are after the Spirit the things of the Spirit.* [6] *For to be carnally minded is death; but to be spiritually minded is life and peace.*
>
> [7] *Because the carnal mind is enmity against God: for it is not subject to the law of God, neither indeed can be.* [8] *So then they that are in the flesh cannot please God.*

As time progressed, God sought another with whom He could establish a more comprehensive, faith-based covenant that would restore what had been lost by Adam in the garden. This faith-based covenant began to unfold during a time of great carnality – a time of idols. God found Melchizedek (Melchisedec in the New Testament) and appointed him to be a high priest.[74] Very little is known about Melchizedek apart from his interaction with Abram as seen in Genesis 14:18-20.

Genesis 14:18-20

> [18] *And Melchizedek king of Salem brought forth bread and wine: and he was the priest of the most high God.* [19] *And he blessed him, and said, Blessed be Abram of the most high God, possessor of heaven and earth:*
>
> [20] *And blessed be the most high God, which hath delivered thine enemies into thy hand. And he gave him tithes of all.*

Melchizedek was the King of Salem (possibly Jerusalem), and he was declared to be a priest of God. His communications with God are unknown, but they were definitely not in accordance with the Law of Moses or the Levitical priesthood of Aaron as these would not occur until 500 years later. He had a direct relationship with God, much the same as the one that Abraham developed. Melchizedek honored God by faith not out of obligation because there was no established law. He was a precursor to Jesus in that Jesus would be a priest after the order of Melchizedek as prophesied in Psalms 110:1-4.

Psalms 110:1-4

[1] The Lord said unto my Lord, Sit thou at my right hand, until I make thine enemies thy footstool. [2] The Lord shall send the rod of thy strength out of Zion: rule thou in the midst of thine enemies. [3] Thy people shall be willing in the day of thy power, in the beauties of holiness from the womb of the morning: thou hast the dew of thy youth. [4] The Lord hath sworn, and will not repent, Thou art a priest for ever after the order of Melchizedek.

Later, we see that a new priest was needed to solve the problems that man faced with the Law. This new priest was Jesus, who followed the faith-based priesthood of Melchizedek described in Hebrews 7:11-12.

Hebrews 7:11-12 *(ERV)*

[11] The people were given the law under the system of priests from the tribe of Levi. But no one could be made spiritually perfect through that system of priests. So there was a need for another priest to come. I mean a priest like Melchizedek, not Aaron. [12] And when a different kind of priest comes, then the law must be changed too.

The writer of Hebrews makes a sharp distinction between law -based and faith-based priesthoods. The function of the law-based priesthood was to bring offerings for sins before God on behalf of the people. The Levites, who were the priests, had to perform the task yearly in accordance with the laws that God gave to Moses. The prophecy that was written in Psalms 110:4 clearly indicated that a specific priesthood would be revived well after the establishment of the Law. It was not to be a priesthood that was prescribed by the Law, it was faith-based and followed the pattern established by Melchizedek. Jesus acted according to this priesthood. As the high priest, He did not offer a yearly sacrifice for the people as did the Levitical priests. Instead, Jesus offered Himself as a one-time sacrifice to pay the price for the sins of every person that ever lives upon the earth. His sacrifice is faith-based since our salvation is obtained by placing our faith in His sacrifice on the cross. This is why His priesthood is said to be like the faith-based priesthood of Melchizedek in Hebrews 5:8-10.

Hebrews 5:8-10

8 Though he were a Son, yet learned he obedience by the things which he suffered; 9 And being made perfect, he became the author of eternal salvation unto all them that obey him; 10 Called of God an high priest after the order of Melchisedec.

Abram was blessed by Melchizedek in Genesis 14:19. Then, God struck a deal with Abram, the son of an idol maker. This deal or covenant was based on the same kind of faith that Melchizedek exercised as a high priest. Abram's faith allowed God to change his name to Abraham. Through his willingness to sacrifice his son, Isaac, Abraham paved the way for God's mysterious plan to restore the human condition through Jesus, the most amazing gift of life the world has ever seen. The covenant God made with Abraham is the most comprehensive of all time and is still with us today. It set up the sacrifice of Jesus and gave us our salvation through Him *(see p. 151)*. Abraham and Melchizedek were both known to God because they allowed themselves to be led of the Spirit *(see p. 177)*. The interaction between Melchizedek and Abraham is further detailed in Hebrews 6:20 - 7:7.

Hebrews 6:20-7:7 *(ERV)*

20 Jesus has already entered there and opened the way for us. He has become the high priest forever, just like Melchizedek.

1 Melchizedek was the king of Salem and a priest for God the Most High. He met Abraham when Abraham was coming back after defeating the kings. That day Melchizedek blessed him. 2 Then Abraham gave him a tenth of everything he had.

The name Melchizedek, king of Salem, has two meanings. First, Melchizedek means "king of justice." And "king of Salem" means "king of peace." 3 No one knows who his father or mother was or where he came from. And no one knows when he was born or when he died. Melchizedek is like the Son of God in that he will always be a priest.

4 You can see that Melchizedek was very great. Abraham, our great ancestor, gave him a tenth of everything he won in battle. 5 Now the law says that those from the tribe of Levi who become priests must get a tenth from their own people, even though they and their people are both from the family of

Abraham. [6] Melchizedek was not even from the tribe of Levi, but Abraham gave him a tenth of what he had. And Melchizedek blessed Abraham—the one who had God's promises. [7] And everyone knows that the more important person always blesses the less important person.

Here we discover that the lineage of Melchizedek is unknown. This almost implies an eternal presence, probably referring to his spirit of faith as opposed to the obligatory performance of a law. The priesthood of Jesus is compared to this faithful priest, and the hierarchy of Melchizedek over Abraham is revealed through his blessing. The first Biblical reference to the concept of tithing is also revealed to be faith based. Tithing is not rooted in any type of legal obligation because there was no established law. Abraham voluntarily gave one tenth of his increase to the faith-based priest of God.

These and many others were sensitive to the voice of God and the leading of His Spirit. They avoided the distractions of their time and made God their priority. They were led when there was no precedence, no guidance, no writings, no law and no Bible to give them direction. They heard God through His Spirit by *faith*. They received His direction by *faith*. They took action by *faith*.

Under The Law

The condition of man had declined from the purity of the covenant of Abraham. A significant change occurred with the establishment of the Law under Moses. The covenant based on *faith* faded into one that demanded *legislation*. Man had become stubborn and unwilling to exercise faith and let the Spirit lead him. God found it necessary to bring him face to face with his frailty and helplessness in the only way he would listen, in a carnal, human way through the Law.

From establishment of the Law of Moses until Jesus' resurrection, most contact with God was reduced to the ritual observance of the Law with the exception of some specific, unique individuals. The Law was given to demonstrate the futility and arrogance of man in his attempt to make himself worthy of any position with God. It was tangible because it was written. It could be easily seen, touched, and felt by man. However, over a period of years, it became exalted above the faith that joined Abraham in covenant with God.

The intent of the Law was to drive man to understand his need for God, but instead the Law became an object of near worship and became a great distraction to being led by the Spirit. This manifested itself most severely during the earthly walk of Jesus. Galatians 3:15-25 makes this very apparent as it ties together the covenant with Abraham, the purpose of the Law and the revived priesthood that manifests in Jesus.

Galatians 3:15-25 *(ERV)*

15 Brothers and sisters, let me give you an example from everyday life: Think about an agreement that one person makes with another. After that agreement is made official, no one can stop it or add anything to it, and no one can ignore it.
16 God made promises to Abraham and his Descendant. The Scripture does not say, "and to your descendants." That would mean many people. But it says, "and to your Descendant." That means only one, and that one is Christ.
17 This is what I mean: The agreement that God gave to Abraham was made official long before the law came. The law came 430 years later. So the law could not take away the agreement and change God's promise.

18 Can following the law give us the blessing God promised? If we could receive it by following the law, then it would not be God's promise that brings it to us. But God freely gave his blessings to Abraham through the promise God made.

19 So what was the law for? The law was given to show the wrong things people do. The law would continue until the special Descendant of Abraham came. This is the Descendant mentioned in the promise, which came directly from God. But the law was given through angels, and the angels used Moses as a mediator to give the law to the people.
20 But when God gave the promise, there was no mediator, because a mediator is not needed when there is only one side, and God is one.

21 Does this mean that the law works against God's promises? Of course not. The law was never God's way of giving new life to people. If it were, then we could be made right with God by following the law.
22 But this is not possible. The Scriptures put the whole world in prison under the control of sin, so that the only way for people to get what God promised would be through faith in Jesus Christ. It is given to those who believe in him.

23 Before this faith came, the law held us as prisoners. We had no freedom until God showed us the way of faith that was coming.
24 I mean the law was the guardian in charge of us until Christ came. After he came, we could

be made right with God through faith. [25] *Now that the way of faith has come, we no longer need the law to be our guardian.*

According to this passage, observance of the Law does not constitute being *"led of the Spirit"* (Galatians 5:18). The Law was given to be a teacher, to bring awareness of sin, and to look forward to Jesus, the redeemer of that sin. Many were still led of the Spirit during the time of the Law. However, this did not happen because they only observed the Law and made sacrifices according to its provisions. It happened because they heard and purposed to listen to and heed the Spirit of God.

To some, especially the spiritual leaders of Jesus day, the Law had become the supreme entity set above the person of God. Rather than worship God, they worshiped the Law and made the Law more important than the leading of God and His Spirit. They took their observance of the Law to an extreme and set it up above the purpose of the Law and even above God Himself. Jesus rebuked them for their actions and attitudes several times. They sought to justify themselves and make themselves acceptable to God just as Job had tried and failed to do. They let their intellect overcome their spirit and missed the big picture of what God was doing. They did not want to lose their positions of honor and control over the people. They let their ***Ideolatry*** get in the way.

The New Covenant

Before The Cross

Jesus walked on this earth under the rules of the Law in the Old Testament. He completely fulfilled its requirements and those of the Old Covenant by perfectly observing the Law. However, Jesus not only kept the physical provisions of the Law but also let the Spirit lead Him, thus keeping the Spirit of the Law as well. He summed up the entire Law in just two requirements in Matthew 22:37-40.

Matthew 22:37-40 *(NKJV)*

[37] *You shall love the Lord your God with all your heart, with all your soul, and with all your mind.* [38] *This is the first and great commandment.* [39] *And the second is like it: 'You shall love your neighbor as yourself.* [40] *On these two commandments hang all the Law and the Prophets.*

Jesus was led by the Spirit, not by legislation and rules. His purpose was to walk in the leading of the Spirit, and He fulfilled the Law as a result. He was and continues to be an example to those who will listen and understand that God's desire is to restore, forgive, heal, and provide eternal life to mankind. Jesus laid the foundation for the New Covenant before His death because no one had ever fulfilled or lived perfectly in the provisions of the Law and the Old Covenant. However, the true beginning of the New Covenant came after Jesus' resurrection.

After The Cross

Jesus spoke in depth about what the ministry of the Holy Spirit would be like for us after He ascended to heaven. The Gospel of John provides us with Jesus' words about the Holy Spirit.

John 14:16-17, 26 *(NKJV)*

> [15] *If you love Me, keep My commandments.* [16] *And I will pray the Father,*
> *and He will give you another Helper, that He may abide with you forever*
> [17] *the Spirit of truth, whom the world cannot receive, because it neither sees Him nor knows Him; but you know Him, for He dwells with you and will be in you.*
>
> [26] *But the Helper, the Holy Spirit, whom the Father will send in My name, He will teach you all things, and bring to your remembrance all things that I said to you.*

Jesus plainly states that the Spirit will lead the believer from within. If you believe and accept Jesus, the Spirit will reside in you, guiding and teaching you. We should never expect any direction from the Spirit that does not agree with what God has already said in His Word, and it will never conflict with anything that Jesus did or said in His earthly walk.

One of the ministries of the Holy Spirit, the Helper or Comforter, is to affirm and declare Jesus as described in John 15:26.

John 15:26

> *But when the Comforter is come, whom I will send unto you from the Father, even the Spirit of truth, which proceedeth from the Father, he shall testify of me:*

Jesus knew that we needed direction and guidance and that both would be manifested in us through the Holy Spirit speaking to our spirits.

John 16:13 *(NKJV)*

However, when He, the Spirit of truth, has come, He will guide you into all truth; for He will not speak on His own authority, but whatever He hears He will speak; and He will tell you things to come.

The Holy Spirit was not available to everyone in the times of the Old Testament. The Spirit of God came upon several people for specific purposes, such as giving a prophecy, issuing a warning or providing wisdom. It was not until Jesus ascended into heaven that the Holy Spirit became available to all believers. Jesus said that the Holy Spirit would come as a Comforter in John 16:7.

John 16:7

Nevertheless I tell you the truth; It is expedient for you that I go away: for if I go not away, the Comforter will not come unto you; but if I depart, I will send him unto you.

God's Purposes and Plans for Man

God's plans for man are far less complicated than we imagine. Very simply, He wants us to share His love and have voluntary, eternal fellowship with Him. The Holy Spirit leads us into a willful, quality decision to acknowledge Him as our creator and provider. Then, He asks us to accept redemption from our sins through Jesus' death, burial, and resurrection.

We all will do many things during our lives. We will be involved in many activities, accomplish goals and share in relationships. The Holy Spirit wants to impart God's guidance into our hearts when we interact with others and make decisions or life choices, but we have to allow Him to do so. We demonstrate evidence of our commitment to be led of the Spirit when we display the fruits of the Spirit. These are the nine character qualities that God reveals to us in Galatians 5:22.

Galatians 5:22-24 *(ERV)*

22 But the fruit that the Spirit produces in a person's life is love, joy, peace, patience, kindness, goodness, faithfulness, 23 gentleness, and self-control. There is no law against these kinds of things.

We will know that the Spirit is leading us when we submit our wills to the Will of God and display these virtues of His Spirit in our lives.

However, the flesh is a powerful force that struggles against the Spirit because it does not want to submit as we see in Galatians 5:16-17.

Galatians 5:16-17*(ERV)*

> [16] *So I tell you, live the way the Spirit leads you. Then you will not do the evil things your sinful self wants.* [17] *The sinful self wants what is against the Spirit, and the Spirit wants what is against the sinful self. They are always fighting against each other, so that you don't do what you really want to do.*

However, allowing the Spirit to lead us so that we experience the *fruits of the Spirit* will yield success, fulfillment, contentment, and joy in everything that we do. This is how the believer in Christ lives in the way of the Spirit and overcomes the flesh.

Man as a "New Creature"

God's Provision

God's Divine Guidance leads us to become a New Creature in Christ through His New Covenant. The dead, sinful nature that we inherited from Adam leads to self-centered destruction, but God offers to *recreate us*. In the flesh, man is a three part being made up of a ***spirit*** that has a ***soul*** and lives in a ***body***. The body and soul (the mind, will, and emotions) are not recreated by God on this earth. The job of the individual is to recreate his or her mind, will, and emotions by following the instruction of the Holy Spirit through God's Word. The new creature that results will be a regenerated spirit that can overcome the body and soul. However, we have to be willing to submit to His guidance and make the change.

God has done the bulk of the work in this covenant relationship. Not only did He make us, but He also made a way for us to overcome the challenges that we face. He also provided the tools for us to get the job done. All we have to do is take hold of our responsibilities and do our part. It is as simple as trusting in Him.

Man's Responsibility

The simplicity of God is quite amazing if we take the time to examine it. It is human intellect or ***Ideolatry*** that makes things complicated. Many times, the confusion that we feel is the result of looking for ways around

His clear direction. If a person does not want to submit and follow, he or she will find ways to subvert the process. Rules and regulations that sound official or spiritual are frequently the results of man's efforts to make himself acceptable. These become traditions and entrench themselves in the minds of men, making God's leading nearly impossible. Jesus accosted those of His day about this very thing in Mark 7:6-13.

Mark 7:6-13 *(ERV)*

> [6] *Jesus answered,"You are all hypocrites. Isaiah was right when he wrote these words from God about you:*
>
> *'These people honor me with their words, but I am not really important to them.* [7] *Their worship of me is worthless. The things they teach are only human rules.'*
>
> [8] *You have stopped following God's commands, preferring instead the man-made rules you got from others."*
>
> [9] *Then he said,"You show great skill in avoiding the commands of God so that you can follow your own teachings!*
>
> [10] *Moses said, 'You must respect your father and mother.' He also said, 'Whoever says anything bad to their father or mother must be killed.'*
>
> [11] *But you teach that people can say to their father or mother, 'I have something I could use to help you, but I will not use it for you. I will give it to God.'* [12] *You are telling people that they do not have to do anything for their father or mother.*
>
> [13] *So you are teaching that it is not important to do what God said. You think it is more important to follow those traditions you have, which you pass on to others. And you do many things like that."*

Jesus' direction is plain. We need to follow the Word of God and not the words of men. Neither God nor His Spirit will ever lead contrary to His already established Word. Following God's Word is the primary responsibility for man. It will allow him to experience *divine guidance* and *walk* in God's plan.

The complexity of the Law served to counter man's tendency to find the loopholes and reinterpret the Law. Man needs to have every situation legislated, and even then the lawyers manage to find ways around the clear intents of laws. However, Jesus made it simple in His approach. When He was being challenged by a lawyer trying to trip Him up, He said there were only two things that needed to be followed as we saw earlier in Matthew 22:36-40.

Matthew 22:36-40

36 *Master, which is the great commandment in the law?*

37 *Jesus said unto him, "Thou shalt love the Lord thy God with all thy heart, and with all thy soul, and with all thy mind.*

38 *This is the first and great commandment.*

39 *And the second is like unto it, Thou shalt love thy neighbour as thyself.*

40 *On these two commandments hang all the law and the prophets."*

If we were truly able to put the needs of others on the same level as our own, there would not be many problems in life. Problems develop when one person wants to put his or her needs above those of everyone else. Every evil that is legislated against in the law results from selfishness. As Jesus noted, things are truly very simple.

The Holy Spirit is available to you to help you transform yourself and, therefore, enjoy the good, acceptable, and perfect will of God. It is your responsibility to do the renewing of your mind. It will not be done for you or against your will. The choice is yours. Your path to achieving that transformation is plain and straightforward as noted in Romans 12:1-2.

Romans 12:1-2 *(MSG)*

1 *So here's what I want you to do, God helping you:*

Take your everyday, ordinary life – your sleeping, eating, going-to-work, and walking-around life – and place it before God as an offering. Embracing what God does for you is the best thing you can do for him.

2 *Don't become so well-adjusted to your culture that you fit into it without even thinking. Instead, fix your attention on God.*

You'll be changed from the inside out.

Readily recognize what he wants from you, and quickly respond to it.

Unlike the culture around you, always dragging you down to its level of immaturity, God brings the best out of you, develops well-formed maturity in you.

The walk of the believer can be easily sidetracked without the leading of the Spirit. God cannot be approached on a carnal level, only on a spiritual one. Renewing of the mind is a requirement, "... *be renewed in the spirit of your mind*" (Ephesians 4:23) and is an intentional process, not an automatic one. The rewards are great, but effort is required. The apostle Paul expressed the struggle in very plain terms in Romans 7:18-19.

Romans 7:18-19 *(NKJV)*

[18] For I know that in me (that is, in my flesh) nothing good dwells; for to will is present with me, but how to perform what is good I do not find.

[19] For the good that I will to do, I do not do; but the evil I will not to do, that I practice.

The triune or three-part nature of man expresses itself in a constant struggle between the *soul*, the *flesh,* and the *spirit*. The leading of the Spirit of God through a renewed mind sets a new course that is fit for the *new creature* that the believer has become. "Looking to Jesus, the Author and Finisher of our faith" (Hebrews 12:2), allows us to understand the way in which God's Holy Spirit leads us and helps us to discern the truth. Being led of the Spirit and walking in the will of God is the most fulfilling life that can be led on this Earth.

Hebrews 12:2

Looking unto Jesus the author and finisher of our faith; who for the joy that was set before him endured the cross, despising the shame, and is set down at the right hand of the throne of God.

God is specific about the thoughts of man. He eloquently points out the differences between man's thoughts and his own in Isaiah 55:8-9. Ignoring those differences is at our own peril. However, understanding that the thoughts of man can be redirected and aligned with God's thoughts can yield immeasurable rewards.

Isaiah 55:8-9

[8] For my thoughts are not your thoughts, neither are your ways my ways, saith the LORD.

[9] For as the heavens are higher than the earth, so are my ways higher than your ways, and my thoughts than your thoughts.

God is not "out to get you," nor does He want evil to come upon you. He wants only good as described in Jeremiah 29:11. The choice is still yours. However, you can choose to accept God's thoughts of peace toward you or reject them and "enjoy" the results. Don't let yourself be confused, God is not.

Jeremiah 29:11 *(NKJV)*
For I know the thoughts that I think toward you, says the Lord, thoughts of peace and not of evil, to give you a future and a hope.

God's expected end for you is restoration, completion, health, prosperity, success, redemption, forgiveness, and ultimately eternal life in His presence.

Using Your Mouth

God is known by many names that describe aspects of His nature and dealings with mankind. We began with identifying Him as the *Creator*, and we find in the Bible that His way of creating is far different than we might have imagined. We do not actually create anything. We simply "re-configure" what is already in existence. We need the nails, wood, steel, dirt, blood, tissues, DNA, etc. with which to build. This is what man calls creating. On the other hand, God actually created by a process that is beyond our ability to conceive. We are compelled to accept this process by faith. At his word, the universe materialized out of nothing, and this does satisfy science.

And God Said

His creation was accomplished by a seemingly simple task, *speaking*. He spoke everything into existence! We can see the description of His method and actions in Genesis 1:1-28.

Creation

1 In the beginning God created the heaven and the earth. 2 And the earth was without form, and void; and darkness was upon the face of the deep. And the Spirit of God moved upon the face of the waters.

The First Day

3 ***And God said****, Let there be light: and there was light.*

The Second Day

*[6] **And God said,** Let there be a firmament in the midst of the waters, and let it divide the waters from the waters.*

The Third Day

*[9] **And God said,** Let the waters under the heaven be gathered together unto one place, and let the dry land appear: and it was so.*

*[11] **And God said,** Let the earth bring forth grass, the herb yielding seed, and the fruit tree yielding fruit after his kind, whose seed is in itself, upon the earth: and it was so.*

The Fourth Day

*[14] **And God said,** Let there be lights in the firmament of the heaven to divide the day from the night; and let them be for signs, and for seasons, and for days, and years:*

The Fifth Day

*[20] **And God said,** Let the waters bring forth abundantly the moving creature that hath life, and fowl that may fly above the earth in the open firmament of heaven.*

The Sixth Day

*[24] **And God said,** Let the earth bring forth the living creature after his kind, cattle, and creeping thing, and beast of the earth after his kind: and it was so.*

*[26] **And God said,** Let us make man in our image, after our likeness: and let them have dominion over the fish of the sea, and over the fowl of the air, and over the cattle, and over all the earth, and over every creeping thing that creepeth upon the earth. [27] So God created man in his own image, in the image of God created he him; male and female created he them.*

*[28] And God blessed them, **And God said** unto them, Be fruitful, and multiply, and replenish the earth, and subdue it: and have dominion over the fish of the sea, and over the fowl of the air, and over every living thing that moveth upon the earth.*

It is clear from these scriptures that when God speaks, things happen. As a matter of fact, *whatever He says* happens. We see a New Testament description of God speaking things into existence in Romans 4:17.

Romans 4:17 *(NIV)*

As it is written:"I have made you a father of many nations."He is our father in the sight of God, in whom he believed-- the God who gives life to the dead and ***calls things that are not as though they were****.*

Jesus spoke of this principle to His disciples in Mark 11:22-24 as He instructed them to have faith in God. We might also call this *the God kind of faith* because it is faith that speaks and things happen. Jesus told them that they could speak in faith to a mountain, and it would obey their command. Then, He made it universal by including anything that they asked for in faith.

Mark 11:22-24 *(NLT)*

[22] Then Jesus said to the disciples,"Have faith in God. [23] I tell you the truth, you can say to this mountain, 'May you be lifted up and thrown into the sea,' and it will happen. But you must really believe it will happen and have no doubt in your heart. [24] I tell you, you can pray for anything, and if you believe that you've received it, it will be yours."

God speaks things into existence that have never existed, and He does it by the *law of faith*. This law is only spoken of once. It is found in Romans 3:27 when the apostle Paul is speaking about grace versus self-righteousness. It is not elaborated upon but refers to our inability to attain acceptability by the works of the law.

Romans 3:27 *(BBE)*

What reason, then, is there for pride? It is shut out. By what sort of law? of works? No, but by a law of faith.

Hidden in the explanation of the grace of God through Jesus in Romans 3:27 is a reference to the *law of faith*. This law refers to belief and trust in God, rather than a trust in self. Faith is a tangible intangible that exists just like the invisible wind. Although you cannot experience it with your physical senses, it is available to you at all times. Conversely, works, or doing things to gain God's favor are *acts of self-righteousness.* Works lead you to believe that you can somehow *earn acceptability* with God. However, Jesus was the only one that was able to do that because He led a sinless life perfectly observing the Law. God says that you can only attain acceptability through faith as written in Ephesians 2:8-9. There is nothing that *you* can do to overcome your sin nature. You need help.

Ephesians 2:8-9

> [8] *For by grace are ye saved through faith; and that not of yourselves: it is the gift of God:*
>
> [9] *Not of works, lest any man should boast.*

Abraham proved his faith (willingness to sacrifice his son) by his works (actions). He did not use his works or actions to justify himself and make himself acceptable. God's favor cannot be earned by works, but it can be acquired by acting on faith. Sometimes, this is a subtle but extremely important distinction in attitude.

God gave up His authority in the earth realm to Adam in the garden, and Adam lost it to Satan. Abraham took it back with his faith when he sealed the blood covenant with God by his willingness to sacrifice his son. *Blood covenant* partners share everything, including authority. Therefore, God as Abraham's covenant partner on earth once again had legal authority to act in the earth. When the time was right, God sealed His side of the covenant with the actual sinless blood of His Son which He used as a substitute to cover the sins of all mankind, including yours. The sacrifice of Jesus was so powerful because He was the perfect Lamb without a blemish of sin. Jesus is God's gift to you through the *law of faith*, not by works.

The full context of Romans 3:23-28 makes this discussion very plain and understandable, but this translation does not use the term *law of faith*.

Romans 3:23-28 *(ERV)*

> [21] *But God has a way to make people right, and it has nothing to do with the law. He has now shown us that new way, which the law and the prophets told us about.*
>
> [22] *God makes people right through their faith in Jesus Christ. He does this for all who believe in Christ. Everyone is the same.* [23] *All have sinned and are not good enough to share God's divine greatness.*
>
> [24] *They are made right with God by his grace. This is a free gift. They are made right with God by being made free from sin through Jesus Christ.*
>
> [25-26] *God gave Jesus as a way to forgive people's sins through their faith in him. God can forgive them because the blood sacrifice of Jesus pays for their sins. God gave Jesus to show that he always does what is right and fair. He was right in the past when he was patient and did not punish people for their sins. And in our own time he still does what is right. God worked*

all this out in a way that allows him to judge people fairly and still make right any person who has faith in Jesus.

27 So do we have any reason to boast about ourselves? No reason at all. And why not? Because we are depending on the way of faith, not on what we have done in following the law.

28 I mean we are made right with God through faith, not through what we have done to follow the law. This is what we believe.

God is the author of faith. It is the way He operates. He speaks according to what He believes and what He speaks comes into existence. There is no question with Him as to the outcome. He knows what it will be because of His faith. We wonder, we hope, and we doubt what might happen when we speak based on weak faith (which is actually doubt). However, God tells us to be like Him in Ephesians 5:1.

Ephesians 5:1 *(KJV)*
Be ye therefore followers of God, as dear children;

Ephesians 5:1 *(ASV)*
Be ye therefore imitators of God, as beloved children;

Ephesians 5:1 - Greek Interlinear Bible					
English	*Be ye*	*therefore*	*followers*	*of*	*God*
Greek	Γίνεσθε	οὖν	μιμηταὶ	του	θεου
Strong's	NT:1096	NT:3767	NT:3402	NT:3588	NT:2316
Pronounced	Gínesthe	oún	mimeetaí	toú	Theoú

The Interlinear Greek Bible reference shows the construction of the verse. These two versions differ in the way the Greek word Strong's NT:3402 is translated. The KJV renders it as *follower,* but it truly means *an imitator*.

"follower" - *Strong's* NT:3402 μιμετεσ (mim-ay-tace') from NT:3401
an imitator: and is translated in the KJV as "follower."

The *King James Version* tells us that we should be followers of God. However, the American Standard Version and others are more specific and tell us to be imitators of Him or to do as He does. This means that we are not just supposed to go where He leads us, but we are to model our actions and words after His example. God creates through words and we are to do the same because He told us to be *imitators* of Him.

God speaks, and things happen. Things change. Things are created as the result of His words. Scientific, carnal man cannot handle this because it can't be explained in human terms. Since science has evolved through human thought, we can see how man's understanding of God might go through a similar evolution. As science is influenced by the next generation of thinkers, philosophers, and scientists, so is man's understanding of God through *religious* thought.

However, this does not alter the fact that God creates through words, and we are supposed to do the same. He gave us the pattern to imitate Him with the *law of faith*, and the responsibility to do it in our own lives. The law of faith causes things to happen regardless of whether they are good or bad. We saw the application of negative faith in Job as he created his reality with his words when he said, "For the thing which I greatly feared is come upon me" (Job 3:27). We see where the process begins in Proverbs 23:7a.

Proverbs 23:7a

For as he thinketh in his heart, so is he….

When we think, we begin the process of belief. Belief comes from our acceptance of the things we think about. These things become our reality, our life, and our filters through which we see the world. Belief is formed through our thoughts, and we begin to speak in line with them. Proverbs 23:7 is talking about forming beliefs. We become what we think in our hearts, which is where our beliefs are formed. The key issue is to begin to believe or have faith in what God says through His Word more than what we come up with on our own or what we base on our experiences and outside influences. Luke 6:45 and Romans 10:10 provide clear explanations about how the words that we speak come out of our hearts and influence our lives.

Luke 6:45

A good man out of the good treasure of his heart bringeth forth that which is good; and an evil man out of the evil treasure of his heart bringeth forth that which is evil: for of the abundance of the heart his mouth speaketh.

Romans 10:10

For with the heart man believeth unto righteousness; and with the mouth confession is made unto salvation.

God does not consider evil, defeat, or failure. He does not ponder negative things. He dwells on His love for you. His thoughts are higher, and His words are more purposeful than ours. He speaks with successful end results on His mind and his words make things happen as described in Isaiah 55:9-11. This is a character quality of God that we are to imitate in our lives.

Isaiah 55:9-11 *(ERV)*

[9] *Just as the heavens are higher than the earth, so my ways are higher than your ways, and my thoughts are higher than your thoughts." This is what the Lord himself said.*

[10] *"Rain and snow fall from the sky and don't return until they have watered the ground. Then the ground causes the plants to sprout and grow, and they produce seeds for the farmer and food for people to eat.*

[11] *In the same way, my words leave my mouth, and they don't come back without results. My words make the things happen that I want to happen. They succeed in doing what I send them to do.*

Being an imitator of God is to follow His lead, to speak into existence your own individual reality in line with God's leading. Like it or not, you do it every time you open your mouth and speak. You speak according to your beliefs and create. The things you speak can generate selfishness, negativity, and destruction or generosity, enthusiasm, and restoration. Negative words are destructive and might come from the influences of ungodly people in your life or your own negative reactions to bad circumstances. We all tend to imitate influential people in our lives. These may be trusted family members, friends, or mentors. They might be the latest celebrity, actor, sports figure or entertainer. While some may be excellent role models, we should be cautious with whom we associate and to whom we give our attention. What we imitate will create our reality.

Fill your heart and mind with those things that are from God, His direction, counsel, guidance, promises, and love. Imitate Him and speak the truth of His Word to achieve lasting success and fulfillment.

Getting Yourself Out Of The Way

Let yourself go beyond your own ***Ideolatry***. Get yourself out of the way. Open yourself up to the possibility that the One that created you has a complete, fulfilling, and satisfying plan for your life, a plan that is rich and fruitful and provides you with everything you need to love yourself and those around you. God continues to reach out His hand to you to ensure your success. You can love God because He loved you first! We see this explained in 1 John 4:18-21.

1 John 4:18-21*(ERV)*

> [18] *Where God's love is, there is no fear, because God's perfect love takes away fear. It is his punishment that makes a person fear. So his love is not made perfect in the one who has fear.*
>
> [19] *We love because God first loved us.*
>
> [20] *If we say we love God but hate any of our brothers or sisters in his family, we are liars. If we don't love someone we have seen, how can we love God? We have never even seen him.*
>
> [21] *God gave us this command: If we love God, we must also love each other as brothers and sisters.*

He has made the first move by providing Jesus for you. It is up to you to build up your faith on that fact. Meditate on it continually and let the promises of His Word penetrate deep into your heart. Speak out about your faith in God and see your life recreated in line with His word. Dare to trust that the character and nature of God is to do only good on your behalf. Believe that He provided Jesus Christ so you can abundantly enjoy the life that He has offered you, both in this life and the life that is to come!

What are some of the things that might prevent you from obtaining all that God has provided for you? It would be a good idea to explore this in your own life. The graphic on the next page contains some possibilities to ponder. Ask God to help you with overcoming any of these issues or others that you may be facing.

Avoid

The Downward Path

Rejection of Jesus
Actively Choosing Evil
Rejection of Authority
Rebellion against God
Need for Personal Power
A Lack of Knowledge of God and His Word
Refusal to Acknowledge the Existence God
Conditioned or Taught Rejection of God
Apathy or a Lack of Spiritual Interest
A Bitter and Unforgiving Heart
The Outright Practicing of Sin
Being Too Busy with Life
An Unwilling Heart
Self-Justification
Self-Importance
Self-Reliance
Selfishness
Pride

To Death

CHAPTER 28

CHOOSE LIFE !

The world has a sin problem. Everyone knows it. Even those that deny that God exists know it. They know it because the concept of right and wrong or good and evil is hard-wired into our very being. This awareness is instinctive in all of mankind, including the occasional sociopath that chooses only to act out evil. We all know the difference between good and evil. The very act of choosing to do evil or wrong rather than good or right means that the individual at the very least sins against his or her own awareness of the two. However, sin goes much deeper than this.

We have already seen that God tells us in Deuteronomy 30:19 that we have options and that there is a choice that we must make. God encourages us to choose life, ***His Life.***

Deuteronomy 30:19 *(NIV)*

> *This day I call heaven and earth as witnesses against you that* ***I have set before you life and death, blessings and curses. Now choose life,*** *so that you and your children may live.*

Sin controls much of the world culture as it works overtime in our society to be accepted as normal. It will always try to justify itself. It will always try to make the individual feel good about engaging in it by advocating for acceptance and tolerance. No manner of rule or law will be able to legislate sin out of the world system or the human spirit. Legislation may provide justification or comfort, but regardless of acceptance by society or the establishment of laws of tolerance of any sin by moral redefinition or diversity, wrong is still wrong and evil is still evil. God has absolutes.

The societies of Sodom and Gomorrah as well as others throughout history have succumbed to the acceptance of sin, evil, and wrongdoing as normal to their own peril. The universal acceptance of sin does not make it go away. It just erodes the spirit of man.

Many religions work overtime to expose things that they define as sin and demand varying levels of disapproval, condemnation, retribution, and punishment to discourage those acts. Some kill or maim if there is disobedience. Others force massive amounts of guilt on their members to persuade them to be obedient. Still others even sell forgiveness of sins.

The difference between religions and God is vast. Religions purport to represent God, but they are man's attempt to put a framework around God and compartmentalize Him. Worse yet, they are hijacked by men in the name of God. Corrupted man institutes religion and sets the rules in an effort to dominate and control other men *(see p. 31)*. Religion requires a high price for redemption from sins through specific actions of strict obedience, submission, financial investment and, in the extreme, murder of those who do not agree with it. However, God is outside the bounds of our human experience and understanding. He has made a way for communication with man to solve his sin problem.

Religions demand adherence, but God provided *free will* to man who can choose to accept or reject Him. God offers to solve man's sin problem through love, not rules. He did put rules in place for the purpose of getting man to understand the depth of the depravity of his sin and the degree to which it pervades every aspect of his existence. He put the laws in place not to demand obedience but to convince man that he could not fix the sin problem himself. He made it clear to man that he needed help, *God's help*, which He provides with love and forgiveness through Jesus.

Because God loves man, He provides this help at no charge. God wants man to want Him. He wants man to acknowledge his sin problem, reach out and receive His solution. God's nature and character is not to demand, but to offer. It is not to condemn, but to set free. It is not to punish, but to forgive. Man and his religions demand, condemn, and punish, but God offers freedom and forgiveness through His own Son to clear the path and make a way for you. Realization of these facts breaks down the barriers that sin creates and opens the door to deeper understanding of who God is and what is character and nature is.

Consider the following:

- There is one God.
- God is right, God is good, and God is Life.
- God exposed disobedience by giving the Law, His instructions for doing right (righteousness).
- There is a difference between right and wrong.
- There is a difference between good and evil.
- There is a difference between obedience and disobedience.
- There are absolutes - acts or behaviors are totally right or wrong, totally good or totally evil.
- Man chooses to do right or wrong, to be obedient or disobedient, or to do good or evil.
- Falling short of God's righteous expectations is called sin.
- Man has a sin problem.
- Man cannot solve his own sin problem by any self-directed means as discussed in Job *(see p. 142).*
- Blood sacrifice is required for sins because *life is in the blood*.
- Man's sins will cause him to die physically and spiritually.
- Sin causes man to be separated from God.
- Religion is a Man's attempt to solve his own sin problem through carnal means such as penance, punishment, financial payments, sacrifice, ritual, etc. Religion controls, but it does not solve the sin problem.
- God made a New Covenant of grace to overcome the unchangeable laws of the Old Covenant as in Esther *(see p. 240).*
- God permanently solved Man's sin problem physically and spiritually by bringing Jesus, His Son, into the world to *shed His Blood* and pay a substitutionary price for the sins of man.
- Once payment for sin is accepted through the Blood of Jesus, a man is seen as righteous and good in the eyes of God.
- It is the responsibility of every human to accept or reject God, Jesus, and His Will for him or her.
- God's wrath is against sin, not you.

Jesus Is The Door To Abundant Life

John 10:9-10 *(NKJV)*

[9] *I am the door. If anyone enters by Me, he will be saved, and will go in and out and find pasture.*

[10] *The thief does not come except to steal, and to kill, and to destroy. I have come that they may have life, and that they may have it more abundantly.*

The Biblical Path To God Through Jesus

John 14:6 *(NKJV)*

Jesus said to him, "I am the way, the truth, and the life. No one comes to the Father except through Me."

Jesus Came To Save The World (And You)

John 3:14-21 *(NKJV)*

[14] *...even so must the Son of Man be lifted up,* [15] *that whoever believes in Him should not perish but have eternal life.*

[16] *For God so loved the world that He gave His only begotten Son, that whoever believes in Him should not perish but have everlasting life.*

[17] *For God did not send His Son into the world to condemn the world, but that the world through Him might be saved.*

[18] *He who believes in Him is not condemned; but he who does not believe is condemned already, because he has not believed in the name of the only begotten Son of God.*

[19] *And this is the condemnation, that the light has come into the world, and men loved darkness rather than light, because their deeds were evil.*

[20] *For everyone practicing evil hates the light and does not come to the light, lest his deeds should be exposed.*

[21] *But he who does the truth comes to the light, that his deeds may be clearly seen, that they have been done in God.*

Jesus Is Knocking At Your Door

Revelation 3:20-21 *(NKJV)*

[20] *Behold, I stand at the door and knock. If anyone hears My voice and opens the door, I will come in to him and dine with him, and he with Me.*

[21] *To him who overcomes I will grant to sit with Me on My throne, as I also overcame and sat down with My Father on His throne.*

Your Ideolatry Is The Core Issue

Your own ***Ideolatry*** has been created by simply living life. Everything that you encounter shapes who you are, how you see things and what you think about. Your choices and the activities you engage in further define your ideolatry. You did not choose the influences that shaped you in your childhood, however, it is your choice whether to make alterations and adjustments that are necessary when you encounter God's truth. He has enabled you with your own *free will* to choose.

Your ideolatry can focus your mind on carnal, human concerns to the exclusion of God or you can choose to follow Him. God's character and nature is to *forgive*, *restore*, *provide for*, *heal*, and *love* every human spirit on the planet. His character and nature is to help you. He is never against you. He gave of Himself through Jesus to ensure your success and eternal life with Him by His grace and through your faith. ***Ideolatry*** that puts human thoughts, ideas, and perspectives above God might be the problem that gets in the way of you receiving and believing Him. Look ***to Him*** not away from Him. There is nothing in our physical lives that carries as much significance as the disposition of our spiritual being. Jesus made that very clear with His words in Mark 8:36-37.

Mark 8:36-37

[36] *For what shall it profit a man, if he shall gain the whole world, and lose his own soul?* [37] *Or what shall a man give in exchange for his soul?*

You alone are accountable for where you will spend your eternity. It is not up to your parents, your siblings, your friends, your husband, your wife or anyone else. It is ***your*** choice and yours alone to accept or reject the God of the Bible and Jesus, His *free gift of grace* to you. He gives you the path to His life because he loves You! This is His Character and Nature.

To Life

Faith
Love God
Accept Jesus
Renew Your Mind
A Humble Attitude
A Heart of Forgiveness
Actively Engage with God
Reject Evil and Choose Right
Thirst for Knowledge of The Word
Acknowledge Your Need for His Help
Actively Practice Good and Reject Sin
Respect God's Authority
Spiritual Life Focus
Reliance on God
Partner with God
Willingly Submit
Acknowledge Sin
Acknowledge God

Follow The Upward Path

God Is *Not* Your Problem.

He Is Your Solution!

CHAPTER 29

GOD LOVES *YOU*!

Your world makes many demands upon you. Thank you for investing your time and allowing this book to speak into your life. Perhaps it has given you a different way to view the one, true God, the God of the Bible, the God who loves you. We have examined how observation establishes a perspective that creates a *relative* version of the truth, but this process may not reveal the *real* truth of the character and nature of God.

God is on your side and has been looking out for you and speaking to you all of your life. Have you been listening? Hopefully, He has been able to speak to you through this book, and you see Him for Who He is. The *real, absolute truth* is that *God **loves you** and wants to spend eternity **with you!***

John 3:16 *(NIV)*

For God so loved the world that he gave his one and only Son, that whoever believes in him shall not perish but have eternal life.

The only requirement that God places on you is that you believe and receive by faith that Jesus Christ is the Son of God and that He died in place of you to assume the penalty for your own personal sins.

Romans 10:9-11 *(NIV)*

[9] That if you confess with your mouth, "Jesus is Lord," and believe in your heart that God raised him from the dead, you will be saved. [10] For it is with your heart that you believe and are justified, and it is with your mouth that you confess and are saved.

I invite you to receive Him in your heart, and say, *"Jesus is my Lord," out loud, right now* and enjoy His Love and His Life for you for eternity!

APPENDIX

Chapter 5 – References to "Truth"

Psalms 33:4

For the word of the Lord is right; and all his works are done in truth.

Psalms 25:10

All the paths of the Lord are mercy and truth unto such as keep his covenant and his testimonies.

Romans 1:22-32

22 Professing themselves to be wise, they became fools, 23 And changed the glory of the uncorruptible God into an image made like to corruptible man, and to birds, and fourfooted beasts, and creeping things.

24 Wherefore God also gave them up to uncleanness through the lusts of their own hearts, to dishonour their own bodies between themselves: 25 Who changed the truth of God into a lie, and worshiped and served the creature more than the Creator, who is blessed for ever. Amen.

26 For this cause God gave them up unto vile affections: for even their women did change the natural use into that which is against nature: 27 And likewise also the men, leaving the natural use of the woman, burned in their lust one toward another; men with men working that which is unseemly, and receiving in themselves that recompence of their error which was meet.

28 And even as they did not like to retain God in their knowledge, God gave them over to a reprobate mind, to do those things which are not convenient; 29 Being filled with all unrighteousness, fornication, wickedness, covetousness, maliciousness; full of envy, murder, debate, deceit, malignity; whisperers, 30 Backbiters, haters of God, despiteful, proud, boasters, inventors of evil things, disobedient to parents, 31 Without understanding, covenantbreakers, without natural affection, implacable, unmerciful: 32 Who knowing the judgment of God, that they which commit such things are worthy of death, not only do the same, but have pleasure in them that do them.

John 1:14-17

14 And the Word was made flesh, and dwelt among us, (and we beheld his glory, the glory as of the only begotten of the Father,) full of grace and truth. 15 John bare witness of him, and cried, saying, This was he of whom I spake, He that cometh after me is preferred before me: for he was before me. 16 And of his fulness have all we received, and grace for grace. 17 For the law was given by Moses, but grace and truth came by Jesus Christ.

John 14:15-17

15 If ye love me, keep my commandments. 16 And I will pray the Father, and he shall give you another Comforter, that he may abide with you for ever; 17 Even the Spirit of truth; whom the world cannot receive, because it seeth him not, neither knoweth him: but ye know him; for he dwelleth with you, and shall be in you.

John 17:17

Sanctify them through thy truth: thy word is truth.

Chapter 10 – "I have done"

This section is presented for in-depth study of the discussion found in Chapter 10 regarding the usage of the implied personal pronoun " I " that is used in Jeremiah 30:15. The translation "I have done" indicates that God did the action. These alternate renderings of the same word, Strong's OT:6213 עָשָׂה, `asah (aw-saw'), used in Jeremiah 30:15 do use the implied "I." These KJV translations are all neutral descriptions not attached to a causative factor or individual. The words in bold in the following scriptures are the translations of the same word, and the subject of the word is shown in parentheses.

Genesis 41:47 *(years)*
And in the seven plenteous years the earth ***brought forth*** *by handfuls.*

Exodus 21:29-31 *(an ox)*
29 But if the ox were wont to push with his horn in time past, and it hath been testified to his owner, and he hath not kept him in, but that he hath killed a man or a woman; the ox shall be stoned, and his owner also shall be put to death. 30 If there be laid on him a sum of money, then he shall give for the ransom of his life whatsoever is laid upon him. 31 Whether he have gored a son, or have gored a daughter, according to this judgment ***shall it be done*** *unto him.*

Exodus 38:24 *(the gold)*
All the gold ***that was occupied*** *for the work in all the work of the holy place, even the gold of the offering, was twenty and nine talents, and seven hundred and thirty shekels, after the shekel of the sanctuary.*

Leviticus 5:17 *(things)*
And if a soul sin, and commit any of these things which are forbidden ***to be done*** *by the commandments of the LORD, though he wist it not, yet is he guilty, and shall bear his iniquity.*

Leviticus 7:9 *(meat)*
And all the meat offering that is baken in the oven, and all ***that is dressed*** *in the fryingpan, and in the pan, shall be the priest's that offereth it.*

Leviticus 7:24 *(fat)*
And the fat of the beast that dieth of itself, and the fat of that which is torn with beasts, ***may be used*** *in any other use: but ye shall in no wise eat of it.*

Leviticus 11:32 *(work)*
And upon whatsoever any of them, when they are dead, doth fall, it shall be unclean; whether it be any vessel of wood, or raiment, or skin, or sack, whatsoever vessel it be, wherein any work ***is done****, it must be put into water, and it shall be unclean until the even; so it shall be cleansed.*

Numbers 32:13 *(generation)*
And the LORD 's anger was kindled against Israel, and he made them wander in the wilderness forty years, until all the ***generation, that had*** *done evil in the sight of the LORD, was consumed.*

Deuteronomy 2:29 *(children of Esau)*
(As the children of Esau which dwell in Seir, and the Moabites which dwell in Ar, ***did*** *unto me;) until I shall pass over Jordan into the land which the LORD our God giveth us.*

Deuteronomy 13:14 *(abomination)*
Then shalt thou inquire, and make search, and ask diligently; and, behold, if it be truth, and the thing certain, that such abomination ***is wrought*** *among you.*

Judges 10:6 *(children of Israel)*
And the children of Israel ***did*** *evil again in the sight of the LORD, and served Baalim, and Ashtaroth, and the gods of Syria, and the gods of Zidon, and the gods of Moab, and the gods of the children of Ammon, and the gods of the Philistines, and forsook the LORD and served not him.*

Judges 11:37 *(thing)*
And she said unto her father, ***Let*** *this thing* ***be done*** *for me: let me alone two months, that I may go up and down upon the mountains, and bewail my virginity, I and my fellows.*

Judges 16:11 *(ropes)*
And he said unto her, If they bind me fast with new ropes that never were occupied, then shall I be weak, and be as another man.

Jeremiah 17:8 *(a tree)*
For he shall be as a tree planted by the waters, and that spreadeth out her roots by the river, and shall not see when heat cometh, but her leaf shall be green; and shall not be careful in the year of drought, neither shall cease ***from yielding*** *fruit.*

Ezekiel 25:12 *(Edom)*
Thus saith the Lord God; Because that Edom ***hath dealt*** *against the house of Judah by taking vengeance, and hath greatly offended, and revenged himself upon them.*

Ezekiel 25:15 *(Philistines)*
Thus saith the Lord God; Because the Philistines ***have dealt*** *by revenge, and have taken vengeance with a despiteful heart, to destroy it for the old hatred.*

Ezekiel 38:12 *(people or nations)*
To take a spoil, and to take a prey; to turn thine hand upon the desolate places that are now inhabited, and upon the people that are gathered out of the nations, ***which have gotten*** *cattle and goods, that dwell in the midst of the land.*

Ezekiel 46:23 *(a row of building)*
And there was a row of building round about in them, round about them four, and it was ***made*** *with boiling places under the rows round about.*

Habakkuk 3:17 *(fields)*
Although the fig tree shall not blossom, neither shall fruit be in the vines; the labour of the olive shall fail, and the fields ***shall yield*** *no meat; the flock shall be cut off from the fold, and there shall be no herd in the stalls.*

Chapter 12 – "Covenant"

This section is for in-depth study of covenant and the concept of binding for all time. These are references regarding how God makes an everlasting covenant.

Genesis 17:7

And I will establish my covenant between me and thee and thy seed after thee in their generations for an everlasting covenant, to be a God unto thee, and to thy seed after thee.

Psalms 89:34-37

34 My covenant will I not break, nor alter the thing that is gone out of my lips. 35 Once have I sworn by my holiness that I will not lie unto David. 36 His seed shall endure forever, and his throne as the sun before me. 37 It shall be established for ever as the moon, and as a faithful witness in heaven. Selah.

Psalms 105:8-10

*[8] He hath remembered his covenant for ever, the
word which he commanded to a thousand generations. [9] Which covenant he made with Abraham,
and his oath unto Isaac; [10] And confirmed the same
unto Jacob for a law, and to Israel for an everlasting
covenant.*

2 Chronicles 13:5

Ought ye not to know that the Lord God of Israel gave the kingdom over Israel to David for ever, even to him and to his sons by a covenant of salt?

Hebrews 13:20-21

*[20] Now the God of peace, that brought again from
the dead our Lord Jesus, that great shepherd of the
sheep, through the blood of the everlasting covenant,
[21] Make you perfect in every good work to do his
will, working in you that which is wellpleasing in
his sight, through Jesus Christ; to whom be glory for
ever and ever. Amen.*

Chapter 13 – "Dominion"

This section is presented for in-depth study of the discussion found in Chapter 13 regarding the word *dominion*. The wide range of Hebrew words that are rendered *dominion* have varying depths or strengths of meaning. The 11 words range in meaning from governance such as *rule*, *govern*, *reign*, *realm* or *empire* (OT:4474, OT:4475, OT:4896, OT:4910, OT:4915, OT:7300 , OT:7980, OT:7985), to a *marriage relationship* (OT:1166), *indebtedness* (OT:3027), *prevail* and *take* (OT:7287). It is in this last sense (OT:7287) that God gave *dominion* to Adam and Eve to subjugate the earth. This is the highest level of *dominion* that God could provide to them. All of the Hebrew words are rendered with additional English words in the *King James version* except OT:4896 which is only used once in Job 38:33 when God was challenging Job about his self-righteousness. God was pointing out that He had total OT:4896 *dominion* over all of creation.

OT:1166 בָּעַל, *ba`al (baw-al'); a primitive root; to be master; hence, (as denominative from* OT:1167*) to marry: KJV - have dominion (over), be husband, marry (-ried, X wife).*

OT:4474 מִמְשָׁל, *mimshal* (mim-shawl'); *from* OT:4910*; a ruler or (abstractly) rule: KJV - dominion, that ruled.*

OT:4475 מֶמְשָׁלָה, *memshalah* (mem-shaw-law'); *feminine of OT:4474; rule; also (concretely in plural) a realm or a ruler: KJV - dominion, government, power, to rule.*

OT:4910 מָשַׁל, *mashal (maw-shal'); a primitive root; to rule: KJV - (have, make to have) dominion, governor, X indeed, reign, (bear, cause to, have) rule (-ing, -r), have power.*

OT:3027 דאי יָד, *yad (yawd); a primitive word; a hand (the open one [indicating power, means, direction, etc.], in distinction from* OT:3709*, the closed one); used (as noun, adverb, etc.) in a great variety of applications, both literally and figuratively, both proximate and remote [as follows]:*

KJV - (+be) able, X about, + armholes, at, axletree, because of, beside, border, X bounty, + broad, [broken-] handed, X by, charge, coast, + consecrate, + creditor, custody, debt, dominion, X enough, + fellowship, force, X from, hand [-staves, -y work], X he, himself, X in, labour, + large, ledge, [left-] handed, means, X mine, ministry, near, X of, X order, ordinance, X our, parts, pain, power, X presumptuously, service, side, sore, state, stay, draw with strength, stroke, + swear, terror, X thee, X by them, X themselves, X thine own, X thou, through, X throwing, + thumb, times, X to, X under, X us, X wait on, [way-] side, where, + wide, X with (him, me, you), work, + yield, X yourselves.

OT:4896 מִשְׁטָר, *mishtar (mish-tawr'); from* OT:7860*; jurisdiction: KJV - dominion.*

OT:4915 מֹשֶׁל, *moshel (mo'-shel); (1) from* OT:4910*; empire; (2) from OT:4911; a parallel: KJV - dominion, like.*

OT:7300 דוער רוּד, *ruwd (rood); a primitive root; to tramp about, i.e. ramble (free or disconsolate): KJV - have the dominion, be lord, mourn, rule.*

OT:7287 האדאר רָדָה, *radah (raw-daw'); a primitive root; to tread down, i.e. subjugate; specifically, to crumble off: KJV - (come to, make to) have dominion, prevail against, reign, (bear, make to) rule,- r, over), take.*

OT:7980 שָׁלַט, *shalat (shaw-lat'); a primitive root; to dominate, i.e. govern; by implication, to permit: KJV - (bear, have) rule, have dominion, give (have) power.*

OT:7985 שָׁלְטָן, *sholtan (Aramaic) (shol-tawn'); from* OT:7981*; empire (abstractly or concretely): KJV - dominion.*

Chapter 18 – "The Sovereignty of God"

This section presents additional scriptures that relate to the sovereignty of God.

Daniel 4:24-25

24 This is the interpretation, O king, and this is the decree of the most High, which is come upon my lord the king: 25 That they shall drive thee from men, and thy dwelling shall be with the beasts of the field, and they shall make thee to eat grass as oxen, and they shall wet thee with the dew of heaven, and seven times shall pass over thee, till thou know that the most High ruleth in the kingdom of men, and giveth it to whomsoever he will.

Daniel 4:34-35

34 And at the end of the days I Nebuchadnezzar lifted up mine eyes unto heaven, and mine understanding returned unto me, and I blessed the most High, and I praised and honoured him that liveth for ever, whose dominion is an everlasting dominion, and his kingdom is from generation to generation: 35 And all the inhabitants of the earth are reputed as nothing: and he doeth according to his will in the army of heaven, and among the inhabitants of the earth: and none can stay his hand, or say unto him, What doest thou?

Romans 9:15-23

15 For he saith to Moses, I will have mercy on whom I will have mercy, and I will have compassion on whom I will have compassion. 16 So then it is not of him that willeth, nor of him that runneth, but of God that sheweth mercy. 17 For the scripture saith unto Pharaoh, Even for this same purpose have I raised thee up, that I might shew my power in thee, and that my name might be declared throughout all the earth. 18 Therefore hath he mercy on whom he will have mercy, and whom he will he hardeneth.

19 Thou wilt say then unto me, Why doth he yet find fault? For who hath resisted his will? 20 Nay but, O man, who art thou that repliest against God? Shall the thing formed say to him that formed it, Why hast thou made me thus? 21 Hath not the potter power over the clay, of the same lump to make one vessel unto honour, and another unto dishonour? 22 What if God, willing to shew his wrath, and to make his power known, endured with much longsuffering the vessels of wrath fitted to destruction: 23 And that he might make known the riches of his glory on the vessels of mercy, which he had afore prepared unto glory.

1 Timothy 6:15-16 (ERV)

15 God will make that happen at the right time. God is the blessed and only Ruler. He is the King of all kings and the Lord of all lords. 16 God is the only one who never dies. He lives in light so bright that people cannot go near it. No one has ever seen him; no one is able to see him. All honor and power belong to him forever. Amen.

Revelation 4:11 (ERV)

Our Lord and God! You are worthy to receive glory and honor and power. You made all things. Everything existed and was made because you wanted it.

Chapter 21 – Acts 5:3 – The Pulpit Commentary

It was given to Peter on this occasion, by the Holy Ghost, to read the secrets of Ananias's heart, just as it was given to Elisha to detect Gehazi's lie (2 Kings 5:25,26); and the swift punishment inflicted in both cases by the word of the man of God - leprosy in one case, and sudden death in the other - is another point of strong resemblance. To lie to the Holy Ghost. It is only one instance among many of the pure spiritual atmosphere in which the Church then moved, that a lie to the apostle was a lie to the Holy Ghost under whose guidance and by whose power the apostle acted. Ananias's fraud was an ignoring of the whole spiritual character of the apostles' ministry, and was accordingly visited with an immediate punishment. The death of Ananias and Sapphira was a terrible fulfillment of the promise, "Whosesoever sins ye retain, they are retained" (John 20:23).

Chapter 21 – Gehazi's Greed – 2 Kings 5:20-27 (ERV)

20 But Gehazi, the servant of Elisha the man of God, said, "Look, my master has let Naaman the Aramean go without accepting the gift that he brought. As the Lord lives, I will run after Naaman and get something from him." 21 So Gehazi ran to Naaman. Naaman saw someone running after him. He stepped down from the chariot to meet Gehazi. Naaman said, "Is everything all right?" 22 Gehazi said, "Yes, everything is all right. My master has sent me. He said, 'Look, two young men came to me

*from the group of prophets in the hill country of
Ephraim. Please give them 75 pounds of silver and
two changes of clothes.'"23 Naaman said, "Please,
take 150 pounds." He persuaded Gehazi to take the
silver. Naaman put 150 pounds of silver in two bags
and took two changes of clothes. Then he gave these
things to two of his servants. The servants carried
these things for Gehazi. 24 When Gehazi came to the
hill, he took these things from the servants. He sent
the servants away, and they left. Then he hid those
things in the house.*

*25 Gehazi came in and stood before his master. Eli-
sha said to Gehazi, "Where have you been Gehazi?"
Gehazi answered, "I didn't go anywhere."
26 Elisha said to him, "That is not true! My heart
was with you when the man turned from his
chariot to meet you. This is not the time to take
money, clothes, olives, grapes, sheep, cows, or men
and women servants. 27 Now you and your children
will catch Naaman's disease. You will have leprosy
forever!" When Gehazi left Elisha, his skin was as
white as snow! He was sick with leprosy.*

Chapter 25 – "Wrath"

These are additional Hebrew words translated in the *King James version* as the word *wrath*. They are also translated using a wide range of other English words.

טא,הָפא' אַף, Strong's OT:639; from OT:599; properly, the nose or nostril; hence, the face, and occasionally a person; also (from the rapid breathing in passion) ire: KJV - anger (-gry), + before, countenance, face, + forebearing, forehead, + [long-] suffering, nose, nostril, snout, X worthy, wrath.

האמךּהש חֵמָה (khay-maw'), Strong's OT:2534; or (Dan 11:44) chema' (khay-maw'); from OT:3179; heat; figuratively, anger, poison (from its fever): KJV - anger, bottles, hot displeasure, furious (-ly, -ry), heat, indignation, poison, rage, wrath (-ful). See OT:2529.

נוורואהש חָרוֹן (khaw-rone'), Strong's OT:2740; or (shortened) charon (khaw-rone'); from OT:2734; a burning of anger: KJV - sore displeasure, fierce (-ness), fury, (fierce) wrath (-ful).

הפאסתאק קָצַף (kaw-tsaf'), Strong's OT:7107; a primitive root; to crack off, i.e. (figuratively) burst out in rage: KJV - (be) anger (-ry), displease, fretself, (provoke to) wrath (come), be wroth.

הפךּסתךּק קֶצֶף (keh'-tsef), Strong's OT:7110; from OT:7107; a splinter (as chipped off); figuratively, rage or strife: KJV - foam, indignation, X sore, wrath.

Chapter 25 – Korah – The Full Account

This account of Korah from Numbers 16:1-50 relates the extent and severity of the penalties for disobedience and rebellion. Moses interceded for the entire congregation, then decreed a sentence on Korah and his clan based upon his judgment of guilt.

*1 Now Korah, the son of Izhar, the son of Kohath, the son
of Levi, and Dathan and Abiram, the sons of Eliab, and
On, the son of Peleth, sons of Reuben, took men: 2 And they
rose up before Moses, with certain of the children of Israel,
two hundred and fifty princes of the assembly, famous in
the congregation, men of renown: 3 And they gathered
themselves together against Moses and against Aaron, and
said unto them, Ye take too much upon you, seeing all the
congregation are holy, every one of them, and the Lord is
among them: wherefore then lift ye up yourselves above the
congregation of the Lord,*

*4 And when Moses heard it, he fell upon his face: 5 And he
spake unto Korah and unto all his company, saying, Even
to morrow the Lord will shew who are his, and who is holy;
and will cause him to come near unto him: even him whom
he hath chosen will he cause to come near unto him.*

6 This do; Take you censers, Korah, and all his company;

*7 And put fire therein, and put incense in them before the
Lord to morrow: and it shall be that the man whom the
Lord doth choose, he shall be holy: ye take too much upon
you, ye sons of Levi.*

*8 And Moses said unto Korah, Hear, I pray you, ye sons
of Levi: 9 Seemeth it but a small thing unto you, that the
God of Israel hath separated you from the congregation of
Israel, to bring you near to himself to do the service of the
tabernacle of the Lord, and to stand before the congregation to minister unto them?*

*10 And he hath brought thee near to him, and all thy
brethren the sons of Levi with thee: and seek ye the priesthood also?*

*11 For which cause both thou and all thy company are
gathered together against the Lord, and what is Aaron,
that ye murmur against him?*

12 And Moses sent to call Dathan and Abiram, the sons
of Eliab: which said, We will not come up: 13 Is it a small
thing that thou hast brought us up out of a land that
floweth with milk and honey, to kill us in the wilderness,
except thou make thyself altogether a prince over us?
14 Moreover thou hast not brought us into a land that
floweth with milk and honey, or given us inheritance of
fields and vineyards: wilt thou put out the eyes of these
men? we will not come up.

15 And Moses was very wroth, and said unto the Lord,
Respect not thou their offering: I have not taken one ass
from them, neither have I hurt one of them. 16 And Moses
said unto Korah, Be thou and all thy company before the
Lord, thou, and they, and Aaron, to morrow:

17 And take every man his censer, and put incense in them,
and bring ye before the Lord every man his censer, two
hundred and fifty censers; thou also, and Aaron, each of
you his censer.

18 And they took every man his censer, and put fire in
them, and laid incense thereon, and stood in the door of
the tabernacle of the congregation with Moses and Aaron.
19 And Korah gathered all the congregation against them
unto the door of the tabernacle of the congregation: and
the glory of the Lord appeared unto all the congregation.

20 And the Lord spake unto Moses and unto Aaron, saying,
21 Separate yourselves from among this congregation, that
I may consume them in a moment.

22 And they fell upon their faces, and said, O God, the God
of the spirits of all flesh, shall one man sin, and wilt thou
be wroth with all the congregation?

23 And the Lord spake unto Moses, saying, 24 Speak unto
the congregation, saying, Get you up from about the
tabernacle of Korah, Dathan, and Abiram. 25 And Moses
rose up and went unto Dathan and Abiram; and the elders
of Israel followed him.

26 And he spake unto the congregation, saying, Depart, I
pray you, from the tents of these wicked men, and touch
nothing of theirs, lest ye be consumed in all their sins. 27
So they gat up from the tabernacle of Korah, Dathan, and
Abiram, on every side: and Dathan and Abiram came out,
and stood in the door of their tents, and their wives, and
their sons, and their little children.

28 And Moses said, Hereby ye shall know that the Lord
hath sent me to do all these works; for I have not done
them of mine own mind. 29 If these men die the common
death of all men, or if they be visited after the visitation of
all men; then the Lord hath not sent me. 30 But if the Lord
make a new thing, and the earth open her mouth, and
swallow them up, with all that appertain unto them, and
they go down quick into the pit; then ye shall understand
that these men have provoked the Lord.

31 And it came to pass, as he had made an end of speaking
all these words, that the ground clave asunder that was
under them: 32 And the earth opened her mouth, and
swallowed them up, and their houses, and all the men that
appertained unto Korah, and all their goods.

33 They, and all that appertained to them, went down alive
into the pit, and the earth closed upon them: and they
perished from among the congregation. 34 And all Israel
that were round about them fled at the cry of them: for
they said, Lest the earth swallow us up also.

35 And there came out a fire from the Lord, and consumed
the two hundred and fifty men that offered incense.

36 And the Lord spake unto Moses, saying, 37 Speak unto
Eleazar the son of Aaron the priest, that he take up the
censers out of the burning, and scatter thou the fire yonder;
for they are hallowed. 38 The censers of these sinners
against their own souls, let them make them broad plates
for a covering of the altar: for they offered them before the
Lord, therefore they are hallowed: and they shall be a sign
unto the children of Israel. 39 And Eleazar the priest took
the brasen censers, wherewith they that were burnt had
offered; and they were made broad plates for a covering of
the altar: 40 To be a memorial unto the children of Israel,
that no stranger, which is not of the seed of Aaron, come
near to offer incense before the Lord, that he be not as
Korah, and as his company: as the Lord said to him by the
hand of Moses.

41 But on the morrow all the congregation of the children
of Israel murmured against Moses and against Aaron, say-
ing, Ye have killed the people of the Lord . 42 And it came
to pass, when the congregation was gathered against Moses
and against Aaron, that they looked toward the tabernacle
of the congregation: and, behold, the cloud covered it, and
the glory of the Lord appeared.

43 And Moses and Aaron came before the tabernacle of the
congregation.

44 And the Lord spake unto Moses, saying, 45 Get you up
from among this congregation, that I may consume them
as in a moment. And they fell upon their faces.

46 And Moses said unto Aaron, Take a censer, and put fire
therein from off the altar, and put on incense, and go
quickly unto the congregation, and make an atonement
for them: for there is wrath gone out from the Lord, the
plague is begun. 47 And Aaron took as Moses commanded,
and ran into the midst of the congregation; and, behold,
the plague was begun among the people: and he put on
incense, and made an atonement for the people. 48 And
he stood between the dead and the living; and the plague
was stayed.

49 Now they that died in the plague were fourteen thou-
sand and seven hundred, beside them that died about the
matter of Korah. 50 And Aaron returned unto Moses unto
the door of the tabernacle of the congregation: and the
plague was stayed.

ENDNOTES

1. J. Culpeper, *History of English* (New York, NY: Routledge, 1997) 29-35.

2. "Idea," *Dictionary.com Unabridged*. (Random House, Inc.) 17 Jun. 2011 <dictionary.reference.com/browse/idea>.

3. "Idolatry," *Merriam-Webster Online Dictionary.* 12 Nov. 2008 <www.merriam-webster.com/dictionary/idolatry?show=0&t=1308365990> .

4. "Ideolatry," Dr. Richard Masek and Vickie Wilsterman, Personal Collaboration, 23 Nov. 2008.

5. "SETI," 26 Nov. 2015 <en.wikipedia.org/wiki/SETI>.

6. R. Plutchik, "The Nature of Emotions," *American Scientist* July-August 2001, Vol 89: 344-350.

7. "San Fernando Earthquake," 26 Nov. 2015 <scedc.caltech.edu/significant/sanfernando1971.html>.

8. J.E. Eberhart-Phillips, T. M. Saunders, A.L. Robinson, D.L. Hatch, R.G. Parrish. "Profile of mortality from the 1989 Loma Prieta earthquake using coroner and medical examiner reports." *Disasters* Jun 1994 18 (2): 160–70. PMID 8076160.

9. Risa Palm and Michael E. Hodgson, *After a California Earthquake: Attitude and Behavior Change.* (University Of Chicago Press, 1992) 63.

10. "Northridge Earthquake," 26 Nov. 2015 <scedc.caltech.edu/significant/northridge1994.html>.

11. "2004 Indian Ocean earthquake and tsunami," 26 Nov. 2015 <en.wikipedia.org/wiki/2004_Indian_Ocean_earthquake>.

12. "Dhoku Earthquake and Tsunami," 26 Nov. 2015 <en.wikipedia.org/wiki/2011_T%C5%8Dhoku_earthquake_and_tsunami>.

13. "Tornadoes of 2011," 26 Nov. 2015 <en.wikipedia.org/wiki/Tornadoes_of_2011#cite_note-6>.

14. "Act of God," *American Heritage® Dictionary of the English Language, Fourth Edition.* (Houghton Mifflin Harcourt Publishing Company 2004). 20 Oct. 2008 <www.thefreedictionary.com/act+of+God>.

15. "Act of God," *The 'Lectric Law Library's Lexicon*. 20 Oct. 2008 <www.lectlaw.com/def/a011.htm>.

16. "Act of God," *The Columbia Encyclopedia, 6th ed.*. 2015. Encyclopedia.com. 26 Nov. 2015 <www.encyclopedia.com>.

17. "Religion," *Merriam-Webster Online Dictionary*. 2008. 12 Nov. 2008 <www.merriam-webster.com/dictionary/religion>.

18. "Religion," *Dictionary.com Unabridged*. (Random House, Inc.). 15 Nov. 2008 <dictionary.reference.com/browse/religion>.

19. "Truth," *Merriam-Webster Online Dictionary.* 2008. 29 Nov. 2008 <www.merriam-webster.com/dictionary/truth>.

20. "Relativism," *Merriam-Webster Online Dictionary.* 2008. 15 Nov. 2008 <www.merriam-webster.com/dictionary/relativism>.

21. Robert L. Scott, "On Viewing Rhetoric as Epistemic." *Central States Speech Journal* 18 Feb. 1967: 17.

22. Stephen Hawking with Leonard Mlodinow, *A Briefer History of Time*, (Bantam Dell - Random House Publishers, 2005) 14-15.

23. Hawking 18.

24. Hawking 69.

25. Hawking 69.

26. "An Almost Perfect Universe," 2 Dec. 2015. <http://www.esa.int/Our_Activities/Space_Science/Planck/Planck_reveals_an_almost_perfect_Universe>.

27. "Semantics," *Collins English Dictionary - Complete & Unabridged 10th Edition.* (HarperCollins Publishers). 26 Nov. 2015. <dictionary.reference.com/browse/semantics>.

28. Robert McCloskey, Quote adapted, 26 Nov. 2015, < www.quotationspage.com/quote/26806.html>.

29. "Allow." *American Heritage® Dictionary of the English Language, Fifth Edition.* 2011. (Houghton Mifflin Harcourt Publishing Company 2004) 26 Nov. 2015 <www.thefreedictionary.com/allow>.

30. "Allow". *Dictionary.com Unabridged.* (Random House, Inc.) 26 Nov. 2015. <Dictionary.com dictionary.reference.com/browse/allow>.

31. "Allow." *Collins Thesaurus of the English Language – Complete and Unabridged 2nd Edition.* 1995, 2002. (HarperCollins Publishers). 26 Nov. 2015 <www.thefreedictionary.com/allow>.

32. "Allow," *WordNet® 3.0,* (Princeton University1967, 2006). 22 Nov. 2009 <wordnetweb.princeton.edu/perl/webwn: 9-17>.

33. "Accomplice." *Webster's New World College Dictionary (4th Ed)*, 16 Oct. 2009. <www.yourdictionary.com/accomplice>.

34. "Accomplice," 16 Oct. 2009 <en.wikipedia.org/wiki/accomplice>.

35. "Reason." *Merriam-Webster.com.* (Merriam-Webster, n.d.). Web. 16 Oct. 2009 <www.merriam-webster.com/dictionary/reason>.

36. "Reasonable," *Merriam-Webster.com.* (Merriam-Webster, n.d.). Web. 16 Oct. 2009 <www.merriam-webster.com/dictionary/reasonable>.

37. *Biblesoft's New Exhaustive Strong's Numbers and Concordance with Expanded Greek-Hebrew Dictionary.*) Biblesoft, Inc. and International Bible Translators, Inc., 2006).

38. *Interlinear Transliterated Bible.* (Biblesoft, Inc., 2008).

39. "Covenant," 20 Apr. 2010 <en.wikipedia.org/wiki/Covenant>.

40. Tim Ito, 19 Nov. 2015 "Overview:Hong Kong." 1998 <www.washingtonpost.com/wp-srv/inatl/longterm/china/overview/hongkong.htm>.

41. G. D. Henderson, *Religious Life in Seventeenth-Century Scotland*, (1893 Reprint, Cambridge University Press, 2011) 164.

42. B.V. Johnson, *High On The Mountain.* (Westbow Press, A Division of Thomas Nelson & Zondervan, Bloomington, IN, 2014) 2-4.

43. "Covenant," *International Standard Bible Encyclopedia, Original 1915 Edition*, (Electronic Database, Biblesoft, Inc. 1995-1996, 2003).

44. "Kinship," 17 Apr. 2010 <en.wikipedia.org/wiki/Milk_kinship>.

45. H. Clay Trumbull, *The Blood Covenant*, (1893 John D. Wattles) 6-11.

46. "Terah," *The Columbia Encyclopedia, Sixth Edition.* (Encyclopedia.com 2008). 28 Feb. 2009 <www.encyclopedia.com/terah>.

47. "Sin - Moon god," 28 Feb. 2009 <www.bible.ca/islam/islam-photos-moon-worship-archealolgy.htm>.

48. *Midrash, the Bereshith / Genesis Rabba*, 2 Nov. 2015 <www.sacred-texts.com/jud/mhl>.

49. *Midrash, the Bereshith / Genesis Rabba*, 2 Nov. 2015 <www.sacred-texts.com/jud/mhl/mhl05.htm> 60.

50. "Dominion," *Merriam-Webster.com.* (Merriam-Webster, n.d.). Web. 10 Mar. 2009 <www.merriam-webster.com/dictionary/dominion>.

51. "Deception," 18 Jun. 2010 <www.oxforddictionaries.com/us/definition/learner/deception>.

52. Rick Renner, *Sparkling Gems from the Greek.* (Teach All Nations Books - Division of Rick Renner Ministries, 2003) 908-913.

53. "Self-deception," 18 Jun. 2010 <www.oxforddictionaries.com/us/definition/american_english/self-deception>.

54. "Sovereign," *Merriam-Webster.com*. (Merriam-Webster, n.d.). 16 Oct. 2015. <www.merriam-webster.com/dictionary/sovereign>.

55. "Sovereignty," *Easton's 1897 Bible Dictionary*. 16 Oct. 2015. <dictionary.reference.com/browse/sovereignty>.

56. "Esther," *Encyclopedia of World Biography*. (Encyclopedia.com. 2005) 26 Nov. 2015 <www.encyclopedia.com>.

57. "talent," <https://en.wikipedia.org/wiki/Talent_(measurement)>.

58. The worth of 10,000 talents - Ancient Israel used the weight of a Babylonian talent which is approximately 67 pounds. 10,000 talents = 670,000 pounds. 670,000 lbs X 14.583333 troy oz./lb. = 9,938,331 troy oz. of silver. Current value is $15 USD/troy oz. $15 USD X 9,938,331 troy oz. = $149,074,965.

59. "Grace," *Dictionary.com Unabridged*. (Random House, Inc.). 11 Oct. 2009. <dictionary.reference.com/browse/grace>.

60. "Judge," *Merriam-Webster.com*. (Merriam-Webster, 2009). 3 Nov. 2009 <www.merriam-webster.com/dictionary/judge>.

61. "Judgment," *Merriam-Webster.com*. (Merriam-Webster, 2009). 3 Nov. 2009 <www.merriam-webster.com/dictionary/judgment>.

62. "Condemn," *Merriam-Webster.com*. (Merriam-Webster, 2009). Merriam-Webster Online. 3 Nov. 2009 <www.merriam-webster.com/dictionary/condemn>.

63. "Sentence," *Merriam-Webster.com*. (Merriam-Webster, 2009). 3 November 2009 <www.merriam-webster.com/dictionary/sentence>.

64. H. D. M. Spence, Joseph S Exell (Editors). *The Pulpit Commentary*, (Electronic Database. Copyright ©2001, 2003, 2005, 2006 by Biblesoft, Inc).

65. James Ussher, trans. Larry and Marion Pierce, *The Annals of the World*. (Master Books, Green Forest, AR: 2003) 22.

66. "Punishment," *The American Heritage® Dictionary of the English Language, Fourth Edition*. Answers.com, (Houghton Mifflin Harcourt Publishing Company 2004) 19 Sep. 2011 <www.answers.com/topic/punishment>.

67. "Testament," *Merriam-Webster.com*. (Merriam-Webster, n.d.). 11 Aug. 2013 < www.merriam-webster.com/dictionary/testament>.

68. "Covenant" *Merriam-Webster.com*. (Merriam-Webster, n.d.). 11 Aug. 2013 <www.merriam-webster.com/dictionary/covenant>.

69. "Wrath" *Merriam-Webster.com*. (Merriam-Webster, n.d.). 30 Dec. 2014. <www.merriam-webster.com/dictionary/wrath>.

70. "Facts About Eagles," 30 Oct. 2015 <www.ccbbirds.org/what-we-do/research/species-of-concern/virginia-eagles/facts-about-eagles/>.

71. "Bald Eagle Plumage Stages," 30 Oct. 2015 <www.swbemc.org/plummage.html>.

72. "How do the feathers of bald eagles molt and change color?" <https://americaneaglefoundation.wordpress.com/2011/03/11/how-do-the-feathers-of-bald-eagles-molt-and-change-color/>.

73. Albert Van Helden, *Measuring the Universe: Cosmic Dimensions from Aristarchus to Halley*. (University of Chicago Press, 1985) 4–5.

74. Melchizedek, <christianity.about.com/od/oldtestamentpeople/a/Melchizedek.htm>.

BIBLIOGRAPHY

Agnes, Michael, ed. *Webster's New World College Dictionary (4th Ed)*. Retrieved on 11/16/2015 from <websters.yourdictionary.com/>, 2001.

American Heritage® Dictionary of the English Language, Fourth Edition, Retrieved on 12/2/2015 from <www.thefreedictionary.com>, Houghton Mifflin Harcourt Publishing Company, 2004.

Amplified Bible, The Lockman Foundation, La Habra, CA., ©1954, 1958, 1962, 1964, 1965, 1987.

Bent, A.C. *Life Histories of North American Birds of Prey.* Dover Publications, 1958.

"Bald Eagle Plumage Stages," Retrieved on 11/1/2015 from <www.swbemc.org/plummage.html>.

Benner, Jeff A., "Hebrew Verb Conjugations," Retrieved on 12/1/2015 from <www.ancient-hebrew.org/41_lesson01.html>.

Bible In Basic English, Biblesoft, Inc., ©2006.

Biblesoft's New Exhaustive Strong's Numbers and Concordance with Expanded Greek-Hebrew Dictionary. Biblesoft, Inc. and International Bible Translators, Inc. 2006.

Collins English Dictionary - Complete & Unabridged 10th Edition. HarperCollins Publishers 2015.

Collins Thesaurus of the English Language - Complete and Unabridged 2nd Edition. ©HarperCollins Publishers 1995, 2002.

Contempory English Version®, American Bible Society, ©1995.

Culpeper, J., *History of English,* New York, NY: Routledge, 1997.

Dictionary.com, Unabridged, Retrieved on 12/1/2015 from <dictionary.reference.com>, Random House, Inc.

Easton, M.G., *Easton's Bible Dictionary,* Thomas Nelson, 1897.

Eberhart-Phillips JE, et.al. "Profile of mortality from the 1989 Loma Prieta earthquake using coroner and medical examiner reports", *Disasters* 18 (2) June 1994.

Encyclopedia of World Biography, Retrieved on 10/25/2015 from <www.encyclopedia.com>.

"Facts About Eagles," Retrieved on 11/1/2015 from <www.ccbbirds.org/what-we-do/research/species-of-concern/virginia-eagles/facts-about-eagles/>.

God's Word, God's Word to the Nations Bible Society, ©1995.

Good News Bible, Good News Translation - Second Edition - Today's English Version, American Bible Society. (Formerly known as the "Good News Bible"), ©1992.

Hawking, Stephen, with Leonard Mlodinow. *A Briefer History of Time*. Bantam Dell – Random House Publishers, 2005.

"Hebrew Verbs," Retrieved on 3/10/2012 from <www.hebrew4christians.com/Grammar/Unit_Ten/Introduction/introduction.html>.

Henderson, G. D., *Religious Life in Seventeenth-Century Scotland,* Cambridge University Press, 2011.

Holy Bible - Easy To Read Version, Revised Edition, World Bible Translation Center, ©1999, 2005.

Holy Bible, New International Version®, International Bible Society, Zondervan Publishing House, ©1973, 1978, 1984.

Holy Bible, New Living Translation®, Tyndale Charitable Trust, Tyndale House Publishers ©1996, 2004.

"How Do The Feathers Of Bald Eagles Molt And Change Color". Retrieved on 11/1/2015 from <americaneaglefoundation.wordpress.com/2011/03/11/how-do-the-feathers-of-bald-eagles-molt-and-change-color/>.

Interlinear Transliterated Bible. Biblesoft, Inc. 2008.

International Standard Bible Encyclopedia. (Original 1915 Edition). Biblesoft, Inc., Electronic Database, ©1995-1996, 2003.

Ito, Tim, "Overview: Hong Kong," <www.washingtonpost.com/wp-srv/inatl/longterm/china/overview/hongkong.htm>.

Johnson, B.V., *High On The Mountain,* Westbow Press, A Division of Thomas Nelson & Zondervan, Bloomington, IN, 2014.

"Mechanical Translation of the Torah," <www.mechanical-translation.org/>.

"Melchizedek," <christianity.about.com/od/oldtestamentpeople/a/Melchizedek.htm>.

Merriam-Webster Online Dictionary. Retrieved from <www.merriam-webster.com>, Merriam-Webster, Inc. 2015.

McCloskey, Robert, < www.quotationspage.com/quote/26806.html>.

Midrash, the Bereshith/Genesis Rabba. Retrieved from <www.sacred-texts.com>, 2015.

New Exhaustive Strong's Numbers And Concordance With Expanded Greek-Hebrew Dictionary. Biblesoft, Inc. and International Bible Translators, Inc.. ©1994, 2003, 2006.

Oxford Dictionaries Online, Retrieved from <www.oxforddictionaries.com>. Oxford University Press, 2015.

Palm, Risa, Michael E. Hodgson. *After a California Earthquake: Attitude and Behavior Change.* University Of Chicago Press, 1992.

Plutchik, R. "The Nature of Emotions". *American Scientist*, Vol. 89, July-August 2001.

Random House Dictionary. Retrieved from www.dictionary.com.Random House, Inc., 2006.

Renner, Rick. *Sparkling Gems from the Greek.* Teach All Nations Books - Division of Rick Renner Ministries, 2003.

Scott, Robert L. "On Viewing Rhetoric as Epistemic". *Central States Speech Journal*, 18, Feb 1967.

"Sin - Moon god," <www.bible.ca/islam/islam-photos-moon-worship-archealolgy.htm>.

"Southern California Earthquake Data Center". Retrieved from <www.data.scec.org> and <scedc.caltech.edu/>, 2015.

Spence, H. D. M.; Exell, Joseph S. (Editors). *The Pulpit Commentary.* Biblesoft, Inc. Electronic Database, ©2001, 2003, 2005, 2006.

The 'Lectric Law Library's Lexicon. Retrieved from <www.lectlaw.com>.

The American Heritage® Dictionary of the English Language. Houghton Mifflin Company, 2004.

The American Standard Version, Electronic Database, Biblesoft, Inc., ©1988, 2003, 2006.

The Columbia Encyclopedia. (6th Ed.). Retrieved from <www.encyclopedia.com>. 2008.

The King James Version, Electronic Database, Biblesoft, Inc., ©1988-2006.

The Living Bible, Used by permission of Tyndale House Publishers, Inc., Wheaton, IL., ©1971.

The Message: The Bible in Contemporary Language, by Eugene H. Peterson, ©2002.

The New King James Version, Thomas Nelson, Inc., ©1982.

Trumbull, H. Clay. *The Blood Covenant.* John D. Wattles Publisher, 1893.

Ussher, James, trans. Larry and Marion Pierce, *The Annals of the World,* Master Books, Green Forest, AR., 2003.

Van Helden, Albert. *Measuring the Universe: Cosmic Dimensions from Aristarchus to Halley.* University of Chicago Press, 1985.

Wikipedia. Retrieved from en.wikipedia.org.

WordNet® 3.0. Retrieved from <wordnetweb.princeton.edu>, Princeton University, ©2006.

SCRIPTURE INDEX

ABOUT THE AUTHOR

In 1976, Dr. Rich Masek, DDS, MTh. achieved his degree in Dentistry from the University of Southern California. He recognized that his dental career was important because he knew that God had directed his path. He was accepted by the one dental school he applied to where there were 3000 applicants for 120 student positions. He continued to study God's Word and develop a deepening relationship with Him over the years as he pursued excellence in his profession.

In 1975, Rich married Sheri, his beautiful wife of 40 years, and inherited a ready-made family of three girls whom he later adopted. Realizing his responsibility as the spiritual head of his new family, he began to pursue deeper knowledge of God's Word. His gift of teaching began to take shape through home Bible studies that he taught for over 20 years. He also became involved in local churches, played keyboards and served in media ministries, doing video and streaming internet services.

Rich further developed his God-given gift for teaching. He became an international lecturer and author on esthetic and computerized dentistry, devoting a significant part of his professional career to teaching and the advancement of high technology in dentistry. It was during this time, while also teaching and developing Bible studies in his home, that God gave him the inspiration to write this book.

At Sheri's prompting, Rich joined the classes of Life Christian University at their church. Three years later in 2010, Dr. Rich Masek was awarded his Master's Degree in Theology! Balancing the time for all of the demand of caring for patients, family, professional teaching and university studies made it a bit challenging to pursue the calling of this book, but as Israel inherited the Promised Land in Exodus 23:29-30, *by little and by little*, it was finally completed.

Rich likes to spend time with Sheri, their two Yorkies, three daughters, five grandchildren and two great-grandchildren when he is not being Dr. Masek, providing patient care or busy writing a book. Now that the book is complete, maybe he will have a bit more free time. However, who knows how long it will be before the next project starts!